The Teenage Tarzan

The Teenage Tarzan

*A Literary Analysis of
Edgar Rice Burroughs'*
Jungle Tales of Tarzan

STAN GALLOWAY

Foreword by James Gunn

McFarland & Company, Inc., Publishers
Jefferson, North Carolina, and London

Frontispiece: Edgar Rice Burroughs, circa 1916. Copyright Edgar Rice Burroughs, Inc. All Rights Reserved.

LIBRARY OF CONGRESS CATALOGUING-IN-PUBLICATION DATA

Galloway, Stan, 1959–
　　The teenage Tarzan : a literary analysis of Edgar Rice Burroughs' Jungle tales of Tarzan / Stan Galloway ; foreword by James Gunn.
　　　p.　　cm.
　　Includes bibliographical references and index.

　　ISBN 978-0-7864-3853-2
　　softcover : 50# alkaline paper ∞

　　1. Tarzan (Fictitious character)　2. Burroughs, Edgar Rice, 1875–1950. Jungle tales of Tarzan.　3. Burroughs, Edgar Rice, 1875–1950 — Characters — Tarzan.　4. Burroughs, Edgar Rice, 1875–1950 — Themes, motives.　5. Burroughs, Edgar Rice, 1875–1950 — Film and video adaptations.　I. Title.
　　PS3503.U687Z67　2010
　　813'.52 — dc22　　　　　　　　　　　　　　　　　2009046883

British Library cataloguing data are available

©2010 Stan Galloway. All rights reserved

No part of this book may be reproduced or transmitted in any form or by any means, electronic or mechanical, including photocopying or recording, or by any information storage and retrieval system, without permission in writing from the publisher.

Front cover: *Tarzan the Teenager*. Copyright Thomas Yeates 2010. All rights reserved.

Manufactured in the United States of America

McFarland & Company, Inc., Publishers
　Box 611, Jefferson, North Carolina 28640
　　www.mcfarlandpub.com

In memorium:
Danton Burroughs,
1944–2008

Acknowledgments

Portions of some chapters were published in earlier forms in the following: "On Teaching Tarzan," *Burroughs Bulletin* NS #57 (Winter 2004): 20–26; "Alienation in 'Tarzan's First Love,'" *Burroughs Bulletin* NS #62 (Spring 2005): 19–23.

Portions of some chapters were presented in earlier forms at the following: ECOF (Edgar Rice Burroughs Chain of Friendship) 2002, Woodland Hills, CA; ECOF 2003, Baltimore, MD; Virginia Humanities Conference 2004, Bridgewater College, Bridgewater, VA; Conference on Christianity and Literature 2004, Point Loma Nazarene University, San Diego, CA; Virginia Humanities Conference 2005, Ferrum College, Ferrum, VA; Virginia Humanities Conference 2006, Mary Washington College, Fredricksburg, VA; Byron and Modernism 2007, University of British Columbia; Virginia Humanities Conference 2008, Radford University, Radford, VA.

Financial and material support came from: Faculty Research Fund, Bridgewater College, 2004–2009; George McWhorter, curator of the Edgar Rice Burroughs Collection, Ekstrom Library, University of Louisville; Danton Burroughs, Jim Sullos, and Cathy Wilbanks of Edgar Rice Burroughs, Inc.; Jerry Schneider, Don Falkos, Bruce Wood, and Ken Fuchs; Kristin Standaert, assistant dean for library systems, Illinois Institute of Technology; Richard Utz; Tristan Galloway.

Indispensable help was received from: Bill Hillman, webmaster of ERBzine; various members of ERBlist and ERBCOF-L; Julia Barb, Karen Hammerschmidt [Smith], and Heidi Yoder, student assistants; Michael Ours and Robert Tout, interlibrary loan coordinators, and others at the Alexander Mack Memorial Library, Bridgewater College; Charles Fleis, Department of Foreign Languages, Bridgewater College; Shalom Black, Brenna Fawley [Layne], Katie Forero, Bliss Gordon [Fabling], Karen Hammerschmidt [Smith], Dana Lehman, Carlton Morrison, and Anna Pavlovskaya; students who have prodded my own thinking with their insights.

Grateful thanks are offered to the following for permissions: Edgar Rice Burroughs, Inc., to quote from *At the Earth's Core*; *The Beasts of Tarzan*; *Jungle Tales of Tarzan*; *Llana of Gathol*; *The Monster Men*; *A Princess of Mars*; *The Return of Tarzan*; *The Son of Tarzan*; *Tarzan and the City of Gold*; *Tarzan and* the "Foreign Legion"; *Tarzan and the Golden Lion*; *Tarzan and the Jewels of Opar*; "Tarzan and the Jungle Murders"; *Tarzan and the Leopard Men*; *Tarzan at the Earth's Core*; *Tarzan, Lord of the Jungle*; *Tarzan of the Apes*; *Tarzan the Invincible*; *Tarzan the Terrible*; *Tarzan the Untamed*; *Tarzan's Quest*; and *The War Chief*; copyright Edgar Rice Burroughs, Inc., all rights reserved. Edgar Rice Burroughs, Inc., to quote from unpublished letters to and from Edgar Rice Burroughs, copyright Edgar Rice Burroughs, Inc., all rights reserved. Edgar Rice Burroughs, Inc., to republish various illustrations, copyright Edgar Rice Burroughs, Inc., all rights reserved. Greenwood Press to quote from Erling B. Holtsmark's *Tarzan and Tradition*. Harcourt Brace and Faber and Faber Ltd. to quote excerpts from *Collected Poems 1909–1962* by T.S. Eliot, copyright 1936 by Houghton Mifflin Harcourt Publishing Company and renewed 1964 by T.S. Eliot, reprinted by permission of Houghton Mifflin Harcourt Publishing Company. Wesleyan University Press to quote from Joy Harjo, "The Book of Myths" from *Mad Love and War*, copyright 1990 by Joy Harjo. The Wylie Agency to quote from W.S. Merwin, "The Judgment of Paris," copyright 1970 by W.S. Merwin. Duane Adams to reproduce his illustrations *Tarzan Shoots Goro* and *Teeka*, copyright Duane Adams, all rights reserved. Dennis Brutus to quote from *Still the Sirens*. Patrick Cullinan to quote from "The Text." James Gunn for his kind foreword, "The Magic of Imagination." Erling B. Holtsmark, Rolf Romøren, and Dan Wylie to quote from personal unpublished correspondence. Don Maclennan to quote from *Notes from a Rhenish Mission* and "In a Pot on the Window Sill." Kristin Standaert for the use of the photograph of the Michigan Military Encampment owned by the Paul V. Galvin Library, Illinois Institute of Technology. Stephen Watson to quote from *Return of the Moon*. Dan Wylie to quote from *Original Forest*. Thomas Yeates for the cover art, copyright Thomas Yeates 2010, and other interior illustrations.

Table of Contents

Acknowledgments — vii
Foreword: The Magic of Imagination by James Gunn — 1
Preface — 5
Introduction — 7

1. It All Begins Again: "Tarzan's First Love" — 23
2. Running in Circles: Cycles and Technique in "The Capture of Tarzan" — 44
3. All for One: "The Fight for the Balu" — 70
4. (Un)Natural Theology: "The God of Tarzan" — 87
5. Black and White and In Between: The Perception of Racism in "Tarzan and the Black Boy" — 109
6. The Problem of Good and Evil in "The Witch-Doctor Seeks Vengeance" and "The End of Bukawai" — 140
7. Painful Laughter in "The Lion" and "A Jungle Joke" — 161
8. What You See: Lessons in Appearance and Reality in "The Nightmare" — 185
9. Allegiance and Apathy: Community in "The Battle for Teeka" — 210
10. Shooting in the Dark: The Role of Imagination in "Tarzan Rescues the Moon" — 227

Bibliography — 241
Index — 253

Foreword:
The Magic of Imagination
James Gunn

I couldn't believe my good fortune. In the back closet of my grandmother's house in the small, southeastern Kansas town of Girard, I came upon a stack of books bound, as I recall, in green cloth. I was seven or eight probably — maybe as young as six — and my father brought his family at Christmas and sometimes in the summer from Kansas City to the home where he had grown up. My grandfather, who had been an editor, a publisher, and a printer in Arcadia and then in Girard before he lost the county printing, traveled around the country talking to Masonic lodges and afterwards selling his 1,000-line verse biographies of George Washington and Abraham Lincoln, sending enough money home to buy the sprawling bungalow with the porch that embraced three sides and had an empty lot as a side yard. My grandfather would stop by our home in Kansas City before Christmas and continue on to Girard.

My father had two brothers, one older, one younger (and a younger sister); John and Harold were literary, and the house was filled with more books than I had seen in one place, shelved neatly in the living room in barrister's stacked bookcases with glass fronts. The books that I came upon in my explorations were different. They had been consigned to the oblivion of a closet and the dismissal of being stacked and not shelved, but my heart beat faster as I picked up one of them and began to read. Probably it was *Tarzan of the Apes*; under it were half a dozen, maybe more, of Tarzan's later adventures. One by one I took them from their hiding place and home with me to Kansas City, so engrossed in Tarzan's adventures that I read them in the car — and made myself car sick.

I don't know why I had never explored the back closet before; I might have avoided the back bedroom because it had on the wall a photograph of a stern old man with a gray face that I was afraid of (he was, I think, a great grandfather, and when Harold, always free with salutary facts, told me I had his blood in my veins I screamed that I didn't want his blood in my veins). I never learned who in the family had purchased the McClurg editions, or who had discarded them. My uncles seemed above such adventure stories, although my Uncle John once gave me a volume of H. G. Wells's short stories, and my Uncle Harold was the fun-loving brother who might have condescended to Burroughs. It may have been my father, who was the athletic brother but liked to read, particularly books on contract bridge and the Civil War. In any case, Tarzan was my magic door into the world of popular imagination, and I read my way through all of those great adventures (how I wish I had those books now, in their original glory!) and all the later Burroughs novels I could find. That wasn't easy. The Kansas City Public Library didn't have any Burroughs books. The same critical judgment that had consigned the Tarzan books to my grandmother's back closet decided that Burroughs was unsuitable for public libraries, and only much later did I discover the Mars novels, the Pellucidar novels, the Land-that-Time-Forgot novels; I had to wait for the paperback reincarnations of the Venus novels and the Moon novels.

I must admit that my affection for Tarzan wavered. I preferred the Mars novels to Tarzan once I discovered them, and then the Pellucidar novels and the Land-that-Time-Forgot novels. But Tarzan was the enchanted doorway, like the poster that hung on my grade-school library wall of a window opening on a wondrous scene above the Keats quotation "Charm'd magic casements, opening on the foam/ Of perilous seas, in faery lands forlorn." Faery lands, indeed! It was there in the grade-school library I consumed the fairy tales compiled by Andrew Lang distinguished by color: red, blue, and, the epitome, gold. And there I absorbed the talking animal Dr. Doolittle books of Hugh Lofting. But Tarzan led me to the hero-pulp magazines that my father began bringing home in the depths of the Depression, beginning with the second issue of *Doc Savage* in 1933 when I was ten. Doc Savage was joined by *The Shadow* and *The Spider, Operator #5, Terence X. O'Leary's War Birds,* and *G8 And His Battle Aces,* and they led me to a used-magazine store in downtown Kansas City called Andy's where I discovered stacks of dusty magazines in the back (always the back!) with the magical names of *Amazing Stories, Wonder Stories,* and *Astounding Stories of Super Science.* I could trade two of my hero-pulp magazines for one of those, and fell in love again — this time with stories that had all the adventure of the hero-pulp magazine but the additional appeal of wilder imagination and fantastic ideas bolstered by credible science and rational speculation. The publication of *Famous Fantastic Mysteries* in 1939 sealed the deal. Though it was primarily fantasy (reprinted from the old Munsey pulp magazines *Argosy, All-Story, Cavalier*), it gave me a review of the early traditions of the fantasy and SF genres and the exciting romantic science-fantasies of masters such as A. Merritt.

In the midst of this growing literature of the imagination, I never lost my affection for Tarzan. One always remembers one's first love. While other writers and critics I came across consigned Burroughs to their childish pasts (the back closet again!), I remained in touch with my younger self, and when Ace Books began reprinting the Burroughs books in the 1960s, I bought them all to share with my two sons (and re-read them myself), and they had the same ability to enchant. My younger son even sat down to create his own Burroughsian adventure stories.

Stan Galloway tells you part of that story in his introduction. What he doesn't tell you is that he may be one of the half-dozen finest Burroughs scholars in the world. I take some pride in that — not that I contributed to his scholarship, but he was one of my graduate students, and I have discovered that the accomplishments of your students feel as good as if they were your own. Stan's involvement with Burroughs coincided with his studies at the University of Kansas. His first scholarly presentation and his first scholarly publication date to 1992, but his fascination with Burroughs went back much farther — perhaps to his childhood, like me. His collection of Edgar Rice Burroughs already was substantial enough in 1993 to win first prize in the graduate division of the Snyder Book Collecting contest, held annually by the KU Libraries.

Stan's book tells you much more than my fannish experience. Focused on Burroughs' short stories about Tarzan — an attempt to fill in the gaps left by *Tarzan of the Apes*, *The Return of Tarzan*, and the rest of this voluminous saga — Stan uses the *Jungle Tales of Tarzan* as a way of considering Burroughs as more than a great storyteller, and a way of connecting the Burroughs *oeuvre* to the rest of what we consider canonical literature and mythology as well as classical considerations of philosophy, psychology, theology, and ethics. Along the way he tells the story of Burroughs' remarkable life and even more remarkable career, considers his impact upon the popular literature of his time, including comic books, comic strips and film, and quotes liberally from other critical and biographical scholarship. The best part may be that it will make you want to look up the Tarzan books again or to encounter them (lucky you!) for the first time.

In other words, Stan Galloway makes a strong case for why *Tarzan* should not be relegated to the back closet.

The author or editor of more than 40 books, James Gunn is the director of the Center for the Study of Science Fiction at the University of Kansas. He has been president of the Science Fiction Writers of America and the Science Fiction Research Association. His biography of Isaac Asimov won a Hugo award in 1983.

Preface

This is the only book in existence focused on the adolescence of the fictional character Tarzan. Edgar Rice Burroughs wrote only one collection of short stories dealing with these early years. I chose to cover this collection because it is more easily separable from the other novels, and because it is easier to consider a short story, rather than a novel, at some depth, in the shorter spaces afforded by the chapters of a book. It provides smaller bites, so to speak, at the beginning of one's examination of Burroughs' writing. And for most readers, aside from the generations of fans, this may well be the beginning of any serious consideration given to Burroughs.

There are very few books of literary examination on Tarzan, period. The most important predecessor, for me, is Erling B. Holtsmark's *Tarzan and Tradition*, which compares the Greek writers with the themes and styles used by Burroughs. Holtsmark's Twayne study, a few biographies of varying quality, and Richard A. Lupoff's fan-oriented *Master of Adventure* round out the stable. (There is also the elusive *Investigating the Un-Literary* by Richard Utz, which has been seen by a handful of experts.) For the most part, literary analysis of Burroughs' writing must be done from the ground up.

Just as Holtsmark argued more than two decades ago, the writing of Edgar Rice Burroughs merits closer attention and holds up under traditional literary scrutiny. Of all the writers popular in the second decade of the twentieth century, only Burroughs still has any name recognition outside a limited pool of specialists on the era. Far more noteworthy, of course, is the name Tarzan, which is known globally.

I read Burroughs in my teenage years. Like most, I left Burroughs behind after high school. In graduate school, though, I picked up Tarzan again and, with the literary tools that I had developed in the meantime, began to examine the texts in much the same way as I did Hemingway and Faulkner. The more I examined, the more I found that was worth considering.

This book has a narrow focus. *Jungle Tales of Tarzan* is the core. These are 12 stories that Burroughs set after the death of Tarzan's foster mother, Kala, but before he attains the kingship of the apes. These stories also occur before the entrance of Europeans into his consciousness. The connection of these stories with the earlier-published *Tarzan of the Apes* is taken up on many occasions, but the purpose is not to join the two texts into a continuous whole. Issues in *Tarzan of the Apes* that have little bearing on the *Jungle Tales* are left unexamined in this study. The thematic focus is on the experience that Tarzan had in his formative adolescent years. Intertwined with this exploration, though, are a number of literary considerations, such as the method of narration, the use of literary devices, and patterns of diction.

What sources could not be had through interlibrary loan came from two important sources. The first is the offices of Edgar Rice Burroughs, Inc., in Tarzana, California, where I was allowed access to Burroughs' correspondence files. I also discussed a number of issues with Burroughs' grandson, Danton Burroughs, before his passing in 2008. The second is the Burroughs Memorial Collection at the University of Louisville. George McWhorter, the collection's curator, was always generous with his time in tracking down the answers to questions I had along with identifying the necessary documentation in support.

While the focus of this book is textual, the sources brought to bear are quite diverse. Indispensible, for example, were the letters provided by Edgar Rice Burroughs, Inc. The correspondence in letter-grams and traditional mail between Burroughs and various editors were candid and illuminating. The written references to Burroughs and to Tarzan are spread across decades and continents. Of importance were theses and dissertations, as well as nearly a century of scattered comments in print. Also consulted, at germane intersections with popular culture, were comic books, artists' depictions, and film interpretations.

The book is organized roughly by the twelve stories in *Jungle Tales*. Two of the chapters consider two stories at a time. Each chapter begins with an overview of the printing history and notable adaptations of the story or stories, followed by a plot summary and notes of interest. Within each chapter are a number of thematic considerations. For example, the first chapter considers Burroughs' role as a Modernist writer by comparison with T.S. Eliot, his drawing from Greek sources for form and content, his variation on the standard love story, and his contrast with the story of Adam and Eve. The index is useful for finding themes and techniques that transcend the consideration of a single story.

This book is about how to appreciate more than just the surface of words. Most readers of Burroughs are along for the ride. The escape into a fictitious world where good prevails and evil is squelched is reward in itself. But after the rush of adventure is over, the words still retain power. There is more to Burroughs' writing than what meets the eye, or the imagination. This study will help any reader to see more, imagine more, and understand more of what Burroughs was doing as a writer. It will also provide a window into the life of a writer in 1916, nearly a century ago, in those idyllic days just before the United States entered The Great War.

Introduction

> *"The whole world knows Tarzan"*
> —"Tarzan's Father" (Crist 7)

Tarzan is legend, fable, adventure, bedtime story—a character known the world around. James D. Hart declared him "part of modern mythology" (219) as early as 1950. Tarzan's story is, as Patrick Cullinan wrote in "The Text," "at first, made up," but "[s]ome years later" (215), it has become so universally known that it has taken on a life of its own. Cullinan's text-turned-archetype "began to sing and dance/ moon upon moon upon moon" (216) in much the way Tarzan's story has become a legend in our time. Partakers of any of Tarzan's sundry manifestations often forget that someone had to write the story down, forget that today's character of mythic proportions, whom Sam Moskowitz says "has become one of the literary treasures of America" (2), began as words on a page some hundred years ago.

Edgar Rice Burroughs turned to writing as a way to earn money. Long before, though, he was a storyteller. Irwin Porges, Burroughs' biographer, reports that, as a child, Burroughs would create and tell stories to his mother (14); later he created and told them to his children. So when the inclination to write struck him at age 35, he believed, "Although I had never written a story, I knew absolutely that I could write stories just as entertaining and probably a lot more so than any I chanced to read in those magazines" (Burroughs, "How" 19). *Tarzan of the Apes*, his third story, was printed in the October 1912 issue of *All-Story Magazine*, eliciting "a flood of approving letters from excited readers" (Porges 136). The editors previewed the story in the September issue, calling it "a crackerjack." And readers responded with enthusiasm. As early as mid–September (the October issue was released in late August), Thomas Newell Metcalf, editor for the Munsey Company, asked Burroughs to put his "hyperbolic imagination" to the task of a sequel since their offices had "had some very nice letters apropos of 'Tarzan'" (letter from Metcalf, 18 September 1912). Burroughs was at first hesitant, replying, "About a sequel to Tarzan. Candidly I don't think it would be a go [...]. These sequel things usually fall flat" (letter to Metcalf, 20 September 1912). Ironically, the same letter informs the editor that he has nearly finished his sequel to "Under the Moons of Mars." Metcalf's letter of 11 October referred to "the necessity of a sequel to 'Tarzan.'" *All-Story* began to print the letters, to fuel the interest. One reader — initials A.J.J.—for example, simply declared in the December issue: "to say that it is the best story I ever read would be putting it mildly." The reader continued: "[...] I am burning to find out what became of him" (958). Metcalf wrote light-heartedly on 10 December: "I still get letters about 'Tarzan.' They come in so often and ask for more of your work that I am tempted to believe we had better call the magazine the 'All-Burroughs Magazine.'" Burroughs relented and complied with the collective outcry from readers for more about the ape-man.

By 1916, though, Burroughs had written himself into a corner, so to speak. The wild success of *Tarzan of the Apes* had led him to sequel after sequel, so that after five books Tarzan was destined to be a grandfather and it seemed there was little leeway for the storyline without some significant departure from his relatively coherent five-book plot. At this point, several years after Tarzan's initial success, Burroughs chose to revisit some of the ground that he had skipped over in the first novel, the years of Tarzan's adolescence. Richard A. Lupoff, in *Master of Adventure*, writes that this "delightful" (207) collection "complete[s] a phase in the Tarzan series" because this "first logical grouping of books closes with [a] return to the beginnings of Tarzan" (149). While the sixth book, a collection of short stories entitled *Jungle Tales of Tarzan*, does not provide a concise coming-of-age chronicle, it does provide some glimpses into events that formed (in retrospect) the ape-man that meets and marries Jane in the first two books.

Two important conundrums, though, arise from *Jungle Tales*: Tarzan's age in the course of the stories and the congruence of the events with the earlier-published *Tarzan of the Apes*.

Philip José Farmer, in a charted addendum to *Tarzan Alive*, puts the events narrated in *Jungle Tales* between February 1907 and August 1908. More recently, Alan Hanson, in his meticulous *A Tarzan Chrono-log*, suggests that the events occur between 6 June 1907 and 30 April 1908. Both begin their reasoning from the Greystokes' departure from Dover, in *Tarzan of the Apes*, in May 1888, four years after the Berlin Conference which formalized the European "scramble for Africa." Tarzan's birthday, Hanson says, is 16 October of that year; Farmer argues for 22 November. This would make Tarzan 18 and 19 years old during the events of *Jungle Tales*. By their reckoning, Tarzan is 20 years old when he first sees Jane, less than a year after the completion of the stories in *Jungle Tales*; Hansen cites as evidence the letter she writes while in the Greystokes' cabin, whose door she and Esmeralda securely latched for "the first time in twenty years" (*Apes* 100), which is necessarily an approximation. The letter is dated "February 3 (?), 1909" (*Apes* 130). The evidence for his age, though, is derived from this earlier novel. Within the *Jungle Tales* stories themselves, no dates or ages are given. References to events in other stories within the collection and in *Tarzan of the Apes* are the only relative data.

Artists, too, have confused the matter by depicting a fully muscled Tarzan from these early stories. Joe Jusko, in his comprehensive artistic study, depicts a Tarzan of Schwarzenegger physique, even in his paintings of "The End of Bukawai," "The Nightmare," and "Tarzan Rescues the Moon." Only in "Bolgani Attack," depicting Tarzan's first fight with his father's knife, does a less muscle-bound figure show up. More near the mark is the simple line drawing that accompanied "The Capture of Tarzan" in *Boys' Cinema Weekly* (7 January 1922; see below) and others of that series or the depiction Harry Habblitz did for *Fantasy Illustrated* (see page 10).

While Tarzan's age may be somewhat ambiguous, it does not materially alter a typical reader's understanding of the events. The major difficulty comes when a reader tries to intersperse the stories from *Jungle Tales* into the original narration of *Tarzan of the Apes*. The parameters of the stories in *Jungle Tales* are these: the stories follow a roughly chronological sequence, Kala has been killed before the first story, and Tarzan has yet to defeat Kerchak for the kingship of the apes at the end. When readers try to fit these two books together, reading the opening novel up through chapter 10 works fairly well. This is a handy spot to switch to the stories, but it is not narratively precise. Chapter 11 begins with Tarzan's return to the ape tribe and his retelling

Illustration that accompanied "The Capture of Tarzan" in *Boys' Cinema Weekly*, 7 January 1922.

Illustration by Harry Habblitz for "The End of Bukawai" featured in *Fantasy Illustrated* #3 (Winter 1964). Copyright Edgar Rice Burroughs, Inc. All rights reserved.

of his murder of Kulonga and the subsequent terrorizing and looting of the village. These events supposedly occur the same day as Kulonga's death: "It was not yet dark when he reached the tribe [...]" (*Apes* 74). The chapter in *Apes* then details Tarzan's attempts to master the bow and arrows he had stolen, which leads him to return to the village for more arrows. Upon the return from this second visit to Mbonga's village, Tarzan kills Kerchak. Therein lies the difficulty. Somewhere in this eleventh chapter of *Tarzan of the Apes* the stories of *Jungle Tales of Tarzan* must fit. To add to the incongruity, near the beginning of this eleventh chapter of *Apes*, Tarzan finds the important locket in the cabin along with his father's French diary. No mention of either of these important discoveries enters into *Jungle Tales*.

That in Burroughs' mind the stories should span a larger length seems evident when, in "The Lion," Tarzan's kingship of the apes is noted to be years hence (119). Similarly, in "The Battle for Teeka," the narrator claims that "years before [...] Kulonga [...] had slain Kala" (151). But the passage of years, in both these cases, is impossible if we follow Farmer's or Hanson's chronology and the narrative of *Tarzan of the Apes*. Hanson notes that the original narrative "leaves no room for the events of *Jungle Tales of Tarzan*" and that therefore "time must be suspended to allow room" (24).

Rather than slavishly follow dates and chronology or invent a time suspension, a reader may profit more from reading the stories as exemplary of the kind of events that Tarzan experienced in his adolescence, given details to ascribe a specific time that may not have, in fact, existed in a strict reckoning of the two texts. For example, in the first three stories, Tarzan seems less mature than Hanson's eighteen. His middle-school kind of rivalry with Taug causes many readers to imagine a Tarzan in his early teens, entering into adolescence. Burroughs' narrator in *Tarzan of the Apes* noted that Tarzan "was nearly ten before he commenced to realize that a great difference existed between himself and his fellows" (36). This awakening awareness of difference is integrated into the first of the stories. While Kala's death and Mbonga's village are referenced in "Tarzan's First Love," the important arrows are not. In fact the arrows that Tarzan learns to take from the village are not mentioned until the fourth story in the collection, which may indicate a much larger passage of time than the four months that Hanson allows. The use of arrows is confident in the fourth story and crucial to the last one, though Tarzan has only begun proficiency with the weapon when he ascends to the kingship in *Apes*, an event which does not occur until after these stories have supposedly transpired. Frank J. Brueckel has suggested that the stories, more loosely, "should be interpolated between chapters [9] and [13] of *Tarzan of the Apes*" (43). Therefore it seems more profitable to look at the stories' interrelatedness to *Apes* as more generalized, because the Tarzan at the end of "Tarzan Rescues the Moon" seems much more mature than the wrong-headed boy in "Tarzan's First Love."

With this in mind, readers are invited to consider *Jungle Tales of Tarzan* in loose, rather than precise, relationship to *Tarzan of the Apes*. That the stories are predicated on the events of the earlier novel is without debate. Consider the frame of the first novel. When Burroughs began *Tarzan of the Apes*, he provided a contextualizing frame story in the same way that Joseph Conrad begins *Heart of Darkness*, with a narrative of the teller instead of what might be considered the story proper. Conrad begins his story with the setting of the narrator and his listeners: five men aboard a boat waiting for the change of the tide. Four of the men are identified and described, including Marlow, the major storyteller in the tale. Only the narrator himself remains unidentified while Marlow tells his story at night. Just as Kurtz had been "very little more than a voice" (Conrad 64) for Marlow, so Marlow had been a voice in the darkness for the narrator. The transmission of Marlow's tale, then, is filtered through the unnamed narrator, who wrote it down at some later time than Marlow's telling of it. That is, readers are dependent upon the unnamed narrator's memory and possible distortion. Likewise, Burroughs begins with a first-person narrator who identifies the original teller of the story, but shields his identity as "one who had no business to tell" the story, but who did so because of "the seductive influence of an old vintage" (*Apes* 7). In an attempt to fill in more information regarding this narrator, Lupoff invents the story of Burroughs' acquisition of the plot from Dr. Watson, of Sherlock Holmes fame. In that story, Watson tells Burroughs: "I fear that my agent nor his other client would think that I had any business giving it to you, Mr. Burroughs, or to any other. [...] I ask only that my name not be associated with its publication" ("Case" 69), echoing phrases from the first paragraph of *Tarzan of the Apes*. Lupoff goes on to postulate that Watson and the fictional Burroughs left literary homage to each other, the first in the mention of John Clayton in *The Hound of the Baskervilles*, the latter a reference to "that celebrated sleuth," Sherlock Holmes, in *The Son of Tarzan* (36; all references to this book and all of the Tarzan books are to the Ballantine editions of 1963–64, unless otherwise noted).

In the strict case of Burroughs' narrator, though not Lupoff's, the original teller provides circumstantial corroboration through three salient sources: a "musty manuscript," "official records of the British Colonial Office," and "[t]he yellow, mildewed pages of the diary of a man long dead" (7). From these the narrator must make inferences and suppositions to create the narrative as a whole. The events of *Jungle Tales* could logically come from neither the colonial records nor John Clayton's diary; the contents of the manuscript are unknown as is the identity, and thus the relationship, of the unidentified first storyteller who also relies on memory. A verifiable chronology is far from expected under such circumstances.

Though Burroughs could have referenced a printed copy of *Tarzan of the Apes* while composing the stories contained in *Jungle Tales*, he likely did not, at least in any detailed way. The year 1916 was a flurry of activity, including an extended vacation in California. The previous September and October Burroughs had written *Tarzan and the Jewels of Opar*; October through December he had written *H.R.H. The Rider*; January through March he had written a sequel to *The Mucker*. Porges indicates that at this time Burroughs was "plagued by severe neuritis pains in his shoulder" (Taliaferro identifies this with a more current term: repetitive motion disorder), and that Burroughs had become "exhausted by months of intensive writing" (237). His proposal to write a series of short stories may have come from his desire to be more flexible for recreational and therapeutic travel. The shorter lengths could be accomplished more easily while writing only in evenings and at odd moments. His "Auto Gypsying," as Burroughs called it, begins with a motor trip Burroughs initiated with his family from Oak Park, Illinois, toward Moosehead Lake, Maine, departing in June of 1916. The trip started off badly and "at Morrison's lake, near Coldwater, Michigan, they had made the impulsive decision to cancel the trip to Maine and head to California instead" (Hillman, "Joan"). After a stop to resupply in Oak Park, the Burroughs family gypsied their way to California, where they stayed until April of the next year. Nine of the twelve stories in *Jungle Tales* were written away from home, though only "The God of Tarzan" was written during travel. Burroughs realized the hardship of trying to write while traveling and, when he was delayed in getting the fifth story to the publisher on time, wrote: "I tried to work on the road; but found it impossible" (letter to Ray Long, 13 October 1916). He commented in his journal, "I find that I cannot, or at least do not write on the road" (qtd. in Porges 248). The last portion of the overland trip was hurried so that Burroughs could set up in Los Angeles to write.

Burroughs finished the stories and they ran in *Blue Book*, one a month, September 1916 through August 1917. A.C. McClurg published it in book form in 1919, complementing a run in Philadephia's *Evening Public Ledger*, 31 May through 16 August. Ten of the stories ran serially again in the *Des Moines Sunday Register* in 1930 (minus "The God of Tarzan" and "Tarzan Rescues the Moon"). Sundry comic book adaptations of the stories followed after World War II, both legal and illegal, notably by Charlton, DC, and Marvel. Gold Key's *Story Digest Magazine* ran the entire book condensed and edited for younger readers in one issue, June 1970.

The short story format that Burroughs uses is atypical of his written work, though it was quite popular. Even though the short story has existed for millennia, its prominence as a literary form comes in the nineteenth century. In America, Washington Irving, Nathaniel Hawthorne, Edgar Allan Poe, and others made the form popular in the decades preceding Burroughs' birth. In the Old World, Honoré de Balzac, Anton Chekhov, and E.T.A. Hoffmann made similar contributions. As a literary form, then, the short story was riding high when Burroughs chose to try his hand at it. By the end of the nineteenth century, Harman and Holman report, the genre "came to be thought of as corresponding to a formula" (511). Its formulaic nature diffused in the twentieth century, about the time that Burroughs was at his peak.

All of the Tarzan stories to this point, though, had been novel-length works. Earlier he attempted to market two short stories, without success. Those stories—"The Avenger" and "For the Fool's Mother"—lay unpublished for nearly eighty years, finally becoming available in *Forgotten Tales of Love and Murder*. That Burroughs went to the form in 1916 may reflect the activity that he sensed ahead. Or, he may have just itched to try something new. While the earlier short stories had been comatose, the stories concerning Tarzan were quite successful. The short-fiction "forays outside the jungle," as Adkins (Introduction 9) calls them, were "mawkish and trite," according to Porges, because they were too much like "ordinary life" (280). When it came to the more imaginative content in *Jungle Tales*, Porges claims the Tarzan stories "emerge with a sensitivity and philosophical subtlety not present in his longer works" (280). Lupoff called the collection "a charming group of vignettes" in which each story "reveals some trait in the development of the youthful Tarzan" (*Master* 148). Burroughs, however, was not inclined to agree regarding their accomplishment. Even after the success of *Jungle Tales*, in correspondence with *The People's Home Journal*, Burroughs wrote: "I have an idea that I am not a short story writer" (qtd. in Porges 721 n. 8). Earlier in writing to Robert Davis, one of Burroughs' *All-Story* editors, he had indicated some frustration with his inability to craft a viable short story without Tarzan in it. He had told Davis that he "should like to be able to write a salable short story occasionally" (15 December 1917). But the story in question ("The Little Door") languished unpublished until 2001. In fact, Burroughs marketed very few stories in comparison to his novel-length output and sold even fewer.

The idea of a story sequence was in the literary air. Some of the stories of *Winesburg, Ohio* were published in 1916, though likely Burroughs took no notice of them, nor of Sherwood Anderson's completed collection that received book publication the same year as Burroughs' *Jungle Tales*. Burroughs himself had proposed the idea of a story sequence in 1912 to Donald Kennicott of the Story Press Corporation. His pilot story for the series was "For the Fool's Mother." But the idea died on the vine. Three years later, when Burroughs brings up the idea again to Ray Long, the concept is given approval, but this time the featured character of Tarzan seems to have been the important consideration. And, like Robert Frost's road less traveled, for readers, that has made all the difference.

The stories, though, as David Bruce Bozarth contends, cannot stand as a reader's introduction to the character. While the information in the stories is essential to understanding the development of Tarzan, the general public had already received four novels (a fifth, though written, was sitting at *All-Story* awaiting a November start date when *Jungle Tales* began in the September *Blue Book*), any one of which might have provided a starting point before this return to childhood. The stories do serve a critical function, though. Bozarth says, "*Jungle Tales*, however, in the context of the remaining Tarzan output shows Burroughs exploring the character more fully than he did in later volumes and what little exploration of the character that followed was *based* on the snippets of *Jungle Tales*" ("Jungle Tales"). It serves also, in retrospect, to add new understanding to the earlier tales. This is why many readers today read both *Tarzan of the Apes* and *Jungle Tales of Tarzan* together. Despite its dependency, Bozarth affirms that this group of stories "is the pivotal collection which DEFINES the personality of Tarzan" ("Jungle Tales," all-caps original).

Perhaps in an effort to revive what might have been perceived as success in retrospect, or perhaps because he was getting tired, near the end of his career, Burroughs wrote two more, though unrelated to each other, short stories— "Tarzan and the Champion" and "Tarzan and the Jungle Murders"— published in 1940 then joined for book publication in 1964 with the novelette "Tarzan and the Castaways."

The shorter of the two, "Tarzan and the Champion," pits the jungle-protector against the world heavyweight champion, One-Punch Mullargan, with little doubt as to the outcome, except for the unexpected arrival of cannibals and the tantalizing nearness of the Waziri. Mullargan's ambiguous character development, beginning as a thoughtless hunter ending with some questionable thoughts, leaves the story thought-provoking without being poignant. In the story, a moral theme might be observed if one follows Michael Jackson's claim that "excessive killing," as clearly shown by Mullargan, represents the sexual impulse. "The hunter who impetuously wants to kill all the animals," Jackson says, represents a lack of sexual self-control, as contrasted by the heroic characters who prefer "moderation" demonstrated by "protecting the young and their mothers" (232). Tarzan's character is static. But, this late in Tarzan's literary life, Burroughs had little motivation and even less latitude to show change in his central character. His role in the second story, "Tarzan and the Jungle Murders," will be discussed in chapter 9.

> *No profit grows where is no pleasure ta'en;*
> *In brief, sir, study what you most affect.*
> — Tranio, *The Taming of the Shrew*
> (William Shakespeare, 1.1.39–40)

That Burroughs' works have begun to receive serious consideration from the academic community would surprise many who lived and read in the first half of the twentieth century, including Burroughs himself. He thanked one reviewer of *Jungle Tales* for recognizing that the "stories are written for entertainment and not to compete with the Old Masters as literary achievements" (letter to H.E. Jacobs). He "never intended them to be [...] contributions to classical literature" ("Creator"), Burroughs said in 1923. And, later that year, E.H. Lacon-Watson's article, "'Tarzan' and Literature," labeled his prose, for the edification of *Fortnightly* readers, as "mature and seasoned illiteracy" (1035). That same year Seth T. Bailey referred to "that unimportant style that has made his works famous" (4). In our own day, Alex Vernon writes in the opening of his academic exploration entitled *On Tarzan* that one of his challenges was "the very act of taking seriously a subject as silly as Tarzan" (5); he concludes, disappointingly, that increasingly the character of Tarzan appeals "solely [to] children" (163). Despite some concerns, John Newsinger affirms, though, that "the Tarzan stories nevertheless deserve serious consideration" ("Lord" 60).

That the classroom (middle school to graduate school) has brought him back would astound and possibly appall him. He wrote in 1932: "It is difficult and even impossible for me to take these Tarzan stories seriously, and I hope that no one else will ever take them seriously" ("Tarzan Theme" 29). Likewise, Burroughs referred to his writing in a self-deprecating letter to Thomas Metcalf, after the rejection of *The Return of Tarzan*, as "my incursion into litrachoor" (24 January 1913). Burroughs was also quoted by the *Los Angeles Times* as saying: "I don't think [my writing] is 'literature'"; then he adds, "I'm not fooling myself about that" (Crist 7). But, as Dorothy McGreal attests, "Burroughs always deprecated his work and avoided any pretense of being a literary figure" (14). Allen Carey-Webb says that he uses *Tarzan of the Apes* as a way to ask "fundamental questions about what literature is, who defines the canon and why" (122).

Erling B. Holtsmark relates the instructive story of the Latin writer Vergil, whose great work *The Aeneid* is considered an essential literary work of his century. Vergil, though, "felt the poem was a failure" and instructed that his executors destroy the manuscript. Holtsmark concludes: "The story serves as a pointed reminder that even a great author is not necessarily the best judge of his own work" (*Tarzan and Tradition* 173n; all references to Holtsmark are from this work unless otherwise noted).

John Taliaferro, in his biography of Burroughs, avers that "in his heart of hearts, he yearned to be considered a qualitative peer of those authors" who were published in the reputable literary magazines (175). The sarcasm of Burroughs' statement is apparent, for example, when at the beginning of *Tarzan the Invincible* the narrator tells the reader: "do not tax your intellect needlessly by attempting to decode such fictitious names as I may use [...]" (7). He implies there would be no profit in such speculation. Then swinging to the antithesis of such a claim, he suggests the story may include "food for thought" (7). In the *Blue Book* publication, entitled *Tarzan, Guard of the Jungle* (7 installments: October 1930 through April 1931), this second claim did not appear. The paragraph was added for the book publication, which Burroughs published as the first Tarzan book to be printed by his own corporation, Edgar Rice Burroughs, Inc. The addition of this disclaimer is intriguing as Burroughs tries to find a personally acceptable middle ground between escapism and philosophy. This may be a case of the author either hiding behind false humility or of his genuine ignorance to the stature of his own work. The former may be supported by the fact that near the end of his career, in a private letter to his daughter, he refers to his writing as "classics" and "inspired literature" (letter to Joan Burroughs, 24 January 1941), and earlier he suggested that the things he wrote "might carry a beneficial suggestion of the value of physical perfection and morality" (qtd. in Porges 212; Holtsmark notes this also 276f and 393), much different attitudes than those expressed in published sources. And, in 1935, he said in a letter to Professor J. John Munson, who had inquired about *Tarzan of the Apes* (written more than 20 years earlier), that the book "may be poor literature although, personally, I question that it is so very poor." The latter case, that he was ignorant to his ability, is bolstered by his own childhood paternal relationship; the "unshakable" belief that he failed to "meet the standards of his father" (Taliaferro 16) may have led him to always underestimate his own accomplishments. For example, when Burroughs did not carry out his duty in supervision at Michigan Military Academy, he wrote to his father that his infraction was insignificant compared to the "lost confidence" he felt in their relationship (qtd. in Taliaferro 38). Robert W. Fenton quotes Burroughs, via his daughter, as saying, "My father [...] used to tell me with increasing frequentness—until I was thirty-six—that I always would be a failure" (16). Taliaferro marks Burroughs as, "[o]f all the Burroughs brothers [...,] the one who had sought his father's approval most directly" (45). Either way, whether Burroughs was ignorant or just publicly modest, his opinion has been overshadowed by popular acclaim, and Tarzan continues to earn interest from a variety of quarters.

The begrudging acceptance of science fiction as a subject in higher education has made inroads for Burroughs' name. James Gunn, who as a child "discovered some Edgar Rice Burroughs 'Tarzan' novels in the back closet of [his] grandmother's home" (9; see also this book's foreword), began teaching collegiate-level science fiction in 1969, some 20 years after he began writing for the science fiction market. Gunn identifies the flashpoint in acceptance of science fiction as the late-1950s. The Modern Language Association included it in its annual convention first in 1958. The next year, Kingsley Amis gave his Christian Gauss Seminar in Criticism devoted to science fiction, and *Extrapolation*, the first academic journal devoted to the subject, began publication. In 1978, Gunn estimated that "hundreds, perhaps thousands, of courses are taught in colleges and universities across the country" (13). In this context Burroughs has been brought onto the academic threshold. A 1996 survey in *Science-Fiction Studies* indicated that Burroughs tied at the number 50 spot (with Connie Willis) for authors most frequently assigned in college courses of science fiction, fantasy, and utopian literature (Evans and Mullen 526). *A Princess of Mars* tied at number 58 with more than a half-dozen other novels in the most-widely-assigned category (Evans and Mullen 525). (Others ranked the same include Arthur C. Clarke's *2001* and *Rendezvous with Rama* and Robert A. Heinlien's *Puppet Masters* [Evans and Mullen 525–26].) It appears that Burroughs' place in science fiction courses is comfortable, though not essential.

More remarkable is the entrance of his most famous character, Tarzan, into the classroom. In 1965, Richard Lupoff suggested that Burroughs' name was "running a strong chance of permanence" (*Master* 2) after such writers as Hemingway, Faulkner, Fitzgerald and Sinclair Lewis (1). In the 2005 update of the book, originally titled *Edgar Rice Burroughs: Master of Adventure*, Lupoff notes that of these authors only "Faulkner is holding his own" (1 n.1). To that add the name of Edgar Rice Burroughs.

The disparagement is neither universal nor consistent, however. Lacon-Watson, for example, also told readers of the *Fortnightly* that the stories of Tarzan's adolescence "are told with a certain ingenuity, a really remarkable power of invention, and an immense courage" (1039). In 1939, Alva Johnston named Burroughs as "the greatest living writer" (6) for readers of the *Saturday Evening Post*, though, ironically, Burroughs never published in the *Post*. Johnston claims that, at times, Burroughs writes "in a high literary vein" (59) in the general sense. McGreal has suggested that "Tarzan may well be the only great literary hero produced by the literature of [the twentieth] century" (15). Though Herbert F. Smith makes no allusion to Burroughs in his critical study, *The Popular American Novel 1865–1920*, John Taliaferro concludes that "there can be little question that [Burroughs] was the most widely read American author of the first half of the twentieth century" (13–14) and Russel B. Nye marks *Tarzan of the Apes* as establishing "the greatest popular character creation of all time" (272). In 1997, Neal Wyatt named Burroughs as one who had "enter[ed] the august ranks of writers [...] who have captured the attention of both lay readers and scholars" (84). This leads to an important but perhaps artificial distinction between a good writer and a good storyteller. Thorton Wilder cuts to this bone when he writes: "There is something mysterious about the endowment of the storyteller. Some very great writers possessed very little of it, and some others, lightly esteemed, possessed it in so large a measure that their books survive down the ages, to the confusion of severer critics" (86–87). Though Wilder was not writing about Burroughs, certainly his claim can be applied to what Burroughs wrote. He answers James Van Hise's question, "Can great stories well told ever really be old fashioned?" (6), and affirms Leigh Brackett's claim that "if you can tell a real story[,] your tales will outlive all the John Galsworthys in the world, regardless of how the lady librarians may sneer at them" (Brackett 9).

Tarzan's longevity is reaching a century, and serious connection and comparison with other "classic" authors have begun to appear, for example, two articles from the 1990s, Carey-Webb's comparison with Conrad's *Heart of Darkness* and Richard Allan Davison's article "Edgar Rice Burroughs, Tarzan and Hemingway." Holtsmark was instrumental in breaking the academic barrier with his landmark book, *Tarzan and Tradition* (1981), followed by his study in the Twayne's United States Authors Series (1986). His preface to the former book claims, "I bring [...] methods similar to those I apply to classical literature" ([xiii]), at a time when serious literary study of Burroughs was practically unheard of, "because," Holtsmark continues, "he merits more serious attention than critics and academicians have hitherto given him" (6). (Richard Lupoff's *Edgar Rice Burroughs: Master of Adventure*, published by Canaveral in 1968, is the only book-length study to predate Holtsmark but Canaveral [Ace for paperback] was predominantly a fiction publisher for Burroughs, not a scholarly press.) Holtsmark found resistance, having "to fight through the ingrained prejudices of many of [his] colleagues in the academic community" but was driven by his belief that Burroughs "should be taken seriously as an author who not only knew how to tell a good story but also had a genuine feel for literature and what it can say about the human condition" (letter to Clyde [Bob] B. Hyde).

From a popular angle, legitimacy of Tarzan in the classroom is validated from the publishing of the Signet and Penguin editions of *Tarzan of the Apes* (1990). Richard Utz's difficult-to-find anthology, *Investigating the Unliterary: Six Readings of Edgar Rice Burroughs' Tarzan of the Apes* (1995), is the first full-length exploration of Burroughs' writing in a classroom context, in his case for students preparing for graduate school. One of the arguments that Utz presented to his students was that "literariness was [...] a cultural construction" (7). The outcome was for his students "to produce alternative readings, concentrating sometimes on the very 'unliterary' aspects which have heretofore been utilized to relegate Burroughs' text to the realm [of] the popular and to ostracize it from 'literature' classes at colleges and universities" (8). In doing so, Utz and his students have suggested an academic re-evaluation, based on broader inquiries, of Burroughs' writing.

Tarzan has made several appearances in instructional texts as well. For example, Michael Meyer's *The Bedford Introduction to Literature*, from its first edition (1987), has used an excerpt from *Tarzan of the Apes* in its explanation of the term *plot*. In the 2008 edition, Meyer explains in part: "The following excerpt [...] provides a conventional plot pattern in which the character [...] is confronted with a problem leading to a climactic struggle that is followed by a resolution of the problem" (68–69). After a discussion of the balance between what happens and why it happens, Meyer concludes his paragraph with: "In Burroughs's adventure story, however, the emphasis is clearly on action. *Tarzan of the Apes* may add little or nothing to our understanding of life, but it is useful for delineating some important elements of plot. Moreover, it is great fun" (69). Meyer makes other comments, concerning both plot and background, before providing the scene of Tarzan and Terkoz battling for Jane. Following the scene, Meyer examines the scene for about three pages to define a number of literary terms, including *exposition, rising action, foreshadowing,* and *denouement*.

Meyer's text is not the first to use Tarzan in an academic role. The earliest is *Literature for Composition* by James R. Kreuzer and Lee Cogan, 1965, which Hulbert Burroughs noted in *ERB-dom* #13. This excerpt from *Tarzan of the Apes* looks at the author's tone and diction in the opening paragraphs. The writing assignment links the Tarzan excerpt to excerpts from Jonathan Swift and H.G. Wells, from which the student examines the authors' "problem of having to gain credibility for the fantastic or incredible" (267). Even earlier (1962), Oxford University Press prepared a classroom edition of Burroughs' first novel, *A Princess of Mars*, complete with study questions.

Teachers, besides myself, have taken a hand in integrating Tarzan into the classroom, as several published sources verify. Perhaps the best example, Tony Trigilio's "Staring Back in the Classroom: Genre, Identity, and the Power of Looking," indicates that Tarzan's character is useful "[i]n literature classrooms" to help demonstrate "the reflexivity of contemporary critical theory" (99–100). Specifically, "Tarzan's First Love" can serve as a textual intersection of "psychoanalysis, sociology, cultural studies, and literary studies" (101). This is the earliest academic article to use a story from *Jungle Tales* for analysis. Trigilio cites Carey-Webb's article in affirming that the reader's "own pleasures" must be considered, that we as readers must "look at our looking" in order to understand the power and popularity of such stories, both in Burroughs' day and our own. He arrives at the claim that reading in such a way serves "both as a formal device for reading a text and as a paradigm for reading ourselves" (102).

In 1966, McGreal concluded that Burroughs "would be pleased to know that, finally, excerpts from his works are being included in more and more textbooks, both here and abroad" (14).

A second academic benchmark to consider is the attention Burroughs has gained in graduate schools. Dissertations and theses indicate what is in the academic air. The earliest focused study treating Tarzan seriously, though only in its conclusion, is "From Hesiod to Tarzan : A Study of the Noble Savage in Relation to Romanticism with Special Reference to the Eighteenth Century," which Nina Grun [Shafer] submitted to Smith College in 1939. The study places Tarzan near the end of a long exploration of "the man in the woods, unhampered by civilized convention" (132). Tarzan represents the then-current manifestation of the idea. He and a host of imitators also show a reversal of the noble savage theme, in that they focus "not upon their kinship with nature," Grun observes, "but rather upon their ability to subdue nature" (134).

Not until after the Burroughs boom of the 1960s does Tarzan surface again in such circles, but this time centrally. David William Spradley's master's thesis in 1972 for Stephen F. Austin State University, entitled "The Tarzan Phenomenon," broadens consideration of Burroughs to address issues of "popular values, mass taste, and middle-class norms" (ii). His chapters identify five areas of consideration: American values, frontier values, the search for identity, narrative technique, and myth. Michael Orth's 1974 dissertation for Claremont Graduate School, titled "Tarzan's Revenge: A Literary Biography of Edgar Rice Burroughs," was serialized later in *ERB-dom*. James R. Nesteby's 1978 dissertation from Bowling Green State University—"The Tarzan Series of Edgar Rice Burroughs: Lost Races and Racism in American Popular Culture"—fed into the nation's growing attention to issues of popular culture led by, among others, Ray B. Browne, Nesteby's dissertation director. Nesteby's emphasis is on cultural assumptions of race and the explicit versus implicit attitudes involved. Peter M. Coogan explores this Tarzan-in-popular-culture theme further, though Tarzan is only one of many characters examined, in "The Secret Origin of the Superhero: The Origin and Evolution of the Superhero Genre in America," presented at Michigan State University in 2002.

Phil Burger provided an ambitious thesis to Utah State University in 1987. "Glimpses of a World Past" is "part biography, part social history" (iii), exploring not only Burroughs' pre-writing life but the conditions and influences on and from it, as a way to show that Burroughs has "a valid claim to a place in American letters" (7). The actual literary aspect of the thesis is corralled into the final chapter.

In 1990 and 1996, two important dissertations took Tarzan seriously. Robert E. Conrath wrote "Rethinking the Ape-man: Approaching Tarzan as Object of Critical Discourse" at McGill University, and Daniel Kanyandekwe wrote "Dreaming of Africa: American Writers and Africa in the Twentieth Century" for the State University of New York at Buffalo. Conrath looks at Tarzan as an icon of popular culture; this study coalesces not only the written texts that piqued public interest but also the various media and material manifestations that expanded Tarzan's name-recognition and continue to demonstrate the character's "astounding durability" (n.p. [prefatory abstract]). Kanyandekwe focuses on four writers—Ernest Hemingway, Saul Bellow, and John Updike, in addition to Burroughs—to examine the role that Africa plays in the fictive imagination. His first chapter examines primarily the lack of verisimilitude in the Tarzan stories. The later authors are then explored with comparative connection to Burroughs.

Carey-Webb asks, "What happens when we take Tarzan seriously as a literary text?" (131). This book is a partial response.

Superficially, this book is different than any other study to date, designed to follow the twelve stories that Burroughs put together to make up *Jungle Tales of Tarzan*. The sections begin with a bibliographic history and plot summary, followed by investigation of salient themes and interconnections of the stories. Each chapter, though, may range beyond the story in question to pursue ideas, themes, and images that, like some literary Zambezi, wind through many terrains. In that respect, a discussion of "The End of Bukawai" may say just as much about "The God of Tarzan" as the former. For the reader looking for all the commentary on a particular story, the index is indispensable.

Chapter 1

It All Begins Again
"Tarzan's First Love"

"Tarzan's First Love" was Edgar Rice Burroughs' first attempt at the short fiction genre with his most famous character. Written in five days beginning 17 March 1916, and published in *Blue Book* magazine in September that year, the story became the first of a series of twelve short stories, which were collected and published in 1919 as *Jungle Tales of Tarzan*, which is the title used for the first story in the *Blue Book* and the *Des Moines Sunday Register* publications. It has been reprinted in such places as Martin Levin's anthology, *Love Stories*, and the anthology *High Adventure*, edited by Cynthia Manson and Charles Ardai. The story has been adapted to comic form in Marvel's *Tarzan Annual* #1 (1977) and reprinted in Malibu's *Tarzan: Love, Lies ... and the Lost City* #1 (1992). Joe Kubert incorporated a portion of the story into "A Son's Vengeance" for DC Comics, inserting the fight for Teeka before Kala's death.

In the story, an adolescent Tarzan compares himself to Teeka, a young female ape, whom he considers beautiful. He finds himself resenting attention shown to her by a fellow ape, Taug. Tarzan fights Taug to show off to Teeka and rescues her from a panther. When Tarzan hunts later, Taug grooms Teeka. When Tarzan observes this he leaves the two apes in romantic resignation. In the jungle, Tarzan sees warriors from Mbonga's village build a cage, which later traps Taug. When Tarzan realizes his rival is removed from competition he tries to reclaim Teeka, but in so doing realizes some of the incongruities between himself and the apes. He frees Taug from the cage for Teeka's sake. He concludes, "Tarzan is a man. He will go alone."

"*Edgar Rice Burroughs is a modern of the moderns, both refreshingly forthright and reassuringly sane.*"
— "War and Literature"

Tarzan has been dismissed from literary consideration for a variety of reasons, ranging from the author's geographic ignorance to his infelicitous style.

For example, a letter to *All-Story Weekly* in 1914, signed by "H.P.L." (whom many have identified as H.P. Lovecraft, an important fantasy-horror writer for *Weird Tales* and other magazines), points out the error of including tigers in Africa, and Jerry Griswold cites several "stylistic drawbacks" in Burroughs' *Tarzan of the Apes*, enumerating "passages of wooden and purple prose, occasional episodes of stagey melodrama, and some characters who seem straight from central casting" (104). Most people accept such faults as expected based on the pulp magazines which published his work; such publications, as Robert Zeuschner claims, "had no interest in publishing anything with philosophical or psychological depth." He attempted to move from the pulps to the slicks but with negligible success: *Tarzan and the Lion Man*, published in *Liberty* magazine, is the lone representative to break out of the pulp ranks. Despite the labeling that relegated him outside literary consideration, at least this story, "Tarzan's First Love," is written with more than the slapdash adventure his readers looked for (and the presence of this book argues that every story of the collection holds elements worth study). Here, Burroughs flirts with the Modernist angst of alienation.

Modernism, at its heart, "emphasized the sharp difference between conscious surfaces and unconscious depths of experience" (55), writes Alzina Stone Dale in her critical assessment of T.S. Eliot, a younger contemporary of Burroughs (Burroughs 1875–1950; Eliot 1888–1965). This sharp difference between surface and depth is what Tarzan realizes in the course of the story. On the surface, Tarzan is one of the tribe of Kerchak. He eats where they eat. He travels where they go. He sleeps where they sleep. But a sharp difference exists between him and them.

This difference is embraced in the Disney movie *Tarzan*, a movie which Richard Corliss says shows Tarzan "search[ing] not so much for his mate Jane as for his place in a society of men and apes" (220). The movie, Corliss continues, is "about the pain and triumph of racial or social assimilation" (221). The theme remains salient in Disney's *Tarzan II*, as well, particularly in the Phil Collins song "Who Am I?" This question underlies the first novel and focuses this collection of stories. Barbara Creed says that *Tarzan of the Apes* "is an attempt to define what it means to be human" (162), as a way of answering this question.

Even Taug, who is a childhood friend, sees Tarzan's physical form as different. Taug, whom Holtsmark identifies as a type of "jungle Narcissus infatuated with his own charms" (71), studies Tarzan and concludes "there was no comparison" (*Jungle Tales* 16) between them. Tarzan lacked a "beautiful coat," "broad nostrils," and "blood-shot eyes" (16), all beautifiers that Taug identified in himself. This superficial discrepancy then indicates the underlying differences in nature between the two. Tarzan's capacity for reason is the primary difference. In examining why Tarzan was attracted to Teeka, Burroughs equivocates, saying Tarzan "probably reasoned" (8) that her playfulness was the cause. No other figure in the story is noted as having reasoned. This difference gives him forethought, compassion, altruism, and eventually isolation. When the panther screams, all the apes flee, but the narrator points out: "With the ape-boy [...] it was different" (12). His response to Teeka's danger displays the underlying difference in the way he thinks. He can extrapolate that his own danger is also a danger to others. He sees Teeka's danger and in un-apelike fashion calls for their companions to turn on the intruder. He reasons that "if all those of the tribe who chanced to be present today would charge, Sheeta, the great cat, would doubtless turn tail and run for his life" (12). But the subconscious shallowness of these creatures becomes as clear as the superficial differences. Tarzan is left to face the danger alone.

This profound difference between Tarzan and the apes is illustrated, literally, by Burne Hogarth in his pictorial version of the story. The text indicates: "Tarzan and Taug took to the trees together, the shaggy coat of the fierce ape brushing the sleek skin of the English lordling as they passed through the primeval jungle side by side" (23). From this, one would expect a straightforward movement such as Russ Manning creates (see below). A youthful Tarzan stretches out horizontally to the left, while Taug, above and behind, reaches forward with the same arm in the same direction. The two are clearly companions in proximity and intent. Hogarth's interpretation of the scene (see page 26) opposes Manning's interpretation and shows through the orientation of the two figures the fundamental difference between them. As they travel, Tarzan's and Taug's bodies are oriented in opposing directions, one head first the other feet first. Tarzan swings over the branch, while Taug dives under it. Walter James Miller has pointed out: "Physically they may be traveling together, but mentally they are going in opposite directions" (11). This is the realization that

An illustration done by Russ Manning and published in the first series of the *Burroughs Bulletin* Old Series 15 (1964). Copyright Edgar Rice Burroughs, Inc. All rights reserved.

INSTEAD, TARZAN AND TAUG TOOK TO THE TREES TOGETHER, THE SHAGGY COAT OF THE FIERCE APE BRUSHING THE SLEEK SKIN OF THE ENGLISH LORDLING AS THEY PASSED THROUGH THE PRIMEVAL JUNGLE SIDE BY SIDE.

A panel from Burne Hogarth's pictorial retelling of *Jungle Tales of Tarzan* (1975). Copyright Edgar Rice Burroughs, Inc. All rights reserved.

Tarzan comes to as the story ends, that while he is *in* the world of the apes, he is not *of* that world. Hogarth, of all the comic illustrators, is able to capture, according to Holtsmark, the "unmistakable sense of urgency, vibrant and controlled movement, and aliveness" (106) central to Burroughs' work. He is able to take a visual image and produce in it and through it a psychological interpretation that transcends the words of the caption and gives definition to the reader's own or alternate building sense of Tarzan internally.

Modernist writers, according to Dale, were characterized in their work "by swift perceptions and abrupt juxtapositions of unrelated particulars" (55). In one sense, Burroughs' creation in 1912 of the hyphenated ape-man was just such a juxtaposition embedded in a complex sociological and psychological field (or, in this case, jungle). The character of Tarzan is marked by perceptions much quicker than the apes of nature, as he displayed when he roped the panther that pursued Teeka. The tension between human nature and ape nature drives both the character of Tarzan and the plot of the story.

Between the first appearance of Tarzan and the time that Burroughs wrote "Tarzan's First Love," Eliot wrote one of his most important early poems, "The Love Song of J. Alfred Prufrock," printed in *Poetry*, June 1915. Prufrock represented the tension between timid youth and cynical middle age. Burroughs' tension, while less philosophical, is bolder in the audacity of its circumstance. And, while contemporaneity does not equal relationship, there is certainly a kinship between Prufrock and Tarzan in their recognition of an inability to reconcile incongruent halves.

Eliot's "Prufrock" takes its genesis from Dante's *Inferno*, as Eliot's epigraph indicates. The futility of lasting achievement is implicit in Dante's character Guido da Montefeltro, who speaks only because he is sure that his words can never be taken to those who would be affected by them. He gives life to the words only because he believes they are eternally dead. This co-existence of contraries is the framework within Eliot's poem. Prufrock combines several contraries: youth versus age, life versus death, and thoughtfulness versus complacency, for example. The joining of life and death became especially important for Eliot. The persona of a later poem, "Journey of the Magi," comments, "I had seen birth and death, / But had thought they were different" (*Complete* 69). The implication in *had thought* is that the persona realizes the error of such an assumption. The opposite, the statement implies, is true: birth and death are much the same. In many ways, the Prufrock poem is the Modernist exemplum of William Blake's "The Marriage of Heaven and Hell." Eliot's poem affirms Blake's claim: "Without Contraries is no progression. Attraction and Repulsion, Reason and Energy, Love and Hate, are necessary to Human existence" (248). However, Eliot could not maintain the optimism that one might find in Blake. Eliot ends his Prufrock poem with drowning rather than the less damning oppression of the law that Blake identifies. Eliot's question in "Choruses from 'The Rock'" focuses the issue: "What life have you if you have not life together?" (*Complete* 101). More like Eliot than Blake, Burroughs ends this story in estrangement rather than assimilation, a young man alone in the jungle.

The idea of civilization as a jungle was in the popular imagination. Upton Sinclair had written his landmark novel of insensitive greed and civilized animality a decade earlier (*The Jungle*, 1906). Clarence A. Andrews claims that "[t]he real shock of [Sinclair's] book comes in our realization of the parallel between animal and human" (4), an idea promoted centuries ago by Solomon: "I said in mine heart concerning the estate of the sons of men, that God might manifest them, and that they might see that they themselves are beasts" (Ecclesiastes 3.18). Sir Arthur Conan Doyle made the connection across the ocean at about the same time as Sinclair. In his Sherlock Holmes story "The Adventure of the Empty House," Watson, the narrator, remarks: "I knew not what wild beast we were about to hunt down in the dark jungle of criminal London" (560). In this case the "beast" is expert tiger hunter Colonel Sebastian Moran.

Burroughs begins the story with Teeka, "a most alluring picture of young, feminine loveliness" (7). A newcomer to the Tarzan stories will not know from this that Teeka is an ape. The first intimation that this is the case, delayed by two paragraphs, is the narrator's statement that Tarzan "had known no other associates than the sullen bulls and the snarling cows of the tribe of Kerchak, the great ape" (7). The conflation of human and animal is implicit in the opening description, and an explicit difference between Tarzan and the apes of Kerchak does not come until later in the story when Tarzan begins to compare himself (ironically) to Teeka, juxtaposing her "handsome coat of hair" with "[h]is own smooth, brown hide" (8). This comparison began for Tarzan when he was "nearly ten" (*Apes* 36), in a poolside epiphany; he had gone, in *Tarzan of the Apes*, to a lake bank for a drink with "one of his cousins," where he is "appalled" at the differences in their reflections (37). As Taug does later, Tarzan goes on, in "Tarzan's First Love," to compare his teeth, eyebrows, nose and mouth to Teeka, recognizing his own inferiority: "Tarzan had often practiced making his mouth into a little round circle and then puffing out his cheeks while he winked his eyes rapidly; but he felt that he could never do it in the same cute and irresistible way in which Teeka did it" (8). Here the juvenile copying understates but confirms the parallel between human and animal that Andrews identifies.

Jurgis Rudkus, Sinclair's protagonist, endures the "jungle" of Chicago. Even before Sinclair, British icon and author Rudyard Kipling said in 1891 that Chicago, the first "real city" he had found in America, was "inhabited by savages" and "barbarians" (*American Notes* 207). Burroughs himself was living in Chicago when he began Tarzan's story. The book, Griswold points out, "was started in the midst of one of the country's great economic depressions, by a failed businessman who was writing in a rented office in Chicago and who had seen that it was a dog-eat-dog world out there, a 'jungle' where only the fittest survived" (107; see also John Tucker's "Tarzan Was Born in Chicago"). Certainly, Burroughs reveals just such a parallel in this story (and in other stories involving Tarzan). It is worth noting that Burroughs himself grew up on Chicago's West Side, and between the publication of Sinclair's novel and the writing of "Tarzan's First Love" also lived primarily in the Chicago area (shown in Bill Hillman's "ERB Houses: The Family Tree from 1875–1950"). Jurgis survives by virtue of three things, Andrews says: "his physical strength, his cunning, and his willingness to adapt to any situation" (6). While Tarzan's story's attack on social conditions is subtle compared to Sinclair's, these three virtues imbue Burroughs' character with the same vitality. Tarzan's physical strength is demonstrated early in the story, when he wrestles with the ape, Taug. His cunning shows even more than his strength in this story with his use of the knife and rope in giving himself an advantage over his adversaries. And, it is his adaptation that allows him to release his claim on Teeka and choose in the end to go alone. It is noteworthy also in Sinclair's *The Jungle*, that Jurgis's wife, Ona, betrays her husband with another man while Jurgis is out and that Jurgis later loses his family to the urban jungle of Chicago, just as Tarzan loses Teeka to Taug while Tarzan is away, eventually losing her and his sense of family with the apes in the jungle of Africa. Burroughs makes this city-jungle connection explicit in "The Capture of Tarzan": "The teeming jungle with all its myriad life, like the swarming streets of a great metropolis, is one of the loneliest spots in God's great universe" (24).

This human-animal dichotomy and the use of jungle as metaphor is also a manifestation of Modernist thought. Jurgis's Chicago, Prufrock's London, and Tarzan's Africa all present an alienating environment which threatens to separate each protagonist from meaningful unity with others. In Tarzan's case, David Adams claims, "The jungle represents the unconscious where he must work out his identity as a human being" ("Folklorist" 4). Jurgis and Prufrock attempt the same in their respective environments. The jungle becomes, in the words of Sarkis Atamian, "the unknown, uncharted territories of the soul[,] and the beasts are the challenges of the demons in all of us" (117).

Burroughs accomplishes much in this brief story. It is a story that centers on the quest for acceptance. This desire is not limited to Modernist writers, though. "Tarzan's identity confusion," Vernon writes, "resonates perfectly with that of [an] adolescent reader" (29) today. Tarzan, of course, in searching for assimilation, manipulates and contorts himself by whatever means available to be a "normal" member of the tribe. The modernist conclusion of such a quest, though, is foregone. The appearance of these needs is self-deluding; the Modernist end comes in alienation, loss, and despair. What is most important is the conclusion. Tarzan is left unassimilated; in fact, he is alienated from the very society that he grew up in. This sentiment is often one that is indicative of the Modernist world. Antonis Balasopoulos has suggested that Tarzan's separation from the apes is a positive situation. His claim, that Tarzan's "freedom from Nietzschean *ressentiment* renders him immune to the malaise and discontent of 'civilized' modernity" (206), seems to leap over the events in *Jungle Tales*, for discontent is central to the entire collection.

Tarzan's world, a literal jungle, has him trapped. This becomes a metaphor for Modern existence. The duality of Taug's literal caging and Tarzan's emotional bondage is a significant double binding. First, in Tarzan's attempt to fit into his ape world, he is like Taug, who is physically caged by Mbonga's warriors. Taug is helpless to set himself free in this situation. Likewise, Tarzan is trapped in a cage, a much larger one, made up of the jungle that he calls home. Just as in the Modern age that which should bring comfort brings despair, the home of the jungle is also the cage that bars him from assimilation. This double image reinforces the message and provides, in the end, the ironic context of Tarzan's final statement. Taug's separation from his own kind is short and temporary. The distance from the tribe to the cage is easily covered by Tarzan when he goes to free him. The distance from Tarzan's jungle cage to Europe or America, however, is insurmountable because it is inconceivable. Tarzan has no way to contact a rescuer, nor could he communicate his desire for rescue if someone were to enter his jungle from the faraway Western world. Also, his bondage is as much emotional as physical. He doesn't know who he is; his quest for acceptance is equally a quest for self-identity. Just as Taug lacks the physical dexterity to unlatch the cage that holds him, Tarzan lacks the mental framework to escape the jungle. He has only the fragments, the clues left in the enigmatic cabin by the shore, of what he is looking for. Tarzan's escape is likewise twofold. He needs the physical relocation that would put him back to his hereditary own, and he lacks, as do all adolescents, the emotional maturity to understand who he is. It will take the arrival of a rescuer, physically and emotionally, to free him from his bondage. In this story, no rescuer arrives, and Tarzan is left alone in his metaphoric cage.

The renunciation of his fellows, of course, anticipates and reflects the renunciation at the end of *Tarzan of the Apes*, a book paradoxically written four years earlier but the end of which takes place in the plot line some years later. There, when William Clayton asks Tarzan how he came to be raised in the jungle, Tarzan must respond in a psychological welter of emotions—because Clayton is engaged to Jane, because Clayton is the current Lord Greystoke, a title and social status Tarzan has just learned is his, and because Tarzan believes Jane loves Clayton. Tarzan's denial of all is wrapped up in the terse explanation: "My mother was an Ape, and of course she couldn't tell me much about it. I never knew who my father was" (219). At this point, it is as if Tarzan is claiming an opposing variation of his statement at the end of "Tarzan's First Love": "Tarzan is an *ape-man*. He will go alone." Assimilation, again, is frustrated as Tarzan stands in a different jungle, either literally at the edge of a Wisconsin forest, or metaphorically in the impersonal jungle of civilization. In terms of plot, though, this second alienation is yet to come.

When near the end of "The Wasteland" Eliot writes, "The jungle crouched, humped in silence" (*Complete* 49), the reader might well understand this in terms of Tarzan's jungle, uninviting and alienating. "Tarzan's First Love" ends, at least from a formalist stance, with isolation. As Prufrock is at the ending of "The Love Song of J. Alfred Prufrock," so Tarzan is left drowning emotionally. The irony of the final line in "Prufrock"—"Till human voices wake us, and we drown" (7)—is applicable to Tarzan's situation as well. It is the human voice within him that wakes a consciousness of separation. That consciousness in turn drowns his attempt at assimilation with the apes. The human voice brings both life and death, the paradoxical words of Guido da Montefeltro. The final word is not physical death but the psychic death that accompanies the recognition that in a Modernist world one is truly alone. The wisdom to be gleaned from the experience comes in the individual taking personal responsibility for his or her life. This is a personal journey that must be taken by the individual; no one can take another person's journey. When one tries, frustration is the only result. While the unnamed author of "War and Literature" may have meant something different, the claim that "Burroughs is a modern of the moderns" is surely worth evaluation.

"There is a Helen in every language."
—"The Book of Myths" (Harjo 82)

A modernist reading is only one view from which to read the story. Alva Johnston noted early that there was "a trace of Homer" (7) in what Burroughs wrote, and John Taliaferro states that "Burroughs [...] borrowed heavily from classical literature and mythology" (225). This is not surprising, given that Burroughs himself admitted that he had "studied Latin for eight years, and never was taught [his] mother tongue" (letter to Metcalf, 9 January 1913). Later in life he advised a fan that part of the foundation a writer needs is "an intimate knowledge of the classics" (letter to George Barrett, 5 November 1928). Holtsmark has claimed in detail, in *Tarzan and Tradition,* that Tarzan is a recapitulation of the Greek hero. He writes that Tarzan "may well be Romulus (or Remus), but he is also Heracles, Achilles, Odysseus, Perseus, Telemachus, Orestes," (93) and any number of other heroes of the classical world. Holtsmark identifies Achilles later specifically as a prototype of the "physical prowess" (120) that Tarzan exhibits. Others, too, have identified the mythic element in Tarzan's character and circumstance. Gabriel Soumille, for example, calls Tarzan "barely less than a sun god" (Charles Fleis's translation of the phrase "*à peine moins qu'un dieu solaire*" [300]), invoking a mythological context which he makes more explicit by later comparison to Hercules (302, 304) and more fleetingly to Prometheus (302), Orion, Jason, Apollo, Romulus and Remus (304). Even the film adaptations capture this relationship, as Francis Birrell points out that Johnny Weissmuller, the actor most identified historically with the role of Tarzan in film, looks like "the Parthenon frieze in motion" (661). Surely no one can miss the allusions to Greco-Roman history and mythology, not only in this story but abounding in references throughout Burroughs' works.

In *Tarzan of the Apes,* at a chronological point just after renouncing his kingship of the apes (that is, after the events of *Jungle Tales*), the narrator describes Tarzan in classic terms: "His straight and perfect figure, muscled as the best of the ancient Roman gladiators must have been muscled, and yet with the soft and sinuous curves of a Greek god, told at a glance the wondrous combination of enormous strength with suppleness and speed" (*Apes* 90). Similarly, in "A Jungle Joke," the narrator claims that Tarzan "was full grown now, with the grace of a Greek god and the thews of a bull" (*Jungle Tales* 159). This leads to the summative description in *Apes* that Tarzan displayed a "superb physique" (192).

That Burroughs had some Greek underpinning in his mind in writing about Tarzan is belied in his use of the adjective *Stygian* at several points, notably in "The Witch-Doctor Seeks Vengeance" where it is used to describe the entrance to Bukawai's cave and again in "Tarzan Rescues the Moon." The word derives from the River Styx, which in Greek mythology is the boundary between the mortal world and the underworld or world of the dead. Burroughs always uses it to mean a darkness that is somehow threatening or eerie, not a total lack of light, but a darkness so ill-lit that shapes and shadows are as much imaginary as real. When Tarzan enters Bukawai's cave he is able to find his way because "long use of his eyes in the Stygian blackness of the jungle nights had given to the ape-man something of the nocturnal visionary powers of the wild things with which he had consorted since babyhood" (102). Taug later goes through the "Stygian gloom" (189) to find Tarzan when the apes' order is threatened by the moon's disappearance. The use is not new to *Jungle Tales*, though. In the first novel the narrator says, "Here and there the brilliant rays penetrated to earth, but for the most part they only served to accentuate the Stygian blackness of the jungle's depths" (*Apes* 45). Similarly, in Bou Saada, Tarzan makes his way "[t]hrough narrow, stinking alleys, black as Erebus" (*The Return of Tarzan* 92) to spy on Rokoff. Erebus is that region of the underworld beyond the River Styx through which a soul must pass to reach the darkest region, called Tartarus; Erebus then is a kind of entryway to hell in Greek mythology. Later, in the fifth book that Burroughs wrote featuring Tarzan, Tarzan jokes that the language of the mangani is really Greek (*Tarzan and the Jewels of Opar* 146).

In addition to the modifying place names he employs, in many other instances within the Tarzan canon, Burroughs appropriates character names from mythology. These can be simple allusions, as when Jerry Lukas quotes from Vergil's *Aeneid* in *Tarzan and the "Foreign Legion"* in referencing Juno's well-known hatred. Juno is the Roman name for Hera, the wife of Zeus (Jupiter to the Romans). These can be minor general references, as when in *Tarzan and the Leopard Men*, Old Timer identifies his captors as "three hundred ebon Charons escorting his dead soul to Hell" (84–85). Charon was the boatman on the River Styx who ferried people to the Underworld. Burroughs, here, turns it from a proper to a common noun, making it plural while still retaining the direct relation to its etymological antecedent through the capitol "C." Or, these can be specific characterizations, as when Korak is named "the brawny, half-naked figure of the giant Adonis of the jungle" (*Son* 185). George McWhorter identifies Adonis as a "[s]ynonym for masculine beauty" (*Burroughs Dictionary* 3) because of Aphrodite's attraction to him. He figures in Ovid's *Metamorphoses* and his story is retold in Bulfinch's *Mythology* and Edith Hamilton's book of the same name, where his prowess as a hunter is noted and his boldness brings his downfall. Perhaps the most direct appropriation of things Greek comes also in *The Son of Tarzan*, where Burroughs retrieves the name Ajax from Homer's *Iliad* for the ape Akut. Ajax was a Trojan warrior who competed for Achilles' armor with Odysseus after Achilles' death. The sailors of the *Marjorie W.* give the ape this name because of his great strength; both they and Burroughs obviously knew their Homer.

Tarzan himself does not escape Burroughs' Greek typology. In writing about Holtsmark's book, *Tarzan and Tradition*, Gary Jacobs points out that "Tarzan's distinguished fictional lineage includes such heroes of antiquity as Odysseus and Aeneas" (5B). Jacobs identifies the similarities enumerated in Holtsmark's premise and extends the effect of those similarities: "Tarzan and Odysseus share characteristics that made them popular to large numbers of people" (5B). Holtsmark identifies Odysseus as a source for "more than a few of [Tarzan's] traits," in particular, "his cunning and cautious approach to life"; this comes arguably from the supposition that neither "believe[s] in the innate goodness of man" (113). The wary nature of Homer's Odysseus "is perpetuated in Tarzan, who adopts an attitude of cautious prudence and patience in evaluating new circumstances and alien people. Tarzan's lack of naïve trust in strangers," Holtsmark goes on, "probably saved his life the first time he met whites" (114; Cf *Apes* 100). David Cowart affirms that "the books which deal with the ape-man's childhood and adolescence, *Tarzan of the Apes* and *Jungle Tales of Tarzan*, chronicle a number of archetypal hero-experiences" (222); in Western culture, such archetypes come earliest from Greek sources.

The initial scholarship concerning Burroughs' sources was done by Rudolph Altrocchi in *Sleuthing in the Stacks* (1944). Altrocchi identifies Tarzan's abandonment to nature in terms of the Greek custom of Aryan Exposure, that idea of leaving a child out in the elements so that it will die, à la Moses. Just as Laius and Jocasta abandon the infant Oedipus to die, only to have him adopted by the Corinthian royal couple, so the death of Lord and Lady Greystoke leads to Tarzan's adoption by Kala and the grumbling Tublat. But the wandering shepherd who took the baby Oedipus to Corinth is less common than rescue from within the world of nature. As in the case of Romulus and Remus, Tarzan's mother is an animal, as Altrocchi claims is the case for the majority of abandoned infants in classic literature. Such feral circumstance was common knowledge by the Renaissance, as Antigonus attests in Shakespeare's *Winter's Tale*: "Wolves and bears, they say, / Casting their savageness aside, have done / Like offices [that of nursing young not their own]" (2.3.187–89). And likewise Tennyson picks up the idea at the beginning of *Idylls of the King*, where Cameliard is devolving through the encroachment of wild dogs, wolves, boars and bears; the wolf "now and then, / Her own brood lost or dead, lent her fierce teat / To human sucklings" (15). That Tarzan is raised by apes should not concern readers because, as Altrocchi remarks, "the animal is changed according to the region and climate in which the legend evolved" (88). The choice of apes is plausible if one begins with an African setting. (Of course, the African setting could have been adopted after Burroughs decided on the ape surrogate, also.)

Though most of the legends referenced by Altrocchi use the feral upbringing as a means to explain something about the adult behavior of the protagonist, some "shrewder story-teller" (89), Altrocchi points out, will focus on the details of that upbringing, a position at which he identifies Burroughs. Indeed half of *Tarzan of the Apes* and all of *Jungle Tales* focus on this period of Tarzan's life.

To return to Tarzan, Kala becomes the stand-in for the Queen of Corinth as Altrocchi suggests, and one could "interpret the she-animal in allegorical terms" (83). As surrogate mother, Kala provides more than a chance at life but also special protection. When Tublat, her mate, urges her to abandon the burden that he perceives Tarzan to be, Kala responds with an oath of lifelong protection: "If I must carry him forever, so be it" (*Apes* 35). It is her vigilance that allows him to come to his teenage years.

Tarzan is also likened to Hercules. Cowart likens Tarzan to "the infant Hercules strangl[ing] snakes" (222). (To be honest, though, in the only childhood snake battle that Tarzan endures, in "The God of Tarzan," Histah is dispatched by Tarzan's knife rather than his great strength.) His strength is often referred to as Herculean, and in "The Capture of Tarzan," he makes "Herculean effort" (31) to avoid the pit dug by Mbonga's warriors. When Tarzan falls into Rokoff's trap in Paris, he becomes "a veritable Hercules gone mad" (*Return* 28). Burroughs may have used the Labors of Hercules also to shape Tarzan's adventure in *Tarzan and the Forbidden City*. In this case the challenges are three: to kill a warrior, to kill a lion, and to steal the sacred diamond from the temple. Though she does not use the name of Hercules, Jane, in describing Tarzan to her friend Hazel, claims: "I have not seen him, but Mr. Clayton and papa and Mr. Philander have, and they say that he is a perfectly god-like white man tanned to a dusky brown; with the strength of a wild elephant, the agility of a monkey, and the bravery of a lion" (*Apes* 132). It seems little coincidence then that actor Gordon Scott who played Tarzan in six movies (*Tarzan's Hidden Jungle* [1955], *Tarzan and the Lost Safari* [1957], *Tarzan and the Trappers* [1958], *Tarzan's Fight for Life* [1958], *Tarzan's Greatest Adventure* [1959], *Tarzan the Magnificent* [1960]) also was cast as Hercules in *Hercules and the Princess of Troy* (1965).

The most telling of all the Greek references in "Tarzan's First Love" is the narrator's claim equating Teeka with Helen, whose charms were the instigation of the Trojan War.

The formula of comparison is not new. He had used a similar structure in the previous Tarzan book, which through the vagaries of the publishing industry had not yet been published. In *Tarzan and the Jewels of Opar*, the narrator equates the sacrificial knife of the Oparians with the Crown Jewels of England (64) and by implication the city of Opar with the British Empire. Holtsmark points out that such "comparisons between the British realm and the kingdom of Opar" reveal "the attitudes [Burroughs] wishes the reader to adopt concerning the Oparians" (54). This same reasoning applies in the reference to Helen of Troy.

With Burroughs' many references to the history and mythology of the Greeks and Romans, that he would compare Teeka to Helen of Troy seems less than surprising. Greek characters are used as objective correlatives, both embryonic and mature, to the action. The idea advanced by T.S. Eliot in 1919 that an image or situation could evoke an emotional or unconscious response from a reader, he called an objective correlative: "a set of objects, a situation, a chain of events which shall be the formula of that *particular* emotion; such that when the external facts, which must terminate in sensory experience, are given, the emotion is immediately evoked" ("Hamlet and His Problems" 100). To play somewhat loosely with Eliot's concept, the reader sees Burroughs do this repeatedly, for example by calling one of Korak's assailants "an ebon Hercules"* (*Son*

---

*The Ballantine editions actually spell it "Hercule," omitting the final "s." The McClurg edition clearly has the final "s," while the Burt edition bears a smudged "s." The next reprint, from Grosset & Dunlap, has cleaned up the smudge by removing the letter.

101). The dread of facing a super-muscled foe is inherent in the allusion; the objective element, Hercules, evokes the non-objective emotional response, dread. (Burroughs also identifies Mugambi [*Jewels* 31] with Hercules.) Likewise, when Burroughs chooses to name Helen as an objective correlative for Teeka, he expects both literal and emotional connections to occur. His equation of Helen and Teeka is joined on the emotional plane of pride: "Helen of Troy was never one whit more proud than was Teeka at that moment" (11).

Helen was the daughter of Leda, after the infamous rape by swan-disguised Zeus. As the daughter of a god, Helen was endued with superlative qualities, both in form and force. She grew to become "the fairest woman in the world" (Hamilton 186), and the coveted wife of Menelaus. When she is taken by Paris—sources disagree concerning Helen's volition in this: Hamilton cites her as stolen; Thomas Bulfinch says she elopes with him (169); Euripides even claims the gods hid her and Paris possessed only "a breathing image, form[ed] from air" (132)—Menelaus rallies all Greece to retrieve her from Troy. As a human, having two men fighting for her favor would be attractive to her vanity. As the daughter of a god, having two nations fighting for her possession seems the appropriate scale.

In the literary imagination, she became the ideal of beauty with an undercurrent of betrayal, much as Guinevere became in the Arthurian cycles. When Christopher Marlowe's Dr. Faustus sees her, as the ideal of human female beauty, he asks the timeless question: "Was this the face that launched a thousand ships?" (5.1.99); and one of Faustus's companions claims that she "was the beautifulest in all the world" and "the admirablest lady that ever lived" (5.1.11–13). Marlowe's better known contemporary pulls from that same imagery when Richard III is wooing Lady Anne, after killing her husband. He argues that it was her "heavenly face that set [him] on" (Shakespeare, *Richard III* 1.2.185). She sits in a long line of *femme fatales*, those female figures who entice some hero to his own destruction, La Belle Dame sans Merci from Keats, or Samson's Delilah.

The resonances of Helen's character and story do much to inform, both intellectually and emotionally, the scene where Burroughs compares Teeka to Helen. Without the image, Tarzan and Taug would be simply two rivals for the affections of a lady (albeit, only Tarzan is human). The differences that the story has identified earlier between Tarzan and Taug make it clear that each is representative of a different "people." The European ancestry of Tarzan and the mangani lineage of Taug re-embody the long-standing pride that sets Greece against Troy under Helen's influence. Two nations (even two species, in this case) are brought to bear in microcosm in the conflict over the possession of Teeka.

Burroughs has also set up Teeka as "a most alluring picture of young, feminine loveliness" (7) in the first sentence of the story. Setting aside the comedy of the comparison, Tarzan finds his own features unflattering compared to Teeka's "handsome" (8) ones. She is, to borrow from Marlowe, "the beautifulest" in all of Tarzan's world. The epiphany is sudden. Presumably, he had seen Teeka on other days where the emotional appeal to him was commonplace. On this fateful day, though, the divine enlightenment visits him and changes his future.

Likewise, Paris was not looking for romance when summoned to judge between the three graces. He had a wife, a supernatural satisfier according to the myth. W.S. Merwin, in "The Judgment of Paris," writes that "he had been / happy with his river nymph" (23) before he was made to choose the fairest of the goddesses. Merwin's Aphrodite gives Paris a glimpse of the future in which he sees "one girl," Helen, and realizes there is "no one like her" (24). It is this same kind of image that pulls Tarzan out of a humdrum leopard-eat-leopard world.

Just as Paris is moved to change his behavior, so too Tarzan changes the filial affection to which he was accustomed into romantic and possessive affection. Helen/Teeka causes people to behave differently. She is the Helen of Robert Herrick's poem "His Age," whose "eyes / [shoot] forth her loving sorceries" and cause the recipient of her looks to "Flutter and crow, as in a fit" (33). The crowing that Tarzan does is in the verbal invective he hurls at Taug; he takes on the animal attribute of the tribe: "'Teeka is Tarzan's,' said the ape-man, in the low gutturals of the great anthropoids" (10).

The sense of betrayal is foreshadowed also in this image. After Tarzan defeats Taug, he later finds Teeka "contentedly scratching the back of his rival" (16). This betrayal is the micro-version of Helen's questionable life in Troy, and the amplified betrayal in Helen's sister-in-law, Clytemnestra, who murdered her husband, Agamemnon, upon his return from Troy. Teeka betrays Tarzan's emotional expectations in allowing Taug's attentions after Tarzan's defeat of him. She seems to enjoy the attentions of whichever suitor is convenient, in self-absorbed fashion.

The charging of the situation that Helen's name invokes, Holtsmark points out, establishes an emotional triangle between two men and a woman, a situation that comes not only from Homer but from a myriad of sources both classical and later, a situation that Burroughs had used to good effect in the first Tarzan novel, with Tarzan, Jane, and Terkoz, as well as a number of other places.

> "But love is blind, and lovers cannot see
> The pretty follies that themselves commit."
> —Jessica, *The Merchant of Venice* (Shakespeare, 2.6.37–38)

Tarzan and Jane's relationship is considered "one of the immortal love affairs" (Clareson 189) of twentieth-century literature. Frank M. Robinson says that *Tarzan of the Apes* succeeded, in part, because "Burroughs had been wise enough to frame the tale as a love story." Without the romantic element, the story would have been simply so much derring-do and exoticism. Andrew Rice called Tarzan's relationship with Jane "one of literature's great love stories" and used lines from Burroughs' text to inspire his wedding vows. Nearly every story Burroughs wrote was a variation on this same kind of love story: Man seeks woman through inestimable obstacles and succeeds only at the last page. For Tarzan and Jane this took two books and their story is well known.

The story of Tarzan and Teeka is less well known.

In one respect, "Tarzan's First Love" can be seen as a microcosm of the love story in *Tarzan of the Apes*, a story yet to come in Tarzan's literary life but already in print for the reader. Tarzan's effort to gain Jane's attention is both effective and rejected. In that highly memorable scene when Tarzan rescues Jane from Terkoz, Tarzan did "what no red-blooded man needs lessons in doing" (141). Jane responds to his kiss with dreamy submission. "For a moment — the first in her young life — she knew the meaning of love," the narrator reveals. This is the moment of victorious, glorious bliss Tarzan has dimly looked forward to. But his effective rescue of Jane leads immediately to rejection. The next paragraph shows fickle fate: "[A]n outraged conscience suffused her face with its scarlet mantle, and a mortified woman thrust Tarzan of the Apes from her [...]" (142). At the novel's end, when Tarzan has an opportunity to reclaim Jane, he follows the leadings of hereditary chivalry and renounces any claim for the good and love of the woman.

Likewise, when Tarzan settles down with Teeka after eliminating Taug (though not permanently), he feels his moment of triumph: "[S]he came quite close and snuggled against him, and Tarzan, Lord Greystoke, put his arm about her" (20). The reader credits Tarzan's innocence and ignorance for this scene. Like an inversion of Titania's magic-induced *faux pas* in *A Midsummer Night's Dream*, the incongruity of the situation is visible only to the reader. Fortunately, that is all the further their ill-starred romance goes. As Tarzan mentally reviews his situation in the next paragraph, he again notices the physical disparity between them. He screams in frustration and renounces his claim on Teeka by returning to Mbonga's village to set Taug free.

Readers are left to ask what kind of love story this is. The story has a traditional framework that involves a struggle between two masculine figures for the attention of a female, as pointed out earlier. Not only is Tarzan frustrated, but the reader may be as well.

When Levin assembled his collection of favorite love stories, he provided the parameter that the "story must contain two *live* adults and leave at least one survivor" ([ix]). But exceptions exist to prove the boundary, and Levin goes on to imply that "Tarzan's First Love" strains at the guideline when he writes: "I also allowed Tarzan his fling with Teeka" (x).

Levin further explains that a love story, as he defines it for his anthology, should concern "two creatures who find one another uniquely magnetic," and that their "lives are in some way changed by this feeling" (x). Under this broad parameter, "Tarzan's First Love" qualifies.

Yet, the word *adults* in Levin's qualification may need additional stretching. According to both Farmer and Hansen, Tarzan is about 18 in this story, but the sense is that Tarzan is much younger. A second consideration of the word *adults* in Levin's qualification is the implication also of *human*. While the mangani are something more than current scientific opinion allows for apes, they are nevertheless short of human. But Burroughs extends many human characteristics to the mangani. This is essential for the story to work. The apes have a verbal language, limited reasoning ability, and limited memory. These human-like qualifications are important.

The implicit sexual undertones provide tension as well, though Burroughs did not intend the story to be prurient. The panther enters the apes' territory as a symbol of evil. Atamian speculates that the name's etymology comes from the Arabic word Sheitan, meaning Satan or the devil. Certainly, Sheeta is a disruptor at the very least, and to call him a devil is not insupportable. David Adams identifies Sheeta as "a classic symbol of unbridled sexual passion" ("Twelve") in this story. It is instructive that Tarzan's role in the story is to bridle the beast and restrain him from his death-producing goal. Likewise, Tarzan is charged with bridling his own passion, lest destruction result. When, in "The Fight for the Balu," Tarzan rescues Gazan from the panther, as Adams says, "[T]he old passionate attachment is vindicated" ("Twelve").

No one really wants Tarzan to win in this romantic competition, given the extrapolated consequences implied by Teeka giving birth to Gazan before the third story of the collection. "As a novelist, Edgar Rice Burroughs was a model of morality," Dorothy McGreal points out; Burroughs "drew a sharp line between good and evil and, unlike real life, the two never overlapped" (14). Taliaferro points out that in Burroughs' fiction "[c]onsensual sensual sexual intercourse is conspicuously absent" (65), and, likewise, Vernon confirms that Burroughs' entire Tarzan output constitutes "a remarkably asexual oeuvre" (96). "His women were pure and his heroes were noble," writes Allan Howard, in qualifying "the influence of Victorian morality" on Burroughs' writing. Holtsmark identifies the tension this way: "Tarzan's sexuality is never explicitly explored, but it is nonetheless highly visible" through suggestion and allusion (131). Like the threat of rape that crops up regularly in Burroughs' work, sexual impropriety is "always forestalled" (Taliaferro 65). Part of the suspense that Burroughs creates relies, at least partly, on the *possibility* of something errant occurring. Burroughs is not opposed to the reader thinking about broken taboos. He would agree with Henrik Ibsen's Hedda Gabler who tells her former lover, "You can think it. But you mustn't say it" (201). Before George Orwell coined the term "Thoughtcrime" in his dystopian *Nineteen Eighty-Four* (19), the separation between imagination and action was the same separation between propriety and impropriety. Thus, Tarzan's attraction to Teeka is the inverse of the abduction of Jane by Terkoz to "be the first of his new household" (*Apes* 139). (Antithetically, Robert Rubanowice suggests differently in his undeveloped speculation: "One wonders as Burroughs was writing volume six whether he might have seriously regretted not allowing Tarzan to follow through with his first true love, Teeka [...]" [576]. Rubanowice says this not as a way to consider the man-ape relationship but as a diversion from the perceived burden of Tarzan's marriage to Jane. Burger agrees that Tarzan's marriage "certainly made the writing of adventures about a supposedly free individual increasingly difficult" [*Glimpses* 135]. Rubanowice's suggestion cannot be taken seriously. When Farmer alludes to such relationships, as in *A Feast Unknown*, he does so outside the established ethics of the character.) Burroughs would have never considered such an outcome for Tarzan's actions. Such liaisons must be relegated to whispered inferences of some unnamed ancestor of Oparian lineage. When Macaulay published Burroughs' novel *The Girl from Hollywood* in 1922, Burroughs was offended by the cover illustration which showed a young woman being helped out of her dress in front of a movie cameraman. He complained to Curtis Brown that such a cover "suggests that it is rotten." "The story is intended to be clean," Burroughs contended, and in the same letter stated flatly, "I hate nasty stories" (qtd. in Taliaferro 194).

Altrocchi claims that the sources Burroughs may have used included stories wherein such "ape-man miscegenation" (101) occurs, and in fact is "so frequent as to have become commonplace" (99). If this is true, then Burroughs consciously chose to avoid the covert implications of such an alliance. Indeed, love and sex are not synonymous, as Burroughs makes clear.

The proposed sources that included such bestiality have not been shown clearly connected to Burroughs beyond the report of Altrocchi, and even Altrocchi makes a leap from his report to the sources. The recalled image as Burroughs described it, in Altrocchi's words (Burroughs' original words have not been recovered), includes the female ape throwing *her* baby after the defecting sailor. Thereafter, based on the sources Altrocchi discloses, it becomes *their* baby. Georges T. Dodds has suggested a 1908 dime novel, *The Young Marooner*, wherein the sixteen-year-old protagonist is marooned with apes which he joins for survival, but this source includes only male apes, which leaves out the "mating aspect" that Altrocchi infers and omits the final image of the female ape that Altrocchi attributes to Burroughs.

The idea, if not the actuality, of cross-species sexuality, which is only hinted at in, if not imposed upon, this story, has a long tradition. The Greeks and Romans regularly crossed the boundaries between animal and human, and even added the gods as a compelling catalyst. Holtsmark points out that "Tarzan's first awareness of his sexuality is explicitly tied to the story of the Trojan War and Helen" (130), the subject of the previous section. Wendy Doniger points out that "in our myths we imagine that animals masquerade as humans" (711) and that personification of them is symbolic and natural. Ovid gives repeated testimony to this in his *Metamorphoses*. An example important for this story is Leda, who gives birth to Helen because of her rape by a swan, which is a form chosen by Zeus for this encounter. Here the female is human while the male is not.

But this is not what Burroughs is about. "There is a time and a place for everything, including s-e-x and four letter words, but it's not in Tarzan books" wrote Vern Coriell, in response to a fan who wanted (in Coriell's words) "a Tarzan who uses four-letter words and goes about doing four-letter deeds" (96). Those who have read beyond this story know that Tarzan's attention is basic in a wholesome way. "One thing about s*x in Burroughs's [...] books" writes Richard Lupoff, "there's nothing explicit there that could turn an Iowa schoolmarm gray, even in 1912" ("Barsoom!" [59]); "his love scenes are cloaked in the genteel and flowing talk of his day [...]" ([63]). Holtsmark rightly points out that Burroughs is able to manage "a finely poised equilibrium between humor and the underlying seriousness of the depiction of a youth's first sexual stirrings" (130).

As a love story, though, the ending is significant. In essence, it is not love or emotion but reason that wins out, even if Tarzan's reason is only partially informed. His recognition of his difference from the apes, though intuitive, effects a volitional and unconsciously moral standard in Tarzan's behavior, which leaves the reader as well as Tarzan in what Holtsmark calls "emotional disequilibrium" (142). Tarzan faces an emotionally charged decision, where his attraction to Teeka is seen not in terms of love but in terms of the quest for assimilation. The ending is both the resignation to abnormalcy as well as acknowledgment of reason's triumph over emotion.

His attraction to Teeka in the first paragraphs of the story is emotional. Tarzan takes in evidence to the contrary well before the final renunciation. He sees the animal kingdom in harmonious relationships, not in line with his own situation; but fails to make application of these warnings of incongruence. The observation is relevant to readers as well. In my poem "Teeka," the speaker asks in the second stanza:

> Doesn't it happen
>   in our lives?
> we see, but do not understand,
> we hear, but do not comprehend the thing,
>   the circumstance,
>   that tries to tell us that this
> is not for us right now—
>   perhaps not ever—
> no matter how much we desire it? [Galloway 33, spacing adjusted].

The question is implicit in Tarzan's situation; but more importantly, the question is universal. Truly, such reader identification is one of the reasons for the success of the story.

    "But for Adam there was not found a help meet for him."
                                               —Genesis 2.20

In many ways, "Tarzan's First Love" builds on the story of the Garden of Eden, and especially Adam's placement there. The word *Eden* is subliminally placed on the first page of the story, embedded in the word *credence*. Though the reference to Eden is indirect, the connections are clear. When Jane sees Tarzan in the first novel, she thinks, "Never [...] had such a man strode the earth since God created the first in his own image" (*Apes* 148). And, after Tarzan rescues her from Terkoz, he takes her into the jungle where "she was entirely contented sitting here by the side of this smiling giant eating delicious fruit in a sylvan paradise [... where] she was contented and very happy" (*Apes* 153). The image is Edenic in intent, depicting the bliss of that first pre-sin couple. The editors at *Blue Book* introduced the first story of *Jungle Tales* (Sept. 1916) with the claim that "something of the bloom and radiance of the world's dawn glorifies Tarzan's life in the jungle" (986). That Burroughs had the story of Eden in mind might be further evidenced by the narrator's comment in "The Witch-Doctor Seeks Vengeance" that Tarzan was as "utterly vogue, as was the primal ancestor before the first eviction" (87), an arguably oblique reference to Adam, whom Brenda Cooper calls the "originator of humanity" (*Weary* 319).

This impression even spills over into some of the filmed versions of Tarzan's story. For example, Creed claims that *Tarzan, the Ape Man*, the first of the Johnny Weissmuller films, "is a reworking of the Christian myth of the divine couple who live happily in the Garden of Eden" (160). And Stanley Crouch in another movie review refers to the jungle as "Tarzan's Eden." This motif is appealing. Tim Cloward has pointed out: "We come from the wild — connectedness, Eden. We want more than anything to tell ourselves how to go back again" (4). Burroughs, in comparing Tarzan to Adam, provides a way, at least partially, for readers to identify with the "first man" in themselves, to, in a sense, go back again.

In this story and others by Burroughs, Tarzan is likened to the pre–Eve Adam in the following ways: 1) he is a specimen of physical perfection, 2) he speaks the language of the "first man," and most important, 3) he is surrounded by animals but without intimate companionship.

Adam is expected to be the perfect man. The Genesis account claims "in the image of God created he him" (1.27) and afterward that the creation was "very good" (1.31). Note also that Tarzan's rise to ascendancy is anticipated in God's directive to Adam to "have dominion over the fish of the sea, and over the fowl of the air, and over every living thing that moveth upon the earth" (1.28).

Tarzan's physique was established in the earlier novels as exemplary of the physically perfect man. The narrator, as shown previously, points out "[h]is straight and perfect figure, muscled as the best of the ancient Roman gladiators must have been muscled, and yet with the soft and sinuous curves of a Greek god" (*Apes* 90). When Tarzan reaches the French mission, Father Constantine first sees Tarzan's "superb physique" (*Apes* 192), and the opening scene of *The Return of Tarzan* shows Olga de Coude observe his figure as "[m]*agnifique*" (7). In "Tarzan's First Love," Tarzan's physique is embryonic. The "boyish" (8) protagonist despairs at his own lack of development. In his fight with Taug, even though the narrator notes his "muscles rigid" (10), the muscular maturation of the earlier novels is clearly subsequent in plot: "The ape-boy had as yet never come to a real trial of strength with a bull ape, other than in play, and so he was not at all sure that it would be safe to put his muscles to the test in a life and death struggle" (11–12). But the promise of maturation is hinted at later in the story when the narrator refers to "the mighty thews which, day by day, were building beneath [...] his brown hide" (15).

The second evidence is perhaps more tenuous. When Tarzan saves La in *The Return of Tarzan*, he speaks to her in "the low guttural barking" (170) of the mangani.* La, who has some sense of history in the ruined city of Opar, identifies Tarzan as someone "who speaks the language of the first man" (172). La is uniquely qualified to make this assessment. She is the high priestly descendant among a people isolated for millennia, speculated as contemporary to the Atlanteans. The rudiments of language identified here by La are presumably pre–Indo-European. The first man to whom she refers here may or may not be literally Adam but symbolically his language is the first language distinguishable. Such a claim also indicates her belief that the mangani are closer to human than to beast. The narrator of "Tarzan's First Love" reports, when the mangani flee to the trees in fear of Sheeta then scream defiance from their refuge, that "the progenitors of man have, naturally, many human traits" (14). One of those traits linking them to the human experience is language. When Tarzan brings Tibo to the mangani tribe in "Tarzan and the Black Boy," he does so for the boy to learn an "intelligible form of speech" (72). This is the same language of the first man that La identifies; the tribal dialect that Tibo speaks is as "senseless as the chattering of the silly birds" (72) to Tarzan. It is not until the arrival of Paul D'Arnot, in *Apes*, that Tarzan's verbal linguistic aptitude buds and blossoms. But the story of the Tower of Babel, another Genesis event, is not the concern here.

Most importantly, Tarzan, by circumstance, is in the same place that Adam found himself. The most striking parallel occurs in the search for someone like himself. In the Genesis account, expanded in chapter 2 after the overview of chapter 1, Adam is brought "every beast of the field, and every fowl of the air [...] to see what he would call them" (2.19). First, note the importance of language from the beginning; the purpose of the visitation is to create a linguistic link between the physical and the verbal. Second, that this is more than a naming exercise is indicated in the conclusion of the next verse. After Adam has named the creatures brought to him, the narrative concludes, "but for Adam there was not found a help meet for him" (2.20). Clearly, the purpose of the animals' presence in this scene is to reinforce the difference between the man and the animals and the need for kindred companionship. And that is precisely the

---

*Technically, the word *mangani* is not used in this context. Burroughs coined the term in the fourth book of the series, *The Son of Tarzan*, where Meriem uses it as the base word from which *Tarmangani* and *Gomangani* are formed, meaning in this case simply ape or people without regard for color. Here it is identified as the language of the tribe of Kerchak and the language of the anthropoids. The term is used, however, in *Jungle Tales* to identify the great apes.

motivation in "Tarzan's First Love." Had Tarzan had the input of John Milton's *Paradise Lost* that Frankenstein's creature found, he might have shouted to the skies: "You must create a female for me, with whom I can live in the interchange of those sympathies necessary for my being" (Shelley 138). But Tarzan has neither Milton's commentary nor an embodied Creator from which to ask help.

When Tarzan compares himself to Teeka, the differences that he recognizes are not a matter of species distinction but of his own perceived deformity. He sees "Teeka's great teeth," for example, as "mighty, handsome things by comparison with Tarzan's feeble white ones" (8). His hairlessness is the first obvious difference, but more important is the mental difference. His call to defend Teeka from the panther attack is foreign to the apes. When Tarzan tries to handle the situation, the narrator provides the point of view of the apes in the trees who thought that "Tarzan was not a real mangani" (14).

When Taug is later captured and Tarzan is able to put is arm over Teeka's shoulder in affection, he confirms their point of view. He is shocked by "the strange incongruity of that smooth, brown arm against the black and hairy coat of his lady-love" (20). The irony is obvious. Teeka's hairiness is a marker, for the reader, of beastliness rather than of beauty. He reasons that there is no difference between the male and female leopard or between the male and female monkeys. Even the difference between the male and female lions can be removed with the elimination of the mane. Likewise variations between male and female birds were minimal compared to the difference between Teeka and himself. Holtsmark agrees that "it is significant that the first time [the readers], along with Tarzan, are made aware of a distinction between man and ape, the cardinal point on which the discovery of that difference hinges is precisely the matter of hairiness as opposed to hairlessness" (71). After freeing Taug from the cage where Mbonga's villagers had held him, Tarzan tells his companion, "[F]or Sheeta there is a she of his own kind" (23); and of course for the other denizens of the jungle this remains true as well. He goes on to acknowledge "for all the beasts and the birds of the jungle there is a mate" (23). But for Tarzan there was not found a help meet for him. One can hear the echo of the Eden account when Burroughs writes, "Only for Tarzan of the Apes is there none" (23). His determination to "go alone" at the end of the story is filled with sympathy. The resolution to this alienation is still in the future. He is like Frankenstein's creature, lamenting, "Like Adam, I was apparently united by no link to any other being in existence" (Shelley 124). But for both this creature and Tarzan, there is no God saying, "It is not good that the man should be alone" (Genesis 2.18). Tarzan's alienation, though temporary, is profound and compelling.

In this sense, "Tarzan's First Love" merely sets up the search for companionship that pulses through the collection. Of course, one need only return to the first two volumes of Tarzan to know the outcome, that his Eve will arrive and after many obstacles real and imagined, the two will be married by Professor Porter at the cabin by the little landlocked harbor where Tarzan was born.

CHAPTER 2

Running in Circles
Cycles and Technique in "The Capture of Tarzan"

This second story puts greater emphasis on Tarzan's relationship to Mbonga's village. Burroughs' handwritten journal indicates that he began the story 8 May 1916 and finished it two weeks later, 25 May. He had finished "Tarzan's First Love" on March 21, 48 days earlier. This second story was published in the October issue of *Blue Book*. The story has been adapted to comic form in Charlton's *Jungle Tales of Tarzan* #1 (Dec. 1964), Gold Key's *Tarzan of the Apes* #169 (July 1967), and in DC's *Tarzan* #212 (Sept. 1972), re-titled "The Captive"; Kubert places this adaptation, curiously, *after* the death of Kerchak.

The story summarizes Tarzan's relationship with Tantor, the elephant. Mbonga's warriors dig a pit in the game trail, place spikes in the bottom and cover it with branches. Tarzan witnesses its construction but fails to realize its significance until later when he hears the warriors stampeding the elephant. Tarzan rushes to the place, avoiding a rhinoceros, just in time to stop Tantor from falling into the pit, but he himself slips down the side and strikes his head. The warriors take the temporarily unconscious Tarzan to the village where he is tormented and prepared for a moonlight cannibalistic feast. He calls for Tantor's help. Tarzan frees himself from his bonds and Tantor breaks through the palisade to carry him away.

In this story Burroughs involves the rhinoceros, *Buto* in the language of the mangani, in a scene reminiscent of Tarzan's standoff of seven lions in *Tarzan and the Jewels of Opar*. In the novel, Buto charges Tarzan from behind. At the last moment Tarzan senses danger and turns to find "Buto, the rhinoceros, his little, pig eyes blazing, charging madly toward him and already so close that escape seemed impossible" (*Jewels* 62). "[A]t the instant that he launched [his spear], Tarzan leaped straight into the air alighting upon Buto's back but escaping the mighty horn" (63). Then, "Tarzan of the Apes leaped nimbly into the tangled creepers at one side of the trail" (63) while the rhinoceros pursued the lions. Similarly, in "The Capture of Tarzan," when the hero is rushing to warn Tantor, he encounters Buto. The narrator points out that Tarzan "had met the stupid beast before and held him in fine contempt" (29). In a similar acrobatic fashion, when the rhinoceros raises its horn expecting to make contact, he finds nothing, "for the ape-man had sprung lightly aloft with a catlike leap that carried him above the threatening horn to the broad back of the rhinoceros. Another spring and he was on the ground behind the brute" (*Jungle Tales* 29).

Though Burroughs had written the scene in *Jewels* eight or nine months earlier, *All-Story Weekly* did not begin serial publication of the story until 18 November 1916, more than a year after Burroughs wrote it. For the general reading public, what the author remembered was not yet public knowledge when they read about Tarzan's encounter with Buto in *Blue Book*, which makes the *Jungle Tales* episode the first for readers to see the rhinoceros. Also in terms of storyline, the adventures in *Jungle Tales* occur long before those in *Jewels*. What occurred in any previous encounter, other than the anachronistic scene in *Jewels*, has gone unrecorded.

This encounter with Buto is also interesting from a literary standpoint because the narrator makes light of the situation. The use of understatement — claiming that the reason for its behavior is "of little moment to one whom Buto charges, for if he be caught and tossed, the chances are that naught will interest him thereafter" (29) — takes away the fatal sting, hiding it under an ironic loss of interest. (Some readers will also wonder at the correct use of the subjunctive *be*, since present usage often eliminates the subjunctive, but Burroughs' Latin training made the subjunctive natural to him.)

Another interesting concern is Tarzan's ineptitude in falling into the very trap he waved Tantor away from. James Blish has identified a concept called the "idiot plot" (Wolfe 18), which indicates that the plot may be carried forward not by intrinsic character motivation but because some character is an "idiot," in this case the hero. It is a common tactic near the beginning of much popular fiction and film. However, it may not be as serious a flaw as it first appears. While it may seem rather incongruous that the wise and reasonable Tarzan is the one caught rather than the unreasoning Tantor, it may be expected because the whole idea of a trickster is predicated on the idea that the "trickster is cunning about traps," according to Lewis Hyde, in *Trickster Makes This World*, "but not so cunning as to avoid them himself" (20). Hyde points out that the trickster character from folklore may be "simultaneously stupid and clever" (56), a claim to be explored in chapter 7.

> "And so the circle goes on ever widening, like as the ripples from a stone thrown in the water."
> — Van Helsing, *Dracula* (Stoker 222)

The cycles of life, whether naturally occurring or humanly imposed, provide comfort and stability. T.S. Eliot describes this action:

> The Hunter with his dogs pursues his circuit,
> O perpetual revolution of configured stars,
> O perpetual recurrence of determined seasons,
> O world of spring and autumn, birth and dying!
> The endless cycle of idea and action ["Choruses from 'The Rock'" 96].

While some readers complain that such repetition fails to lead to greater insight, that the treadmill quality of such action is more debilitating than energizing, the technique is a time-honored tool. The pattern that Burroughs chose to use relied on the proposition that the story (and by extension, life itself) "is cyclical in form rather than linear" (Adams, "Folklorist" 3). Holtsmark claims that the repetitive writing that is sometimes attributed to Burroughs pejoratively "and his reliance on formulaic language are not indicia of inferior or uncontrolled writing but rather a measure of his traditionality" (7).

One form of the many cycles that Burroughs employs is what Holtsmark identifies as "ring composition" (36). It is created with "the statement of a given word at or near the beginning [...] and the repetition of this word at or near the end" (36). The purpose or usefulness of this technique goes beyond its unifying appearance. To be most meaningful, its use must be "closely related" (37) to the writer's intended emphasis of the passage; that is, the return is based on a keyword. This circular composition can occur at any level: sentence, paragraph, episode, story, or story collection.

At the sentence level, near the beginning of "The Capture of Tarzan," the narrator relates: "Yet they were alone, for the teeming jungle with all its myriad life, like the swarming streets of a great metropolis, is one of the loneliest spots in God's great universe" (24). The word *alone*, near the beginning, circles back to its relative *loneliest*, to bring the concept full circle within the space of a single sentence. The emphasis on the concept is important in its contrast of appearance and reality both within the sentence and in its connection with the sentence that follows: "But were they alone?" (24). The idea of aloneness is given double illustration in this way.

This works in the scope of a paragraph as well. In the same story, after Tarzan has successfully warded Tantor from the concealed trap that Mbonga's villagers had dug, the narrator begins the paragraph with Tarzan "standing upon the edge of the pit" (31), pleased at the success of his reckless rescue of the elephant. Danger turns to celebration. But the short circle of emotion swings round with Tarzan, at the end of the paragraph, falling "toward the sharpened stakes in the bottom of the pit" (31). The pin-word that joins the circle is *pit*. Physically, Tantor is saved from it and Tarzan himself is snared by it. Symbolically, the pit represents the fall from fortune and prefigures the potential death and burial of the hero. This reversal of fortune, the first of two peripeties that Tarzan experiences in the story, serves to mark the apogee of the circular plot. The emphasis on *pit* enriches the readers' understanding of the situation, illustrating a particular point in the circular construction. The sudden reversal of fortune, from rescuer to victim, marks the rising action. In terms of plot, the fall occurs nearly midway through the story and the remainder of the narration deals directly with the hero's capture and his mechanization of an escape.

This cyclical technique, of course, occurs in larger narrative units, as well. For example, Holtsmark identifies a passage of eight paragraphs in "The God of Tarzan," where Tarzan leaves his death-defying encounter with Mbonga and takes refuge in "a swaying couch among the trees" where he is "absorbed in the solution of his strange problem" (59). This marks the beginning of a contemplative circle. To this point Tarzan has been in physical pursuit of an answer to his question regarding the nature of God. As the action subsides, this interlude marks an intellectual search to his "strange problem" bookended with the references to the "swaying couch" (59, 60). The next morning Tarzan continues his inactive consideration through a succession of twelve questions, which are terminated by a "wail that came [...] at some distance from Tarzan's swaying couch" (60). In the paragraph that begins after this second reference, Tarzan is "electrified into instant action" (60), thereby completing the circle and returning to the action that had been forestalled during this episode.*

This story, "The Capture of Tarzan," affirms the circular form. As each story in the collection is intended to be self-contained, this should come as no surprise. But Burroughs clearly has the story come full circle, with Tarzan's rescue of Tantor in the first half and ending with Tantor's rescue of Tarzan.

Considering the twelve stories of the *Jungle Tales* collection, Holtsmark points out that the stories themselves form thematic rings. The first and last stories—"Tarzan's First Love" and "Tarzan Rescues the Moon"—are united by their emphasis on what Holtsmark calls Tarzan's "socialization," his "relationship to the world of [...] the apes" (43). Likewise the second and eleventh stories—"The Capture of Tarzan" and "A Jungle Joke"—Holtsmark says, focus on Tarzan's "relationship both to the people of Mbonga's village and to the animals of the jungle" (43). Holtsmark enumerates several recapitulations in "A Jungle Joke" that arise from "The Capture of Tarzan," including the trap-setting for an animal (elephant, lion), the treatment of the captives by Mbonga's villagers, the superiority of Tarzan's "man-mind" (*Jungle Tales* 27, 175), the reversal of the rescued animal becoming a rescuer, and the perpetrators (the villagers) becoming the victims of the animal's destructive power.†

Holtsmark concludes that by using this cyclical technique, "thematic elements introduced at the beginning of the work appear towards the end [to] bring the reader full circle" (40). It is as Mr. Lorry, in Charles Dickens's *A Tale of Two Cities*, affirms: "As I draw closer and closer to the end, I travel in the circle, nearer and nearer to the beginning" (241). And what better emblem of that circle than the full moon that features so prominently in that last story, a moon that starts as a circle, loses its circularity, and then regains it in the end. So

---

*For a more detailed reading of this passage, see Holtsmark, *Tarzan and Tradition* 39–40.
†Holtsmark's full account in *Tarzan and Tradition* is found on pages 40–43.

Duane Adams' illustration entitled *Tarzan Shoots Goro* (2000).

important are these regular patterns of return that Holtsmark claims that if they were absent, "the emerging sense of Tarzan's identity and beliefs collapse into a jumbled heap of *passim* observations" (44).

The circle, so carefully crafted in *Jungle Tales*, is the emblem of the literal geometric figure, which must have an opposite side across its diameter. Those ideas shown in the beginning chapters of the book should echo back from the last chapters of the book. This idea is expressed visually in Duane Adams's illustration entitled *Tarzan Shoots Goro*. The composition of this colored pencil drawing is unified through concentric circles overlapping from a number of directions. Primarily, the moon in the upper right corner sends out light, like ripples in a pool, mirrored finally in the convexity of the tree trunks at the left edge. In contrast, Tarzan's bow, the focal point of the piece, curves in the opposite direction, showing the tension between man and nature. A third visual movement comes from the vegetation in the bottom foreground. Giving a nod at the sphericity of the scene, this foliage seems to wrap up and toward the figure of Tarzan, as if the viewer were looking through the broken wall of a tangible bubble.

As another illustration of these rings within the collection of *Jungle Tales*, David Adams points out that Burroughs "roughly alternates his tales between stories describing Tarzan's relationships with the ape tribe and Tarzan's relationships with the natives" ("Jungle Tales"). The variation is the centerpiece — stories five, six, and seven, which carry the extended narration of Tarzan's entanglement with Tibo and Bukawai. In concentric circles from this collective center, the stories alternate with the preceding odd-numbered stories and the succeeding even-numbered stories dealing with Tarzan's interaction with the ape tribe. (Note that the ape life and village life are not mutually exclusive; often Tarzan visits both locales within a single story. For the purposes of this illustration, Adams has chosen the predominant interest in each story for its categorization.)

In terms of reality, cycles occur but only rarely in comparison to the randomness of life. While the circle is a naturally occurring shape, it is usually obscured by the entropy and chaos of everyday life. This is reflected in an observation by Sherwood Anderson, who suggests that there are two types of stories, plot-based fiction and character-based fiction, representing the distinction between order and chaos. "[I]f you want to be a successful writer and make a good deal of money," Anderson suggests, "it is perhaps best to become a plot story writer" ("Man" 57), because character revelation does not require, in fact mitigates against, the cycle implicit in a plot's dénouement. Plot-focused fiction allows the author to impose action — artificial cycles as well as symbols— upon the characters. As if he had Burroughs in mind, Anderson goes on regarding plot-focused fiction: "You can excite the reader. You can even make him believe temporarily the impossible. In our popular stories the impossible is always being done" ("Man" 58). (Incidentally, Anderson chose to focus on the character-based story in his own writing.) The use of these cycles— and they occur in a variety of forms— may not be responsible for any measurable part of Burroughs' popularity, but it may account for some of the reason Burroughs is getting more than a second glance by serious readers.

In order to see the cycle, the reader must be viewing from the outside of the story. Viewpoint occurs within a story as well. The choice of what the narrator tells rests with the author, and just what the author reveals or conceals makes a great deal of difference in what the reader is able to "see."

Burroughs' Tarzan stories generally use a point of view called editorial omniscience. Harmon and Holman's *A Handbook to Literature* defines three distinct aspects to such a point of view: 1) repeated "shifting from the exterior world to the inner selves of a number of characters," 2) unrestricted "movement in both time and place," and 3) "freedom of the narrator to comment on the meaning of the actions" (364).

For example, "The Capture of Tarzan" begins with an objective description of the warriors who are digging the pit. The third paragraph shifts slightly to a different physical point on the trail to identify the perceptions of a reed buck. The narration, though, moves beyond objective description to point out that the human presence is "terrifying" (24) to the animal. "A hundred yards away" (24) begins the next paragraph, again in an external view. Here again, mixed in with the objective view are internal indicators as well. Numa, the reader is told, "had dined well," a fact not objectively evident, and his grunt is both "low" (objective) and "disgusted" (subjective) (24). Already the narrator has displayed two of the three criteria marked by Harmon and Holman regarding multiple shifts spatially and internally. The third element is also present in these paragraphs, that of interpretation. At the end of the second paragraph, the warriors are described objectively: "Sweat glistened upon their smooth ebon skins, beneath which rolled rounded muscles [...]" (23). But to this, the narrator adds an interpretation; the muscles are "supple in the perfection of nature's uncontaminated health" (23). The level of perfection is not objective, nor is the intention of nature. Here the narrator is telling the reader how to interpret the objective information.

The narrative stance is mutable in Burroughs' work. The narrator can be omniscient, relating the thoughts and impressions of one or more characters. The narrator can be objective, providing only those sensory facts that an observer might experience. The narrator can also be editorial, giving the reader information that could not be found in either of these ways and also telling the reader how to interpret such information. Sometimes the narrative includes a phrase, a sentence, even a paragraph, of what is commonly called authorial intrusion, a place where the narrator seems to speak directly to the reader in a matter of little relation to the story, as shown, for example, later in the story with the statement "You will doubt it" (33). Here readers are addressed directly and told what they believe. The same occurs in the opening paragraphs of "Tarzan's First Love." None of these perspectives is wrong, though some may debate the effect of the various modes of perspective.

Taliaferro calls these changes of narrative stance, especially switching from third-person to first-person narration, a "glaring mistake"; though he moderates the seriousness of the charge in his next sentence, stating "worse sins in literature" exist (110). Michael Meyer further moderates the topic, claiming: "Few generalizations can be made about the advantages or disadvantages of using a specific point of view" (*Bedford* 223).

Burroughs also uses a special form of narration when dealing with the non-ape animals, as identified earlier. When animals are the subject of the narrative point of view, the narration often becomes sensory. Again, near the beginning of "The Capture of Tarzan," Numa awakens from a pleasant slumber and through his senses examines his world. Primarily the lion uses his sense of smell to determine his situation, for the two things of interest to him are "the acrid scent spoor of the reed buck and the heavy scent of man" (24). Having a full belly, though, leads Numa away from the things that he identifies. Similarly, Tantor, whose eyes are of little use to him, when startled in the forest, raises his "long, supple trunk [...] quickly to wave to and fro in search of the scent of an enemy" (26). In this instance the "enemy" he has heard is Tarzan. Earlier in the paragraph, Tarzan, likewise, had used his sense of smell to identify Tantor's "familiar, pungent odor" (25). Among dumb animals, these smells are a kind of unwitting language, communication without words.

Tarzan also lives in this wordless environment (though he lives above it as well). The world of the senses precedes the world we perceive through language. Tarzan lives, as Don Maclennan has said, "somewhere before / the world of words was made," a world where "[s]mell spoke before speech" in such tangibles as "river water," "fog," and "cut grass" ("In a Pot on the Window Sill" 8). This sense of smell is primal. It provides a connection between Tarzan, the man (with an untapped language heritage), and the animals, whose interaction with their world comes almost exclusively through the senses.

Given the variability of the narrative stance in these stories, a reader may forget that the first Tarzan story began with a first-person narrator. The narrative frame that Burroughs sets up in *Tarzan of the Apes* is dropped in subsequent Tarzan stories. In fact, the initial novel never returns to its opening narrator, leaving the reader to infer, in the end, the relationship of the two speakers at the beginning of the story to its final revelation. The same technique is used by Shakespeare in *The Taming of the Shrew*, with its Christopher Sly induction, and by Henry James in *The Turn of the Screw*. The Tarzan reader must question whether the sources for the later stories continue to be the tipsy acquaintance, the "musty manuscript," the "dry official records of the British Colonial Office," and the "diary of a man long dead" (*Apes* 7). The use of the unnamed narrator relating events spoken by another is like that of Conrad's unnamed narrator relating Marlow's story, as noted in the introduction. Such an approach can be seen as a form of protection. Chinua Achebe points out that in *Heart of Darkness*, this narrative device can "set up layers of insulation between [the author] and the moral universe of his story" ("Image" 9). This distance provides for multiple layers of ambiguity in determining whether an attitude expressed represents the author, the unnamed narrator, or the speaking source of the story.

Some might mistake the editorial omniscience as a faulty extension of the actual character who begins *Tarzan of the Apes*, the speaker who states: "I had this story from one who had no business to tell it to me" (7). The narrator of this frame could not have witnessed many of the events subsequently narrated. This leads Greg Wahl, for instance, to claim that "Burroughs goes to great lengths to create a narrator we cannot believe" (34). That is, a narrator, following Wahl's argument, cannot be both a character and omniscient. Perhaps this is why the initial narrator has slipped away, or perhaps the narrator, as god of his fictive world, defies the logic that Wahl presents.

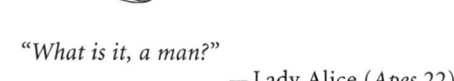

"What is it, a man?"
— Lady Alice (*Apes* 22)

Tarzan is repeatedly referred to as Tarzan of the Apes. Though the apes play no significant role in this story, the fact that Tarzan is of them raises a question that could have been addressed even before now. The question is: what are these apes, and what is their relationship to humans?

Taliaferro, in *Tarzan Forever*, states: "Burroughs's knowledge of apes at the time was understandably vague; scientists had not yet begun to do fieldwork on primate [...] behavior" (76). A summary of what was known in Burroughs' lifetime requires a return to the sources that Burroughs himself might have encountered. What these sources likely were has been analyzed superbly in Atamian's book-length essay, *The Origin of Tarzan*. One of those sources, J.W. Buel, in his book, *Heroes of the Dark Continent*, published in 1889, reports that the first gorilla specimen came to Europe in 1843, indicating that the large apes were only rumor before this verification, 32 years before Burroughs' birth. The animals then described stood five feet high and bore long canine teeth. They are described as imitators of humans. Buel adds the odd statement: "When their young ones die the mothers carry them about, closely pressed to them, till they fall from putrefaction" (89). This, of course, explains why Kala was able to drop her dead child in the Claytons' cabin when she picked up the crying baby Tarzan. Buel goes on to acknowledge that the report contains "a bad admixture of fact and fiction" (89), but he does not point out which information is which, nor did he likely know. R.M. Ballantyne, in his 1886 novel, *The Gorilla Hunters*, gives similar physical information. The hunters, in shooting "one of the rarest animals in the world" (211), were careful to log a description: "Height, 5 feet 6 inches; girth of the chest, 4 feet 2 inches; spread of its arms, 7 feet 2 inches [...]"; in addition to measurements the narrator provides subjective evaluation as well: "The body of this brute was covered with gray hair, but the chest was bare and covered with tough skin, and its face was intensely black. [...] there was something terribly human-like about it, despite the brutishness of its aspect" (212).

A second source identified by Atamian as one of the two primary sources

2. *Running in Circles* 53

GORILLAS—MALE, FEMALE AND YOUNG.

A nineteenth-century illustration of gorillas from J.W. Buel's *Heroes of the Dark Continent*.

from which Burroughs drew in the formative days of Tarzan, Paul Du Chaillu's 1861 book, *Explorations and Adventures in Equatorial Africa*, identifies another distinct species of great ape called the kooloo-kamba (from which Atamian suggests the name Kala is derived). Du Chaillu, whom Daniel Volman also names as "one of the first to provide convincing evidence for the existence of the gorilla" (680), identifies it as an animal that was "less powerfully built than the male gorilla, but as powerful as [...] the chimpanzee [...]" (314). Based on oral evidence, that is, that the locals used a different name for this particular specimen, and by his own observations, he concluded that it was "a new animal," distinctive for its call, its facial whiskers, and a jaw "not very prominent — less so than any of the apes" (317). Most importantly this ape is found in the trees, the very place to which the apes in Kerchak's tribe flee when danger threatens. Du Chaillu also adds that this animal "of all the great apes now known [...] most nearly approaches man [...]" (317). If Burroughs had read this, as Atamian argues, the comparison to humans may have sparked his creation of a "new animal" most closely resembling humans. Experts since have identified the kooloo-kamba as a species of chimpanzee. But the mystery that surrounded the reports of the nineteenth-century explorers made unnumbered variations among ape species possible in Burroughs' mind, a fact evidenced in *The Beasts of Tarzan*, where Tarzan identifies Akut's tribe as "another species" (25). In "The Battle for Teeka," the narrator describes Kerchak's band as "these great, manlike apes which the natives of the Gobi speak of in whispers; but which no white man ever had seen, or, if seeing, lived to tell of until Tarzan of the Apes came among them" (149).

David Livingstone reports that gorillas, called sokos by him in translation from one of the native languages, "often go erect," but are ugly in human terms, "a bandy-legged, pot-bellied, low-looking villain, without a particle of the gentleman in him" (*Last* 323).* He further describes them:

> His light-yellow face shows off his ugly whiskers and faint apology for a beard; the forehead, villainously low, with high ears, is well in the background of the great dog-mouth; the teeth are slightly human, but the canines show the beast by their large development. The hands, or rather, the fingers, are like those of the natives. The flesh of the feet is yellow, and the eagerness with which the Manyuema devour it leaves the impression that eating sokos was the first stage by which they arrived at being cannibals: they say the flesh is delicious. [323].

Livingstone adds that they have keen eyesight, but do not use their canines as a weapon. They eat no meat. Their "speech" is "like fox-hounds" (324). "They live in communities of about ten, each having his own female" (325).

David Day, in his assessment of the apes that Burroughs created, explained that the mangani "are a race of carnivorous, arboreal simians. They are neither gorilla nor chimpanzee, but more intelligent than either, and presumably more

---

*Waller's editorial note says that the soko is "*not* the gorilla," his emphasis, but "is in all probability an entirely new species of chimpanzee" (323). This may be a variant name or species of Du Chaillu's kooloo-kamba.

An 1861 illustration from Paul Du Chaillu's *Explorations and Adventures in Equatorial Africa* of an ape species identified as the kooloo-kamba.

closely related to Man than any other species" (86). He points to Burroughs' own description of Kala as "an ape[:] a huge, fierce, terrible beast of a species closely allied to the gorilla, yet more intelligent; which, with the strength of their cousin, made her kind the most fearsome of those awe-inspiring progenitors of man" (*Apes* 30). And as humanlike creatures, they bear similar body parts, usually set off by some inhuman modifier. Burroughs comments repeatedly concerning various anatomical features of the apes. Tibo, for example, sees not simply apes but "beetling brows," "great fangs," "wicked eyes," "mighty muscles" and "shaggy hides" (73). In terms of behavior, they are likewise similar to humans in certain respects. The apes are apparently polygamous, for example, because when Terkoz is banished from the tribe the narrator explains from the ape's point of view: "The tribe had kept his women. He must find others to replace them" (*Apes* 139). Multiple uses of the plural forms make the issue unmistakable. Many of the indigenous peoples of Africa, analogously, also practice polygamy.

These creatures are clearly not scientifically supported, but invented from suggestions in the less-than-consistent reports of the day. Hart calls the mangani "a race of apes bigger and smarter than gorillas" (219), and similarly Everett Bleiler identifies them as "a species (or genus) of intelligent, gorilloid apes who possess a rudimentary culture and a fairly elaborate language" (103). The spoken language, for example, of the mangani is many times more versatile than that of the modern gorilla or chimpanzee. Because of the words that Burroughs ascribes to the apes, Farmer has logically concluded that the mangani words include "sounds not found in English and seldom found in other languages" ("Language" [14]), though, nonetheless, the speakers of these words must "have teeth, oral cavities, larynxes and pharynxes much like those of human beings" ([15]). Poul Anderson summarizes succinctly: "No such breed of apes ever existed as were supposed to have raised [Tarzan]" (46).

With this imprecision of description on the part of Burroughs and his sources, it is instructive to note what the visual representations of the mangani have been. Artists have depicted Burroughs' apes in various ways. Hal Foster began the comic strip in 1929, with rather rudimentary apes. The panels were small black-and-white images, more suggestive than detailed. Rex Maxon took over the strip. These daily strips were drawn quickly and left little time for finesse. Midway through his career, Burroughs praised his book illustrator, J. Allen St. John, as the best illustrator he had, claiming his artwork "added considerably to whatever success" the books may have achieved (Burroughs, "Illustrator"). He credited the leisure that St. John had to work with and the reference to the printed text that he was able to capitalize on. St. John's apes, though, are more chimpanzee-like than others, a comparison that Burroughs does not put in writing. Foster and Maxon had made them more like humanized gorillas, but the details are minimal. And in reality (if such a claim is relevant), they must be something of a mix between the two. It is not until Burne Hogarth takes over as artist for the Tarzan comic strip in 1937 that this mixture begins to be apparent. A later culmination of Hogarth's metamorphosis is apparent in his book-length study of *Jungle Tales of Tarzan*. (See exemplary panel in chapter 1, page 26.)

Holtsmark affirms that "the naturalistic or zoological accuracy in Burroughs' depiction of ape society is of no more consequence to us than is the theological veracity of Homer's presentation of deity." Homer and Burroughs "both deploy their nonhuman actors the better to [...] comment on the human participants" (66). While the apes might be superficially natural, they are thematically essential. The way Burroughs' apes think and behave, while suspect to a modern primatologist, present meaningful insight from a literary standpoint.

Hal Foster drew the first comics page of Tarzan, retelling the entire first book in pictorial form, in 1929. This panel shows his understanding of ape form. Copyright Edgar Rice Burroughs, Inc. All rights reserved.

The apes may not be scientifically viable, but they certainly are central to many of the themes that Burroughs presents, and many readers have speculated on what the apes might mean beyond their literal selves. One area rich in speculation is the anthropomorphic quality of the apes. Both human and simian characters "are highly individualized beings," says Johnston (60). The animals are representative of human qualities and maintain a kind of consistency that readers ascribe to human behavior. Alan Barnard calls the world of Tarzan's foster family "the humanitarian ape world" (108).

In an early child's story written for his niece and nephew, Burroughs invents a tour guide named Anthropop, a talking monkey. The distinction between animal and human is metaphoric in both writing and speech. When Burroughs was suffering from dysentery at Fort Grant, he described his hospital steward as "an ape named Costello [...] a beast [...] unfit to care for sick men" (qtd. in Taliaferro 40–41). Jonathan Swift had done something similar for satiric purposes in *Gulliver's Travels*. The Houyhnhnms are intelligent, conversant horses ruling over the beast-like humans called Yahoos. In Burroughs' story, *Minidoka*, his use of Anthropop in reversing the expected roles "is intended to shed satiric light on man's mistreatment of animals" (Taliaferro 53). That in this early form Burroughs used the ape as a representative of humans suggests that in the Tarzan stories a similar intention may be appropriate.

The Disney productions have long understood this humanization of animals. Eleanor Byrne and Martin McQuillan have pointed out that the ani-

J. Allen St. John illustrated more Burroughs books than any other. This illustration (1919) was for "Fight for the Balu." Copyright Edgar Rice Burroughs, Inc. All rights reserved.

mated features contain "not so much a rendition of animals as such[;] rather they are anthropomorphic metaphors by which Disney presents the most humanist and traditional of values" (103). In the Disney movie *Tarzan*, "[T]he anthropmorphised ape tribe uphold family values" (Byrne and McQuillan 114). Balasopoulos calls the tribe which raises Tarzan "[t]he debased caricature of the absent Victorian family" (204).

Steve Baker says the belief that "animals are metaphorically indispensable to humankind" is an idea that "proposes a relation between humans and animals" that is "anthropomorphic, attributing [...] all manner of human motives to the animals" (81). Burroughs certainly intends the reader to see the apes for what they say about humans. This was a popular technique, used for example by Conan Doyle. Watson, the participant narrator of Conan Doyle's Sherlock Holmes stories, at several points refers to their antagonists in animalistic terms. For example, Sebastian Moran, a military man and expert tiger hunter, is "wonderfully like a tiger himself" (564), and Holmes repeatedly refers to him in terms of the hunter and the tiger, making Moran the animal. In a later story Watson describes the ambush that he and Holmes are setting in terms of hunting animals, and the human prey bearing animal characteristics. He says the search contains "something of the thrill which the hunter feels when he lies beside the water pool, and waits for the coming of the thirsty beast of prey" (638). He then muses: "What savage creature was it which might steal upon us out of the darkness? Was it a fierce tiger of crime, which could only be taken fighting hard with flashing fang and claw, or would it prove to be some skulking jackal, dangerous only to the weak and unguarded?" (638). Burroughs' narrator does this also, for example when he describes Snipes, from Tarzan's point of view, as a rat (*Apes* 93).

Burroughs also reverses the filter and uses humans to comment on animal behavior. When he does this, the animal comes off nobler in the eyes of the reader. Holtsmark explains the inversion of this concept as well: The violation of a young woman (Jane) "is attributed to the beast Terkoz, and the bestialization of the human Rokoff imports to him characteristics of Terkoz" (134). Thematically, this is important, because Holtsmark indicates that the antagonist in Tarzan's stories "is somehow a beast, in fact or in intent" (135). With that in mind, Holtsmark is able to contend that Canler, the man who attempts to "buy" Jane as a wife in *Apes*, is nothing more than "the 'civilized' analogue to Terkoz" (141).

Philosophically, the relationship between humans and the apes can be supported along the principles of analogy. Using Martin Heidegger's three-part distinction from "Introduction to Metaphysics," Byrne and McQuillan point out that animals "must have some world," while stones "have no world"; both these are differentiated from humans who are "world-forming" (109). The result of this line of thought is that even though an animal does not have as much "world" as humans do, it has the potential to "acquire world and so acquire spirit" (Byrne and McQuillan 109). It is by such reasoning that both writer and reader can extend limited human characteristics to the animals and in doing so implicitly make application of the nature of humanity. "The community of apes is never just a community of apes in Burroughs," Holtsmark argues; "an implied comparison" (64) or contrast between apes and human nature is embedded. This is not because the apes represent ideal society, a utopia of any sort. The apes are certainly as peevish as any human group that could be randomly assembled. The standard human assemblage, "both African black and European white," displays "all its short-comings" quite clearly in contrast to "the 'natural' order of the apes" (Holtsmark 64).

Burroughs used the apes in a way similar to the way Ibsen used trolls in *Peer Gynt* to contrast human behavior. Michael Kahn writes, "I can't believe that Ibsen thought he was just writing about trolls. He is writing about a society which is in reality one thing while pretending it's another [...]." He concludes that the focus for Ibsen was in "social human concerns much more than [it] was in folklore" (qtd. in Donn Murphy). Burroughs, though some will balk at the comparison, also invested more into the ape community than echoing folklore. The human concerns are repeatedly raised while looking at the ape community. It is no surprise to find Gail Bederman's claim that the apes that Burroughs presents the reader are "the original primal humans" (220). The three most important distinctions, Bederman says, between Tarzan's apes and the scientific ape readers know today are their language (discussed in chapter 1), their forms of leadership (discussed in chapter 7), and their use of ceremony (discussed in chapter 4).

Burroughs "shared with millions of his contemporaries" a "life-long fascination with evolution" (Taliaferro 92). As the search for the missing link took form, "the gap [between apes and humans] didn't seem all that vast" (Taliaferro 93). That every Jekyll had within him a Hyde, or every domesticated dog had within it a wolf, showed also that every Baltimore girl had within her a primeval woman and every English nobleman had within him a primeval man. Burroughs' interest in the evolutionary continuity between humans and apes continued, as he worked out variations in later Tarzan novels, including the Waz-don and Ho-don in *Terrible*, the Bolgani in *Golden Lion*, and the DNA-altered "Englishmen" in *Lion Man*. In another typical blending of primate fusion, Ras Thavas in *The Mastermind of Mars*, includes among his vivisectionist experimentation transplanting of the brains of apes into what on Mars constitutes a human body. When the warriors from Mbonga's village capture Taug, the narrator calls him, from their perspective, a "hairy tree man" (19) rather than an animal.

John Fiske, an adherent of natural theology, popular when Burroughs lived in Chicago, suggests four signal features of humans to distinguish them from apes: 1) "the greater progressiveness" of wider variation in a single generation, 2) "more or less permanent family relationships," 3) "articulate speech," and 4) "the duration of infancy" (86–87). Little is said to confirm or deny the first characteristic regarding the apes, but the second and third criteria are clearly marked in the stories as mangani attributes. The fourth one, the duration of infancy, separates the mangani from humans. The premise of *Jungle Tales* is that the apes with whom Tarzan had grown up had matured more quickly than Tarzan. This was shown in the first novel, when Kala was urged to leave the child behind. The narrator supplies maturational information: "The little apes [...] were as far advanced in two or three moons as was this little stranger after twenty-five" (35). While Tarzan is entering adolescence in the first story of *Jungle Tales*, Taug has become "a huge, sullen bull ape, somber and forbidding" (9), just as all the apes Teeka's age "were rapidly becoming surly and morose" (8). This blending of characteristics sets the apes somewhere between the scientifically supported ape and humans.

Conrath, in *Rethinking the Ape-Man: Approaching Tarzan as Object of Critical Discourse*, identifies the 1758 edition of Linneaus' *Systema naturae* for some crucial distinctions in humans. This scientific standard identifies various forms of humanity by region and by theory. *Homo europeus, homo americanus, and homo asiaticus* are clearly regional designations. Admixed are other groups less geographical, including *homo ferus* and *homo sylvestris*. Humans from the regional categories that have been returned to primitive existence, like Tarzan and Mowgli, are what comprise the *homo ferus* group. The *homo sylvestris*, though, are intended, though pre-dating Darwin, as a kind of missing link, a moving from ape to human in the "hypothetical ape-like ancestor of both" (Morris). Conrath explains this category as "an inverted *homo ferus*" (25). He goes on: "Rather than being man in a regressed, animal state, *homo sylvestris* represents the possible emergence of man *from* an animal state" (25). Conrath certifies, "The great apes that bring up Tarzan, the *mangani*, are *homo sylvestris*" (25). He reasons that "they possess a rudimentary language, and social and family behavior, which though rather animalistic, are structurally quasi-human" (25–26). It is this intermediate state between ape and human that Burroughs intended. Not only in *Jungle Tales* but sown into the other novels as well, Burroughs refers to the apes by names and descriptions that make it clear that Kerchak's tribe, and by extension all the mangani, represent something that must be identified as the "phylogenetic ancestor of modern man," Holtsmark argues (83). In this collection, Burroughs states that "the progenitors of man have, naturally, many human traits" (14), referring to the apes, and he calls them "the primal seeds of humanity" from whom "the ancient progenitor [...] took the first step out of ape-hood toward humanness (120)." In the first novel, the narrator establishes that Kala is a member of "those awe-inspiring progenitors of man" (*Apes* 30). He reinforces this belief when at the Dum-Dum the narrator reveals that at the "dawning [of] humanity[,] our fierce, hairy forebears danced" in the first ceremonies (*Apes* 51). Holtsmark also notes in three books following *Tarzan of the Apes* that Burroughs calls them "first men" (*Return* 173), "forerunners of primitive man" (*Beasts* 22), "fierce hairy progenitors of primitive man" (*Beasts* 33), and "great hairy primordial men" (*Son* 90).

The differentiation between the monkey and the ape is also important in understanding Burroughs' intent. The monkey (Manu) is seen as a lower form in the evolutionary scheme. Two books before *Jungle Tales*, in *The Son of Tarzan*, Burroughs explored the shared language between the two. Etymologically, the narrator reveals that "root words were so similar" in the language of the monkeys and the language of the apes "so as to suggest that the language of the Manus was the mother tongue" (*Son* 82). More important than the similarities, though, are the differences. The narrator goes on to point out that "[d]reams, aspirations, hopes, the past, the future held no place in the conversation of Manu" (82). While Meriem, the character on whom the narration is focused in this passage, is human and understands these things, the barrier is not intellectual but linguistic. It is her comparison between "the poverty of [the monkey's] vocabulary" (82) and the relative ability of the apes' language that yields this distinction. This would indicate that the apes that Burroughs has created have at least the rudimentary ability to dream, aspire, and hope because they can understand that the present has a *before* and an *after*.

Another comparison, detailed at some length in Holtsmark's book, is between the apes and the pantheon of Greek gods. He sets out the claim that "more than a few points of contact" exist connecting the apes with the "anthropomorphic gods" (67) that the Greeks and Romans described. He identifies several similarities, including the "authoritarian patriarch[al]" (67) ruler, the rising of the younger to forcefully take away the leadership of the older, and the clearly defined method of attaining the leadership position.

Holtsmark says that "Burroughs' apes owe an inestimable debt to the gods of classical literature, and [are] understood as a continuation of its divine machinery" in Tarzan's world (84). "As the gods in ancient literature may be used to represent ideas and attitudes about what is right or wrong with human character and action, so the animals come to be used by Burroughs in a contrapuntal or antithetical technique for the development of his ideas about man's civilization and the way life is lived in it" (86). Just as in early civilization, he adds, the females are fought over (sometimes by their own manipulation), leading at least once to a ten-year war, and those who have social power are often difficult to handle. "[A]s the Olympian family," Holtsmark elaborates, "with its virtues as well as its many defects, [the apes] always [present] at least an implicit parallel to the human world, so the familial and social activities of animals appear always to be involved to some extent in the world of Tarzan and other men" (77). In the same manner as the gods of classical mythology came to represent "a kind of magnifying glass through which the humans may be seen more accurately," so also do the apes "permit the reader to gain insight into the psychological and spiritual workings of humans and their relationships with each other" (77).

The family life is "fundamentally carefree" (68) with a danger of disunity because of disagreements; and, there is a ruling council with arguable power. These are elements of the Greek pantheon just as surely as they are of the mangani tribes.

The emotional make-up of Taug and Teeka especially is modeled on human emotions. The correlations are clear enough that the apes' emotional responses can be readily understood by readers. For example, the narrator gives the apes the capacity for sadness. When Tarzan tells Teeka that Taug will be killed by the Gomangani, he sees "a wistful expression and a troubled look of sorrow" (20) in her face. Likewise, "Taug felt sorrow as any other father might feel sorrow" (149) when he finds the body of Gazan where it had fallen during the violence of Teeka's abduction. Teeka feeds in "loneliness" (20) while Taug is away. When Tarzan commits indignities upon Taug, Taug determines to be revenged upon him (44), and when Teeka is abducted, Taug feels "the overmastering desire for revenge" (149). Hatred marks the apes' response to Numa, the lion (121) and at times their response to Tarzan (187). The apes can fear as well, as when Sheeta is seen (12) or Histah threatens, that single denizen of the jungle that also inspires loathing (61). The apes, also, are capable of love, as shown when Teeka enters the embrace of the snake in an effort to rescue her child (61), and, of course, "[i]n her wild, fierce way Kala had loved her adopted son" (17). Corollaries such as loyalty and friendship also are shown when Tarzan and Taug attempt to rescue the abducted Teeka (152) and when Taug sides with Tarzan against the other apes (186). At the beginning of "Tarzan and the Black Boy," the narrator claims the apes have the capacity for contentment (64) and enjoyment (65). These emotions through which Burroughs humanizes the apes set them apart from the other animals of the jungle.

Holtsmark sees these emotional attributes as "strongly reminiscent of the gods of ancient literature" (72) and concludes, "The apes, like the gods, have been humanized" (73).

Other speculation about what the apes represent comes from Eric Cheyfitz and Brenda Cooper. Cheyfitz argues that the apes are representative of "the 'mob' for which they unabashedly stand" (21). Cooper suggests that the apes present "traces" of "black people [who] are savage or absent" (*Weary* 103). Her claim seems inaccurate regarding *Jungle Tales*, where Mbonga's people frequent ten of the twelve stories. She complains about the "blurred boundary between apes and local, black people" (*Weary* 106), by citing a passage from Cheyfitz and another author, stemming from Burroughs words only at a distance.

Exactly what the ape might have represented to Burroughs is indeterminate. Tony Crisp suggests that the ape to a reader's subconscious might "represent a world of human experience [that] human beings have lost and feel sorrow at its absence" (32). The consciousness of self, "with its labyrinth of ideas and decisions" (Crisp 32), has caused humans to lose "a sense of oneness with life around them. Animals have enormous remembered wisdom," Crisp says, and by this he means not only instinct but also "complex social codes" (32). These instincts and codes are "still accessible to humans who can listen to the unconscious, and discover the enormous wealth of information they have about such things as social behavior and body language. The ape can depict this wisdom [...]" (32).

From a developmental point of view, it is natural that Tarzan would accept the apes as equals, and that the blacks of Mbonga's village should be distinguished only by a prefix, as *gomangani*, shows them simply as a variation rather than something entirely different. Tarzan, too, is one of the prefixed variations. James Serpell reports that children fail to "make a clear distinction between humans and non-humans" as is shown when they "begin responding socially toward animals [...] as if they were persons" (172). Serpell takes his cue from Sigmund Freud who claimed, "Children have no scruples over allowing animals to rank as their full equals" (*Totem* 126). This is Tarzan's situation when his adoption in infancy confuses the breast of Alice the mother with the surrogate breast of Kala the ape.

Claude Levi-Strauss established another line of thought about the relation of humans and animals. This totemic discourse identifies, as Richard L. Tapper has said, "a system of classification of nature [which is] employed to express the nature of relations between human groups and individuals" (50). This system suggests that the study of the interconnectedness of humans and animals is metaphoric rather than, or at least in addition to, literal. The focus is that the comparisons reveal things about humans themselves. Tapper divides the uses of these metaphoric treatments of animals into two categories: the animal as model of behavior and the animal as contrast to model behavior. Burroughs employs both categories. As noted above, Rokoff and Canler are worse than beasts, and a number of people from Mbonga's village might be added to the list. On the other hand, Sheeta is shown as a contrast to proper behavior because "of all the jungle folk, [only Sheeta] tortured his prey" (*Apes* 76). This first category suggests, as Mary Midgley believes, that "humans are capable of worse and more-motivated evil than animals" (Tapper 57). Rudyard Kipling identifies this propensity in his poem "The Hyaenas," where the hyenas are shown disinterring the bodies of dead soldiers but are implicitly more honorable than humans because they do not soil a man's reputation. The hyenas that accompany Bukawai may be seen, then, as purer beasts because their behavior is more natural than their master's.

In this way, Tapper argues, the animals serve "a moralizing and socializing purpose" (51). They become momentary foils by which to judge their human counterparts. The socializing message can vary widely, depending on the readers' predilections. A Marxist might read the apes as the lower class, a metaphor for the working man in apposition to the nobleman Tarzan, who reaps the fruits of their labor. This is seen even more pointedly in Tarzan's relation to the cannibal tribe's offerings of food and weapons. A psychologist might read the apes in terms of human development, as a view into the brain of a child, as indeed many nineteenth-century anthropologists believed was demonstrated in a kind of continuum from beast to human, where each higher form attained a higher measure of cognitive development against the human child. W. Winwood Reade, for example, pointed out in 1864: "The negro imitates the white man as the ape imitates the negro" (30); or later Freud wrote: "There is a great deal of resemblance between the relations of children and of primitive men towards animals" (*Totem* 126). An ecofeminist reading, as provided for example by Jonna Higgins, suggests that Tarzan embodies "men's preeminent position over women and nature" (17); that is, the apes represent both nature and women who, as a group, have been "mutually devalued as the non-male Other" (18).

But for all the humanizing attributes that Burroughs gives the mangani, some scientists question whether there is an absence of such traits among the animal kingdom. Midgley, for example, points out that "quite complex aspects of things like loneliness and play and maternal affection, ambition and rivalry and fear, turn out to be shared with other social creatures" (14). The list rambles across Burroughs' depiction of the apes with high correlation. Rodney Needham points out also that much of the behavior of the mangani corresponds to present-day observations concerning apes. For example, the striving in single combat for supremacy in the group, he says, "seems to be common behavior among primates" (22). Concerning the Dum-Dum, Needham says, "Burroughs was more right than he could have known," and he cites "significant positive correlation between percussion and rites of passage" (23). The apes represent an entire spectrum of human behavior.

"I wonder," I said reflectively, "what an elephant's soul is like!"
—from Dr. Seward's diary, *Dracula* (Stoker 273)

While the apes are certainly the most prominent of the animal types in Tarzan's life, this story highlights the special kinship that he finds with Tantor the elephant. In what Holtsmark calls a "supporting role" by a "nonhuman participant" (84), the elephant in this story is to Tarzan what Tornado became to Zorro in later years, coming to the rescue at the sound of whistle.

Holtsmark points out that Tarzan's "remarkable friendship with Tantor" is characterized by "stability and endurance" (86), a fitting symbol of the elephant's size. This important relationship serves as "a solid counterweight" (87) to the dangers of daily jungle life and to the increasing anti-sociability of the apes. Burroughs' narrator calls Tantor a "good listener" (*Jungle Tales* 184), which is why he can provide "solace and quiet friendship" (Holtsmark 87). Tantor is "the symbol of eternal peace," according to David Adams ("Twelve") and "the peaceful constant," according to Burger (*Glimpses* 30), of Tarzan's world.

Holtsmark speculates that the name Tantor was created "from the Latin adjective *tantus*, 'so great,' becoming a noun by the addition of the common Latin agent suffix-*or*. Tantor should, therefore, mean 'he who is so great,' which, one must admit, is not without merit as an apt name for the huge pachyderm" (98). Porges agrees: "Somehow *Tantor* seems appropriate for a towering, majestic, and kindly elephant" (194). Crisp suggests that elephants represent, from the unconscious mind, "[t]he enormous potential power of life" (34). Perhaps the name loses some of its majesty since the Disney hypochondriac has given a different rendition.

Just as the apes are interpreted in a number of ways, so the elephant is multivalent. Hillman points out, "it is easy to see the dog personae in his description of other faithful beasts" ("The ERB / Jack London Connection I"), and here he includes elephants as exemplary. Tarzan's call for Tantor functions similarly to a dog whistle, though in this case it is audible to every creature of the jungle. Burroughs considered several characteristics inherent in elephants. When A. J. Spiro, an editor at the *New York Evening Journal*, asked for a letter in support of a campaign to acquire an elephant for the Brooklyn Zoo, Burroughs complied, naming elephants exemplars of "dignity, poise and patience" (qtd. in Porges 452).

Holtsmark lists Tantor as the only non-ape who is "divine in its self-sacrifice and compassion" (72). He uses "divine" in the classical pantheistic manner, and indeed Tantor's rescue of Tarzan in "The Capture" does smack of the classical *deus ex machina*. The idea of sacrifice for another is central to the story. First, Tarzan risks himself to save Tantor from the piked pit. When he revives as a captive in Mbonga's village, in Kubert's graphic rendition, Tarzan thinks explicitly, "Tantor is saved ... But — Tarzan has taken his place!" ("Captive" 11).

When the various incarnations of these stories are probed, the back formation of them seems to support, as the editors of *Blue Book* said, "the tang of the imperishable fairy tales" ("Tarzan, Lord of the Jungle"). The role that Tantor plays in this story is straight out of such traditional tales. In such stories, "the Helpful Animal, like the Wise Old Man, often appears when the hero has reached an impasse and cannot see a way out of his dilemma," explain Harold Schechter and Jonna Gormely Semeiks, in "The Helpful Animal and the Holy Fool" (265). Their discussion cites Simpleton from Grimms' "The Queen Bee," who is aided by "grateful creatures whose lives he has previously saved" (Schechter and Semeiks 265). This is akin to the story of the lion that Androcles befriended. After Androcles saved the lion from a painful thorn in the paw, the lion in return saved the life of Androcles years later in the coliseum. A quick comparison might connect the sharpened spikes in the pit to the thorn in the lion's paw, though Tarzan averts the initial impaling. The palisade wall of Mbonga's village becomes the coliseum where Androcles was sentenced to death. In both cases, the man and animal leave the danger together, reunited.

"When Tarzan is in trouble," Holtsmark points out, "the loyal Tantor rescues him in great style" (87). This is the first time in Tarzan's literary life that such a rescue has occurred, though Burroughs had used the device earlier to rescue Korak in *The Son of Tarzan*, and returns to it in "Tarzan and the Jungle Murders" in 1939. Nor is this the last time that Tantor arrives in *deus ex machina* fashion in *Jungle Tales*. In "Tarzan Rescues the Moon," Tantor again rescues Tarzan from the threat of overwhelming odds. The surprising arrival of the elephant in this last story, Holtsmark points out, "has overtones of the *deus ex machina*, the 'god from the machine,' made popular in Euripidean tragedy" (87). "Tantor, like one of these rescuing divinities, not only physically dispels the attackers, but also quite literally lifts Tarzan up on his back and lumbers off with him to the safety of Tarzan's cabin by the sea" (87). In this miraculous fashion, Tarzan is just as surely saved as the day his father's knife slew Bolgani in the beating fists of the child.

That Burroughs chooses the elephant and not the lion is immaterial (though later Tarzan does have just such a lion named Jad-bal-ja, who rescues him first in *Tarzan and the Golden Lion* and most memorably in *Tarzan and the City of Gold*). In his early years, the focus of *Jungle Tales*, an elephant seems more benignly appropriate, though Tantor's carnage in Mbonga's village is anything but benign. Schechter and Semeiks point out that "the Helpful Animal may be a member of virtually any species" (265), and that "[s]ometimes, of course, the kind of Helpful Animal found in a work will depend on the story's locale. In such jungle tales as the Tarzan and Bomba series, for example, the Helpful Animals are, predictably, elephants, chimps, and lions [...]" (266).

Some readers balk at the plausibility of Tantor's actions in this story. That he could have fallen into the staked pit seems right enough. J.H. Williams, who spent much of his adult life living and managing elephants in the Burmese jungle, points out that "wild elephants are not always suspicious of danger" (43). His headlong flight from the warriors toward the pit seems quite plausible. That Tarzan could turn him from his single-minded stampede strains a bit more. And that he would return to the village at Tarzan's call is beyond the scope of most readers. In setting forth the situation, the narrator follows five questions with a kind of procatalepsis, "You will doubt it" (33), directly addressing the reader and anticipating the reader's objection, followed by its answer in the passive negative affirmation: "[I]t is not to be doubted [...]" (33). But the narrator does not intend the reader to wholly doubt. By raising the questions, the narrator hopes to short-circuit potential counter-arguments before the reader can raise them, by a conditional agreement.

The tension between verisimilitude and what Samuel Taylor Coleridge calls "poetic faith" or "that willing suspension of disbelief" (285) is important, and the breaking point between them falls in different places for readers. The narrator attempts to deflect the potential of failed verisimilitude with the statement, "Elephant hunters may be right when they aver that this animal would not have rendered such service to a man, but to Tantor, Tarzan was not a man — he was but a fellow jungle beast" (36). Even among human-elephant relations there is some speculation that elephants make personal choices. Dan Wylie, in his extended study, *Elephant*, claims that "[d]eep mutual affection" attends the "5,000-year-old history" of interaction between the two species (114). Williams believes that the claim of the indomesticability of African elephants "is not entirely true" (33). He points out that Hannibal's famed elephants may have been African. Wylie goes even further to claim in relation to Hannibal's venture, that "North African elephants were [...] trained like their Asian counterparts." He adds, "[T]hey are no less tractable" (*Elephant* 128). In corroboration, he adds that Egyptian hieroglyphics "distinguished between wild and trained elephants" and that Sumerian artifacts support the existence of tamed elephants, or, at a minimum, humans riding elephants (116). Another support is the incredible memory that is popularly ascribed to elephants. Wylie confirms that elephants have "an unusually large temporal lobe," an area "associated with memory" based on current brain mapping (50). In *Son*, Burroughs had Tantor recognize the villainous Malbihn many years after their initial contact—when Malbihn had killed Tantor's mate. And, the narrator's claim that Tantor did not see Tarzan as human mitigates much of the scientific speculation and observation because the situation is irreproducible.

When the narrator states that "[s]ometimes Tarzan wondered if Tantor reciprocated his affection" (27), the reader is not particularly aroused. Scientists seem divided on the issue, ranging from those "who regard the attribution of emotional states to animals as illegitimate anthropomorphism" to those who see the elephants as "kindred species" (Wylie, *Elephant* 61). Wylie comes down on the more sympathetic side, affirming the "capacity for altruism" would appear, as in humans, "highly developed" (59). The context of Burroughs' statement, Tarzan's affection for Tantor, makes this a minor but relevant mystery. Like any effective foreshadowing device, it does not rise out of the text and beg for address. It comes not at the beginning—in fact, it comes in the twenty-second paragraph of eighty-two—nor is it the first or last sentence of its paragraph, where it might receive greater emphasis. But it does exactly what it should because it is, as Harmon and Holman define foreshadowing, "[t]he presentation of material in a work in such a way that later events are prepared for" (235). The dénouement of the story depends on the answer to this implied question. The narrative does the same thing in other places. For example, in "The End of Bukawai," when the witch-doctor sees his hyenas while tying Tarzan in preparation for torture, the narrator states, from Bukawai's point of view: "He knew that they but waited for the time when he should be helpless" (112). The placement is similar, embedded within the context of a greater concern, yet it points to the story's dénouement.

Three paragraphs before the question of Tantor's affection, the narrator explicitly tells the reader: "At his bidding, Tantor would come from a great distance—as far as his keen ears could detect the shrill and piercing summons of the ape-man [...]" (26). But this revelation is downplayed by the immediate application of Tarzan's ability to direct the course of the elephant while riding "upon his head" (26), thus diverting attention from the principle to a ready application that belies its importance.

At Tarzan's realization of his capture, the narrator again plants a foreshadowing statement: "he did not cast about for outside aid now [...]" (32), this time in the negative. The emphasis is on Tarzan's self-reliance, but the inclusion of the adverb *now* indicates that the time may come when "outside aid" might be sought. The narrator continues this negative foreshadowing in a series of five rhetorical questions regarding Tantor's motivations, concluding with the statement: "[I]t is to be doubted that Tantor would have attempted to overcome his instinctive fear of the black men in an effort to succor Tarzan" (33). Even in denying the potential, the idea is presented. Upon a second reading, the foreshadowing, as usual, becomes more obvious.

In other ways Burroughs embeds foreshadowing as well. The story begins with the warriors digging the mysterious pit. That the pit will be important later in the story is assumed and its foreboding presence abides in the first half of the story. When the story opens with the description of the warriors digging the pit, the reader is forewarned that someone or something will surely be endangered by it. Many verses from the Bible predict the use of the pit as a trap, for example, Isaiah 24.18, which says, "And it shall come to pass, that he who fleeth from the noise of the fear shall fall into the pit; and he that cometh up out of the midst of the pit shall be taken in the snare [...]." (Whether Burroughs read from it or not, Harmon and Holman point out that the Bible, in its King James Version, is "[t]he single book that did the most to mold present English prose style" [442, emphasis removed]; its effect culturally is inestimable.) In the case of this verse, it is the intent of Mbonga's warriors to create noise to produce fear in Tantor, from which he will flee, and in doing so fall into the pit that they have prepared. When this is foiled, the second part of the verse comes into play. Because Tarzan falls into the pit in his attempt to avert Tantor, he is raised up, unconscious, and bound, or snared.

On the opposite end of foreshadowing is the lesson learned. When one event results in a distasteful consequence, the intelligent actor will learn to avoid a similar situation in the future. James Ward illustrates the principle this way: "A fox who has once escaped from a trap will not be caught again, if the same sort of snare is used; recognizing the resemblance between the old situation and the new he will refrain from touching even a more tempting bait" (449). Tarzan never again falls into such a pit, nor does Burroughs record Tantor making such a mistake. Both live to keep the circle moving in its perpetual revolution.

CHAPTER 3

All for One
"The Fight for the Balu"

Blue Book (Nov. 1916) bills "The Fight for the Balu" on its contents page as "one of the most keenly exciting exploits of Tarzan." Burroughs wrote the story from 26 May to 1 June 1916, two weeks before his family trip that would keep them away from Chicago until spring of 1917. The *Des Moines Sunday Register* re-titled the story in newspaper fashion: "Tarzan Fights Huge PANTHER To Rescue Infant Ape!" The story has been adapted to comic form in Charlton's *Jungle Tales of Tarzan* #1 (Dec. 1964) and in DC's *Tarzan* #213, re-titled "Balu of the Great Apes," reprinted, divided into two parts, in DC's *Tarzan the Untamed* #252–253 (Aug.–Sept. 1976) and again in *Edgar Rice Burroughs' Tarzan: The Joe Kubert Years* #1 (Dark Horse, 2005).

Teeka gives birth to Gazan shortly before the story opens. Showing more interest than Taug, Tarzan tries to touch the baby and is bitten by Teeka. When Taug comes to defend his offspring, Tarzan ropes him and suspends him from a nearby tree, head down. When the other apes begin to taunt and jeer at Taug, Tarzan decides to set him free. In her interest in the scene, Teeka sets her baby beside her, and Sheeta, the panther, begins to slink toward Gazan. Tarzan sees the danger and rushes toward the baby. Tarzan and Sheeta deadlock over the infant. The other apes gather around them, and as the leopard reaches for the infant, Tarzan attacks. Teeka sweeps her baby to safety and urges the bull apes to join Tarzan in his struggle. When Tarzan's leg is raked open, Taug leads the others into a pulp-pounding attack against the panther. Afterward, Teeka allows Tarzan to hold Gazan while she licks his wounds. Taug joins them.

This is one of two stories in the collection with no interaction with Mbonga's village, making this a purely man-ape exploration. The other, "The Battle for Teeka," occurs in the penultimate spot.

Tarzan tries to establish teamwork in this story, and manages at least to plant the seed of the idea. The apes are habitually self-centered, especially the males. This attention to self both physically and emotionally is a barrier that Tarzan must get the apes to address and overcome because the opposite of teamwork is selfish protection of the ego, which mitigates the safety supposedly implicit in numbers. Until a person (or an ape) can let go of the perceived desire to protect the self, the person cannot understand the role of integration into a team. In current society, "egotistical maleness," as Edward Rothstein calls it, is "the epitome of contemporary villainy" (E1). And it is the scourge of Kerchak's tribe. While Kerchak, oddly, is not present in the collection of stories, his legacy from *Tarzan of the Apes* is clearly one of egotistical dominance. The other apes likewise care for themselves and scatter at the first sign of trouble. The maternal instinct is the only real counter to the each-one-for-self principle of the tribe. Fiske suggests that all cooperative efforts sprang from the initial instinct of motherhood. "As the maternal instinct had been cultivated for thousands of generations before clanship came into existence," he says, "so for many succeeding ages of turbulence the patriotic instinct, which prompts to the defence [sic] of home, was cultivated under penalty of death. Clans defended by weakly loyal or cowardly warriors were sure to perish" (Fiske 104). Tarzan attempts in this story to move them many generations, by Fiske's theory, toward the more human role of cooperation. This movement has inherent in it the noble savage as a contemporary signifier and leads eventually to the role and use of tools, the rudiments of technology.

"*In her wild, fierce way Kala had loved her adopted son*"
—*Jungle Tales* 17

The role of the mother is one of the most basic of all nature. From the mother figure come the protector, the nurturer, the teacher, and a host of other interpersonal roles. Fiske explains: "Before such divine things as love and self-sacrifice could spring up from their cosmic roots and put forth their efflorescence, it was necessary that conscious personal relations should become established between mother and infant" (121). Teeka's protectiveness of Gazan in this story shows the maternal instinct at work. Even Tarzan, whom she knows and trusts in other situations, is not trusted in the newness of motherhood. Fiske, again, supposes that "the relation between mother and child must have furnished the first occasion for the sustained and regular development of the altruistic feelings" (121). The adults of the tribe, aside from the mothers for the infants, show no concern for the fate of others. At the beginning of "The Lion," the narrator sets exactly the scene when at the lion's charge "huge bulls trampl[ed] upon little balus" while "only a single she held her ground [...], a young she inspired by new motherhood to the great sacrifice that her balu might escape" (118). The other apes must be goaded into action because no personal advantage could be seen in risking life for the sake of another. The sense of self and other exists individually. Only rarely, as in the case of an intruder ape from another tribe in "The Battle for Teeka," does the self take on a corporate identity, here because of the educational scenarios that Tarzan has led them through.

Tarzan knows the characteristic is insufficiently developed, and so asks them to stay behind (at least in part) rather than join the pursuit only to fall away to the distraction of a caterpillar a hundred yards farther on. It is the love for the infant that Teeka demonstrates repeatedly that Tarzan wants to extend in principle to the entire band. Fiske suggests that just such a progression occurred in human pre-history. "The capacity for unselfish devotion called forth in [the mother-child] relation," he says, can be transferred to "the conduct of individuals not thus related to one another" (121). The role of the mother is crucial, he says, because "[o]f all kinds of altruism[,] the mother's was no doubt the earliest; it was the derivative source from which all other kinds were by slow degrees developed" (121). The ability to show concern for someone other than the self springs first from the mother protecting her child. Later, then, the role of the father, as demonstrated by some animals, takes on a parallel role. Eventually, the concern is extended to those in the larger family and then finally the animal grouping—band, tribe, herd, whatever the name. Fiske concludes that "the first appearance of real maternity was an epoch of most profound interest and importance in the history of life upon the earth" (Fiske 122), because from it all other forms of concern were born.

Kala, Bederman notes, "showers Tarzan with a pure, selfless devotion any human mother would be proud to emulate" (223), "[i]n her wild, fierce way" (*Jungle Tales* 17), Burroughs' narrator adds. The beginnings of altruism, as Fiske calls the opposite pole of egotism, were likely unrecognizable in prototype. It is only as one response built on another that a primitive type of others-awareness was built and passed on. And of course there are no records of its development, but the supposition is appealing. Barnard says that Kala "represent[s] something in the 20th-century Western view of the maternal instinct, of 'primitive' woman, or of 'primitive' society generally which readers find both appealing and plausible" (108). Because maternal love is witnessed in current society, readers assume something like it has existed in previous generations; and, certainly since written records have existed, readers can be assured that a mother's love is central in civilization in a variety of circumstances. "[T]he 'natural' love of mother and child," Cheyfitz concludes, "can translate across racial boundaries" (20)—and the reader might just as profitably substitute *species* for *race*—a condition that does not translate well for the males in Kerchak's tribe.

But this does not negate the role of the father. At the beginning of the story, Taug is identified as Gazan's father, even though it is Tarzan who elicits the most interest in the child. When Teeka rebuffs Tarzan, though, Taug enters into the dispute against his childhood friend. Whether other males had done so before, or whether Taug is a turning point in the development of the mangani is unclear. In "The Battle for Teeka," Taug, the narrator says, "felt sorrow as any other father might feel sorrow" and that "God implanted in the savage bosom that paternal love" (149). And so despite the fact that Taug had become "a huge, sullen bull ape, somber and forbidding" (9), some seeds of otherness had germinated. That he had grown up with Tarzan (one must assume that Taug is a younger playmate, since the apes mature more quickly than humans)—had "romped," fished, "baited Tublat and teased Numa" together (9)—may support a conclusion that his interaction with Tarzan has moved along the developmental line more than any other generation and more than any other influence. Taug, then, has become the rudiment at least of a father in his concern for his offspring. And there are few father roles revealed in the Tarzan stories.

Tibo's father, Ibeto, is one of the marginalized fathers to note. The narrator reveals that he captured Momaya from another tribe years earlier, making him a valuable warrior to Mbonga, even if he is not prosperous. The reader learns that Ibeto "never had owned more than three goats at the same time in all his life" (94–95). Though it is not demonstrated in the tale of Tibo, the paternal role is also important, if for no other reason than he provides a context for Momaya and Tibo to reside in Mbonga's village. In the earlier *Tarzan of the Apes*, the narrator identifies Mbonga also as a father; it is his son Kulonga who kills Kala.

Yet in many ways, Balasopoulos contends, Tarzan's story depends on fathers. The heritage of John Clayton, through the artifacts of the cabin, are the essential pin on which the first novel hinges. Balasopoulos argues that the first novel "both repeats and inverts, Defoe's *Robinson Crusoe*" (206). Burroughs had been given a copy of *Robinson Crusoe* in 1883 for his eighth birthday, a book which he kept in his personal library in adulthood. In Daniel Defoe's groundbreaking story, young Robinson finds himself breaking away from the father's advice and influence; he "frequently expostulated" with his father (and mother) for "being so positively determined against what they knew [his] inclinations prompted [him] to do" (Defoe 16). The father had said earlier, "That boy might be happy if he would stay at home; but if he goes abroad he will be the most miserable wretch that was ever born" (16). Robinson as a young adult chooses to make that break from the father, and is haunted by it ever after. Tarzan, too, experiences a break from the father, though, as an infant, his break is not by choice. It is through this interpersonal rebellion that Robinson establishes his independence from his father and begins to institute dependence of slaves under him, followed by the domestication of the island and acquisition of Friday; fatherhood and imperialism are linked in this way. Tarzan, likewise, rebels against his foster father, Tublat, ironically with the knife of the biological father, as a first step toward independence, a step that is made effectual with the death of Kala. At the end of *Jungle Tales*, Tarzan has yet to take the next step, that of dominion over others, but that is the next major action that must take place when one returns to the *Apes* narrative. The repetition of the Defoe plot is recognizable. Its inversion, too, is evident, when the reader realizes that Tarzan is unwittingly seeking to be reunited with the father. The defeat of Tublat turns out to be double-sided. "The primal scene of rebellious patricide," as Balasopoulos sees it, "comes to signify not the temporary dethronement of despotic power but its triumphant restoration" (206). The rule of one father is replaced vicariously by another. And through the power of that dead father, Tarzan becomes ruler of the apes. His doing so exposes his attempt "to symbolically undo the premature and traumatic break with the ancestor's defeated figure, to close the gap," Balasopoulos says, "between the father's interrupted imperial mission and his own" (206). Tarzan's rise to the kingship of the apes becomes the recapitulation of the father's initial charge to investigate — and implicitly read, preside over — the natives, much as a father presides over his household.

Teeka's motherhood is the spark that ignites Tarzan's latent desire to have a charge of his own. The parental theme is emphasized by the short declaration that begins the story: "Teeka had become a mother" (37). Though she had "retained her childish delight" (37) longer than others of the tribe, she is compelled to change when she experiences motherhood. Tarzan is emotionally hurt when she does not freely hand the child into his care. Teeka's protectiveness is instinctual, that is, untaught. In "The God of Tarzan," she propels herself into the coils of the snake to rescue her baby, an action otherwise repulsive to any ape. Later, in "The Battle for Teeka," Toog, the interloping ape, is able to exploit her maternal devotion to her child to kidnap her.

But the apes are not the only maternal examples that Burroughs provides in these stories. Momaya, of Mbonga's village, presents the obvious foil to Tarzan's attempt at motherhood. In "Tarzan and the Black Boy," Tarzan takes Tibo from Momaya when the two are "farther down stream [from the village] than usual" (69). Momaya is gathering food, as was expected of an industrious mother, while her child plays nearby. Tarzan ropes Tibo beside the "river [that] winds close beside the village" (69) and carries him away "into the depth of the jungle" (71). That the first mention of Momaya is at the water's edge is significant. Joanne Stroud, in her foreword to Gaston Bachelard's book, *Water and Dreams*, claims that water represents, at least in some instances, "the spring of being, [that is, specifically] motherhood" (ix). It contains "strongly feminine characteristics" (ix), which Bachelard affirms (14).

Tibo's mother's name, Momaya, derives from the maternal *mo-* and *ma-*, from which come the English words *mother* and *maternity*. The familiar *Mommy* is embedded within the Africanized construction with the feminine— *a* suffix. Holtsmark even suggests that the name is an "Anglo-Greek appellative calque" (177n), meaning Mother Earth. Nothing particularly subtle informs the name, and the character is clearly meant to represent the maternal principle that Tarzan is searching for. Her actions in later stories are clear comparisons by which the reader can assess Tarzan's efforts and temperament toward motherhood. The reader sees the parental protective instinct in her when she responds to Tarzan's abduction of Tibo. When the great white "god" of the forest is dragging her son away and she cries out and "leap[s] fearlessly" at him; the narrator records: "In her mien Tarzan saw determination and courage which would not shrink [...] from death itself" (70). Rather than engage with her, one arm holding the tied child, he takes to the trees, "just as the infuriated mother dashed forward to seize and do battle with him" (71). He is impressed with her protective response, as she continues to cry and "menace" him after he is out of sight, and he muses that the village would be more "formidable" (71) if the male villagers had similar pluck.

Because she believes Tibo has been taken by supernatural means, she consults the witch-doctor of the village but gets no satisfactory aid. In desperation and against the express commands of her husband and the village chief, she sets out to consult the leprous outcast Bukawai, "who was in friendly intercourse with gods and demons" (76). Such an act strained "her great mother love" (76), because Bukawai was not altogether safe, nor was his help certain. Far from safe, Bukawai was considered to produce magic more evil than the local witch-doctor. But Momaya's love for her child drives her beyond reason. The narrator explains that "[m]other love, however, is one of the human passions which closely approximates to the dignity of an irresistible force" (77). This is the corollary to Teeka's attack of the snake in "The God of Tarzan." Nor, when Tibo is returned, at the end of "The Witch-Doctor Seeks Vengeance," does Momaya's "shrewish tongue" (76), which had threatened Tarzan and scorned the village witch-doctor, mellow. Bukawai's and Rabba Kega's attempts at extortion are met with derision as she cries, "Momaya will show you some magic of her own" (105). The "vixenish" (77) woman then takes a nearby stick and, because Bukawai has already fled, pursues Rabba Kega through the village, striking him whenever she was able.

Tarzan's efforts to mother Tibo fail because he attempts a role that he is not capable of, at least at the level of maturity that he has attained in this story sequence. Rather, he becomes an interruption to the normal relationship displayed between Momaya and her son. He is not the father figure, which is absent in Tibo's first story, but an intruder. Holtsmark calls him a "supposititious father" and "a foundling father" (156), qualifying him by modifiers that make him no real father at all. Instead, Tarzan attempts to be a parent without the maturity to do so and "soon realizes he cannot be a father by force" (Holtsmark 156).

The instinctual desire for family that Tarzan tries to pacify in this story is important. He has lost his first, biological family to death at an early age. He has lost his second, adoptive family to death just recently. And now Tarzan is attempting to set his world right by forming a third, artificial family by taking Tibo. Holtsmark points out: "When the family is in order, the world is in order and makes sense; when the family is split and relationships are not clear, the world itself is disjointed" (157); and Tarzan certainly has felt the disjointedness of his world. As these first three stories have shown, the family unit is not peculiar to any particular world. Rather, its universal nature makes it central in the lives of everyone whether black or white, animal or human. And it is a place in a family — as child or parent or both — that Tarzan seeks.

To see Tarzan as both parent and child is not contradictory. Everyone has the potential to be both. As Augusto Centeno points out: "Several theories are always possible at one and the same time, each possessing its own kind and degree of validity" (3). Just as it is not contradictory to suggest that a specific person can be parent, child, wage-earner, performer, and so on, it is not contradictory to propose multiple readings or understandings of a single person or, to extend the idea, of a single text.

As a writer—or simply as a human, Sherwood Anderson would say— Burroughs is using his writing as a means of "trying to struggle through the tangle of human relations" (Anderson, "Man" 46). And human relations have taken some varied priorities over the centuries, especially as conjectured in the pre-historical context and its perceived presence in "savage" representations of our historical era.

> *"They don't seem really savage."*
> —David Innes, speaking of the
> Sagoths (*At the Earth's Core* 27)

Much has been said over recent centuries regarding the noble savage, a term coined by John Dryden in his verse play *The Conquest of Grenada*. Ursula K. LeGuin contends that "Tarzan is a direct descendant of the [...] Noble Savage" (447), among other antecedents. This root of the noble savage goes back at least to Jean Jacques Rousseau, who postulated that the less civilizing a person had, the nobler his or her principles. Rousseau popularized the idea in the eighteenth century. In the opening to *Emile*, he writes: "Coming from the hand of the Author of all things, everything is good; in the hands of man, everything degenerates" ([9]). This idea of the corrupting influence of human relationships is central to his idea, which culminates in the proposal that the less "civilizing" a person has the nobler his sentiments. Mark Twain comments similarly through Huckleberry Finn, who finds his natural inclinations superior to all of the Widow Douglas's attempts to "sivilize" him, "considering how dismal regular and decent the widow was in all her ways" (11). To be fair, the nobility of the uncivilized is but one aspect of Rousseau's often contradictory philosophy. But the idea of the natural man was picked up by the Romantics and has survived in various incarnations ever since.

Among the characteristics expected of the noble savage are a harmonious relationship with nature, exquisite health/physique, a selfless innocence, and innate wisdom. In several degrees these qualities are indicated in Tarzan. His jungle life, though fraught with dangers, is essentially harmonious and symbiotic. His form is "[m]ighty and muscled" (*Jungle Tales* 68) much like Mbonga's men whose "rounded muscles, [are] supple in the perfection of nature's uncontaminated health" (23). His innocence allows him to be attracted to Teeka and his selflessness underpins his many attempts to create unity among the apes. His reasoning ability allows him to create things and understand cause-effect situations much to his own benefit.

3. All for One

Interest in the noble savage, as Grun points out, is "indicative of an unflagging interest in the man of nature" (132). Tarzan, she indicates, writing in the 1930s, was representative of "the contemporary fictitious Noble Savage" (133). The way the figure was treated in "the modern Noble Savage story is decidedly different" (Grun 133) from its eighteenth-century counterpart. In the twentieth-century popular version of the theme, she writes, the focus is on "the savage [trying] to discover his civilized identity" (133). In particular, Tarzan represents the congenial blending of the savage and the civilized. He must have a dual heritage to accomplish this, a tacit condition of the feral story. Tarzan's nobility comes not from his feral childhood, but from "an inherent strength, [...] by virtue of birth and breeding, enabling him to rise above the degradation that accompanies a life of bestiality" (Grun 135). Newsinger affirms that the heredity that matters to Burroughs "is not Tarzan's humanity [...] but his English aristocratic heritage" ("Lord" 60), and Hart identifies Tarzan not just a child but "a sprig of British nobility" (219). "The struggle between Tarzan and an ape for the possession of a girl, and the sudden awakening of the gentlemanly virtues in the breast of the victorious Tarzan, [are] symptomatic" (Grun 135) of the struggle between the divided heritage. A distinct difference exists between the fictional story of a prehistoric man such as Burroughs' Nu of the Niocene or Jack London's Big Tooth and the feral child that Tarzan represents. Grun acknowledges this when she says the then-contemporary depiction of the noble savage "is a child of civilization rather than of nature; he is expedient, fierce, dissatisfied with his life, constantly at war with his environment, and decidedly unspiritual" (135). Tarzan is not a noble savage, then, in the sense that Rousseau is associated with; instead he is simply the raw juxtaposition of *noble* and *savage*, in a literal sense.

Tarzan displays and endures these traits in various ways in *Jungle Tales*, ranging from his ostracism by the other apes, through the struggles with flora and fauna of the jungle, to the inconclusive search for a higher being spurred by his reading. But, the stories of Tarzan and other incarnations of the noble savage indicate "the eternal interest in the primitive, and the desire [of the reader] to share, if only vicariously, a life that is not surrounded by the complex paraphernalia of a civilized existence" (Grun 135). When Burroughs was asked by an editor for some of his personal adventures, he responded, "I am one of those unfortunates who always gets to a fire after it is out." Like so many of his readers, he added, "I get my adventure, vicariously, through Tarzan" (letter to Leo Margulies, 30 January 1940). Burroughs represents the average man in this respect, but reading the exploits of Tarzan can invigorate, "endowing the reader with a Promethean sense of power" (Hart 219–20).

In Burroughs' early years, primitivism was in vogue, typified, for example, by the Polynesian primitivism of Paul Gauguin's *Where Do We Come From* (1897–98) or the Scythism of Igor Stravinsky's *Rite of Spring* (1913). Primitivism celebrated people close to nature, uncorrupted by civilization, based on the idea that inherent nobility flourished outside the civilizing influence. Hart, in his literary assessment of America called Tarzan "a joyous symbol of primitivism" (219). Harmon and Holman cite Tarzan as a "testimony to the durability of the idea" (372). As such, the narrator in "The Capture of Tarzan" points out that "he was not handicapped by the second-hand, and usually erroneous, judgment of others" (28). His purity and success come from his lack of contamination from civilization.

Balasopoulos presents the idea, by way of Hayden White, that the purpose of the popular notion of the noble savage was not to elevate the savage so much as it was to "belabor the nobility" and to defy "the notion of genetic inheritance" (Balasopoulos 209 n.9). This runs counter to Burroughs' vision. Tarzan's nobility is, of course, secured from the earliest narration, when his parents are identified as lord and lady; and, his ape upbringing can be nothing other than savage. The conceptual blending of *noble* and *savage* is made literal through Burroughs' narrative. Balasopoulos does acknowledge the difference that Tarzan represents as "a hero who both recapitulates the eighteenth-century originary fantasy of the 'noble savage' and inverts its political implications" (205). In this way, Tarzan can function as both the representative of civilization and its antithesis, both the poison and the antidote, both the law and the outlaw, the Wyatt Earp and the Robin Hood.

But for all the comparison, Burroughs, according to Taliaferro, was not aware of either Rousseau's or Nietzsche's ideas concerning superhumanity (14). Holtsmark adds, "Unlike Rousseau [...], Burroughs most decidedly did not believe in the perfectibility of man" (144). And Conrath adds this insight to the discussion: "In the case of wild men and feral children it will become evident that the issue is divided between scientific plausibility and literary imagination, 'myth' and 'reality' [...]" (17). Burroughs himself said, "I do not believe that any human infant or child, unprotected by adults of its own species, could survive a fortnight in such an African environment as I describe in the Tarzan stories"; if survival were somehow managed, such a being would "develop into a cunning, cowardly beast [...] under-developed from lack of proper and sufficient nourishment, from exposure to the inclemencies of the weather, and from lack of sufficient restful sleep" (*The Daily Maroon*, University of Chicago, 31 May 1927; qtd. in Fenton 44–45). This polar dichotomy, Conrath points out, is essential in Farmer's collection, *Mother Was a Lovely Beast*. Farmer identifies the two essential elements of the Tarzan character as, first, the "represent[ative of ...] the collective unconscious of humanity" through his feral identity, and, second, the role of actual man (xi).

The ideal of active masculinity, identified and explored in John F. Kasson's book *Houdini, Tarzan, and the Perfect Man*, was important at the turn of the century, when Burroughs was himself searching for vocational identity. Tarzan is, in Taliaferro's assessment, "the embodiment of Teddy Roosevelt's 'strenuous life'"; he also identifies him as "a latter-day Leatherstocking [with] exuberant physicality and solid pedigree" (15). Burroughs' admiration for Roosevelt was unquestioning, and is explored more in chapter 5. Roosevelt's manliness was attractive and charismatic, especially to Burroughs who saw himself as sometimes lacking in personal verve. Jeff Berglund would agree with Burger's claim that "[t]he American Adam was incarnated in Leatherstocking [and] Tarzan" (*Glimpses* 124) among other characters. Tarzan is "the self-made man [...] fulfilling the prophecy of a new beginning in the wilderness" (Bergland 75). Just as Huckleberry Finn proposes to "light out for the territory ahead of the rest" (Twain 283), Tarzan has gone before the reader to demonstrate the nobility and vibrancy of the natural life. Tarzan contained all the missing vitality that any reader might want.

Just as Defoe's *Robinson Crusoe* was important in understanding the role of the father, so it provides a context also for the role of primitivism. Conrath identifies it in the establishment of two types of "savages": the "Adamic" ones and the "'underdeveloped,' socially and mentally retarded" ones (20). For Crusoe, Friday represents that first class and the cannibals from whom he is rescued comprise the second group. Conrath goes on to say that "Burroughs' popularized version centuries later, is a similar panegyric for the innocent savage" (20). Burroughs reveals both types, though. The villagers under Mbonga are much the compatriots of Friday's oppressors, while the Waziri, whom readers meet in *The Return of Tarzan* represent the Adamic, innocent group that Conrath identifies along with Tarzan. Similar to Friday's companionship with Crusoe in British literature is Chingachgook's relationship with Natty Bumppo (Leatherstocking) in American literature. Such companions, Conrath claims, are "personage[s] whose humanity was never in question" (21).

From the middle of the nineteenth century on, conceptions of the noble savage have also had to deal with Charles Darwin. Burroughs owned a copy of Darwin's *The Descent of Man*, though Taliaferro, who apparently inspected the copy, points out that "he never got much beyond sketching a monkey on the title page" (14). Porges affirms that "Tarzan's development illustrated Darwin's ideas" (364). His Darwinian ideas, though, were likely formed through the popular media rather than directly from Darwin's work. Burroughs' incorporation of Darwinian thought though is not unique. Rather, as Holtsmark contends, it "was part of the common literary property of the day" (144) used by innumerable writers, most now forgotten. Holtsmark continues, "Burroughs views Tarzan's personal growth and development as the recapitulation of human evolution in the form of a single individual" (145). This one man becomes a kind of "paradigm for the human race" (145). In one article, Burroughs explained that he "was mainly interested in playing with the idea of a contest between heredity and environment" ("Tarzan Theme" 29). These are the two poles at work in popular Darwinism.

Holtsmark points out that "Burroughs keeps reminding us of our zoological phylogeny," and from the "cultural vantage" of popularized Darwinism "he could not help seeing something of the beast in man's background" (72). He elaborates that Burroughs in the various Tarzan books "obviously offers the notion that there is much of the beast in man and much of man in the beast"

(82). His reason for doing this is both artistic and personal. Holtsmark believes: "For Burroughs the idea of Darwinian evolution is a central theme for validating his own position in the age-old controversy over the relative contribution of nature and nurture to the development of the individual" (144). Burroughs was a lifelong supporter of evolutionary theory in its popular form. In the 1930s, when his thinking had perhaps solidified more fully on the matter, Burroughs declared that evolution was simply "an immutable law of Nature" (Burroughs, "Evolution" 76). Holtsmark suggests that one of the reasons the Tarzan character has retained popular interest is his relationship to the idea of a missing link (83). That link, though, is insufficient in itself to arouse continued interest. The appeal is from the nobility of this natural man, the American Adam, the noble savage, that undergirds the character.

> "Have you a piece of rope and a knife?"
> — Jean Valjean, *Les Misérables* (Hugo 340)

If Tarzan had not had some transcendent quality, no one would know his name. Burroughs credits his literal survival to his hereditary intelligence. He claims in *Tarzan of the Apes* that Tarzan "would have died as he had lived — an unknown savage beast in equatorial Africa," if it had not been for "that little spark which spells the whole vast difference between man and brute — Reason" (86). Such reason manifests itself in the ability to create tools and, in short, create things by extrapolating from simple cause-and-effect observations. Byrne and McQuillan claim that "[i]t is not speech which makes us human but the use of techne" (115). And such technological innovation sets Tarzan apart from the apes in his world.

Most demonstrative of all in displaying his reason at work, in Tarzan's formative years, especially those chronicled in *Jungle Tales of Tarzan*, is the primitive bit of technology found in the rope. Tarzan's use of the rope goes through a progression: from a means to manipulate his environment, to the application of a repeatable and effective procedure, followed by or concomitant with an understanding of the principles at work.

When Burroughs set Tarzan into his jungle home, one of his purposes was to contrast the young ape-man with his civilized counterpart, often identified simply as Lord Greystoke, a title which Tarzan will inherit when he claims his due at the end of *The Return of Tarzan*. He does this to answer, as Grun suggests, "whether virtue and manners are part of civilization, or an innate part of man's character" (132). Early in *Jungle Tales*, Burroughs sets up the contrast like this: "Lost to Tarzan of the Apes was the truth of his origin. That he was John Clayton, Lord Greystoke, with a seat in the House of Lords, he did not know, nor, knowing, would have understood" (8). At several points Burroughs intertwines the explicit comparison between the landed lord in England and the lord of the jungle, usually to satirize the complaints of the former. In *Tarzan of the Apes*, Burroughs makes the first explicit comparison in terms of Tarzan's dining: "Lord Greystoke wiped his greasy fingers upon his naked thighs [...]; while in far-off London another Lord Greystoke, the younger brother of the real Lord Greystoke's father, [...] when he had finished his repast [...] dipped his finger-ends into a silver bowl of scented water and dried them upon a piece of snowy damask" (67). On another occasion, in *Jungle Tales*, Tarzan "finding a comfortable crotch high among the trees, composed himself for a night of dreamless slumber, while a prowling lion moaned and coughed beneath him," as "in far-off England the other Lord Greystoke, with the assistance of a valet, disrobed and crawled between spotless sheets, swearing irritably as a cat meowed beneath his window" (91). Later, in a similar situation, Burroughs narrates that Tarzan "slept as well that night as he did on any other night, and though there was no roof above him, and no doors to lock against intruders, he slept much better than his noble relative in England, who had eaten altogether too much lobster and drank too much wine at dinner that night" (*Jungle Tales* 105). When Tarzan voiced his victory cry to the jungle inhabitants, "[b]irds fell still, and the larger animals and beasts of prey slunk stealthily away"; in contrast, the narrator adds, "[I]n London another Lord Greystoke was speaking to *his* kind in the House of Lords, but none trembled at the sound of his soft voice" (*Apes* 79).

Burroughs begins "The Witch-Doctor Seeks Vengeance" with a purposeful and elaborate contrast — the longest he ever published — between Lord Greystoke in England who was "shooting pheasants [...], immaculately and appropriately garbed," with the help of twenty-three game flushers (87) and Tarzan who was hunting without helpers. "Later that day, in England," the narration continues, "a Lord Greystoke ate bountifully of things he had not killed [...] quite ignorant of the fact that he was an impostor and that the rightful owner of his noble title was even then finishing his own dinner in far-off Africa" (88).

Heredity is the strength that Burroughs credits with Tarzan's superiority. When the young Tarzan faces down Sheeta the panther, in "Tarzan's First Love," he does so "with the same courageous resignation with which some fearless ancestor went down to defeat and death on Senlac Hill by Hastings" (14). His appeal to the thousand-year-old battle, the most recent to defeat British soldiery, affirms the hereditary fortitude intended within the ape-boy.

Despite Burroughs' attempt to discredit civilization and exalt the natural man, the technology of civilization becomes important in Tarzan's rise to superiority over the jungle denizens. Byrne and McQuillan claim that "Tarzan's privileged position relies on his use of technology" (113).They mention in particular his "spear, knife, [and] lasso" (113). While Burroughs repeatedly contrasts civilization negatively with Tarzan's jungle existence, the technology of civilization, however primitive it may be, is essential in Tarzan's survival.

The return to the cabin in *Apes* is a turning point in Tarzan's development.

His re-acquaintance with the cabin of his birth comes, as Taliaferro says, from "a strange, unfathomable yearning, combined with sheer animal curiosity" (77). That cabin is the embodiment of both his personal and cultural history. For Tarzan's father, "the home-building instinct" is so strong, Catherine Jurca says, that "with no training and few tools he constructs a structurally sound, well-ventilated, beautiful cabin" (490). This is the natural course for "the Anglo-Saxon aristocrat" (Jurca 490) that John Clayton embodies. The cabin, then, Jurca goes on, "and the treasures it safeguards are imagined as transcendental agents of cultural transmisson" (491).

Burroughs is enigmatic when, in "The Nightmare," he claims that "the moss-grown cabin [...] with its contents was the sole heritage left by his dead and unknown father to the young Lord Greystoke" (133). In "The Battle for Teeka," a peculiar circumstance allows the technology of civilization to save Tarzan's life, though the adolescent ape-man is unaware of the process, nor can he duplicate it. Earlier in the story Tarzan had discovered a box of "cylindrical bits of metal" which were "quite green and dull, coated with years of verdigris" (147). He finds them attractive when polished and drops a handful of them into the bag he carries with him so that he can polish them later. At the climax of the story, Teeka hurls them at some attacking apes of another tribe who had outnumbered and overwhelmed Tarzan and Taug. The resulting explosion sends the attackers running and leaves Tarzan dumbfounded. Burroughs makes the connection of this technological wonder explicit, claiming "the dead father of Tarzan of the Apes, reaching back out of the past across a span of twenty years, had saved his son's life" (159). "[T]he father," Holtsmark comments, "in a sense never dies" (152).

The most memorable item that Tarzan takes from the cabin of his birth is the hunting knife that he carries ever after. Before finding the knife, Tarzan felt inferior to the apes. The knife, though, becomes an equalizer of sorts. In facing Mbonga, in "The God of Tarzan," the narrator makes an effort to identify the knife with his heredity, identifying it as "his long, keen knife, the knife that John Clayton, Lord Greystoke, had brought from England many years before" (58). It is this knife that saved him from an attack by Bolgani the gorilla, and which, later, leads him to defeat Kerchak to become king of the apes. But the knife is not a reproducible technology for Tarzan in his adolescence, nor does it need to be as long as he retains possession of his hereditary artifact. Only once does Burroughs record Tarzan fashioning a knife of his own, in *The Beasts of Tarzan*, where he makes one of flint after landing on Akut's island.

It is the rope that demonstrates most clearly Tarzan's technological application of inherited reasoning ability. Tarzan's invention of the device comes early in *Apes*. The narrator does not record a particular moment of epiphany, instead summarizing: "Early in his boyhood he had learned to form ropes by twisting and tying long grasses together" (40). The Disney adaptation in *Tarzan II* incorporates the rope into the young Tarzan's character. When he asks Zugor to help him find his identity, Zugor identifies the rope as one of the distinguishing elements that sets him apart from the other animals. Being able to use the rope to secure bananas from the treetops or pull a friend to safety makes Tarzan positively different in this adaptation. Unlike Tarzan concluding in "Tarzan's First Love" that he was a "man," however, Zugor proclaims him a "tarzan," having no vocabulary to express the idea of humanity.

Tarzan finds this technological wonder first as a toy and then as a tool in his development from disfigured ape to superior man. His mastery of the rope sets him beyond his companions and assures his rise to leadership within the ape tribe.

When Tarzan's father is put ashore, he must use whatever forms of technology are available to him, ranging from physical principles to tangible materials. As he goes about building shelter for Lady Alice and himself, he picks out "four trees which formed a rectangle about eight feet square, and cutting long branches from other trees he construct[s] a framework around them, about ten feet from the ground, fastening the ends of the branches securely to the trees by means of rope, a quantity of which Black Michael had furnished him from the hold of the *Fuwalda*" (*Apes* 21). This "snug little nest" (*Apes* 22) serves and preserves them until they are ready to move into the cabin that Lord Greystoke builds over the course of the next month.

These ropes no doubt had long since rotted before Tarzan could have used or learned from them. However, the "superior intelligence and cunning" (*Apes* 40) that he inherited from his father provided a productive mental workshop for the fun-loving ape-boy. Whether Tarzan ever saw the remains of these or other ropes is conjectural. Burroughs provides no objective lesson to teach Tarzan the principle of rope making, but claims simply that he learned to do it. The narrator credits that he "originated" the idea in contrast to the limited mental abilities of his ape companions (*Apes* 40). His first use for the ropes is entertainment, which the practical joker in Tarzan sees in creating discomfort to others, especially Tublat. But a rope across a path to trip someone soon loses its humor, and Tarzan must do more with this wonder that he has created. The narrator explains: "By constant playing and experimenting [...] he learned to tie rude knots, and make sliding nooses; and with these he and the younger apes amused themselves" (*Apes* 40), though his ape playmates were able only to poorly mimic Tarzan's proficiency. When Tarzan accidentally lassoes "one of his fleeing companions, retaining the other end in his grasp," he thinks: "Ah, here [is] a new game, a fine game" (*Apes* 40). "[P]ainstaking and continued practice" (*Apes* 40) at this game more than entertains the young Tarzan. In "The End of Bukawai," the narrator points out that the ape-boy "was always inventing new ways in which to play. It is through the medium of play that he learned much during his childhood" (106). Like Victor Frankenstein, Tarzan is "guided by an ardent imagination and childish reasoning, till an accident again changed the current of [his] ideas" (Shelley 40). The one accident regarding the rope is detailed in a flashback. Tarzan mistakenly lassoes a branch instead of the ape he intended. The resultant ability to swing from such a prepared toy taught him specifically the principles of friction and centrifugal force. The rope-play was instructive, and — it gave him a useful tool, a new weapon in the daily fight for survival. In "Fight for the Balu," the narrator makes this transition explicit: "At the ape-man's side swung his long grass rope — the play-thing of yesterday, the weapon of today" (40).

The reader learns that Tarzan takes to carrying the rope with him because he finds it useful. In "Tarzan's First Love," he wears it "[c]oiled about his shoulders" (10); even in adulthood he continues this practice, as noted for example in *Tarzan and the City of Gold*, where the narrator points out that "the loose coils of his grass rope lay across one bronze shoulder" (10). At some point the plant fibers are supplanted by leather, as the narrator in *Tarzan and the Jewels of Opar* points out: "At his side hung a long, rawhide rope — a natural and more dependable evolution from the grass rope of his childhood" (79). But this seems to be an exception. This rope is carried "fast[ened] at his waist" (80). The rope, no matter how carried, was an essential part of Tarzan's "clothing," as Burroughs points out in *Tarzan the Untamed*, because without it, "Tarzan would have felt quite as naked as would you should you be suddenly thrust upon a busy highway clad only in a union suit" (13).

In his adolescent phase, Tarzan continues to see the rope as a plaything. In "Tarzan and the Black Boy," he uses it to entertain the baby Gazan (68), and in "The End of Bukawai" he relates the joy of swinging (105–08). The physical principles of motion and momentum, in the latter case, come to him, Holtsmark claims, because he was "[a]lert [...] to the possibilities inherent in any novel situation" (107).

But toys quickly give way to tools in Tarzan's mind. In "Tarzan's First Love," he sees Mbonga's villagers using ropes to drag the cage that has captured Taug along the jungle trail to their village. Even before this event, he has used ropes to extend his own reach. The first use described in *Tarzan of the Apes* is to retrieve things, in this case a fleeing companion. This unnamed ape is the first of many creatures, friend and foe, who are thus caught short by Tarzan's rope. It is in this fashion that he acquires his *balu*, Tibo, in "Tarzan and the Black Boy" (70). And immediately prior to the events related in *Jungle Tales*, the rope is the primary weapon Tarzan uses to avenge Kala's death in the pseudo-lynching of Kulonga before the hunting knife cuts life from the warrior.

Not only is the rope useful for retrieving things, but it also functions to keep others bound. In "The Fight for the Balu," Tarzan strings up Taug by the legs so that he can talk with Teeka and see her baby unmolested. In "The End of Bukawai," the rope restrains first Tarzan when he is captured by Bukawai and then Bukawai himself when Tarzan turns the tables. Later, in "A Jungle Joke," Tarzan sees a young goat tied inside a lion trap. After freeing the animal, he replaces the bait with Rabba Kega, the witch doctor from Mbonga's village. The rope functions even in a very traditional way, after the arrival of Europeans in the harbor, when Tarzan ties a spade to himself so that his arms can be free to carry the treasure chest he has exhumed.

The first hunting use Burroughs records for Tarzan's rope is to grab "many [...] smaller animals" (58) in *Tarzan of the Apes,* in a chapter entitled "The Tree-Top Hunter." As the boy learns the uses of this new tool he tests its limits when Horta the boar pulls him from a branch and charges him in return. Later, in "Tarzan and the Black Boy," he has learned his lesson, and instead of holding the rope, he "made it fast about the stem of the tree above the branch from which he had cast it" (68). An even stronger test of the artificial restraint is made on Sheeta the panther in the opening and closing stories of *Jungle Tales.* To save Teeka, Tarzan lassoes Sheeta in a desperate forty-foot cast. He "drew the noose taut, bracing himself for the shock when Sheeta should have taken up the slack" (13). After some matadorial maneuvers, Tarzan races for the trees, leaving the rope behind. In doubling back, the panther tangles the rope in a bush and finally snaps it free after Tarzan is safely in a tree. In "Tarzan Rescues the Moon," when presumably he has developed more finesse, the narrator reports that Tarzan had once roped Sheeta and tied him safely to a tree (183). His proficiency in such tasks is magnified in *Tarzan the Untamed,* when in an extended narration, Tarzan ropes Numa the lion, hangs him suspended by the rope while he bags and hog-ties the beast as a part of his revenge in "When the Lion Fed."

These uses might easily be interpreted as weapons rather than tools, depending, perhaps, on whether the intent is restraint or assault. Certainly the latter is true in the case of Kulonga. Tarzan also assaults Tublat repeatedly, "[heaping] many indignities [...] upon him by means of the hated rope," usually by "jerk[ing] him ridiculously and painfully from his feet" or nearly garroting him by swinging him by the neck from an overhead branch (106).

Tarzan has indeed understood the principles at work, and he has developed a duplicable process. "Tarzan and the Black Boy" opens with Tarzan "braiding a new grass rope" (64). On this occasion "he added an extra strand" (64) to make the product stronger. He makes new ropes on several occasions, after losing them around the necks or bodies of stronger animals than he can manipulate. That the process became second-nature is evident when as an adult he is marooned on an island and immediately proceeds to "[braid] a long grass rope — such a rope as he had used so many years before to tantalize the ill-natured Tublat, and which later had developed into a wondrous effective weapon in the practised hands of the little ape-boy" (*Beasts* 30).

A final example to show that Tarzan understands the technology of rope-making is illustrated in the fact that he learns also how it can be destroyed. In "The End of Bukawai," the narrator recalls a time through a flashback when a 13-year-old (according to Hanson) Tarzan had learned the delight of swinging on the rope; that event also taught him the physical principle of friction. Repeated abrasion from the tree bark against the grasses wore through the rope, nearly killing the boy when he fell forty feet. That he learned not to swing so long without repairing the rope is creditable, but he also learned to apply his knowledge: "the very thing that had once all but killed him proved the means of saving his life" (108). The moment of connection occurs when Bukawai has tied him to a tree with Tarzan's own rope, rather like the bait of a trap, a pattern used later in "A Jungle Joke." While the hyenas are building up the courage to attack him, the epiphanic moment comes, "[l]ike a flash of the cinematograph upon the screen" (113). Remembering the principle from his earlier debacle, "[i]mmediately he commenced to draw the rope rapidly back and forth across the tree trunk" (114). Applying the principle that reason has taught him, Tarzan escapes by undoing the very technology he has created.

While most readers looking for technology would turn to computer and industrial applications in literature, well represented by the cyberpunk movement in literature sprouting out of such works as William Gibson's *Neuromancer* and Ridley Scott's film adaptation of Philip K. Dick's "Do Androids Dream of Electric Sheep?" re-titled *Blade Runner*, technology begins long before. As Burroughs has said, reason, and thus technology, begins with "the primal ancestor before the first eviction" (87). And for Burroughs there is no better exemplar of the primal ancestor in the modern world than his own character, Tarzan.

CHAPTER 4

(Un)Natural Theology
"The God of Tarzan"

"The God of Tarzan" was the fourth short story Edgar Rice Burroughs wrote in "The New Stories of Tarzan." Written the week of 7–13 July 1916 (Friday through Thursday), while camping near Coldwater, Michigan, and published in *Blue Book* magazine in December that year, the story is a rare exploration for Burroughs of the spiritual dimension of his most famous character. In the table of contents, the *Blue Book* editors called it "the most thoughtful" as well as "one of the most exciting of these unique tales." Ray Long, the editor who accepted the story, replied privately that it was "the best of the bunch so far," perhaps because it heightened "a peculiar poetical sort of quality" that was indefinable (letter to Burroughs, 17 July 1916). Holtsmark has praised the story for its "pantheistic profundity" (108). Within this story Burroughs also explores the language/literacy connection introduced in *Tarzan of the Apes*, and begs the question of children's literature and its impact. The story has been adapted to comic form in Charlton's *Jungle Tales of Tarzan* #3 (May 1965), Gold Key's *Tarzan of the Apes* #169 (July 1967), and Marvel's *Tarzan* #9 (Feb. 1978). An audio presentation of the story is available online from the Prometheus Radio Theatre.*

In the story, an adolescent Tarzan has been teaching himself to read from books found in his father's cabin. He is able to hunt down approximate meanings of the words but does not understand the meaning of the word *God*. He asks some of the apes. The first has no answer. The second sends him to ask the moon, but the moon does not answer. Tarzan next visits the village of Mbonga and confronts the witch doctor, who he determines is a fraud. Leaving the village, Tarzan grapples with Mbonga who tries to kill Tarzan. Tarzan releases him when he sees the pitiable fear in the old man. Tarzan ponders the world around him as well as his response to Mbonga. When Tarzan hears screams, he goes to rescue Teeka and her baby from a snake. He decides that it is God who inspires inexplicable responses in people. God had caused him to have pity on Mbonga and had made Teeka rush into danger to save her child.

---

*This presentation is in two parts, read by Steven H. Wilson, available at http://cdn4.libsyn.com/prometheus/200719.mp3 and http://cdn4.libsyn.com/prometheus/2007-20.mp3.

He identifies God's goodness with the beauty of nature. The story ends by reinstating doubt in Tarzan's question, "Who made [...] the snake?" (64).

> "For the invisible things of him [God] from the creation of the world are clearly seen, being understood by the things that are made, even his eternal power and Godhead"
>
> — Romans 1.20

Finding God through nature is certainly no new track, but it is a track that Burroughs avoided before this story. Later, when responding to the Scopes trial for the International Press Bureau, he simplifies the difficulty by suggesting that God and Nature are the same: "[O]ne cannot think of God and Nature as separate and distinct agencies" ("Evolution" 76).

Owen Gingerich, astronomer and professor at Harvard University, summarizes the argument of natural theology to be "that the Book of Nature, with its astonishing details [...] suggests a God of purpose and a God of design." Simply put, natural theology, a type of argument from design, suggests that God's nature and purposes can be inferred from study of the natural world. The idea was popularized by William Paley in his 1802 work *Natural Theology; or, Evidences of the Existence and Attributes of the Deity, collected from the Appearances of Nature*. Natural theology provides evidence of a creator, but as Gingerich has pointed out, "arguments from design [...] simply can't be construed as proofs [...]." The whole product of natural theology is logical inference. Gingerich goes on to say that natural theology is most useful when it "deals with hints and coherencies, not proofs."

The Magdalen Metaphysicals, a group including C.S. Lewis, debated the nature and interrelationship of such concepts as language, philosophy and religion, coming to the conclusion that "religion might begin with experience, but it was ultimately a matter of intellectual truth," according to Dale. "They all sought to reunite joy, reason, and virtue, a quest they thought came from a natural longing for an Absolute whose object is not in this world" (56). The God for which Tarzan searches is much like the Absolute identified by the Magdalen Metaphysicals. The desire to search for such is embedded within human nature. It is this nature that separates Tarzan from the flippant response of Numgo claiming to be God and the distinct apathy that the apes have for Tarzan's questions.

Burroughs leads Tarzan in a quest for such coherencies in this tale. Tarzan makes correlations, but the story ends not with proof but with another question. It is just such teasing out of hints and coherencies that enrich a literary text. As Sherlock Holmes sees a recovered hat and reveals its owner to have "had foresight, but [...] less now than formerly, pointing to a moral retrogression, which, when taken with the decline of his fortunes, seems to indicate some evil influence, probably drink, at work upon him" (Conan Doyle 203), so the student of literature examines seeming irrelevancies and varied details to establish coherence. The narrator in "The Capture of Tarzan" tells the reader that Tarzan "compared judgments, reaching conclusions—not always correct ones, it is true, but at least he used his brain for the purpose God intended it" (28). "The God of Tarzan" creates a ready platform to examine authorial assumptions and reader response. The quest that Tarzan takes up is not abstract, even though the concept of God may be. The process of literary analysis can be studied here without much philosophical or theological labor.

To set up the scenario, Burroughs must find a way to acquaint Tarzan with the concept of God. That Burroughs conceived Tarzan, at least sometimes, as a created being rather than (or at least in addition to) a new variation in the evolutionary chain is shown in the next adventure he wrote, *Tarzan the Untamed*, where Tarzan shows no outward sign of emotional distress: the narrator comments, "[T]he God who made him alone could know [his] thoughts" (11). Additionally, near the end of World War II, having seen first-hand some of the horrors that the human race was capable of, he wrote to his daughter, Joan: "I have always been just a little bit cynical about homo sapiens. But now I guess that I shall have to admit that God made a pretty good job when he whittled him out" (qtd. in Taliaferro 344). His admission is frank without being contemplative. In "The God of Tarzan," Burroughs prepares Tarzan's mind through linguistics, specifically through his labored but innate grasp of language, honed through an implied series of intuitive leaps, as examined later in this chapter.

The next leap is from linguistic intuition to theological intuition. Tarzan's reasoning of God is based on his reading, but his conclusions are unbelievable for some readers. However, some readers might identify Robert Browning's poem "Caliban Upon Setebos" as a plausible comparison to Tarzan's natural theology. Few readers would affirm the theological reasoning of Browning's Caliban, much like Tolkien's Golem, a creature adapted from Shakespeare's *The Tempest*, but the process of reasoning between Caliban and Tarzan is similar. Many distinct correlations can be made between the two. Both Caliban and Tarzan refer to themselves in the third person, represent the beast in man, attribute to God characteristics from themselves, look to the moon for God, acknowledge God as creator of things, see the snake as a destructive force, and believe God allows no direct revelation of himself. The first two commonalities relate to the characters themselves. Caliban's naïve reference to himself as "This Caliban" (259, l. 264) is manifested in Tarzan in his memorable statement at the end of "Tarzan's First Love," "Tarzan is a man. He will go alone" (*Jungle Tales* 23). Notice that both refer to themselves in third person. In the present story when he addresses the moon, Tarzan refers to himself in third person six times, while using the personal pronoun only once: "I am Tarzan" (51), where the name is used as a predicate nominative instead of the subject. Similarly when he interrogates the witch doctor, Tarzan refers to himself in third person seven times, while resorting to a single "I." Also, as Caliban "[e]mblematiz[es] the bestial in man" (Loucks 252), so Tarzan represents the dichotomy of the "beast-man" (*Jungle Tales* 58), where one who is a hereditary member of parliament exhibits "nothing human in the bestial growls that rumbled up from his deep chest; [...] nothing human in the bared fangs, or the catlike leaps" with which he attacks Mbonga (58). The remaining characteristics, dealing with the characters' reasoning and assumptions, will be taken in the larger course of this section.

James F. Loucks points out that Browning's poem was likely spurred into being by the publication of Charles Darwin's *Origin of the Species* and the ensuing debate over the missing link. Popular Darwinism was also influential in Burroughs' creation of Tarzan. Unlike Tarzan's story, Browning's poem "has little to do with Darwinian theory," Loucks explains (252). Instead, he says, "Browning's subject is man's inveterate tendency to create God in his own image" (252). This idea, outside the Bible, goes back at least as far as the Greek poet-philosopher Xenophanes who argued, for example, that a horse would make his god very much like a horse. Browning chose, as an epigraph for the poem, Psalm 50.21: "Thou thoughtest that I was altogether such a one as thyself." The same can be said of Tarzan's reasoning when he tries to puzzle out the defining characteristics of God. Don Marquis identifies this propensity in his 1915 poem, "The God-Maker, Man": "As the forehead of Man grows broader, so do his creeds; / And his gods they are shaped in his image, and mirror his needs" (49). Caliban first acknowledges the Creator as the one who made "the sun, this isle, / Trees and fowls here, beast and creeping thing" (254, ll. 44–45). Setebos is his name for God and his dwelling place is the moon. (In lines 24–25, Caliban identifies the moon as the dwelling place of Setebos. To say that Setebos is another name for God is an oversimplification, though. Setebos is the malevolent side of Deity, contrasted with Quiet, the benevolent aspect of God.) Caliban then speculates on his own choices, if he were the Creator, and concludes that natural law would be at his caprice. Tarzan considers the concept of God taken from the books he found in his father's cabin and struggles with the idea that "God [is] mightier than Tarzan" because Tarzan "acknowledged no equal in the jungle" (49). Like Caliban, Tarzan conceives of God in terms of himself and "hope[s] that God would not prove a belligerent God" (52). This idea correlates with Freud's psychology of growth and of the ego. Tarzan's delight still in games of tag, for example, shows an ego that sees itself as the center and therefore the most important aspect of the universe, just as a child thinks and feels.

From the suggestion of Numgo and Mumga, fellow mangani, Tarzan decides to see if God is in the moon, whose name is Goro in the language of the great apes. Tarzan climbs a tree and calls out, "Tell me, Goro, are you God!" (50). That Browning is more philosophical than Burroughs is of little debate. Burroughs and Browning share the same beginning point but thereafter go their own directions. Browning is both philosophical and theological. Burroughs is simpler in content and diction and, aside from the fact that Tarzan uses the subjunctive correctly, more suited to the voice of the character. For example, the challenge Tarzan makes to Goro is unusually sophisticated but with a straightforward syntax: "Tell me [...] if you be the great king who sends Ara, the lightning; who makes the great noise and the mighty winds, and sends the waters down upon the jungle people when the days are dark and it is cold. Tell me, Goro, are you God?" (50).

In the end Tarzan understands the incorporeality of God, that is, power without body. Tarzan thinks: "The flowers and the trees were good and beautiful. God had made them. He had made the other creatures, too, that each might have food upon which to live" (63–64). And, this leads David Adams to conclude, as do many readers: "Tarzan's God is the source of good and the beautiful" ("Jungle Tales"). That which is pleasant and beneficial become markers of God's presence in Tarzan's world, which produce, as Bob Zeuschner says, "an intense subjective feeling of awe and amazement at the wonder and power of Nature."

Tarzan realizes that self-sacrifice is a manifestation of God, that God brings good despite his own desires and holds his "knife from the throat of the old Gomangani" (63) when he would have killed the village chief. This lesson makes a lasting imprint, causing the narrator in the next story to comment with obvious reference that Tarzan "knew neither fear nor mercy, except upon rare occasions when some strange, inexplicable force stayed his hand" (68). It is this inexplicable staying of violence that later allows Terkoz to live, an event that causes the other apes to consider Tarzan "[s]trange because he had had it in his power to kill his enemy, but had allowed him to live — unharmed" (*Apes* 88). These inexplicable things, to Tarzan, are the essence of God.

As a side note, the character of Mbonga* is depicted by Burroughs as an adequate, though not brilliant, leader for the village. When Tarzan discovers that he is "a very old man with a scrawny neck and wrinkled face" (*Jungle Tales* 59), he realizes the impression obtained from a distance changes under scrutiny. This nobler, more distant, character is emphasized in Kubert's graphic rendition of "The Captive" for DC Comics. When Tantor picks up Tarzan in the village, Kubert has Mbonga step in front of the elephant to contest his rescue. Tarzan turns Tantor from running Mbonga down, saying, "He is an enemy ... but, a brave one! Do not harm him...!" (17). This response is out of place in the stories Burroughs wrote, though it picks up the attitude that Tarzan shows

---

*A possible antecedent to Burroughs' village chief may be found in *The Zambesi Expedition*. David Livingstone reports an incident of a rebellious leader named Bonga. He was "son of another half-caste chief, who bade defiance to the Tette authorities, and had a stockade at the confluence of the Zambesi and the Luenya" (32). When some distant defectors came to him, "[t]he superstitious savage put them all to death" (32). Livingstone then relates this story: "Bonga once caught a captain of the Portuguese army, and forced him to perform the menial labour of pounding maize in a wooden mortar. No punishment followed on this outrage. The Government of Lisbon has since given Bonga the honorary title of Captain, by way of coaxing him to own their authority; but he still holds his stockade" (33). This Bonga, younger in age than Burroughs' character, may have plausibly been forced to flee Portuguese authorities, moving northwest into Tarzan's territory. This is not the only speculative source for Mbonga, though. Farmer, in *Tarzan Alive*, suggests the name comes from a phrase in a native dialect, "*Mi bonga* meaning 'I take'" (46), and Atamian prefers Mbango, a recurring man in Du Chaillu's *Explorations*, as his genesis, insisting Burroughs had "no need to go from a verb to a noun" (65), as Farmer did. Neither, though, considers Livingstone's story.

toward Bulabantu in "Tarzan Rescues the Moon." Previous to the close scrutiny in "The God of Tarzan," Mbonga had been near Tarzan on only one occasion, when he had quelled the mob that surrounded the captive Tarzan so that their victim could be made a feast spectacle that evening. Mbonga's leadership "restored quiet and order" (34) among the people, and "like all good rulers," when the melee broke out, Mbonga "circled in the safety of the background" (35). Nothing of his personal appearance is stated, nor of Tarzan's opinion of him. When Mbonga reappears in "The God of Tarzan," the narrator labels him the village's "[w]ise old patriarch" (56).

The corollary to Tarzan's withholding the knife comes in Teeka's likewise inexplicable action of choosing to enter the coils of the snake out of love for her child. Of all the creatures of the jungle, only the snake is seen as reprehensible, a "repulsive foe" (*Jungle Tales* 61). "[T]hat she had voluntarily rushed into that deadly embrace" "filled him with the greatest wonder" (61). Tarzan needed this objective example of someone taking action contrary to inclination in order to understand his own decision to spare Mbonga. This is precisely the principle at work in the controversial ending of *Tarzan of the Apes*, when Tarzan chooses to forego his own desire for what he believes will please Jane. His love for her is characterized by deference born out of these childhood examples with Teeka and Mbonga. Not only does he make the decision to leave Jane to his cousin, but prior to that decision he yielded to her request to release Canler; in *Return*, he does the same for Rokoff at her urging. This existence of a force beyond his own reason, the inexplicable, is the basis for his understanding of God.

The kicker line to the story — "Who made Histah, the snake?" (64) — is cousin to William Blake's exploration in the poem "The Tyger." Blake's question goes beyond the question of who created evil, though. Initially, Blake's poem asks of the tiger, "What immortal hand or eye / Could frame thy fearful symmetry?" (85). The emphasis here is on creative power. The final stanza of the poem alters the question, substituting the word *dare* for *could*. This change shifts the emphasis from power to motivation, hinting even at audacity, the capricious kind of God that Caliban imagined. And Caliban, too, identified the destructive force of Setebos with the snake in a simile for an ocean wave sent to flatten Caliban's handiwork (see ll. 207–10). Tarzan doesn't answer either question.

The snake, as a symbol for evil, sometimes brings skepticism from readers, especially those acquainted with cultures where the snake is given greater esteem. Tarzan's thoughts and reason seem too conventionally Western, given his nearly blank theological slate, despite the many undescribed books in the Greystoke cabin. Rather than an anthropological reflection, the orthodoxy that Tarzan mirrors is more likely that of the cultural milieu that Burroughs lived in. That is to be expected because Burroughs is not commenting on literal jungle life but on the jungle of modern life. Burroughs likely did not give the inclusion of the snake as a symbol of evil a second thought because it was a well-established image in his day. Snakes are "degenerate collateral kin" (125) to the dinosaurs, according to Fiske, a popular lecturer on history and evolution in Burroughs' younger days. It was common to consider snakes as "objects of dread and loathing to higher creatures" (Fiske 126). And Sherlock Holmes asks the rhetorical question: "Do you feel a creeping, shrinking sensation, Watson, when you stand before the serpents in the Zoo, and see the slithery, gliding, venomous creatures, with their deadly eyes and wicked, flattened faces?" (Conan Doyle 645). So in Tarzan's jungle, not only does Tarzan consider the snake "repulsive," but "[t]he apes, too, loathed the terrifying reptile and feared him even more than they did Sheeta, the panther, or Numa, the lion. Of all their enemies there was none they gave a wider berth than they gave Histah, the snake" (*Jungle Tales* 61). When Tarzan defeats the snake he does not voice the cry that would signal victory in battle because "to him Histah was not an animal" (63) — not an enemy in the sense of a predator or a challenger from any other division of the animal kingdom but some malignant force lacking animal identity. Whether that comes from the lack of limbs or the unusual method of locomotion is impossible to say; Tarzan knew only that it "differed in some peculiar way" (63) from everything else that lived in the jungle. T.S. Eliot has linked the theme, somewhat in answer to Blake, in "Choruses from 'The Rock'":

> The great snake lies ever half awake, at the bottom of the pit of the world, curled
> In folds of himself until he awakens in hunger and moving his head to right and
>   to left prepares for his hour to devour.
> [...]
> Be not too curious of Good and Evil [112].

In "The Hippopotamus," Eliot writes "the True Church remains below / Wrapt in the old miasmal mist" (31). While one may debate whom Eliot's True Church represents, certainly the limit set by the "miasmal mist" can be profitably compared to the barrier between reason and faith. Tarzan has reached the limit of reason and ends not with answers but further questions. Reason has led him through a fog only to find that more fog waits ahead. Caliban had concluded that Setebos withheld direct knowledge of his purposes and forced his creation to play a guessing game in how to please him — "Discover how or die" (257, l. 218). Such caprice leaves Caliban cowering at feared wrong guesses, hiding and reading divine retribution into every discomfort. But Tarzan is not led to fear or despair by his limited understanding. Limited reasoning is still profitable. In "Choruses from 'The Rock,'" Eliot uses another image that may accurately portray Tarzan's viewpoint, a world of "little light, that is dappled with shadow" (113). With *some* light — in this case sufficient for Tarzan — the human mind can find satisfaction. After all, one suspects that Tarzan can make nearly as quick progress through the jungle on an overcast day as in brilliant sunshine.

The leap of faith that Tarzan lacks in moving from the natural world to the supernatural is one that he *does* make in terms of bugs to words. The intuitive leap that allows him to understand the abstract nature of written words is precisely the kind of leap that would move him from reason to faith. At this point Burroughs separates the linguistic from the spiritual. In spiritual terms,

Burroughs has chosen not to move his character beyond the tangible. Much later, in 1934, when the issue was pressed upon him, Burroughs replied, "It seems to be an inexorable law that, spiritually, man never arrives anywhere. He reaches a point where he seems to be arriving somewhere, and then the pendulum swings back" (letter to George Vaughn). Such a claim matches Tarzan's spiritual movement in this story. He is able to identify God as an invisible force who is all-powerful in nature, but he is unable to leap beyond that to a personal God. He "seems to be arriving" but it is at this point that the pendulum swings for Tarzan. Burroughs indicates that "Tarzan almost had arrived at something tangible" (60), but for Tarzan this *almost* is insurmountable. A.W. Tozer, a Protestant theologian contemporary with Burroughs, credits Canon Holmes with identifying "the inferential character of the average man's faith" (49). While Tarzan is far from average in most every category, here the *almost*, which marks the average man, cannot, even for Tarzan, become reality, and God must remain at the level of inference. The proof lies in the final story of the collection where, despite this small epiphany, Tarzan still struggles with "the untrained man-mind groping through the dark night of ignorance for an explanation of the things he could not touch or smell or hear and of the great, unknown powers of nature which he could not see" (177).

Burroughs never again displays such purposeful speculation regarding God in his elaboration of Tarzan's life. Tarzan's belief appears to become a social one, reflecting the society of the author rather than the society of the story. Tozer suggests that many Americans "have heard about [God] from others"—as Tarzan did from the books in his father's cabin—but have put faith "into the back of their minds along with various odds and ends that make up their total creed" (49). While nature is sufficient to suggest the existence of God in the story, residual doubt and uncertainty remain as a part of Tarzan's embryonic creed, as the final question indicates. Tarzan, like Burroughs, falls into another category of spiritual seeker for whom "God is an ideal, another name for goodness, or beauty, or truth; or [...] law, or life, or the creative impulse back of the phenomena of existence" (Tozer 49–50). These conceptions of God come from the Greek traditions rather than the Hebrew. God, for the Greeks, is "immanent in the world and manifested at every moment through the orderly sequence of its phenomena" (Fiske 142), but never is defined in the more personal terms of Jewish or Christian traditions. The idea of evolution that undergirds Burroughs' thinking has led "to the Greek conception of God as the power working in and through nature without interference or infraction of law" (Fiske 147), an impersonal force and ultimately unknowable.*

A fully realized conception of God based on nature alone, then, Tarzan finds ultimately impossible. When Tarzan is introduced to Jane, his sense of the divine is reshaped by Burroughs' romantic sensibilities, where the narra-

---

*Though Fiske argues that "it is practically misleading to apply the term Unknowable to the Deity that is revealed in every pulsation of the wondrously rich and beautiful life of the Universe" (Fiske 150).

tor tells the reader that Tarzan came as close to worshipping Jane as he came to worshipping anything because he "knew no god" (*Apes* 135).

More than a decade later, in *Tarzan at the Earth's Core*, Burroughs returns briefly to the spiritual nature of his character. Here, Tarzan is described as "intensely religious," though he "subscribed to no creed" (42). He no longer ponders theology but lives by several assumptions that the reader might infer come from this particular story. Even later within the *Jungle Tales*, the reader finds that Tarzan continues to use his own experience and observation to explain the world he lives in; the narrator in "Tarzan Rescues the Moon" explains the logic whereby Tarzan identifies "the three principal seats of emotion" as "his throat, epidermis, and the hairs of his head" (180). The reasoning from physical response found in this passage reflects the same kind of reasoning that had led to theological conclusions in "The God of Tarzan." The narrator proceeds: "When Kala had been slain a peculiar choking sensation had possessed his throat; contact with Histah, the snake, imparted an unpleasant sensation to the skin of his whole body; while the approach of an enemy made the hairs on his scalp stand erect" (180). These seats of emotion are separate from God, apparently, though related to the conclusion that compassion is imposed from a supernatural source. Tarzan has no physical location to seat the compassionate response and so designates God as the source. Apprehension, on the other hand, has a physical location based on the connection to the hairs standing upright when an enemy approaches. The reasoning ascribes to God those responses that lack a physical concomitant.

The narrator in *Tarzan at the Earth's Core* tells the reader that Tarzan was "like the majority of those who have always lived close to nature" (42). This reference to nature as the primary "text" on theology reinforces the natural theology explored in "The God of Tarzan." This later narrator goes on: "His intimate knowledge of the stupendous forces of nature, of her wonders and her miracles had impressed him with the fact that their ultimate origin lay far beyond the conception of the finite mind of man, and thus incalculably remote from the farthest bounds of science" (42–43). While this affirmation that scientific inquiry is insufficient to answer questions concerning God may seem to contradict the impulse of natural theology, it is not science that embodies the insufficiency so much as the "finite mind of man." Paley himself called the inference of God in natural theology "an immense conclusion" (468), but a necessary one. Tarzan sees nature as revelatory but doubts his own ability to understand it entirely. The narrator goes on to explain that "while he [Tarzan] realized that he knew nothing of such matters," he "liked to think" that God was "personal," and "that after death he would live again" (43). By "personal" Burroughs likely means that God has a personality rather than the more conservative view that ascribes personal attention to every human, as in the traditional salvation message. This same attitude rises which Burroughs, in correspondence with an astronomer, wrote: "I can appreciate, in a small way, the swell time God had in creating the universe" (qtd. in Poul Anderson 47).

Paley had credited God with a personality in his *Natural Theology*, based on the logic that "that which can contrive, which can design, must be a person. These capacities constitute personality, for they imply consciousness of thought" (462). This conclusion uses *personality* in a broad sense, but it is in just such a broad sense that the narrator intends its usage in this passage. Faith, according to the author of the biblical letter to the Hebrews, "is the substance of things hoped for, the evidence of things not seen" (11.1). Tarzan's reasoning here, the things he "liked to think," falls short of evidence and substance. To call Tarzan's desire to "live again" faith is too generous. His reasoning here, again, is predicted in "Tarzan Rescues the Moon," when the narrator says, "The secret of life interested him immensely. The miracle of death he could not quite fathom" (179–80). Tarzan had no experience with life after death, but his imagination has supplied such a possibility. In "The Nightmare," for example, he sees the head of a man he had killed earlier that evening attached to the head of a snake. The man is apparently seeking retribution as his "jaws opened to seize" Tarzan before "the apparition disappeared" (135). This man has, in a sense, lived again.

Burroughs provides tantalizing snippets of theology but never a full discussion that surpasses Tarzan's musings in "The God of Tarzan." So when, in his personal letter to Vaughan, nearly twenty years after writing the story, Burroughs writes that he believed in "an inexorable law, that, spiritually, man never arrives anywhere," he credits that there are movements and leanings, but that they last no longer than a "pendulum swings" before reversing themselves. Beyond that Burroughs records no faith. Zeuschner has gone so far as to claim that faith in Tarzan's characterization "is irrelevant. It is replaced by self-confidence and courage." Now, those characteristics can be readily found in every story.

Another ironic aspect of Tarzan's search for God is the fact that the villagers from whom he seeks an answer consider him some kind of deity. When Momaya returns to the village under Tarzan's protection, "she walk[s] with God" (86). He is called a demigod in the opening story and compared to a Greek god in the penultimate; he is referred to as a god seventeen times, a devil-god twenty-six times, and a demon twelve times, these last two appellations largely from the viewpoint of the two witch-doctors. Tarzan does not realize the ways of God are mysterious to both parties. The village and Tarzan seem to be looking for god in the other.

Alternatively, the apes, to the best of their fuzzy reasoning, placed the powers that Tarzan ascribed to God in the moon. Numgo specifically identifies the moon as the source of power "because the Dum-Dum always was danced in the light of Goro" (49). And later, in "Tarzan Rescues the Moon," Taug asks with concern, "How shall we dance the Dum-Dum without the light of Goro?" (189). Confusing concurrence with causality, Numgo and Taug have pointed to the closest thing to worship that the apes have, the Dum-Dum. Burroughs calls this rite of the apes as the source of "all the forms and ceremonies of modern church and state" (*Apes* 51). *Jungle Tales* does not include a description of this "savage orgy" (158), but refers to it in several of the stories, beginning with

"The God of Tarzan." In the first novel, Burroughs sets the scene: "In the center of the amphitheater was one of those strange earthen drums which the anthropoids build for the queer rites the sounds of which men have heard in the fastnesses of the jungle, but which none has ever witnessed" (51). The apes gather under the full moon to celebrate "important events in the life of the tribe" (52), ending, paradoxically with the tearing apart and eating of some foe, ape or non-ape, with brutal violence. In preparation, the earthen drum is beaten, while the males assemble in a line of dancers in mock battle. When the frenzy reaches its peak, they rush upon the corpse with furious abandon. Burroughs also refers to the Dum-Dum as "the council chamber of the great apes" (*Return* 190). Kipling had a Council Rock in the *Jungle Books*, where Mowgli's rejection from the pack takes place, and Burroughs may have had some similar proto-governmental function in mind that was never fully developed. In *Son*, Korak and Akut witness a Dum-Dum that proclaims a new king. Akut brings Korak to the site to introduce him to the tribe, giving the gathering a kind of citizenship-granting status, a status which the two fail to receive.

Surprisingly, several antecedents to the Dum-Dum are possible. David Livingstone's *The Last Journals of David Livingstone, in Central Africa, from Eighteen Sixty-Five to His Death* may provide a seed for the Dum-Dum, claiming that apes "make a drumming noise, some say with hollow trees, then burst forth into loud yells" (324); then in rephrasing Livingstone says they "beat hollow trees as drums with hands, and then scream as music to it" (325). Reade reports: "My informant asserts that he saw once not less than fifty [chimpanzees] so engaged, hooting, screaming, and drumming with sticks upon old logs" (184, 187n). He also says that "the habits of the gorilla differ [...] from those of the chimpanzee" in no "material respect" (187).

A possible literary antecedent may be found through Jack London. London, admired by Burroughs, died on 22 November 1916, five months after the completion of this story. In his 1906 novel, *Before Adam*, London creates a prehistoric, language-less people who participate in a similar ritual called the hee-hee. Even the name is similar in its repetition of a simple syllable. London records the first occurrence when several of the men had been "drawn together by mutual rage and the impulse toward cooperation" (170). While first one, then another, voices his rage at their oppression, until all are gibbering together, something magical happens: "Some one seized a stick and began pounding a log. In a moment he had struck a rhythm. Unconsciously, our yells and exclamations yielded to this rhythm. It had a soothing effect upon us; and before we knew it, our rage forgotten, we were in the full swing of a hee-hee council" (170). And just as Burroughs had supposed of the Dum-Dum's embryonic nature, so London's narrator claims that "the hee-hee council was an adumbration of the councils of primitive man, and of the great national assemblies and international conventions of latter-day man" (171). The cathartic nature of the hee-hee and Dum-Dum may be inferred, as in each, "with mad antics, leaping, reeling, and over-balancing, [the participants] danced and sang in the sombre twilight of the primeval world" (London 172), as a way to bring unity and control to disparate and impotent life.

The setting of the Dum-Dum is important. In *Apes*, the narrator points out that "the only opening into the little, level arena was through the upper branches of the trees" (51), and in *Return* the narrator claims that not even Tantor could force his way into the natural amphitheater because of the thick tangle of vines and "creepers of huge girth" (190). It is more secluded than any other place in the jungle. Holtsmark claims that such a setting provides "psychological ambience" (8). The Dum-Dum is more than a meeting place. It marks major moments of triumph over other apes. It is in this context that Tarzan kills his foster father in Oedipal fashion. It is here that Tarzan later kills Kerchak and becomes king of the tribe. Holtsmark points out that "the physically entangling growth of the jungle serves as an obvious commentary on childhood's emotionally entangling relationships that must be severed" (8–9). In killing these older rivals, Tarzan takes their place within the community of the great apes. The Dum-Dum includes a nearly obscured community function, as it does in London's hee-hee, as it does in Kipling's *Jungle Books*, and as it does in the Greek councils of mythological Olympus. When, in "The Lion," the narrator says that Tarzan "had wrested for himself a place in the councils of the savage beasts" (119), a reader may think more readily of the classical pantheon or of Kipling's council Rock, than of the Dum-Dum, which Bederman identifies as "the earliest of all human rituals" (220).

The beginning point of the Dum-Dum has, in summary, at least three branches. It first points to a kind of religious expression, second marks a type of governmental power, and third provides a community-building civil function. On this last claim, Berglund likens the Dum-Dum to the horrific feasts of Mbonga's village, calling the apes' version an embodiment of "cultural rituals of revenge cannibalism" (57). The cannibalism practiced in the Dum-Dum is dual in interpretation. As an ape, Tarzan would have thought of enemy apes as his own kind, and therefore would have developed a positive attitude toward the eating of one's enemies, no different than eating Horta, who is also an enemy. Freud suggests that the reasoning behind cannibalism is based on the belief that by ingesting parts of an opposing body, "one at the same time acquires the qualities possessed by him" (*Totem* 82). (This quality of transference is not limited to cannibalism, though; Freud says much the same thing in *The Ego and the Id* regarding the eating of animals, where "the attributes of animals which are incorporated as nourishment persist as part of the character of those who eat them" [19 n.2].) But, as a human, he is technically not eating his own kind, because apes and humans are different species. Tarzan's participation in the rite, according to Berglund, shows that he "does not question his adopted society's ritual of warfare cannibalism" (57). But the claim is too adamant in its interpretation. Tarzan has shown that true cannibalism, as occasioned by his examination of Kulonga, is unacceptable, as explored in chapter 7. What matters most is the community participation of the Dum-Dum as it reflects similarities with Mbonga's village.

"A is for Archer [...] B Is for Boy"
—primer in the Greystoke cabin (*Apes* 43)

Though the title of this story forefronts its theological aspect, certainly other connections are both possible and necessary. One of those is the idea that the Tarzan books are for children. Burroughs did not aim for a children's market—"*Tarzan of the Apes* was not written primarily for children" (Burroughs, "Edgar")—though he was not opposed to derivative works for children, eventually adding of his own accord the adventures of the Tarzan Twins, Dick and Doc in 1927.

The Whitman Big Little Books, beginning in 1932 and adding their illustrated version of *Tarzan of the Apes* in 1933, tapped a market that might have been whetted by the production of Foster's illustrations used in *The Illustrated Tarzan Book No. 1*. The introduction claims the Foster book to be "the first of Mr. Burroughs' famous novels to be published in picturized or strip form" ([3]). Each illustration mounts 4–8 lines of type, recounting the story.

Grosset & Dunlap moved their Tarzan reprints to a series entitled Books for Boys and Girls in 1948, following their World War II editions commonly referred to as the Madison Square editions, presumably targeting the younger audience as a more likely body of readers.

Disney, of course, saw the potential this direction as well in adapting *Tarzan of the Apes* to their animated feature line, complete with peripheral spin-offs. Irene Trimble uses the Disney image of Tarzan to lead off her children's picture book, titled *What Makes a Hero*. Under the text of the title question crouches Tarzan, his hair trailing to the left of the page, as if he has just swung his head to look at the reader. The next page also features an image of Tarzan carrying Jane away from threatening baboons, with text that emphasizes the importance of helping someone who is in trouble. The remaining heroic characteristics are illustrated with other Disney heroes, including Hercules, Aladdin, and Buzz Lightyear, current favorites in their appeal to children.

The seeds of a number of children's stories can be found in *Jungle Tales*. These connections do not indicate Burroughs as a source, but rather they indicate that the impulse and motifs that Burroughs incorporates are the same as those used profitably by children's authors both before and after he wrote *Jungle Tales*.

Hans Christian Anderson's fairy tales include the story of "The Ugly Duckling" (1844). In many ways this story serves as an overarching backdrop to the entire *Tarzan of the Apes/Jungle Tales* assemblage. Tarzan is the swan's egg dropped into a duck's nest. He is similar to the members of his host family but enough different to bring ridicule. This is especially important in "Tarzan's First Love." In trying to win Teeka's affection, Tarzan assumes a compatibility between them based on homogeneity. While friendships certainly can cross species lines, the overlooked differences are insurmountable for complete assim-

Hal Foster's panel for Tarzan's discovery of himself in letters. It was published in newspaper syndication before being collected into Foster's 1929 book, *The Illustrated Tarzan Book No. 1 Picturized from the Novel Tarzan of the Apes by Edgar Rice Burroughs.* Copyright Edgar Rice Burroughs, Inc. All rights reserved.

ilation. In this story, Tarzan notices the contrast between his skin, his nose, his teeth and Teeka's and labels his own shortcomings as "feeble" (8). In the first novel, Tublat, Tarzan's foster father, urges Kala to abandon the "burden" (*Apes* 35) because he sees no hope of the child ever maturing into something useful. In that novel, Tarzan is "nearly ten" when he first notices "that a great difference existed between himself and his fellows" (36). Tarzan finds his nose and teeth are far too small to make him like his playmates. This is the inverse of Andersen's ugly duckling, whose features were too large to match his comrades, but the attempted ostracism that follows is the same.

And many works following the publication of *Jungle Tales* incorporate similar themes and motifs. Frank Ashe's children's book, *Happy Birthday, Moon*, may come to the minds of some readers as Tarzan tries to talk to the moon. Like Tarzan, in Ashe's book Bear tries to get closer to the moon when he gets no response to his greeting. Bear thinks that the distance may be too great for the moon to hear his voice and devises a way to get closer. His attempts, though, bring no perceptible improvement to the situation. Tarzan is surprised to find once he is in "the highest point within his reach [...] that Goro was as far away as when he viewed him from the ground" (50). Certainly this observation strains the reader's sense of verisimilitude. The sudden de-sophistication of Tarzan in this scene, particularly when his search for truth is very real, works against the story. One would have to assume that Tarzan had never noticed the lack of difference in the moon's size between the two vantage points of the ground and the highest tree. In the reader's view, Tarzan's lack of insight is unsatisfying, unless Tarzan is suddenly far younger than established in other areas of the book. The reader of Tarzan's story has too much sophistication to accept Bear's naiveté for Tarzan.

Another children's book identified as bearing similarities to this tale is P.D. Eastman's *Are You My Mother?* Here the comparison is not to the reasoning of the main character but to the sequential search returning to the starting point. In Eastman's book, a bird hatches to find its mother missing and goes in search of her, asking in turn a kitten, a hen, a dog, a cow the title question, before being returned to the nest in time for the mother bird's arrival. Tarzan's search might be seen in similar terms: Tarzan asks the ape Numgo, the moon, and the witch-doctor, "Are you God?" before returning figuratively to where he began, that is, the world of nature.

Another story in the collection, "The Nightmare," prefigures two important images from Winnie-the-Pooh's adventures. The first comes when Tarzan is watching the villagers gorge themselves. One nameless villager comes to Tarzan's attention: "It was evident to Tarzan that the old fellow would eat [...] until there was no more meat" (130). As Tarzan watches he remembers a time when he had seen a hyena "eat his way into the carcass of a dead elephant and then continue to eat so much that he had been unable to get out of the hole through which he had entered" (131). In a less grisly way, A. A. Milne does just that in Pooh's visit to Rabbit's house. Pooh takes advantage of Rabbit's hospitality and eats the entire pot of honey. Upon trying to exit through Rabbit's front door, Pooh finds himself inextricably wedged, though he refuses to admit it. When Rabbit asks, "Hallo, are you stuck?," Pooh responds, "Just resting and thinking and humming to myself" (15). Rabbit's house has taken on the benign form of Burroughs' dead elephant. The second comes from the hallucinations that Tarzan experiences after food poisoning. In much the same manner as Tarzan experiences a phantasmagoria of enemies — a lion, an eagle, a human-headed snake — attempting to kill him, Pooh, in the Disney adaptation, experiences those dread heffalumps and woosles in a variety of fantastic forms attempting to steal his honey. In both cases the dreams are preceded by eating something prized as well has keeping it from some undesirable threat.

Even though Burroughs insisted "Tarzan does not preach; he has no lesson to impart, no propaganda to disseminate," he does add his caveat: "Yet, perhaps unconsciously, while seeking merely to entertain I have injected something of my own admiration for certain fine human qualities into these stories of the ape-man" ("Tarzan Theme" 29). Tapper affirms that "animals are good to think with, and good to teach with" (51). As a source for character-building in children, the Tarzan stories have been identified in Theodor Rebarber's report for the U.S. Department of Education for fostering in readers aged 9 and above the character qualities of careful thinking, self-reliance and self-knowledge.

Of course one of the pleasures derived from children's books is what Baker calls "the playful relation of seeing and not seeing" (146). The reader acknowledges intellectually that animals cannot talk, but chooses to set aside the demand for verisimilitude in order to enjoy the fantasy of a world where such things *could* happen. Burroughs plays with, indeed strains at, at times, this willing suspension of disbelief. In children's literature, the anthropomorphism given to animals is adopted with no alarm. When Tarzan dons the skin of a lion, in "The Lion," to the apes of the tribe he *is* a lion; when he does it in Mbonga's village, he *becomes* a lion. For a child reader this is no different from the Big Bad Wolf who mysteriously is mistaken for Red Riding Hood's grandmother. For the reader who wants to believe, there is no problem.

> "*Of what a strange nature is knowledge! It clings to the mind when it has once seized on it like a lichen on the rock*"
> — Frankenstein's creature, *Frankenstein* (Shelley 115).

Tarzan is a self-taught reader. Burroughs intended that he be so from the beginning. His proposal to his editor consisted of a three-sentence overview, concerning "the scion of a noble English house," "adopted by a huge she-ape," who "learn[s] to read English without knowledge of the spoken language" (letter to Metcalf, 6 March 1912). This process is introduced in the novel when Tarzan enters the long-abandoned cabin of his parents when he is "over ten years old" (*Apes* 43). There he begins his first book, "a child's illustrated alphabet," with "A is for Archer" (43). Repeatedly over the years, Tarzan returns to the cabin to investigate the books, and the narrator of *Tarzan of the Apes* claims that "by the time he was fifteen he knew the various combinations of letters which stood for every pictured figure in the little primer and in one or two of the picture books" (49).

"Through literacy," Vernon suggests, "through symbols, he conceptually separates himself from the animals around him" (173). In these picture books and primers that the Greystokes intended to educate their child, Tarzan finds a different kind of hunt from the physical, which Burroughs takes up again in "The God of Tarzan." This mental hunt stimulates Tarzan's curiosity and satisfies him in ways inconceivable to Kerchak's tribe. In addition to the literal hunting ground of the jungle, the dictionary becomes his mental hunting ground, "following up the spoor of a new thought through the mazes of the many definitions which each new word required him to consult. It was like following a quarry through the jungle — it was hunting, and Tarzan of the Apes was an indefatigable huntsman" (48). The words become, in Vernon's conception, the attractive forbidden. Like Adam's tree at the center of the garden, literacy becomes for Tarzan "the irresistible temptation that will forever cast him out of his idyllic garden" (173), which leads Vernon to conclude that Tarzan's story is an "allegorical flight" from Eden (174).

The intellectual leaps required for Tarzan to move from his perception of language as "little bugs which ran riot upon the printed pages" (48) to abstract concepts strain many readers' suspension of disbelief. Critics have objected to the relationship of sound and meaning as derived only from the written symbols. As early as 1914, readers objected to Tarzan's linguistic ability in the first Tarzan story. One of the early writers was "H.P.L." (readily identified as H.P. Lovecraft). In a letter to the editor, he faults Burroughs, whom he has just identified as "[a]t or near the head of your list of writers": "[W]e behold the hero, before he has learned the relation between vocal sounds and written letters, writing out his name, Tarzan, which he has known only from the lips of his hairy associates." Lupoff, a Burroughs critic in the 1960s, calls this "a valid objection" and attributes this element to "Burroughs' boundless faith in the ability of man" (*Master* 188). Many people have weighed in on Tarzan's ability to teach himself to read. Charles Caruso simply comments that Tarzan came by the ability "[p]ainfully, but with blue-blooded tenacity" (104).

This aspect of Tarzan teaching himself to read has been the sticking place for many readers, who claim it couldn't be done. Altrocchi claims, for example, "it certainly is unbelievable that a child quite alone in the jungle, no matter how atavistically brilliant, even though he found some books, could possibly learn to read and write" (92). Altrocchi's only explanation for such an occurrence is that Tarzan must be "super-normal" (92). And in the larger scheme, Tarzan's linguistic aptitude might well be called super-normal. His linguistic ability does not stop with his acquisition of written English. David Adams has counted 29 languages/dialects specifically mentioned in the Tarzan series as languages in which Tarzan communicated. Adams further speculates that "Tarzan undoubtedly knew many of the Bantu languages" ("Burroughsian"), though they are not mentioned by name in the texts.

In a story wherein the reader has already accepted the feral upbringing of Tarzan, this matter of linguistic aptitude seems a less weighty matter. Just as Macbeth admitted, "[T]o be king / Stands not within the prospect of belief" (Shakespeare, *Macbeth* 1.3.73–74), so the reader may claim Tarzan's ability to learn language without a teacher is unbelievable, yet in both stories the unbelievable occurs.

Burroughs needed an articulate hero. Just as he acknowledged that the feralism of his story did not accord with scientific findings, so does his transference of spoken and written words differ from any scientific documentation. For his plot, though, Tarzan needed the ability to communicate. Creed affirms that "the thing which clearly sets [Tarzan] apart from the apes is his ability to learn language" (162). By this, she certainly means written language, as the great apes themselves have spoken language. Rolf Romøren points out that the simplified film versions of Tarzan have "marginalized" an important emphasis in Tarzan's character, "the importance of language acquisition and literacy for acquiring [humanness]*" ("Light"). Romøren cites Conny Svensson's book *Tarzan i slukåldern* (*Tarzan in the Book Devouring Age*) where identification comes not so much with the death-defying feats of the young Tarzan but "more with the diligent schoolboy of the wilderness, deprived of his teachers" (qtd. in Romøren, "Light").

And since the event comes not from an attempt at scientific accuracy, it may well be intended to represent something other than itself. Maggie Kilgour reminds the reader: "All action [...] reveals some meaning which is behind or underneath it [...]" (227). "Burroughs begs his readers," Berglund argues, "to view Tarzan's act of reading allegorically: the primitive being yearns for knowledge" (54). The chapter in *Apes* where Tarzan experiences this "epiphanic moment" (Berglund 54) is entitled "The Light of Knowledge." Berglund, in his insightful article "Write, Right, White, Rite: Literacy, Imperialism, Race, and Cannibalism in Edgar Rice Burroughs' *Tarzan of the Apes*," points out that for all the interest in action that Burroughs creates, "he seems more concerned with arming his character with literacy: reading, writing, and inevitably, speaking [...]" (54). Because Tarzan is more intelligent than his companions and quite probably more so than any companions he might have had in a civilized upbringing, he "sees nothing wrong," Holtsmark says, "with the pursuit of intellectual and [...] academic interests" (108). Holtsmark continues in analyzing the importance of Tarzan's intellectual pursuit: "Certainly the whole narrative about his learning to read underscores not only the eagerness with which he embarked on the acquisition of knowledge but also the great delight and joy he found in giving himself over to these diversions" (108). For Burroughs, then, "reading and writing is natural to man as a consequence of his innate ability to think" (Byrne and McQuillan 109). Literacy is innate; its potentiality and foundation lie in every human — only its development differs from person to person. Bleiler notes that Tarzan's "achievement of literacy must surely be one of the greatest intellectual feats in history" (103), but of course Tarzan is not a figure from history but from literature.

Other literary characters record the astounding difference reading brings to life. The best parallel is that of Mary Shelley's creature in *Frankenstein*. The creature spies on the De Laceys who are teaching an Arabian girl English. While the emphasis is on learning to speak, Shelley slips in this one-sentence paragraph during the creature's confrontation with his creator: "While I improved in speech, I also learned the science of letters as it was taught to the stranger,

---

*Actually, Romøren used the word *humaneness* in his original text, which he indicated to me later to be an error. "I should of course wish," he said, "that literacy could make us more humane as well, but life (and language) doesn't seem that simple" (personal e-mail).

and this opened before me a wide field for wonder and delight" (113). So well does the creature learn written language that *Paradise Lost*, no primer in its complexity, becomes a primary text. This provokes a search for the Creator, a confused issue because of his genesis at the hand of Victor Frankenstein. To the point, though, Shelley provides even less justification for the creature's ability or method of learning written language than does Burroughs with Tarzan. Byrne and McQuillan distinguish him from "Mary Shelley's Rousseau-taught monster" (109), because Tarzan has no teacher, except the books found in his father's cabin. Those books and the world of nature are enough to answer most of his questions.

Other stories that Burroughs might have known, where a character learns to read, though in a different context, include Poe's "The Gold Bug," and Conan Doyle's "The Adventure of the Dancing Men." In these stories, the hero must learn to interpret written symbols and create meaning. Poe's hero, Legrand, sets the ground for later literary decoders, through his simple substitutions. In the latter case, Sherlock Holmes is able to make simple letter substitution by statistics and intuition. Critics have criticized Conan Doyle for Holmes's intuitive leaps as well; Alastair Fowler, for example, in affirming "Holmes' professedly scientific method," acknowledges that his reasoning is "notoriously hard to follow" (157) because "Holmes depends on assumptions" (159). In both these cases, though, the reading comes in the form of translating one written form into another written form. Burroughs complicates matters by making his an issue of translating from a spoken language into a written one, when Tarzan writes his name on the note he leaves at the cabin. This event, committed in the initial tale of Tarzan, is not repeated in *Jungle Tales*. Even so, Johnston believes that the way Burroughs portrayed the matter with Tarzan "is better than" (59) either of these two stories.

In "Tarzan and the Black Boy," the issue of communication is important in showing Tarzan's understanding of language. When Tarzan tries to communicate with Tibo, the results are mutually frustrating. Tarzan cannot understand Tibo and Tibo cannot understand Tarzan. Perhaps unconsciously, Burroughs has echoed the biblical dictum: "Therefore if I know not the meaning of the voice, I shall be unto him that speaketh a barbarian, and he that speaketh shall be a barbarian unto me" (1 Corinthians 14.11). At this uninitiated state, Tarzan thinks his is the only language and arrives at the "obvious" conclusion that Tibo needs to be educated in the speech of the mangani. The "violent babble of uncouth sounds" (34) that Conrad labels the speech of the natives is to Tarzan "as senseless as the chattering of the silly birds" (71–72); Tibo's "speech was not talk at all" (71). Tarzan plays the role of an unwitting Prospero to a terrified Caliban. In Shakespeare's play, Prospero becomes the master-tutor for the creature he finds on the island, explaining:

> I pitied thee,
> Took pains to make thee speak, taught thee each hour
> One thing or other. When thou didst not, savage,

> Know thine own meaning, but wouldst gabble like
> A thing most brutish, I endowed thy purposes
> With words that made them known [*The Tempest* 1.2.356–61].

The superior attitude inherent in Prospero's speech might inform the grand assumption that Tarzan makes regarding Tibo, that his own linguistic background was the standard against which all other attempts at speech are measured. The reader, of course, is able to realize that Tarzan's speech is not superior to the language of Mbonga's village; both are effective in their prescribed contexts.

If reading represents superiority, then the source of that reading may also represent a similar dominion. Romøren identifies Tarzan's discovery of the cabin as an essential step in his maturation because "books and letters [are] an efficient way to supplement his (human) recollection" ("Light"). The cabin is an important setting for this essential task. The cabin, according to Balasopoulos, "contains all of the civilized present in condensed form"; that it "so magnetically attracts Tarzan" (203) is emblematic of, among other things, Tarzan's budding aptitude for learning. When Tarzan is eleven, he discovers "the right combination" (*Apes* 42) of manipulations to open the door to that "source of never-ending mystery and pleasure" (*Apes* 41). Upon a subsequent visit to the cabin, he takes the time to "learn the mechanism of the lock" (*Apes* 47), so that he could understand the relationship of the lock to the door and its frame. This initial investigation foreshadows the larger learning of relationships, those of the marks on the page to each other in varying combinations. When the narrator of "The God of Tarzan" begins the story with the reference to this or a similar occasion, he packs it with the image of understanding relationships. In finding inferred meaning in some of the relationships that "puzzle his young head" (48), Tarzan inches indefatigably from one side of his hyphenated appellation to the other, from the ape side of *ape-boy* to the other. Balasopoulos points out that despite the evolutionary overtones that Burroughs charges his novel with, the scene and the accomplishment have nothing evolutionary in them. The cabin represents four things: "a veritable arc of Western knowledge, an ensemble of linguistic and pictorial signs which explain the world and one's place in it, a lesson in technical know-how, [and] a warehouse of secrets of identity and implements of power" (Balasopoulos 203). In absolute terms, then, nothing is evolving. Rather, Tarzan is learning facts and mental processes that are common in civilization but mark his own personal ignorance. The discovery is the Keatsian Cortez staring at the Pacific. Keats is not the first to read Homer. He is led by the help of a book, Chapman's translation, to an understanding that had been available to others, through other translations, or available to even the original Greek listeners. It is the imagined Cortez staring at the Pacific after Balboa had discovered it for the European world. It is this personal education that Burroughs focuses on in Tarzan's self-literacy. Tarzan personalizes the information, through "the controlled replication of what already exists" (Balasopoulos 203) or is already known commonly in other parts of the world.

In response to Tarzan's search for identity through his reading, Balasopoulos points out that it is "the image (rather than the sign) [that] defines Tarzan's own identity formation" (209 n.4). That is, Tarzan finds more meaning in the pictures of the books than in the words of the books. We see this when he comes upon the word *God* and has no picture with which to solidify meaning. In a sense, his search is for the missing picture. Cheyfitz points out that "pictures are fantasized [...] as a universal or ur-language" (15), a language that can speak where words fail, a language that existed before words came into use.

Tarzan is distinguished from every other entity in his jungle by this ability to read. This is no simple difference. Berglund makes a triple-faceted entity of textuality, literacy, and civilization, in contrast to its counterpart, made of orality, illiteracy, and barbarity. In doing so, he shows the interrelatedness of Tarzan's ability to read as a contrast to Mbonga's villagers. Tarzan's resistance to cannibalism, then, is a by-product of his literacy; Berglund claims that "Tarzan's knowledge about the morality of cannibalism comes to him via the found books" (55); he later clarifies that the books did not tell him explicitly that cannibalism was wrong, rather "he has intuited [this] from his readings" (65). His argument, of course, hinges on the claim he makes, that "cannibalism is complexly enmeshed within a discourse about orality and written literacy" (55). Chapter 7 will develop the significance of cannibalism in greater detail.

Berglund also finds importance in the re-creation of letters, claiming that "Burroughs bewitches his readers into assuming that it is entirely natural for his character to be delighted by the magical marks he has left" (67). He continues that today's readers conjecture "a clear cause-and-effect relationship between literacy and social class and power" (68). If this is the case, then Tarzan's heritage predisposed him to his literate capacity. Berglund concludes: "What has become clear in Burroughs' absurd rendition of Tarzan's learning to read is that the skills of literacy operate to instantiate cultural regimes of knowledge. Literacy is not a set of neutral skills devoid of ideological underpinnings" (66). Tarzan reads, then, because he is noble. And those who do not read, one might suppose, cannot reach a level of nobility.

Berglund points out, "Before he finally closes the gap between his written and spoken (or unspoken) identities, except for his name, Tarzan does not record the oral ape language in English characters" (69). The meaning of his name, white skin, is lost when it is translated into English sounds that are gibberish, as the reader assumes all the ape language appears to be. R.G. Collingwood points out that "in a child's original acquisition of his mother tongue every word he is to use must first be explained to him; and it is actually supposed that this comes about by its mother, or other instructor, pointing to the fire and saying 'fire' [...]" (227). He says though that such an assumption is in error. "The reason why no mother teaches language in this way," he goes on, "is that it could not possibly be done; for the supposed gestures of pointing and so forth are themselves in the nature of a language" (227). Despite the implausibility of this aspect of Tarzan's self-education, Altrocchi points out that "miraculous auto-didacticism is also a traditional element in a certain branch of forsaken-babe stories" (92), though he provides no examples.

Another reason Burroughs needed Tarzan to attain significant linguistic aptitude is the character's role as liaison between groups and as self-translator. Cheyfitz points out the linguistic ability of Tarzan in comparison to Natty Bumppo. Tarzan was called "the Natty Bumppo of the African jungle" ("Old" 67) by editors at *Ellery Queen's Mystery Magazine*. In James Fenimore Cooper's *The Prairie*, like the "linguisters in the settlements," "[h]e can talk to the Pawnee, and the Konza, and the Omaha, and he can talk to his own people" (293). Likewise, Cheyfitz explains, "Tarzan is a translator" (15). In the first novel, Tarzan speaks the language of the mangani and learns to read and write English before the arrival of Europeans. Oddly he never understands that the people of Mbonga's village speak a language. His experience with Tibo and Momaya might have suggested this to him, but he lacked sufficient insight at that point of his maturity. After his encounter with Paul D'Arnot, in which Mbonga's village is effectively wiped out, he learns to speak first French and then English in short order. In the next novel, he learns Arabic and then Waziri, his first native African language. Somewhere unrecorded in this time he also learns "the mongrel tongue of the West Coast" (*Return* 169).

Cheyfitz argues that language acquisition is a fitting indicator of Tarzan's self-searching, as well. "Tarzan's search for identity," he says, "is a linguistic search, in which he is literally translated from ape into man" (15). Jurca, also believes the importance of Tarzan's literacy lies in what it teaches Tarzan about himself. One of the primary distinctions that Tarzan learns from the picture books is the division between humans and the other creatures of the jungle, especially the apes. She concludes: "writing exists to teach men who they are and to make them proud of their distinguishing characteristics" (492). Tarzan's learning to read is a major step in his quest for identity. When he identifies this difference between himself and his companions, an identification that is slowly forming in the collection of these tales, his separation becomes complete. While he occasionally chooses to dwell with the great apes on other occasions in other novels, never does he feel at home or stay long. One major reason for this, Cheyfitz reveals, is linguistic: "Tarzan cannot fully converse with the apes because written English cannot translate into their impoverished tongue" (16). This very lack is illustrated in the story when the apes are confused by Tarzan's attempts to find God. Following the belief that literacy is power, it is immediately after these twelve stories that Tarzan defeats the linguistically impaired Kerchak to become king of the tribe. Because he is "unable to converse fully with the apes," Cheyfitz argues, "Tarzan can only dominate them" (16). Though, to be fair, his leadership is temporary, and he outgrows his place among the apes. His search for God has led him to find a portion of his identity exactly where he started, in the books of his father's cabin.

CHAPTER 5

Black and White and In Between
The Perception of Racism in "Tarzan and the Black Boy"

Burroughs finished this fifth of the *Jungle Tales* 13 October 1916 in Los Angeles, from whence he wrote the rest of the stories. When Long indicated that the editorial office was pleased with the story, Burroughs replied with typical self-doubt: "Am mighty glad you liked the story. I am always fearful that you won[']t" (letter 30 October 1916). Oddly, he does not note the date he began the writing. The amount of time between this story and its predecessor is the largest gap in the collection. When Burroughs finished "The God of Tarzan" in July, he was at Camp Branch in Michigan. His hairpin decision to strike for California followed, and apparently little or no writing took place while his family was westering. The family stayed in Los Angeles from 23 September through March of the next year.

A comic version of the story appeared in Gold Key's *Tarzan of the Apes* #170 (Aug. 1967). The story is also retold inside an original story published in the British *Tarzan of the Apes* #18 (29 October 1971), titled "Bukawi's Revenge." In this departure, Jane is captured by Bukawi (so renamed) in revenge for Tarzan foiling his attempt to get "three goats, two new skins, and new cooking pot" (14) from Momaya so many years earlier. The messenger who comes to tell Tarzan of Jane's abduction retells a version of Tibo's time as Tarzan's balu. Burroughs pitched a second record album set to Decca after the success of the dramatized *Tarzan of the Apes*. The story Decca bought was "Tarzan and the Black Boy," retitled *Tarzan and the Little Black Boy*, which was recorded 16 June 1942 on a 3-disc set of 78s. Each side lasted approximately 3 minutes, making a total of about 18 minutes for the story. The same actor, Elliott Lewis, gave voice to Tarzan and M'Bonga.

In the story, Tarzan makes a new rope while Gazan plays alongside. While hunting, he realizes that he might fit in if he had a child of his own. He comes upon a boy, Tibo, playing along the river near his mother and uses his rope to capture him. Tarzan takes him to his tribe but the apes want nothing to do with the boy. Tarzan takes him away, beginning to realize that caring for a child demands much work. Tibo cries and refuses food, though eventually he begins to trust Tarzan. The boy's mother, Momaya, goes first to her village witch-doctor then to an outcast witch-doctor, asking for help in retrieving her stolen child. She cannot and will not pay the price the outcast Bukawai asks. Tarzan comes upon a lioness grieving over a dead cub and intuitively understands that Momaya must be grieving as well. Tarzan hides Tibo so that he can go hunting. Tibo sees his mother returning to her village after the disappointing visit to Bukawai and they are reunited. Tarzan returns at the moment a lion attacks. Tarzan saves them and Tibo pleads with Tarzan, with the mangani words he has learned, to allow him to go home with his mother, in return for a daily food offering left outside the village gates for him (this is verified beginning with chapter 12 of *Apes*, when Tarzan discovers "food always standing at the foot of the tree which was his avenue into the palisade" [*Apes* 83]). Tarzan relents and escorts them back to the village. Tarzan again feels lonely; Tibo and Momaya feel elated; and Bukawai, who has followed and observed, vows revenge.

When the narrator claims that "imagination is but another name for super-intelligence" (75), he echoes a theme from Jack London. Burroughs thought highly of London. Hillman lists London as one of Burroughs' favorite authors and goes so far as to call London a mentor for Burroughs (as does Taliaferro [20, 105]), though no correspondence between the two ever occurred ("The ERB / Jack London Connection I"). Burroughs even considered inviting him to join the board of directors for a film company he was working on in 1916. London died, however, before Burroughs made contact. London's *The Call of the Wild* was high in the popular imagination and no doubt Burroughs recalled, if not in word, in concept what London's narrator had said regarding Buck, that the "quality that made for greatness" in him was "imagination" (24). That Buck can rise to the leadership of the sled team is not based solely on strength. When Buck takes on Spitz, the lead dog, London's narrator notes that Buck could fight not only as an animal "by instinct, but he could fight by head as well" (35).

Also of note in this chapter, Momaya is a sympathetic woman and the narrator points out that she was not originally from Mbonga's tribe but came into it as a possession of war. Reade claims that while the father is too selfish to care about the needs of his children, "[t]he maternal instinct which we see so powerful in the mere animal creation is not absent from the negress" (206). Momaya here is corollary to Kurtz's African woman in *Heart of Darkness*. This is the only woman in Conrad's story to draw something of a favorable response. Achebe points out that because "she is in her place," she "can win Conrad's special brand of approval" ("Image" 8). That is, because she is an African woman, she can be admired in ways that a European woman would not care for. Against a backdrop of "[d]ark human shapes [...] flitting indistinctly against the gloomy border of the forest," "a wild and gorgeous apparition of a woman" enters the scene (Conrad 77). This woman, as Momaya had been when Tibo is abducted, is ready to take on tremendous odds, to confront the entire boatload of foreigners to get back her beloved Kurtz. Conrad describes her as "treading the earth proudly"; "[s]he carried her head high"; "[s]he was savage and superb, wild-eyed and magnificent" (77). So might the reader imagine Momaya.

This story, like many of the others, displays a new tactic in Tarzan's search for personal definition. The story highlights sameness and difference, especially in regards to racial attitudes, as Tarzan explores another part of the continuum of his identity. The comparisons and contrasts show aspects of Tarzan's dual nature as well.

> "[...] far above and beyond material benefits will be that higher good, that [...] will come, in a blotting out of sectional differences and racial animosities and suspicions, in a determination to administer absolute justice [...]"
> — Booker T. Washington, Atlanta Exposition Address, 18 September 1895 (Washington 224)

Readers who have not read widely do not know the racial climate in which Burroughs wrote. And the terms by which the complaints are made are often ill-defined. When Rothstein wrote about the Disney adaptation, he felt compelled to preface his praise for the original novel with a caveat concerning racial stereotypes which "marred it" (E1), a claim backed up with no specific citation. That Burroughs' words offend some readers is not the same as Burroughs' personality being racist. Prejudice takes many forms and many names, not all of them damning.

The charge of racism has become prevalent. Midgley defines it as "the offence of treating somebody—for whatever reasons—in a way determined by race, not by individual qualities and needs" (99). She calls it in reality "an ill-formed, spineless, impenetrably obscure concept" (99). One distinction she makes is between belief and prejudice, for they are two distinct attitudes. People can believe different things without being prejudiced. "A belief is not a prejudice simply because it indicates a difference," Midgley explains (101). In application to a whole range of writers at the turn of the twentieth century, the prejudices and differences sometimes become tangled.

Today many acknowledge a kind of cultural blindness to racial issues that are now high profile. Meyer writes that from "a twenty-first-century perspective" the story is often seen as "an unfortunate manifestation of the period's assumptions" (Afterword 299), especially regarding racial issues. Words and attitudes that have far and sharp political and social ramifications were a century ago depoliticized speech—"discourse which treats its subject as universally accepted, scientifically established, and therefore no longer open to criticism by a political or theoretical opposition" (Brantlinger 168). The current concern regarding racism, McWhorter points out, "did not exist in the popular consciousness when the first Tarzan story was written" ("No" 34). And Peter Mwikisa affirms that Conrad, an older contemporary of Burroughs, "did not foresee an African readership" when he wrote his famous short novel, *Heart of Darkness*. For Burroughs, Africa was only vaguely a real place. The popular image, whether from explorers' accounts or from fictitious interpretations, had never been rendered with the objective accuracy that is expected by today's readers. Dorothy Hammand and Alta Jablow point out that "the Africa of anthropology and that of popular 'literary' conception" (13) did not coexist at the end of the nineteenth century. The popular version ruled alone, and this is the only Africa that Burroughs knew, the Africa of Buel and Du Chaillu and of Haggard and Conrad. This Africa was inhabited by "a few stock figures [who] are never completely human" (Hammand and Jablow 14) in a world almost as imaginary as Barsoom and Pellucidar, other imaginary places created by Burroughs. The inhabitants, whether antagonists or compatriots, were clearly imaginary and meant to represent a particular fictive cipher and not a particular African people.

Poul Anderson's summary of Burroughs' output following the paperback boom of the 1960s points out that in Burroughs' work, "[r]acial stereotypes are common"; but then he adds parenthetically an important acknowledgement: "However, almost all writers of that period used them, and Burroughs does picture Tarzan's black friends, the Waziri, [by contrast] as an admirable people" (46). Holding a writer accountable to standards that were not valued in his day is specious. The argument has been inflicted on writers as diverse as London, Kipling, and Conrad, as well as Burroughs, all writers at the end of the nineteenth century and beginning of the twentieth.

The case of Conrad, whose *Heart of Darkness* was serialized in 1899 and published in book form in 1902, is instructive. Achebe led the charge against *Heart of Darkness* in a 1975 lecture at the University of Massachusetts, claiming that Conrad "portrays Africans as lacking the power of expression, devoid of recognizable humanity, [...] as cannibals who should stay in 'their place'" (Carey-Webb 123). Achebe calls Conrad "one of the great stylists of modern fiction and a good storyteller" ("Image" 3); contrarily, he also calls him "a thoroughgoing racist" ("Image" 11). *Heart of Darkness* fails as great art, Achebe says, because it "parades in the most vulgar fashion prejudices and insults from which [people have] suffered untold agonies and atrocities," and it challenges the human identity of blacks ("Image" 15). Achebe asks, "Were there people there [in Conrad's depiction of Africa]?" followed by the colloquial response: "Well ... not really, you know ... people of sorts, perhaps, but not as you and I understand the word" ("African" 4). The callousness of white attitudes toward blacks cannot be written off; those attitudes existed. Huckleberry Finn's off-hand comment typifies this attitude when he answers questions regarding a riverboat explosion. Aunt Sally asks, "Good gracious! Anybody hurt?" Huck's response — "No'm. Killed a nigger" (Twain 216) — rightly demonstrates the dehumanization that occurred in nineteenth-century America, an attitude that was perpetuated well into the twentieth. Burroughs was ten when *The Adventures of Huckleberry Finn* was published. During Burroughs' lifetime, that callousness wore thin.

Conrad's Africa is "the antithesis of Europe and therefore of civilization" ("Image" 3), Achebe says; in *Heart of Darkness*, the self-congratulatory refinement of the Western nations contrasts with the silent animality of an imaginary fecund wasteland. The Africa portrayed in *Heart of Darkness*, he says, is "where the wandering European may discover that the dark impulses and unspeakable appetites he has suppressed and forgotten through ages of civilization may spring into life again in answer to Africa's free and triumphant savagery" ("African" 5–6). Conrad's narrator, Marlow, says:

> It was unearthly, and the men were — No, they were not inhuman. Well, you know, that was the worst of it — this suspicion of their not being inhuman. It would come slowly to one. They howled and leaped, and spun, and made horrid faces; but what thrilled you was just the thought of their humanity — like yours — the thought of your remote kinship with this wild and passionate uproar. Ugly [51].

The problem that Achebe identifies is not a literary one but a cultural one, though the two problems, like prejudices and beliefs, are difficult to divide. Achebe correctly identifies the problem as "the willful tenacity" of European nations to cling to the stereotyped image, though he admits that this Western response "is more [...] reflex action than calculated malice" ("Image" 18). Based on an essay by Frances Singh, Carey-Webb argues that Conrad's fiction is "profoundly compromised by an acceptance of nineteenth-century anthropology" (124). Brenda Cooper confirms that "[w]hen Conrad depicted the interior of Africa as dark, wild and savage, he was not being entirely original. Over many years," she continues, "certain ways of seeing Africa, certain conventions of how to describe this continent had been well established, conventions Conrad developed, refined, modified and perplexingly, also interrogated" ("Boat" 64). And Achebe himself acknowledges that "Conrad's yelling crowds were [...] a hand-me-down" (*Home* 26) inherited not only by Conrad but the bulk of writers from that generation. He half-excuses Conrad, when he says, "It was certainly not his fault that he lived his life at a time when the reputation of the black man was at a particularly low level" ("Image" 13), but he refuses to allow the contemporary culture of the author to mitigate the seriousness of his charges of racism.

The same may be said of Burroughs, that he has appropriated the conventions previously established and modified them to suit his needs. Some may argue that his interrogation of these conventions is muted, compared to Conrad's, but his establishment of John Clayton's mission — "to make a peculiarly delicate investigation of conditions in a British West Coast African Colony from whose simple native inhabitants another European power was known to be recruiting" people into forced labor (*Apes* 7) — marks the story's beginning as one of just such interrogation. The scrutiny regarding this interrogation in

Conrad shows the ambivalence that seems to underlie *Heart of Darkness*. That "Conrad seemed to interrogate the greedy and exploitative, ivory hunting nature of colonialism, even as he reinforced it discursively" (Cooper, "Boat" 65), points to a critical ambivalence that confuses as well as illuminates the issue. Tarzan is also such an ambivalent character, Cooper says, "on that razor edge between facilitating and betraying, often looking in both directions simultaneously" (*Weary* 4). As in the Janus figure from Roman mythology, left and right, forward and backward are instilled within the same character.

That the text of *Heart of Darkness*, or the Tarzan stories, or any other text, does not line up with a reader's current political views, does not, as Carey-Webb points out, make it "somehow [...] less worthy of analysis" (126). He goes on: "To cease paying attention to a text, or to minimize its importance, because it is 'racist' is to suggest that racism is not an important object of investigation [...]" (126). Brenda Cooper suggests that the racial stereotyping and colonial assumptions do not negate other aspects worth studying. "Along with its investment in the social order, great literature philosophises about life, ponders the tentacles of death, the paradoxes of existence, of love and beauty, birth and disease, pain and desire" ("Boat" 65). She points out also that the ability of the text to explore these things is not dependent on the writer's intentions. Such works explore these concerns "unwittingly as the enduring conventions of how to depict [various people groups] are ingrained in tradition" ("Boat" 65). It is this tradition — "that white racism against Africa is such a normal way of thinking that its manifestations go completely unremarked" — that so enraged Achebe ("Image" 12). Such a tradition, he pointed out, led to "the dehumanization of Africa and Africans" (Image" 12).

Because the topic is important, Carey-Webb says, he asks readers to look at *Heart of Darkness* and *Tarzan of the Apes* together "to gain a more complicated understanding" (127) of the two books. Meyer agrees that acknowledging that "such attitudes were pervasive in the culture" of the early twentieth century is "a strategy that doesn't excuse or mitigate [those attitudes] but that attempts to create a better understanding" (Afterword 299). Carey-Webb points out thematic, political, and philosophical similarities, including their portrayal of "Africans as primitive, racially inferior types lower down the scale of social evolution" (127). The difference between Conrad and Burroughs, Carey-Webb says, is not in their racial depictions but in Conrad's use of a less accessible, "highly 'literary' language" (128). Carey-Webb complains, anachronistically, that both authors "oppose the brutalities of Belgian colonialism, [but] seem to accept and perhaps even admire the more 'restrained' and 'effective' British version" (128). That either Tarzan or Kurtz would be able to survive, Carey-Webb attributes to their supposed European superiority, an assumption he implies should be questioned.

Kurtz, in Conrad's novel, can be compared to Tarzan in a number of ways. Mwikisa, for example, marks Kurtz as "the criminal, the prosecutor, and the judge," made all the more entrancing because he can "carry out these three roles simultaneously." Kurtz has become criminal, a reader assumes from the piked heads surrounding his camp. He has become a law unto the village that has rallied around him, again based on the assumed servility of the villagers. Tarzan, too, may be seen as a murderer, and therefore a criminal, from the time he kills Kulonga, on through the innumerable, mostly unnamed, victims of Mbonga's tribe. He is the prosecutor who follows Kulonga to examine his guilt. And finally he is the judge and executioner when he stabs Kala's slayer through the heart with his father's knife. The difference may lie in the readers' perceived justification. In current popular thought, the revenge for the death of a loved one is more justifiable than murder to increase ivory production. The attribute that Marlow identifies with Kurtz is a lack of self-control: "Mr. Kurtz lacked restraint in the gratification of his various lusts" (74). This lack of self-control, paradoxically, leads to control over the indigenous people, nearly to the point of worship. Mwikisa identifies that to these "simple inhabitants[,] Kurtz is taken for a God [...]." Tarzan, as the last chapter showed, is viewed similarly. In both cases, a certain lack or loss of maturity may be reckoned the basis for their actions.

Burroughs' belief in a hierarchy of races, Taliaferro suggests, was typical of his era (94). "For his generation, Burroughs was not exceptionally condescending in his attitude toward blacks, both American and African," he says; but, in firm ambivalence, he adds: "Nor was he particularly enlightened" (107), meaning that Burroughs did little to question the stereotypes in his fiction, knowing that the shorthand of stock characters made characterization less of a burden, a bit like the cook who uses the same ingredients in similar proportions, without examining or questioning the recipe book. Taliaferro goes on: "Having never been to Africa, he swallowed too easily the stereotype of the benighted, violent, superstitious Negro aborigine" (107). But visiting that continent would have remedied nothing, if Conrad's example is of any value. Conrad had witnessed events from which Marlow's narrative derives, yet the blacks remain more nameless and indistinct than those that Burroughs described. And many of the sources examined here relied on eye-witness African accounts. Taliaferro cites this narrative statement from *The Beasts of Tarzan* in support of Tarzan's implicit racism: "Tarzan had always found that it stood him in good stead to leave with natives the impression that he was to some extent possessed of more or less miraculous powers" (57). He finds this in support of Burroughs' "assumption that a Great White Bwana is better equipped to solve the problems of Africa than are Africans themselves" (108). Taliaferro's evidence, though, seems ill-applied, as the statement in *Beasts* applies little to solving problems, and largely to making an impression. It is identical to the village chief: "Mbonga used the superstitious fears of his people to his own ends" (*Jungle Tales* 57). Taliaferro's assumption, though, is illustrated in the recent movie *Blood Diamond*, released a century after Conrad and Burroughs wrote, where, Joe Queenan claims, "a selfless Caucasian [...] ensures that truth and justice prevail in sub–Saharan Africa, something the local black community has been unable to effectuate" ("Tarzan's Children"). Barbara Ransby identifies Leonardo DiCaprio, the film's protagonist, as "a modern-day Johnny Weissmuller" and concludes that the movie reinforces "the age-old racist stereotype that Africa is lost without European sympathy." Queenan points out that a whole genre of movies operate on the racial theme of the white protector, where "beleaguered black folks marooned in forlorn, blood-drenched African nations get to see justice done because of the heroic efforts of some truly fabulous white people." He complains that with such a set-up, "every black person in the film is either a victim or a monster" ("Whiter") because the emphasis is on the "white savior" ("Tarzan's Children"). Such modern usage may be analogous to what Conrad and Burroughs were doing as well, though in their day no protest was raised.

Claiming that "Burroughs was no more or less prejudiced than many of his white contemporaries or that he was often judgmental of whites," Taliaferro argues, in concert with Achebe, "neither negates nor forgives his racism" (132). Such an attitude seems ungracious, as Patrick H. Adkins points out, because neither Conrad nor Burroughs "lived in a world that could scarcely have conceived of the social standards to which [Taliaferro] holds them accountable" ("*Tarzan Forever*"). Burger, in his addendum to Lupoff's book, points out that Burroughs' "work unashamedly reflects the era in which it first appeared, warts and all" ("Forty" 236). Because of this he was "stuck with cultural blinders of which he was unaware" (239). Taliaferro, Burger asserts, suffers from the same problem when he judges "Burroughs' perceived racial views" ("Forty" 239) by the standards of a later generation. Nonetheless, the racial problem is indeed, as Burger says, a "thorny issue" ("Forty" 251).

Where are the specific offenses in *Jungle Tales*? In "Tarzan and the Black Boy," when the narrator refers to Tibo's "dull, Negroid mind" that lacks "the divine spark" of imagination (75), the handy stereotype rises in Burroughs' prose to offend readers of later generations. The adjective *Negroid* can be read as racially representative. While there is no scientific evidence that stands today's tests that would support such a view, at the beginning of the twentieth century that was not true. Even as late as World War II, the American military "equated [...] low black test scores with a lack of native intelligence" (Murray 63–64) rather than a lack of educational opportunity. The attitudes of the ready plots of the day included stereotypical elements. The attitude that denigrated blacks came part and parcel out of the social milieu from which Burroughs pulled his plots. When Howard writes, "His writing conformed to the pattern of the markets of his day," he includes the attitudes of both editors and readers of the second decade of the twentieth century. This was an era that treated blacks and other groups as second-class citizens. For example, the U.S. government instituted the military draft shortly after Burroughs had completed *Jungle Tales*: Burroughs' notes indicate he completed "Tarzan Rescues the Moon" on 18 March 1917; the military draft began 5 June the same year. Initially, black men were allowed to fill the ranks of the already-established black units, which totaled four.

The integration of blacks and whites within the military did not occur in any meaningful way in Burroughs' lifetime. (Desegregation of units was made possible by Truman's Executive Order 9981 in 1948, but all-black units continued to exist until 1954. The transition occurred largely during the Korean War.) Whites and blacks were kept separate. In the processing of military applicants, white men were not to be examined by "colored doctors" (see Paul Murray's entire article for evidence of how "deeply entrenched" racism was "among the branches of the Wilson government" [Murray 60]). Provost Marshal General E. H. Crowder reported to the Secretary of War, at the end of 1918, that the role of "the negro in the great world drama," that is, as participant in the war, should be seen as "but another proof of the complete unity" of the country (193); "His race furnished its quota," he goes on, even though "opportunities for enlistment were not opened to him to the same extent as to whites" (194). He then goes on to say, in a paragraph meant to show how fairly and equally blacks had been treated in the military, that blacks were "still the slave, to a large extent, of superstition fed by ignorance" (194). Despite unequal practices that Crowder seems not to credit as important and that Murray documents, Murray points out that the citizenry of the day provided a "virtually complete absence of complaints against discrimination in the draft" (60)—that is, no one voiced outrage at the unequal treatment of blacks in the military. Even *The Crisis*, edited by W.E.B. DuBois, Murray notes, reported news on the war but made no editorial comment on the unequal attitudes and treatment toward blacks. One might presume that the role and treatment of blacks was similarly unnoticed, or at least not commented upon, by the public at large in other arenas.

In looking at the world in Conrad's and Burroughs' lifetimes, one would be hard pressed to single out a "black civilization" (though Burroughs creates one in the futuristic Abyssinian Empire of his 1915 novel *Beyond Thirty*). At twelve, Burroughs received a letter from his brother, George, encouraging him to read *A Brief History of Ancient, Mediaeval, and Modern Peoples*, which the family owned. This book's introduction presents the matter-of-fact claim: "The only Historic Race is the Caucasian, the others having done little worth recording" (Steele 10). The only Africans acknowledged in the ancient world were the Egyptians. The imagination that is lacking in Tibo is that "which builds bridges, and cities, and empires" (*Jungle Tales* 75). When the narrator says that blacks have such imagination "only a little" (75), he is referring to the scope of history as seen through the eyes the European-derived historians. Having lived through the height of the British Empire, which may be embedded in the lowercase reference above, Burroughs, from a historical point of view, finds no qualms in referring to a "dominant race" (75); though such dominance is more political and historical in the minds of today's readers than the long-held belief in intellectual dominance. To Burroughs' credit, even among the "dominant race" only "one in a hundred thousand" possesses the "super-intelligence" (75) that Tarzan holds. The emphasis is on Tarzan's ascendency rather than a uniform racial paucity.

When the reader considers what was touted as scientific knowledge when Conrad and Burroughs were being educated, it is more difficult to find blame. For example, Reade's classic anthropology book, *Savage Africa*, written in 1864, details much of European "knowledge" in the second half of the nineteenth century. In it a reader finds several ideas which show up again, perhaps in Conrad's and definitely in Burroughs' writing. Reade covers the Atlantic side of Africa and identifies Free-town as the capitol of "our principal colony upon the coast" (25). This is the town from which Tarzan's parents "vanished from the eyes and from the knowledge of men" (*Apes* 9). Reade points out that "intellect [is] a product [...] which is not copious" in blacks (30). He goes on to say that "[a] certain skill in mechanics, without the genius of invention; a great fluency of language, without energy in ideas; a correct ear for music, without a capacity for composition — in a word, a display of imitative faculties, with an utter barrenness of creative power — there is your negro at the very best" (33). He then goes on to say that even this depiction is valid for only a very few and "to show such trained animals as fair samples of the negro is to make an exhibition of black lies" (33), in the same way that claiming a performing circus animal represented its species. Conrad similarly depicts "the savage who was fireman" on the steamer Marlow is directing upstream. His description sounds much like the description Reade makes in his anthropological text. "He was an improved specimen; he could fire up a vertical boiler. He was there below me, and, upon my word, to look at him was as edifying as seeing a dog in a parody of breeches and a feather hat, walking on his hindlegs" (Conrad 52).

"The existence of cannibalism, which some authors have ventured to deny, is supported by clouds of authors," says Reade (135). One of his interviewees identified the typical choice for cannibalism was the prisoner of war (137), which we see in D'Arnot's case in *Tarzan of the Apes*, and which we might infer, without the literal war, in Burroughs' short story "The Capture of Tarzan." Reade also describes "the gorilla dance," which is accompanied by, among other instruments, a "sounding log" (164). Reade suggests that gorillas climb trees and are polygamous. These are characteristics of Burroughs' apes and the dance is similar to the Dum-Dum explored in the last chapter.

As for his anthropological study of the black inhabitants of the African coast, Reade repeats uncited predecessors who "have asserted that the negro belongs to a distinct species; that is to say, that he is as widely separated from our own race as the wolf is from the dog or the zebra from the horse" (397). Such an attitude today is labeled pseudo-speciation, which Midgley defines as "the tendency for human beings to regard their cultures as if they were actually separate species" (109). Certainly the difference between what is taught and what is caught, so to speak, has been debated and weighed differently through the ages.

Reade provides his objective evaluation of skin color and hair texture, clearly heritable traits, but includes, as if also objective, such bizarre comments and comparisons as:

- "A negro will take up a live coal in his hand and light his pipe from it without suffering any pain" (397).
- "As with the lower animals, the brain retreats to the back of the head" (398).
- "[A]s in apes, the great toe is separated from the others by a wide space. The foot is frequently used by the negro as a hand" (398).
- They differ in blood (it is "thicker and blacker than ours" [411]), in bile, and in semen (399).
- They have "less intelligence" (404).
- The blackness of their skin "is the color of disease" (409).
- "[T]he growth of the brain in the negro, as in the ape, is sooner arrested than in those of our race" (399).

He summarized that "the negro, speaking physically, approaches the ape" (399), then adds that in a number of other features, "the negro approaches the child; for all these features are found in the foetus or child of the Aryan race in its different periods of development" (399). "Thus it has been proved," Reade concludes, "by measurements, by microscopes, by analyses, that the typical negro is something between a child, a dotard, and a beast. I can not struggle against these sacred facts of science" (Reade 399).

Reade adds his social assessment that blacks "do not merit to be called our brothers, but let us call them our children. Let us educate them carefully, and in time we may elevate them, [but] not to our own level — that, I fear, can never be —" (430). Even after Burroughs wrote his *Jungle Tales*, Winifred Kirkland perpetuates a similar belief in her 1918 treatise *The Joys of Being a Woman*, where she claims: "The duskier race stands at the same point of evolution with the child" (31).

Holtsmark, too, qualifies Burroughs' "patronizing attitude" as a product of his era and therefore not a reason to offer "blanket condemnation" (5). Rather his views were seen by his contemporaries as verified by science. Brian Street writes similarly, "[A]t the turn of the century [...] anthropologists themselves proceeded" by means of racial character designations. "The collective representations of other cultures" he concludes, and here the case of Mbonga's village is central, are "grounded in the scholarship of the period" (77).

Even if Burroughs never read the works that seem to lay a foundation for his African perceptions, the summer that Burroughs was 17, he worked at the Chicago World's Fair, which Frederick Starr labeled "a practical study in anthropology" (610). The World's Columbian Exposition celebrated the 400th anniversary of the permanent connection between Europe and the Americas by Christopher Columbus. One reviewer asserted: "The influence of the Exposition on the taste of the country cannot be overestimated" ("Through" 9). Burroughs first visited the Exposition with his drill regiment from Michigan Military Academy. The squad camped for two weeks on the Midway close to the Kilaueau volcano, in the shadow of the world-debuted Ferris Wheel, the

The drill regiment from Michigan Military Academy spent two weeks camped at the 1893 Chicago World's Fair, before the summer that Burroughs worked the grounds. Photograph courtesy of Paul V. Galvin Library — Illinois Institute of Technology. Used by permission.

exposition's "crowning feature" (McDowell 411). The Midway was a mile-long avenue crammed with global representations of ethnic groups. While the purpose was strictly educational in intent, the press used the opportunity to point out the superiority of whites. Edward B. McDowell wrote, in *Frank Leslie's Popular Magazine,* of the natives of Dahomey (from today's country of Benin): "Sixty-nine of them are here in all their barbaric ugliness, blacker than buried midnight and as degraded as the animals which prowl the jungles of their dark land." He places them beneath their American counterparts because they have not "learned the language of civilization." "It is impossible," he concludes, "to conceive of a notch lower in the human scale" (415). The author of "Through the Looking Glass," an article summarizing and reminiscing at the close of the fair, pointed out the "opportunity" for "the scientific mind to descend the spiral of evolution, tracing humanity [from] its highest phases" represented by the accomplishments displayed at the Chicago fair, "down almost to its animalistic origin" (9); the author fosters geographic and moral confusion as well, claiming the Dahomey represent "the Ethiopian race," which "thrives on slavery" (9). John C. Eastman, writing for *The Chautauquan,* found them "more closely allied with the cruel and superstitious practices of savagery than any other country represented in Midway" (603). He refers his readers to Henry Stanley, Livingstone, and du Chaillu, as if these living people were illustrations of their writings, and indicates an uneasiness people had with their weaponry, lest they might "use their spears for other purposes than a barbaric embellishment" (604), in this reconstructed village that Starr calls "a real glimpse of negro Africa" (619). The Columbian Exhibition was called "an exhibition of patriotism" ("Through" 9), but Bederman claims, in retrospect, that the exposition served to "assert the power of white manhood" (217). The cultural exhibits were seen by many as contrasts to the glory of America. The fair was a spectacular demonstration to the world that America had come of age, and that Chicago, no longer a backward industrial center could compete with the aesthetics of Paris. Hillman adds his conclusion: "Almost all of the wondrous adventures and the fantastic worlds that [Burroughs] would eventually transcribe to paper 20 years later can be linked to events that he experienced at the Chicago Columbian Exposition ("Edgar Rice Burroughs' Remarkable Summer"). After his military duty was complete for the academic year, he drove the grounds, along with his brother Coleman, for the rest of the summer, giving rides in a "horseless surrey" promoting the power of batteries, manufactured by his father.

Given the state of popular "knowledge," Burroughs' depiction of Africa and Africans is more understandable. While the Africa he presented seems inaccurate today, it was and is, as Bederman suggests, "a recognizable version of a popular primitivist fantasy" (220), derived in a general way from the Dahomey exhibit at the World's Fair, if not from a number of other sources available at that time. That fantasy has as much to do with Eden, as was discussed earlier, and evolution as it did with a real geographical location. Bederman calls Burroughs' Africa "a place of origins, frozen at the moment the earliest human beings appeared on earth" (220), a description especially apt regarding Burroughs' earlier novel *The Eternal Lover.* This fantastic setting also serves a literary purpose, Mwikisa points out, "providing [...] a foil against which [Anglo] superior virtues can be made manifest." This literary use, though, is suspect, says Mwikisa, because using "racist imagery simply as rhetorical devices" will "severely compromise the merit of the works in which they are used," an idea reflected from Achebe.

The reader may also take into account that among the most popular books of the latter part of the nineteenth century were the chronicles of various explorers. While not necessarily scientific even in their own day, they were considered credible. *In Darkest Africa,* for example, Henry Stanley's bestseller of 1890, speaks repeatedly of the indigenous people in belittling terms. For example, "[t]hese forest natives [...] are cowardly, and at the same time vicious" (1.132); or of the Zanzibaris who accompanied him inland, "these men appeared to possess neither instinct nor reason, neither perception nor memory. Their heads were uncommonly empty" (1.182). (A 1939 Associated Press article, entitled "Edgar Rice Burroughs, Tarzan Creator, Was Never In Africa," claims that the sources for *Tarzan of the Apes* were a "50-cent dictionary" and Stanley's book.) Even Livingstone, the altruistic missionary whom Stanley went in search of — a man who bristled at "the stupid prejudice against color" (*Missionary Travels* 2.19) — referred to the people he served as "savages" (*Missionary Travels* 1.9). The pattern of these exploration accounts "move from adventure to adventure against a dark, infernal backdrop where there are no other characters of equal stature — only bewitched or demonic savages" (Brantlinger 176). *Jungle Tales of Tarzan* seems to fit the description without exception.

Collingwood, author of the influential 1947 text *The Principles of Art*, points out in reference to Freud, "the 'oddities' of savage behavior" of the Africans "are only such points as seem odd to a modern European, i.e., the points in which that difference consists" (77n). In this Collingwood and, before him, Freud seem to echo Montaigne's observation that "men call that barbarisme which is not common to them" (244). It is such a frame that allows Livingstone to champion and belittle the native people within the same work. Hammond and Jablow point out that such "ethnocentrism is a nearly universal human attitude" (15). They justify the generalization with the claim that people are so habituated to their individual background and conditions that their behavior shows the "inevitable expression of basic human nature" (15). Collingwood continues: "So, in still plainer English, Freud's programme is to reduce the differences between non–European and European civilizations to differences between mental disease and mental health" (77n). Freud's subtitle to *Totem and Taboo* is "Some Points of Agreement between the Mental Lives of Savages and Neurotics." Freud's definition of *savage*, though, deals not with certain proscribed behavior, but simply with the assumption that "those whom we describe as savages" present a "picture of an early stage of our own development" (*Totem* 1), an idea in line with Reade and other early anthropologists.

Collingwood says,

> It was excusable in Locke to classify savages with idiots [...] for Locke and his contemporaries knew practically nothing about them. But it was very far from excusable in nineteenth-century anthropologists, who knew that the peoples they called savage, [...] understood enough of the connexions between causes and effects in nature to perform delicate operations in metallurgy, agriculture, stock-breeding, and so forth [59].

That Collingwood could excuse a seventeenth-century writer based on cultural ignorance but not a nineteenth-century one seems instructive in principle. Locke, he tacitly argues, didn't have the cultural information to make the same conclusions that later writers would have. While the evidence that Collingwood identifies may have been available at the end of the nineteenth century, its interpretation differed from that of twenty-first-century writers.

Teddy Roosevelt inspired patriotism in Burroughs; Burroughs even volunteered for Roosevelt's Rough Riders, though he was not selected, which is no surprise after Burroughs' discharge from the cavalry because of a heart condition. Roosevelt's championing of "civilization" over "backward people" (Beale 33) can be ascribed to Burroughs as well. Roosevelt, though, did not base levels of civilization on race but on economy. Howard K. Beale suggests that "unlike many other Americans [Roosevelt] did not limit the possibility of progress to white men but expected Negroes, Filipinos, and Chinese ultimately to develop [...]" (31). Beale cites Roosevelt's review of C.H. Pearson's *National Life and Character: A Forecast*, wherein Roosevelt wrote,

> If any one of the tropical races ever does reach a pitch of industrial and military prosperity which makes it a menace to European and American countries, it will almost necessarily mean that this nation has itself become civilized in the process; and we shall then simply be dealing with another civilized nation of non-aryan blood [...] without any thought of their being ethnically distinct" [367].

This makes sense when the reader considers that Roosevelt believed that race was a product of "acquired characteristics and [...] the effect of geographic environment" (Beale 29), which means no race is "permanently or inherently inferior" (Beale 30). Burger adds his opinion that Burroughs was "not as racist" (*Glimpses* 57n) as Roosevelt had been in his class consciousness.

Holtsmark claims that racism "was part of the cultural baggage of [Burroughs'] age, but it is still one of those uncomfortable areas that anybody writing on Burroughs [or Conrad] today must come to some kind of terms with"; "Burroughs was not the reflex-racist that he is often credited with being, but certainly held a kind of 'unconscious racism,'" a term borrowed from Orth, a type of racism that was "typical" of the times (letter to Martin Williams). Mwikisa affirms that in Burroughs' day, these attitudes "were not instantly objectionable phenomena," especially compared to the responses of today's readers. Rather, they were seen by the popular press as honorable and altruistic pursuits. "You have to judge any creative work against the milieu in which the author/artist/whatever worked. You just don't expect Rembrandt and Dali and Lichtenstein to do the same work" (Lupoff "Barsoom!" [55–56]).

In context, within the Tarzan stories, Tarzan's attitude toward blacks changes over the course of time. When Tarzan kills Kulonga, the narrator qualifies his action: "He knew nothing of the brotherhood of man. All things outside his own tribe were his deadly enemies" (*Apes* 70). Mbonga's tribe is his introduction to the human race, "the brotherhood of man" that is invoked by the narrator, and Taliaferro points out that "the 'jabbering,' superstitious cannibals of Kulonga's tribe" (79) did not make a good first impression.

At this point chronologically, Mbonga's villagers are the only other humans that Tarzan knows, and they are not a positive introduction for him. Mbonga and his tribe are given more detail in *Jungle Tales* than any other book. Remember that Burroughs had already written five novels chronicling Tarzan's life from birth to grandfatherhood. And in those and later volumes a variety of black men are described. Busuli is a strong Waziri warrior whom Tarzan befriends in *Return* and Muviro leads the Waziri admirably in *Tarzan Triumphant*, to name but two.

The men of Mbonga's village are not bad because they are black. Their skin color has no bearing on their character. They are bad because they are selfish and depraved under Mbonga's leadership. Mbonga's village is not a microcosm of the black world for Burroughs. In the previous novel (and indeed since the second Tarzan novel), Burroughs provided a counter to the cannibals with the Waziri. In *Tarzan and the Jewels of Opar*, the narrator writes: "Lord and Lady Greystoke with Basuli and Mugambi rode together at the head of the column, laughing and talking together in that easy familiarity which common interests and mutual respect breed between honest and intelligent men of any races" (158). Statements like this are important to show the balance that ERB provided in racial terms for characters that he created. The people of Mbonga's village do not represent "an absolute expression of Burroughs's own attitude towards dark-skinned human beings" (Needham 24). They are a specifically created group and they serve a specific fictive purpose. And while their depravity is unpleasant, the narrator of *Apes* points out that "that arch hypocrite, Leopold II of Belguim" was responsible for "still crueller barbarities" (158) than Mbonga's people. Cruelty is unacceptable in polite society, and Burger goes so far as to state that one belief clearly portrayed in Burroughs' life, as well as his writing, is "that one's inhumanity is made apparent through cruelty" (*Glimpses* 27–28). Of course, every person is part of a race; but more important was the fact that every person was foremost composed of a personal character making individual choices. Mbonga's village is, under the leadership of a despicable man, depraved. The Waziri, under the leadership of Mugambi or Muviro, are noble.

Mbonga's village, according to the narrator in "A Jungle Joke," held interest for Tarzan because of the variety of actions that were found in none of the other denizens of the jungle but them. Tarzan finds three hindrances to forming a positive relationship with the villagers. The narrator comments: "If it hadn't been for their black faces, their hideously disfigured features, and the fact that one of them had slain Kala, Tarzan might have wished to be one of them" (161). Of the reasons, the first two are cosmetic. The blackness of the face gave them no advantage over the apes of Kerchak's tribe. In the first story, Tarzan grappled with his differentness and this no doubt contributed illogically to his discounting of the villagers on the basis of their skin color. The second is a matter of cultural awareness. The Dahomey exhibit that Burroughs had visited at the World's Fair contained people who were "frightfully scarred"; John Eastman explains that "voluntary incisions made in the cheeks [were] believed to enhance their beauty" (604). While Tarzan had learned that creatures looked different, he had not attributed, apparently, a neutrality to those differences. In the matter of his own hairlessness he had first taken the difference as a negative aspect of his own condition, as seen in the early stories of the collection. In *Tarzan of the Apes*, though, the narrator points out that during his adolescent years, after the events of *Jungle Tales*, "he learned to shave — rudely and painfully, it is true — but, nevertheless, effectively" (90) in an attempt to match the pictures in the cabin books.

In "The God of Tarzan," the narrator states clearly that "his relations with the people of Mbonga, the chief, were the antithesis of friendly" (52). These people, it is worth pointing out, represent no specific group of people. They are created for fictional purposes, as Needham says, "from conventionally prejudicial components" that were "not out of scale with contemporary stereotypes" (23), elements of which were gleaned from a variety of popular sources already examined. So, when writers like Newsinger claim that "the way Burroughs portrays black people in his Tarzan stories tells us considerably more about him and the culture in which he was situated than it does about the realities of the lives of the black people living in tropical Africa" ("Lord" 64), their emphasis skews the intentions of the fiction. Newsinger believes that "relations between black and white [are] one of [the] central themes" ("Me" 80) of the stories. While Tarzan relates to the villagers in nearly every story, the interaction functions to define Tarzan, not the others. Burroughs did not intentionally distort the culture of any people group. So while it lacks political correctness for today's reader, it may provide some historical accuracy of American social conditions just before World War I.

When Taliaferro says that Esmeralda, a character included in *Apes* admittedly for comic relief, clearly indicates "that 'domestic' blacks are scarcely more sophisticated than the African natives" (80), he misses the intent. Esmeralda is of a different sort altogether. The stock character that Esmeralda represents is of a type long established in literature. That she is black is but a variation on the stock country bumpkin, who can be found of any hue. She draws not a little from Richard Sheridan's Mrs. Malaprop. Regarding Burroughs' use of dialect, contemporary readers likely found nothing outrageous. Nineteenth-century writers, like Twain, valued dialectical representation highly. In a nonfiction context, Crowder's 1919 government report quotes one soldier responding "I'se not gwine *to* France. I'se gwine *through* France" (195, original italics). Esmeralda's diction is similar.

Taliaferro compares Burroughs reversal of skin color among the Martian races to the satirical work of Jonathan Swift. In Martian perceptions, it is the white-skinned people that are most closely allied to the apes of the planet, which are also white. The most noble of the Martian races, called the First Born, are black. Taliaferro is quick to discount this as a reliable counter of the author's own sentiment. He attributes this inversion to "playfulness" on Burroughs' part, rather than a "progressive view of race," though he cites no precise evidence for this interpretation aside from the generic proof he labels "nearly every Tarzan story" (94).

Taliaferro has little good to say about the collection of stories that comprise *Jungle Tales*. He labels them as "considerably less able-bodied," "underweight vignettes" (131). "[F]requent slights against blacks," he says, end up "[o]vershadowing the general lightheartedness" (131) that characterize these stories. And even though he has claimed that Burroughs' stereotyping was commonplace in his generation, he judges that these remarks "must have been received as mean-spirited" (131). He cites three statements, then, in support. The first comes from "Tarzan and the Black Boy," at the moment Tarzan first sees Tibo. The narrative calls him "for a black, handsome" (70). The impression that Taliaferro leaves is that the narrator is suggesting a lower standard for blacks in terms of beauty, even using quotation marks around the word *boy*, as if it were an inappropriate word for a ten-year-old. Two factors mitigate against this interpretation. First, as noted earlier, the narrator's point of view is not the expected omniscient or objective but rather a limited blend, capable of providing impressions made upon the characters while not obliged to maintain such a perspective. Here a legitimate interpretation is that this is what Tarzan sees, not necessarily what an impartial bystander would see. The narrative notes, in addition to Tibo's skin color and his pleasing appearance, two other important characteristics: the straightness of his form and the litheness of his movement, characteristics important to Tarzan. In terms of form, Tarzan thinks, "Here was a balu fashioned as he himself was fashioned" (70). The point of the paragraph is Tarzan's identification with the boy, not the boy's racial inability to meet some "white" standard, as Taliaferro implies. Additionally, again written from Tarzan's point of view, the narrator adds: "Of course this one's skin was black; but what of it?" (70). Tibo's skin color held no inhibition for Tarzan because he did not know if his own skin color were not some aberration. The black skin color is the same barrier that keeps him from integration with Kerchak's apes. Tarzan, as the sole living representation of white skin, as his name indicates, sees that he is different. His difference from the apes, at this point, is a source of shame rather than pride; likewise his closer similarity to Mbonga's villagers cannot be made without also noting differences, including the sensitive issue of skin color.

The off-handed manner in which the narrator embeds "for a black" in Tarzan's assessment of Tibo may offend some readers. Taliaferro takes the phrase ultra-seriously when he claims that "[t]he very gratuitousness of his remarks [...] — the implication that his sort of bigotry was fair play and on some level entertaining — is proof enough that the hurt was intentional" (132). Taliaferro leaps the gap between "intentional" and understandable without a bridge. Burroughs' audience was different than today's readership. Nothing he wrote was published without first going through an editorial sieve, in this case *Blue Book*'s Ray Long. The earliest cries of racism in his books begin to surface after Burroughs' death, parallel to the civil rights movement in America.

Taliaferro also pulls out two statements from "A Jungle Joke." The first is that "Tarzan's chief divertisement" was "baiting" the people of Mbonga's village (162). The second is that their cruelty differs from his own: theirs "the wanton torture of the helpless," Tarzan's "the cruelty of necessity or of passion" (169). Mbonga's village constitutes the entire universe of humans for Tarzan, who has not seen another man or woman since his adoption into Kerchak's tribe. The assumptions and interpretations made by Tarzan are incomplete. He relates and compares is own experience as the initial judgment of both Kerchak's tribe and Mbonga's village. As for his own "baiting" of the blacks, Tarzan fails to see that he falls into the "wanton torture" category that he attributes to Mbonga's people. Vengeance for Kala's death might have "justified" Kulonga's death as an act of passion — though one might also assume that the life-for-a-life principle so common in Western culture was not present in Tarzan's "culture" nor triggered from his heredity as his revulsion for cannibalism had been — but Tarzan is blinded to the fact that his continued killing of the villagers differs only in circumstance from the torture of captured people inside the village walls. It is not until Tarzan is older and has reflected upon the difference between the jungle and civilization that he begins to question his attitude toward blacks. But the seeds of change are in this collection. First, Tarzan has pity on Mbonga. Next he protects Tibo and Momaya. A later seed occurs in the final story of *Jungle Tales*, when Bulabantu, natural enemy of the mangani, stands his ground. Tarzan defends him when the apes begin to attack. His first conscious decision to treat blacks differently comes from the tutoring of D'Arnot at the mission of Father Constantine. The lesson is internalized in *The Return of Tarzan*, as Tarzan stalks a black man to take his possessions:

> [N]ew thoughts presented themselves to the ape-man — thoughts born of the refining influences of civilization, and of its cruelties. It came to him that seldom if ever did civilized man kill a fellow being without some pretext, however slight. It was true that Tarzan wished this man's weapons and ornaments, but was it necessary to take his life to obtain them? [123].

The conclusion of the matter is: "The longer he thought about it, the more repugnant became the thought of taking human life needlessly" (123). When he then saves the life of Busuli, instead of killing him, he finds the result pleasantly surprising:

> How close he had been to killing this man whom he never had seen before, and who now was manifesting by every primitive means at his command friendship and affection for his would-be slayer. Tarzan of the Apes was ashamed. Hereafter he would at least wait until he knew men deserved it before he thought of killing them [125].

A significant tension exists in Tarzan's assessment of Mbonga's people. His introduction to them, via the death of his surrogate mother, puts them in a negative frame from the beginning. Another deterrent listed by the narrator added to their skin color is their "hideously disfigured features" (161). The disfigurement that Tarzan sees is not identified at this point of the narrative. Likely he refers to Tibo's mother, who had filed teeth; a slit lip that "support[ed] a rude pendant of copper [...] exposing the teeth and gums of her lower jaw"; various other piercings to nose, ears, forehead, and cheeks, filled with wooden and metallic ornaments; and, tattooing on her chin and nose (69). In addition to that, the narrator reports that Tarzan sometimes felt "a strange revulsion" for them "which he could not interpret or understand" (161), but which he called hate.

In the same passage, though, the narrator says, again from Tarzan's implied point of view, that these people from Mbonga's village "aroused his imagination," and "their ways were interesting" (161). And Tarzan "wished to be one of them," the narrator says, "sometimes" (161). The narrator continues outside Tarzan's perspective, "from them he learned much more than he realized" (161–62). It is clear that Tarzan's perception is limited in his assessment of the blacks living near him. The hate that he feels toward Mbonga's people is generalized until D'Arnot explains that skin color is not a determinant of character. This occurs when Tarzan and D'Arnot are making their way, in *Tarzan of the Apes*, to a port where they can find passage to civilization. When Tarzan sees some blacks working in a field he prepares to kill them because "[t]hey are black" (*Apes* 191). He has known no other black men besides those from Mbonga's village. Their animosity toward Tarzan had conditioned him to respond in animosity himself. Just as the lion was always a danger, he reasons that black men were consistently so. He asks if he should wait and address a charging lion to determine if he is indeed friendly. D'Arnot advises him: "Wait until the blacks spring upon you [...] then you may kill them. Do not assume that men are your enemies until they prove it" (*Apes* 191). And in this way, after the events of *Jungle Tales*, Tarzan learns that character and skin color are not related, in what David Adams calls "[a] revolution from the primitive code to a civilized one" ("Jungle Tales").

When Tarzan tells Olga de Coude, in *The Return of Tarzan*, that he thinks that blacks "are in most ways lower in the scale than the beasts" (38), he says so, first concerning the males' inability or disinclination to protect their women; from a literary point of view, he may be recalling the aggressiveness of Momaya in defense of Tibo in "Tarzan and the Black Boy." There the narrator says that Tarzan "meditated upon the possibilities which might lie in the prowess of the Gomangani [blacks] were the hes as formidable as the shes" (71). Secondly, he says this before he meets the Waziri tribesmen later in this book. His first night in the Waziri village, Tarzan is "impressed by the symmetry of their figures and the regularity of their features [...]. [T]he faces of the men were intelligent and dignified, those of the women ofttimes prepossessing" (*Return* 126).

That Tarzan sees writing, when he pencils a note to the cabin inhabitants, as communication only between white humans and not as a means of communication among black humans may be construed as a racial cut. However, the reader must consider that Tarzan is putting together his own imperfect understanding of the world. He has never seen writing in Mbonga's village. His experience in the books is a white experience.

In a later novel, *Tarzan the Terrible*, Burroughs creates a race of tailed humans (an attempt at filling the "missing link" for Darwin enthusiasts), which is divided by what Burroughs would consider three non-essential differences:

religious beliefs, hairiness, and skin color. The narrator identifies their cultural blindness: "Not even the fact that they appeared to be equals in the matter of intelligence made any difference" to their hostility to one another, because "one was white and one was black" (22). Clearly the narrator sees skin color as arbitrary in terms of the qualitative differences between the two groups. Near the end of his life, Burroughs provides support to an open attitude toward blacks. In one of his last novels, *Llana of Gathol*, John Carter observes that the First Born "are an exceptionally handsome race" and "their black skins, resembling polished ebony, add greatly to their beauty" (63). That Burroughs has racial intent in the passage cannot be missed, when John Carter qualifies the claim with "I am a Virginian; and it may seem strange for me to say so" (63). Regarding earlier works, Leslie Fiedler speculates that "surely Burroughs must have had some dim sense that he was writing about the American racial situation in encoded form" (188). By the end of his career, the encoding is more thoughtful and explicit. Burroughs artist Russ Manning correctly assesses the situation when he writes, "Tarzan is above prejudice and intolerance" because he "mistrusts the entire human race, particularly 'civilized' man and put his trust in the individuals, black, white or animal, who have proved themselves worthy of it" (letter).

Burroughs suffered from racial charges much earlier than the concern for Africans, for his portrayal of Germans in *Tarzan the Untamed*. Though the 1921 novel had not been published in German, reports of its contents had been published and had punctured sales of the other German-language Tarzan books. Burroughs responded at the request of his German publisher, with a letter addressed "To My German Readers." He claimed, "I never knowingly offend honorable and decent classes of society" (qtd. in Taliaferro 204). He also provides a comparison of Northern attitudes toward the South before and after the American Civil War. He pointed out (without foundation) that children of pre–Civil War South were taught that "Yanks grew horns and were the authors of hideous crimes" (qtd. in Taliaferro 204). Only after great struggle and reconciliation, he said, did such erroneous beliefs become corrected. Burroughs later writes to a fan: "There is nothing personal in my use of any nationality for my villains. I have used Americans as well as Russians, and, as you will understand that I must have a heavy [...] I am bound to step on someone's toes [...]" (letter to Fred Anger 21 July 1934). Burroughs died before the analogous Civil Rights movement of the 1950s and 60s. He also pointed out for German readers that he targeted people who were "cruel, ruthless, arrogant" (qtd. in Taliaferro 204) rather than people of a particular ethnic heritage.

A decade after *Jungle Tales*, Burroughs did take a stand against the accepted racism of the day, in regards to Native Americans. When he offered *The War Chief* to *Blue Book*, Donald Kennicott responded with a rejection, not on the basis of the writing, but because, he said, "[W]e would get in big trouble if we offered [readers] an American Indian story [...] from the Indian's point of view." He adds that he personally found his treatment of the subject "quite right," but conceded that "magazines like ours can't undertake to educate the public" (letter to Burroughs 12 December 1927). Andy MacDuff (Shoz-Dijiji) comes from the seed of the "Caledonian savage" and the Cherokee (3). The sympathy Burroughs shows toward Native Americans is surprising. That he does not accord the same sympathy toward African tribesmen marks, according to Taliaferro, an "inconsistency [that] was doubtless lost on him, and he was not alone in his selective progressivism" (217). When Burroughs tried to sell *The War Chief* to *The Country Gentleman*, he found popular American tastes, at least as perceived by H.C. Paxton, unsympathetic. Paxton acknowledged the dealing with Native Americans in the previous century as "one of the most shameful chapters in American history" but countered that the American readership wanted to see such "savage peoples in fiction" only in the role of "the staunchly loyal follower of the white leader" (qtd. in Taliaferro 218), Fran Striker's Tonto to the Lone Ranger, for example.

Bozarth, one of Burroughs' outspoken-without-fawning defenders, concludes that "any attempt to overlay today's 'politically correct' attitudes upon a work that was written in an earlier era [...] is a ridiculous attempt to rewrite history" ("Interracial Marriages"). In another place, Bozarth claims that "it would be unfair to apply the social conventions of this era to an earlier time" ("Jungle Tales"). Such anachronistic application, Atamian says, is "a disgusting falsehood" (94). Adkins affirms that "interracial love is always portrayed positively" ("*Tarzan Forever*") in Burroughs' writing. Bozarth argues that claims of racism need to be more balanced. In regards to interracial marriage, Burroughs was far ahead of his contemporaries. Though Tarzan is often considered as the most important representation, he is not Burroughs' sole representation. Many heroes defy cultural expectations and marry interracially in Burroughs' books, as we see in his first book, *A Princess of Mars*, for example, where John Carter marries a "red" woman on Mars. Other heroes include Gordon King who marries the Cambodian Fou-tan in *Jungle Girl*; Shoz-Dijiji, raised Apache in *The War Chief* and *Apache Devil*, who takes Wichita Billings for a wife; and Tony Rosetti, in *Tarzan and the "Foreign Legion,"* who marries Sarina, a woman of mixed heritage. This does not include many other interspecies relationships that occur in his science fiction stories. The lack of consideration of such evidence stains the reputation, Bozarth says, of a writer who "was a shining example of tolerance and understanding" ("Interracial"). Bozarth identifies two aspects absent in the mature Tarzan that exist in the early Tarzan: "killing for pleasure" and "black-baiting" ("Tarzan: Man or Beast?"). These things appear to be left behind in Tarzan's maturation catalyzed by his contact with civilization.

When *Tarzan the Ape Man* hit the theaters in 1932, the treatment of black porters by the white safari leaders, Taliaferro suggests, "must have provoked a healthy amount of outrage" (255). But Taliaferro gives no supporting documentation; he does provide positive comments from *Variety* magazine and the *New York Times*. While Taliaferro's claim appears unfounded, the earliest suggestion that Burroughs' blacks were unsavory to black viewers comes in a 1940 charge not about the books or about the movies but regarding the savage stereotypes in the "funnypapers" (Logan 429).

With a written text, the images are of the readers' making. When artists are brought into consideration, the representation of race becomes even more difficult to manage. Stanford W. Carpenter points out that Tarzan in graphic form, comic-book adaptations in particular, "has a particularly rich history of racialized imagery" (195). Graham J. Murphy affirms that racism in Tarzan comics is "coded in the linguistic/visual hybridity of the comic book genre." While Burroughs obviously did not write the comic adaptations, they still bear some important continuity with the problems initiated in the text. While Tarzan has accepted the Waziri as fellow men, for example, he still retains a superiority over them. As Carpenter says, the "'uncivilized' African occupants (the fictitious dark skinned Waziri) regard Tarzan, and all that he represents, as their lord and savior" (207). Carpenter points to an opening panel of the *Tarzan Versus Predator at the Earth's Core* mini-series where, just as it did in Conrad's *Heart of Darkness*, the jungle represents "the flip side of modernity" (207), which includes "its dark skinned inhabitants [...] to serve as a counterpoint to the civility and progress represented by Tarzan" and others (205). The panel that comes closest to his description has Muviro in fluffy loincloth and headdress with his back to the viewer, effaced. But when Ambassador Sneftly calls the Waziri belittling names, Tarzan responds: "These 'savages,' Mr. Ambassador, are neither my children nor my servants"; he adds in the next dialogue box: "They are my friends" (Simonson n.p.). Carpenter's point is that such dialogue is undercut by the visual placement by the artist putting Muviro, as representative of all minorities, in a subordinate position. Walter Simonson, who scripted the mini-series thinks too much is made of the lack of visual prominence of the Waziri, whom he described to Carpenter as "co-equal but not co-billed" (Carpenter 209). He points to the scene where Tarzan goes to rescue the Waziri, but finds they have already freed themselves (in "Part Three: The Ancient of Days"). Weeks says that since the Waziri were not the primary focus of the plot, he used, in Carpenter's words, "readily identifiable stereotypical images," including the headdress design used by Kubert decades earlier (211). Weeks continues his rationale, saying, "I used to be self-conscious about racial representations but you have to rely on certain racial characteristics [...]. We need a certain amount of racial stereotyping in this medium" (Carpenter 211). Carpenter ends his assessment with the weak disclaimer: "[M]ost of the characters in use [in Burroughs writing, in particular] were created for a White reading public and in an era in which there was no concern for the representation of ethnic others" (212).

Charles R. Saunders, an African American writer, gives allowance for writers like Conrad and Burroughs: "In the late nineteenth and early twentieth centuries, it was fashionable to believe that Africa was the 'Dark Continent,' that all its people were lower on the cultural and evolutionary scale than whites, that Africans had no history or civilization [...]" (Bell 90). Saunders implies that readers must understand the world that these writers lived in was different from the one current readers perceive, and that these writers should not be condemned for the world they lived in.

To conclude, as Taliaferro does, that because of this Burroughs is "guilty of a form of cruelty that surpassed anything he ascribed to the black Africans in his fiction" (132) is at least anachronistic if not unreasonable. Henryk Zins says the same of Achebe's charges against Conrad.

Does the unconscious and unintentional nature of the depictions nullify the offense to readers? Not likely. Today's readers have been sensitized to issues that are real and prickly. Several of the casual statements in *Jungle Tales* will rub the prickles and raise eyebrows. Is it right to blame the writer for the offense? No more than it is acceptable to accost a man who has bumped into another on the dance floor unintentionally. The disturbance may be real without the offense.

When Cheyfitz, Marianna Torgovnick, and Jurca, for example, point out Tarzan's superiority in terms of race and gender, while the claims are true, one must note that the Tarzan character is superior to every conceivable foil. That is part of his characterization. Tarzan is also superior to white European men (many of them depicted clearly as despicable), but the outcry on their account has gone unsounded.

It seems the evidence, variable by definition, suggests that Burroughs is a racist and *not* a racist, that he presents ideas that are read as derogatory toward other races, yet does so in cultural reflex, without malice. Walt Whitman, an American poet of Burroughs' father's generation, writes near the end of his famous poem "Song of Myself":

> Do I contradict myself?
> Very well then I contradict myself,
> (I am large, I contain multitudes) [79].

Readers are left to sort out the contradiction, with the realization that some seeming discrepancies are irreconcilable and coexistent.

"I learned to recognise the thorough and primitive duality of man"
— Dr. Jekyll, *Dr. Jekyll and Mr. Hyde* (Stevenson 84–85)

This concept of being two things at once, or in vacillation, is important not only for understanding the author, but more importantly for understanding the character of Tarzan. "Duality must exist," Stroud says, "for the imagination to be engaged" (viii). Bachelard further clarifies: For anything "to engage the whole soul, there must be a *dual participation* of desire and fear, a participation of good and evil, a peaceful participation of black and white" (12, italics original). In nature, this duality is established as night becomes day becomes night becomes day, ad infinitum. Many novelists have capitalized on this duality inherent in the human condition. Perhaps the most notable, Feodor Dostoevsky, in his early work *The Double*, focuses on the complexity of the duality of a human temperament. In Dostoevsky's work, this is accomplished, Ruth Mortimer explains, by the use of "one or more 'doubles' in the characters who surround [another], characters who represent different, frequently opposed or repressed, aspects of his own nature" (106). In barer terms, Robert Louis Stevenson does this in *Dr. Jekyll and Mr. Hyde*. Later in the Tarzan novels, Burroughs will introduce this idea explicitly through the character of Estaban Miranda. In *Jungle Tales*, the narration sets up a number of symbiotic opposites by which the reader comes to understand Tarzan's character more precisely.

The narrator in "A Jungle Joke" suggests that the cave man and modern man are the same: "Always, everywhere, man is man, nor has he altered greatly beneath his veneer since he scurried into a hole between two rocks to escape the tyrannosaurus six million years ago" (167). And while this seems a quite acceptable claim when regarding the base nature of villains, in this context Rabba Kega, the nobility of ancient man is also a common theme in Burroughs' writing.

The most important duality expressed in these stories is that of human and ape. For example "the spark of martyrdom" joins the two poles of "the wild ape and the glorious women of a higher order" (*Jungle Tales* 158). The ape and the modern woman, Kala and Lady Alice, are polar opposites, but their willingness to give their lives for the protection of their mates or their children joins them. Holtsmark claims, "The comparison between Lady Alice and Kala is one of the sustained synkrises of the novels, and it underscores the duality of Tarzan's origins" ([92]). While Fiske claims, "Psychologically, [humans have] travelled so far from apes that the distance is scarcely measurable" (49), some differences are certainly worth observing. The contrasts within these myriad similarities are instructive. Tarzan is not just one identity contrasted with another. He is both human and ape. This duality is demonstrated in the very hyphenation of the term *ape-man*. It is one thing made of two natures. What Williams was taught — "[Y]ou can take a man out of the jungle, but if he is born to it you cannot take the jungle out of a man" (12) — seems to point to Tarzan's situation precisely. The ape nature and the human nature are both needed to complete the personal identity of the hero.

Even the film versions of the story mirror this duality, for it is a core concept of Tarzan's character. Added to this is the singular relationship of Tarzan and a character created for the 1932 *Tarzan the Ape Man*, the chimpanzee Cheeta. (Burroughs did not create this character.) The success of the role brought it back for a number of Tarzan movies. The success comes in part, claim Schechter and Semeiks, from the two characters who "form a single unit — a unit which stands for the fusion of the 'higher human faculties,' such as reason and morality, with the 'lower,' animal level of our nature" (268). This makes Tarzan a "complete human being [...] a healthy combination of intelligence, virtue and animal spirits" (Schechter and Semeiks 268). The character of the monkey Nkima, who debuts in Burroughs' novel *Tarzan and the Lost Empire* (1929) and may have been the genesis of the Cheeta character, functions similarly but in a less noticeable way than does Cheeta. Before Nkima, all of the monkeys in Tarzan's Africa were called Manu.

Duality is demonstrated in a number of other applications as well, ranging from syntax to plot. Holtsmark identifies the following passage as illustrative of the "polar expressions" (14) that Burroughs often incorporates syntactically. When Tarzan considers how to make Tibo into his own child, he thinks the following:

> He would tend him carefully, feed him well, protect him as only Tarzan of the Apes could protect his own, and teach him out of his half human, half bestial lore the secrets of the jungle from its rotting surface vegetation to the high tossed pinnacles of the forest's upper terraces [*Jungle Tales* 70].

The care that Tarzan projects is two-fold, polar. He will deal with the physical through food and protection and he will deal with the mind through teaching. The union of the body and the mind marks the joining of the poles, just like the jungle floor and the treetops invoked in the comparison. It is similar to the three-part Hebrew idea of body, soul, and spirit, representing the entire person. The polar structure that Burroughs chooses here, simplifies the concept without losing the essential tension of the two elements. Through this dual form of care, "[...] Tibo will be made into a complete man" (15) Holtsmark concludes, because Tarzan's care extends to all areas of human need along the body-mind continuum. Holtsmark points out that Tarzan represents the physical and the intellectual; because of this he "is able to bridge the two worlds of knowledge and action" (109). In doing so, the contrast between the two is given living tension.

Another variation on the duality of mind and body comes in the dichotomy of nature and nurture. Tarzan is made of both his heredity, which Burroughs puts heavy weight upon, and the environment in which he is raised. For example, in the first novel, after Tarzan watches the sailors bury the treasure chest, the narrator reveals: "Tarzan of the Apes had a man's figure and a man's brain, but he was an ape by training and environment." The hereditary intelligence given him "told him that the chest contained something valuable," while his environmental "training had taught him to imitate whatever was new and unusual" (*Apes* 127).

Another form of duality is represented by binary code. Either something is, or it is not. "It is an undeniable fact that we cannot know anything whatever except as contrasted with something else" (Fiske 34). And sometimes that "something else" is an absence. Wylie examines this concept in a poem of his poetic alphabet, *Original Forest*. Wylie's "hoofprint punched in mud" (n.p.) relies on the unreadable base of mud to provide shape to the hoofprint, in its very nature something created by absence. The mud is pushed away to make the "nothing" that brings meaning to the viewer. The mud is not readable, but without it the hoofprint cannot exist. This poem initiated by the letter "I" reinforces the nature of identity, because human identity is built on the distinction between the "I" and the "other." The poem begins: "If only I could read fully, / everything would become a sign." But everything cannot be readable, just as a dual nature cannot congregate at a single pole. The words of this page serve as illustration. The paper means nothing, but the ink which has been formed into letters must have the nothingness of the page on which to create meaning. The ink and the paper represent the two poles of the text. "For meaning to have meaning," Wylie said in an interview, "it needs to have that void or that meaninglessness, or that chaos behind it in order to attach to the mind. Somehow in the symbiosis between them it makes meaning meaningful." In the same way, the jungle existence that Tarzan leads cannot be properly understood without the missing civilized life that he "should" have lived. Burroughs provides the concept of this absence in several layers, but most pointedly in the direct comparison of Lord Greystoke in England at several points within the stories. The tension between civilization and jungle "serves to underscore the incradicable duality of his nature" (96).

At the level of plot, this contrast is a recurring theme Burroughs uses of two social groups forced by circumstances to live together, often in the form of two cities, as seen in *Tarzan, Lord of the Jungle*, *Tarzan and the City of Gold*, and *Tarzan and the Forbidden City*. David Adams points out that "the positive and negative poles provide a balance, so the cities are often in reality more alike than different" ("Folklorist" 5). In the differences, a multitude of similarities surface to make a whole culture, no matter how the superficial differences vary. Burroughs established this idea with the Waz-don and the Ho-don tribes in *Tarzan the Terrible*.

In "The Nightmare," the duality of dream and reality is explored, which is the subject of chapter eight.

"Who am I?"— *Moses*, Exodus 3.11

All of the stories in *Jungle Tales* explore some aspect of Tarzan's quest for identity, beginning with "Tarzan's First Love." As Tarzan sees the various animals in pairs he recognizes the linking of like species, lion with lioness, ape with ape. This is one of the important themes incorporated into the Disney production of *Tarzan II*. The Phil Collins theme song for the film, "Who Am I?," captures that search; it "sets just the right tone," says Betty Jo Tucker. The song occurs in the production while Tarzan imitates the behavior of various animals, trying to fit in. Brain Smith, director and co-writer of the film, explains in the DVD bonus features, "We like to think of it as being kind of a little lost tale of

Tarzan's youth" ("Bringing"). Certainly the same premise was the foundation for Burroughs writing *Jungle Tales of Tarzan*. Smith explains that in the first Disney *Tarzan* film, Tarzan grows up during the song "Son of Man." The idea for *Tarzan II* sprang from this scene in the first film. "At the beginning of the song he starts off as a young boy and there's a series of events and some transitions and suddenly he's an adult. And we were kind of wondering, well, what happened to him during that time period" ("Bringing"). The same wonderings, nearly a century earlier, prompted Burroughs to write his own sequel from the same premise but with a different name. In both, the who-am-I question is central.

In "Tarzan's First Love," Tarzan takes his first step in identifying himself as being separate from all the other creatures in the jungle because there is no female counterpart for himself. In "Tarzan and the Black Boy," he makes another attempt at being like the others by raising a child. Here, nearing the midpoint of the book, the desire to belong has shifted from the personal to the corporate. He has displaced the need for personal companionship with the acceptable alternative of the parental role.

The most important event that Burroughs records in the first novel regarding Tarzan's search for identity comes when he sees his reflection next to that of a companion ape. The incident at the pool is one of the most effective, Johnston says, where the adolescent hero sees that he is "not a trueborn ape"; in that mirrored reflection, Tarzan "discovers what a poor relation of the higher anthropoids he really is" (59). This is a disturbing discovery for the boy, and it plants the seed of isolation even before his interest in Teeka reinforces his difference. Johnston finds Tarzan "as reserved and contemplative as Hamlet" (59). And the Shakespearean reader might well imagine Tarzan lamenting: "Now I am alone. / Oh, what a rogue and peasant slave am I!" (2.2.549–50). Hamlet's disillusionment with his situation leads to solitary contemplation. Both Tarzan and Hamlet could identify with the words of Agur the prophet, "Surely I am more brutish than any man" (Proverbs 30.2). Both feel shut out; both believe that no one understands the situation into which they have fallen.

Before beginning *Jungle Tales*, Burroughs completed *Tarzan and the Jewels of Opar*. Because of the sale to competing editors, as noted, the public got the first stories of *Jungle Tales* in *Blue Book* before *Tarzan and the Jewels of Opar* began serialization in *Argosy* (18 November through 16 December). Central to the plot of *Tarzan and the Jewels of Opar* is the quest for identity. In this earlier instance, though, Tarzan has lost his memory from a blow to the head while gathering jewels in Opar. While Tarzan cannot remember who he is, he is jealously sure that he desires the "pouch of pretty pebbles" (85) which has been stolen from him. Holtsmark points out that in "the search of a pouch of jewels, the jewels [are] symbolic of identity. The tale is the classical one of the search for self" (26). Tarzan has lost his identity in the loss of his memory and the jewels become the key to unlock that psychological chest. It seems ironic that a reader at the end of 1916 could have been reading about Tarzan's search for identity both as an adolescent, in *Jungle Tales*, and as an adult, in *Jewels of Opar* at the same time.

One method that Burroughs uses to reveal identity to the reader, without explicit recognition by the character, is through modifiers of motivation. In "Tarzan's First Love," Tarzan's fingers are called "relentless" (22), when he chokes Taug's guard. The modifier, of course, does not truly refer to the fingers but to the determination of the fingers' owner; that is, Tarzan is relentless in pursuit of this particular goal. As Holtsmark says, the word "probes beneath the surface of those fingers and suggests something about the mind and heart that direct their action" (103). Likewise, in "The Capture of Tarzan," in the melee of violence that attempts to subdue Tarzan, one cautious warrior notes Tarzan's "merciless teeth" (35). Again, it is not the teeth that can show mercy; that is possible only for the owner of the teeth. Similarly, in "A Jungle Joke," when Tarzan abducts Rabba Kega, the hands upon the witch doctor's throat are "cruel" (165). The revelation of cruelty is lost upon Tarzan, the doer, but revealed to the reader. By doing this, the narrator, through the choice of character-indicating modifiers, is able to leave the reader with revelations of a character's identity without making declarative statements concerning it.

Cheyfitz argues that Burroughs' first Tarzan novel "is a romance of identity" (14), or an "evolutionary romance of identity" (19), which he compares to James Fenimore Cooper's *The Pioneers*, written nearly a century earlier (in 1823). While this antecedent fits more neatly Burroughs' later pair of Apache novels—*The War Chief* and *Apache Devil*—the comparison is still instructive. The hero is known to the reader as one thing (in Tarzan's case, a British nobleman) while the hero himself identifies himself with another group (Kerchak's apes), just as it is revealed at the end of Cooper's novel that Oliver Edwards's half-breed identity was adoptive rather than literal, leaving him the white grandson of Major Effingham. Likewise, Tarzan's ape identity is adoptive as revealed to him near the end of the first novel by the confirming telegraph from D'Arnot regarding the fingerprints in Lord Greystoke's diary.

When Tarzan takes food from Mbonga's village, he commits more of himself than if he were to take nuts from a hollow log where Manu had squirreled them away. Kilgour points out that "to eat the food of others is to become one with them, and so to be alienated from one's true home and identity" (48). The precedent comes from Homer. When Odysseus and his crew eat with Circe, they commit themselves unwittingly to her land, and are treacherously kept under her spell. When Tarzan, in "The Nightmare," takes food from the village cooking pot, he is inadvertently identifying with the cannibal tribe, an identity which he literally cannot stomach. The ensuing sickness purges him of his error just as surely as if he had heard Dante's Ulysses number him among his crew: "Consider well the seed that gave you birth: / you were not made to live your lives as brutes, / but to be followers of worth and knowledge (*Considerate la vostra semenza: / fatti non foste a viver come bruti, / ma per seguir virtute e canoscenza)"* (26.118–20). Tarzan breaks this identification, this evil enchantment, in "The Nightmare," through his vomiting.

The rejection that Tarzan has dealt with stems from the hatred Tublat directs toward him. Tublat urged Kala to abandon the infant, and the mutually tormenting relationship between Tublat and Tarzan reinforced the question of Tarzan's inclusion in Kerchak's tribe. It is a rejection similar to what the creature fashioned by Victor Frankenstein faces when he is abandoned by his creator.

Kilgour writes:

> The gothic hero [...] is frequently an orphan, and the structure of the novel recalls the Greek romances, in which the narrative moves toward the revelation and restoration of identity. [...] sometimes, as in the case of Oedipus, the revelation of identity is disastrous. The gothic hero or heroine is both isolated and alienated by being orphaned, but also finally bound rigidly by family ties he or she cannot know about and discovers too late. The past takes on even more terrifying and monstrous forms when it remains buried and unknown, when one cannot tell where one has come from or who one's father is but is still tied to a source one cannot see or remember [176].

His own identity is wrapped up beneath many layers, not the least important of which is his name. The first syllable, *tar*, means *white* in the language of the great apes. The irony that tar is a black substance cannot escape English readers. This irony is unknown to Tarzan, though. It is his whiteness that makes him different from all others in the jungle. The whiteness is both prestige and stigma, much like the whiteness of Herman Melville's whale, Moby Dick. Tarzan is revered by Mbonga's villagers in much the same way that the whale is revered by the crew of the *Pequod*, with a "rather vague, nameless horror" (Melville 199). Ishmael, the narrator of Melville's novel, states plainly: "It was the whiteness of the whale that above all things appalled me" (Melville 199). He wrestles with the concept:

> Though in many natural objects, whiteness refiningly enhances beauty, as if imparting some special virtue of its own, as in marbles, japonicas, and pearls; and though various nations have in some way recognized a certain royal pre-eminence in this hue; even the barbaric, grand old kings of Pegu placing the title 'Lord of the White Elephants' above all their other magniloquent ascriptions of dominion; and the modern kings of Siam unfurling the same snow-white quadruped in the royal standard; and the Hanoverian flag bearing the one figure of a snow-white charger; and the great Austrian Empire, Caesarian, heir to overlording Rome, having for the imperial color the same imperial hue; and though this pre-eminence in it applies to the human race itself, giving the white man ideal mastership over every dusky tribe; and though, besides, all this, whiteness has been even made significant of gladness, for among the Romans a white stone marked a joyful day; and though in other mortal sympathies and symbolizings, this same hue is made the emblem of many touching, noble things—the innocence of brides, the benignity of age; [...] [Melville 199–200].

He goes on to name, among other things, "the white belt of wampum" as a sign of honor among Native Americans, the ermine collar of the judge, the purest fire, Jove "made incarnate in a snow-white bull," "white robes [...] given to the redeemed" in John's book of the Revelation, and the whiteness of God on the throne (200). He ends the two-page sentence, though, with this caveat: "yet for all these accumulated associations with whatever is sweet, and honorable, and sublime, there yet lurks an elusive something in the innermost idea of this hue, which strikes more of panic to the soul than that redness which affrights in blood" (200). He goes on to name the albino and the corpse as representative of the repulsive whiteness in humans. The double nature of whiteness is epitomized in his statement: "whiteness is not so much a color as the visible absence of color; and at the same time the concrete of all colors [...]" (206).

Tarzan's whiteness is his stigma as well as his identifying determiner. Mbonga's villagers refer to him by his color, for example in "A Jungle Joke," as "the white devil-god" (168), and respond to him with awe. His whiteness is his signifier, and in these stories the signifier is negative far more often than positive. His situation is much like the situation in the adventure of Arthur Gordon Pym and the crew of the *Jane Guy*. In Poe's tale, they find on the island of Tsalal, a black tribe to whom "*white* had all the qualities of a *taboo*," a color which "inspired them with both veneration and terror" (Bonaparte 330, italics original). Poe's narrator notes that whenever these inhabitants are confronted with white things, "they appeared to recoil" (849), including such things as "the schooner's sails, an egg, an open book, or a pan of flour" (850), as well as the white skin of the sailors.

Freud postulates that as one's identity forms, "one's inner center is an alien, for the self is built out of lost objects of desire that have been introjected as a means of accepting their loss" (Kilgour 229). By introjection, Kilgour explains Freud's intention to invoke "the mental assimilation of external objects which, lost as possessions, become internalized and identified with the self" (229). Tarzan has lost the surface of his heritage and is left with intriguing symbols in the cabin and its contents.

Later Tarzan has a more mature, more cynical view of who he is. In *Tarzan and the City of Gold*, his companion Gemnon offers the philosophy: "We are what we are born [...]; some men are beasts, some are men, some are men who behave like beasts." Tarzan responds with one of his rare smiles and the words: "But none, thank God, are beasts that behave like men" (90). It seems that while the duality of his heritage cannot be erased, it can be understood. The events of *Jungle Tales* set a framework from which a mature understanding of those differences can be made.

CHAPTER 6

The Problem of Good and Evil in "The Witch-Doctor Seeks Vengeance" and "The End of Bukawai"

The *Blue Book* contents page (February 1917) labels "The Witch-Doctor Seeks Vengeance" a "vivid narrative of tumultuous life in the dark African jungle." Burroughs wrote the story in the first five days of November. Its companion story, "The End of Bukawai," was written a month later, 8–11 December 1916. The *Des Moines Sunday Register* re-titled the stories "Revenge" and "Trapped." "The End of Bukawai" has been adapted to comic form in *Fantasy Illustrated* #3 (Winter 1964) and in Marvel's *Tarzan Annual* #1 (1977).

"The Witch-Doctor Seeks Vengeance" begins with an elaborate comparison of the current Lord Greystoke in England involved in an aristocratic version of hunting. The scene moves to the jungle, where Tarzan moves toward Mbonga's village in pursuit of some entertainment. He is distracted and irritated by the "great wailing" (89) of a single voice. When he drops into the village to effect "a violent termination" (89) to it, he discovers Momaya. He does not understand her desperate pleas to him, but later in the jungle he recognizes Tibo's footprints among those of Bukawai's entourage. He investigates and finds Tibo guarded by Bukawai's hyenas, while the witch-doctor tries to extort a payment from Tibo's family. Mbonga's witch-doctor, Rabba Kega, challenges Bukawai to a contest of magic. While the village watches the chicanery of the two, Tarzan rescues Tibo and returns him to the village. Bukawai flees and Rabba Kega gets a howling chase from Momaya through the village.

"The End of Bukawai" begins with a flashback to a time when Kala and Tublat still fostered the boy Tarzan. Tarzan lassoes Tublat and torments him. He also makes two important discoveries concerning his rope. First, he discovers the physics of a pendulum, including the ideas of centrifugal force, pivots, and inertia. Second, he learns the principle of friction as a destructive force. This second principle becomes crucial in the "present-day" portion of the story. Several months after Tarzan's embarrassment of Bukawai at Mbonga's village,

Tarzan is rendered unconscious in a storm. Bukawai finds the breathing form and takes him to his cave where he can enjoy torturing Tarzan to death. He ties Tarzan to a tree then rouses him. He wants to watch his hyenas eat Tarzan alive. Tarzan, recalling the lesson regarding friction, manages to wear through his ropes before the hyenas do him damage and puts Bukawai tied in his place, awaiting the return of his own hyenas.

Before beginning "The Witch-Doctor Seeks Vengeance," Burroughs wrote to Ray Long (16 October 1916), asking if the series of short stories would end with six or be extended to twelve. Apparently the commissioning of these stories began orally, as the first written mention of them occurs in a letter to rival editor, Robert Davis at Munsey's offices. Because Long and Burroughs both lived in Chicago at the time and were members of the White Paper Club, it is reasonable that they discussed business in person as well as through writing. In setting up what became *Tarzan the Untamed*, installments of which were billed as short stories, Long ends his note of 2 October 1918 with the question, "Hadn't we better talk it over?" His next letter, dated 7 October, begins: "Just to get our informal agreement on the new Tarzan stories on paper." Something similar may have occurred with *Jungle Tales*, without the written follow-up.

On the day that he began writing "Tarzan's First Love," Burroughs sent a "Night Letter" via Western Union to Davis: "Have been asked for a series of twelve six thousand word Tarzan stories for monthly publication." He offered Davis a chance bid on the stories. Davis responded that he was interested only in serial fiction from Burroughs. That Burroughs might have been tired of the obligation these stories held on him is suggested by this reference in October to a shorter series, since clearly he described it himself as twelve stories the previous spring. Also, the September issue of *Blue Book*, where "The New Stories of Tarzan" began had informed readers that the adventures would number twelve (986). Because Burroughs had been traveling, it is quite possible that he had not seen the issue bearing the announcement, or, because it ran on the page previous to his own story, did not read it. After his submission of "Tarzan and the Black Boy," he commented to Long: "Will do the best I can with the balance of them, though I must admit that I can't see where the stuff is coming from" (30 October 1916). After completing "The End of Bukawai," in correspondence with Davis again, Burroughs wrote ambiguously, "I offered you the short stories [*Jungle Tales*] and you couldn't see them — neither can I" (20 December 1916). The final three words of the sentence carry no elaboration, but they may have indicated a perceived lack of inspiration for completing the series. Two days later, though, he began the next story.

When Long received "The Witch-Doctor Seeks Vengeance," he responded with some disapproval of the story, "the first [story]," he said, "over which I have not been enthusiastic" (letter to Burroughs 16 November 1916). The first of his two objections was an overt comparison, primarily at the beginning of the story, between Lord Greystoke and Tarzan. Burroughs responded that when he had done a similar comparison in *Tarzan of the Apes* it had been received well. He gave permission, though, for the references to be taken out. In this regard, the *Blue Book* version differs from the eventual book publication. Long excised the first four paragraphs of the story (481 words) and replaced it with two sentences (18 words): "Tarzan had been hunting. Now, having eaten of his kill, he was drinking deep at a jungle stream" ("Witch-Doctor Seeks Vengeance," *Blue Book* 744). As a stand-alone story, Long felt justified, no doubt, in keeping the story focused entirely on the jungle action.

The second objection that Long registered in the letter is the return of Tibo, who, he said, "was all right for one story, but he was not a good character for two." Burroughs made no justification to the carryover of Tibo's character. Ironically, or perhaps as a power maneuver, Burroughs took the character of Bukawai, who had appeared in the same two stories, "Tarzan and the Black Boy" and "The Witch-Doctor Seeks Vengeance," and featured him in a third story, "The End of Bukawai," begun three weeks later (8 December, after Long's initial letter of 16 November).

This double story forms an extended narrative that continues Tarzan's exploration of contrasts in the forms of good versus evil and nature versus civilization. These stories also explore the idea of distortion of nature, what Sherwood Anderson called *grotesque*, particularly as seen in the hyenas that Bukawai keeps.

"[A]ll human beings [...] are commingled out of good and evil"
— *Dr. Jekyll and Mr. Hyde* (Stevenson 89)

Related to Tarzan's philosophical exploration of the nature of God, which occurred in "The God of Tarzan," is the nature of good and evil, and the attendant hypocrisy that follows its discussion. T.S. Eliot claims in "Choruses from 'The Rock'": "However you disguise it, this thing does not change: / The perpetual struggle of Good and Evil" (98). Just as Tarzan reasoned the qualities of God based on his observations in nature (after the enigma of the written word), the existence of evil is suggested at the end of the story when Tarzan asks, "Who made Histah, the snake?" (64). Ralph Earle observes that "one cannot explain the insidious influence of evil in this world without postulating a personal agent behind it" (57). The stories of Bukawai provide that personal dimension, at least of one sort.

The difference between good and evil is often overt in Burroughs' writing. This is a corollary to the point of view of the narrator or the main character. Tarzan, of course, represents good in the stories, while Bukawai is the embodiment of evil. This is an extension of the idea of duality explored in the previous chapter. Atamian argues that the inspiration for Bukawai's name comes from Du Challu's story of the Bakalai people. These people were particularly superstitious. Atamian summarizes: "Evil spirits, witchcraft, magic — the spirit of the demonic world is the theme, Bakalai is the name [...]" (66).

6. The Problem of Good and Evil 143

The evil man is characterized by his focus on himself to the detriment of those around him. In Psalm 10, a number of parallels are clear between the generic wicked man and Bukawai. A portion of the psalm says:

> The wicked in his pride doth persecute the poor: let them be taken in the devices that they have imagined. For the wicked boasteth of his heart's desire, and blesseth the covetous, whom the Lord abhoreth. The wicked, through the pride of his countenance, will not seek after God: God is not in all his thoughts. His ways are always grievous; thy judgments are far above out of his sight: as for all his enemies, he puffeth at them. He hath said in his heart, I shall not be moved: for I shall never be in adversity. His mouth is full of cursing and deceit and fraud: under his tongue is mischief and vanity. He sitteth in the lurking places of the villages: in the secret places doth he murder the innocent: his eyes are privily set against the poor. He lieth in wait secretly as a lion in his den: he lieth in wait to catch the poor: he doth catch the poor, when he draweth him into his net. He croucheth, and humbleth himself, that the poor may fall by his strong ones. He hath said in his heart, God hath forgotten: he hideth his face; he will never see it [verses 2–11].

The words of the wicked man are characterized by boasting (about his own desires), blessing the covetous, cursing, deceit, fraud, mischief, and vanity. In particular, the face is used to represent the character of the man. The eyes present a window to the soul, it is said. Here, they are "set against the poor." Burroughs uses the eyes similarly as a way to reinforce a character's integrity, or lack of it. Even the number of Bukawai's eyes is confused, much less his use of them/it. In "The Witch-Doctor Seeks Vengeance," Bukawai "open[s] his eyes in well-simulated amazement" (99), when he encounters Momaya, who threatens to "tear [his] eyes from [his] head" (99). Burroughs confuses the issue, though. Later in the scene, the narrator says Bukawai "blinked his one eye angrily" (102); it would have worked more believably for Bukawai to lose the eye between the two stories instead of during a scene at Mbonga's village with no one noticing; then later in the next story, the narrator states that Bukawai "could not believe the witness of his own eyes" (111). In "The End of Bukawai," the narrator reinforces the point that the witch-doctor has only one eye, when by contrast he claims "but had he had a dozen eyes he could have found no beauty" (111). He has lost his depth perception; the world has become two-dimensional for him, and beauty may represent that third dimension lost.

Eyes reveal much about other characters as well. Mbonga has "greedy eyes" (36), and under Tarzan's grasp there is "terror in the man's eyes" (59). But Tarzan's eyes can be found "dreamily devouring the object of their devotion" (7); his eyes are "keen" (21, 92, 135, 153), "practiced" (24), "cold" (115), "quick" (138), "alert" (152), and "jungle-trained" (135), all speaking of the discipline by which he encounters his world. Emotionally, Tarzan's eyes might be "sparkling in anticipation" (164), or ambiguously "glittering" (164). And Tarzan sees in Teeka's eyes "a wistful expression and a troubled look of sorrow" (20), revealing her concern over Taug's fate.

Repeatedly the psalm identifies wickedness with taking advantage of the poor. Momaya represents the poor of the village. She does not have the exorbitant price that Bukawai demands for his dubious services. The wicked man treats others with disdain. He puffs at them in public. Like some humanized puffer fish, he makes himself to be much larger in danger and in importance than he is in actual substance. He hides in the shadows, though, most of the time, in the "lurking places" and in "his den." Literally, Bukawai's cave is the embodiment of verse 9, but with the substitution of the hyena for the lion. The intent remains; the evil man is carnivorous, eating those people around him as a means of staying alive. The metaphor is made literal with the lion image in the psalm and the hyena application in these stories.

The wicked man also is identified by his disavowal of any power higher than himself. He will not acknowledge the authority of Mbonga and chooses to live outside Mbonga's authority. He sets himself up as an equal rather than a subordinate. His deference to the spirits is false, in that he has no clear relationship with actual spirits and the ones that he names are simply a part of his manipulative sham. In doing so, he tries to set himself outside accountability. If there is no human to whom he must show obedience, he believes there is no spiritual power to whom he will be required to answer as well. This is anarchy; if he were to actually have people under his subjugation, he would be a despot. He does not believe that any god will require accountability from him; therefore, he becomes a god unto himself.

The result of such an attitude is death. Murder is the hallmark of evil. From the time of Abel's death, the causeless taking of another's life has been evil's iceberg tip. Bukawai plotted Tarzan's death, though he was unable to carry it out, and he was willing to kill Tibo rather than return him without reward.

Later the psalmist identifies God as "the helper of the fatherless" (verse 14). While readers identify with Tarzan's resourcefulness and his ability to outmuscle and outwit his various adversaries, it is easy to forget that Tarzan is indeed an orphan. And while it would be inaccurate to conclude that every orphan is on the side of good as opposed to evil, certainly the opposition between Tarzan and Bukawai is brighter, in view of the psalm, realizing that Tarzan is the potential recipient of divine favor.

The judgment that the psalm reserves for the wicked man at the beginning of the passage quoted above is that he will suffer in the ways that he intended others to suffer, that he will "be taken in the devices that [he] ha[s] imagined" (Psalm 10.2). This is the mirror image of the Golden Rule: "Do unto others as you would have them do unto you" (a popularized form of Luke 6.31). This principle is clear: those who are merciful receive mercy from others, while those who delight in taking advantage of others, will soon be taken advantage of themselves. Bukawai does not believe this. As the psalm says, in his heart he believes that adversity will not visit him even though he is the cause of adversity to any that he meets. Ultimately the reader understands the return of the imagined device when the hyenas that he had intended eat the bound Tarzan, it is implied, will return to eat their impotent master.

6. The Problem of Good and Evil

When Burroughs was a child, his father was dismissed from jury duty because he did "not believe in fanaticism anywhere" (court transcript; qtd. in Hillman, "Major"). In this instance the elder Burroughs was referring to Roman Catholicism. His son later found it convenient to dismiss all religious form as suspect. This suspicion is reflected in "The God of Tarzan" when the young protagonist watches the witch-doctor in a "weird ceremony": "Tarzan witnessed strange things that night, none of which he understood, and, perhaps because they were strange, he thought that they must have to do with the God he could not understand" (53). Human reason provides the litmus test of understanding. Because the knowledge of God cannot come completely through reason, error is attributed by the observer, in this case, Tarzan. When the error is known by the perpetrator as well, this becomes hypocrisy. If there were an unpardonable sin in Burroughs' universe, it would be just this kind of falseness. His writing stance toward religion consistently condemns hypocrisy. Bukawai is only one of many figures who substitute the form of godliness for the reality of it.

Montaigne points out that human nature is inherently flawed, "prying narrowly into [others'] faults we are blinded in ours" (249). This principle comes of course from the teachings of Jesus who warned his followers of hypocrisy in Matthew 7.1–5; one must tend to the personal "beam" before helping remove another's "mote." Characters like Bukawai have taken such narrow prying and made it a livelihood.

Earlier in 1916, Burroughs proposed a story about the biblical Cain. When Davis gave an ambivalent approval for the story, Burroughs responded to his hesitancy with: "Because I am not religious[,] don't think that I couldn't write a religious story. It's just a matter of imagination, and I can easily imagine myself a religious bigot [...]" (letter to Davis 24 January 1916). For Burroughs, bigotry, a form of hypocrisy, is inseparable from religious thinking. The religious figures, every witch-doctor of Tarzan's Africa, or the therns of Barsoom, consistently reveal in Burroughs' works the worm of hypocrisy at their hearts.

When Bukawai and Rabba Kega face off in front of the trio of Mbonga, Momaya, and Ibeto, near the end of "The Witch-Doctor Seeks Vengeance," Rabba Kega grabs the attention of his audience by surreptitiously dropping some dry leaves into a fire container and then pretending that he is "communing with the spirits within" the smoking vessel (102). That the narrator calls the leaves dry is sensible on the literal level, but the adjective is also important at a more symbolic level. The word has associations with more than lack of moisture. Eliot, for one, invests the word with associations of spiritual lack of life. He begins, for example, his "Gerontion" "in a dry month" (21) and ends it with "a dry brain in a dry season" (23). The dryness, while literal, is indicative of the internal lifelessness of modern existence. Cornell scholar David Daiches confirms: "Dryness has always been for Eliot the basic symbol of life without faith and hope" (117). When applied to Rabba Kega, this faithless and hopeless life is indicated by the dry leaves with which he deceives the company.

Daiches says further, in his commentary on Eliot, that "the life of man without the organizing and vitalizing spirit, without religion, faith, a sense of value" can be "[n]othing but a dry and meaningless desert" (117).

Lifelessness as a connotation of dryness goes back to Ezekiel, whose vision of the valley of dry bones shows the contrasts between the dry, spiritless bones and the living men they become. Ezekiel describes the bones as "very many" and "very dry" (37.2). These bones, even when miraculously reassembled into skeletons with muscle and flesh added, remain lifeless until the wind brings life. The prophet understands the vision figuratively, when the voice of God says, "Our bones are dried and our hope is lost" (Ezekiel 37.11). The analogy is explained, except the bodies are revived not with wind but when God's voice says, "I shall put my Spirit in you, and ye shall live" (37.14). The Hebrew word for *spirit* is *ruach*, a word which is translated as wind, breath, and spirit. It is the same word in the creation passage where "the Lord God formed man of the dust of the ground, and breathed into his nostrils the breath of life; and man became a living soul" (Genesis 2.7).

With Rabba Kega, the absence of value and faith is displayed in the dry leaves. He is spiritually dead, a counterfeit, and all his sleights-of-hand used to simulate genuine spiritual life simply betray the sham of his efforts. It is this revelation that Momaya responds to at the end of the story, showing the entire village that such fraudulence is intolerable.

Eliot provides more than an illustration of dryness, though. His poem, "The Hollow Men," seems applicable as well. As B.C. Southam says, "the hollowest of them all" is "the most deceived and self-deceiving" (204). The analogue of Eliot's hollow men provides a slightly different reading of the witch-doctors' characters. It may be, as Southam says of men beside the Acheron in Dante's *Inferno*, that they "have never been spiritually alive, never experienced good or evil, having lived narrowly for themselves" (204). In this reading, both Bukawai and Rabba Kega are ignorant of their own emptiness. Instead of purposely extorting and deceiving the villagers, they sincerely believe they have the powers that they represent; although, their imperfection must be equally clear to them. But their sincerity moves them from the group of charlatans into a group of sincerely mistaken people. Southam goes on: "[T]he hollow men are not narrowly the conspirators; they are all mankind" (205). In this way, the witch-doctors serve as representatives of the readers, and serve as a caution and reminder of their own imperfection.

Southam claims that Conrad's *Heart of Darkness* "is possibly the most important single literary experience in Eliot's poetry from 'Prufrock' onwards" (205). "Conrad's story is full of hollow men — empty of faith, of personality, of moral strength, of humanity" (205). The witch-doctors, no matter by what name, in all of Burroughs' stories are just such hollow men.

Eliot began the poem "Gerontion" in 1917, the same year that *Blue Book* published "The Witch-Doctor Seeks Vengeance," though Eliot reading any of the stories in *Blue Book* is unlikely. Eliot worked on the poem for two more years, until it was published in *Poems, 1920*. Eliot's "Gerontion" suggests that people are deceived by "whispering ambitions," and they are "guid[ed ...] by vanities" (22). Bukawai and Rabba Kega give, as does the abstract "history" of Eliot's poem, "[w]hat's not believed in, or if still believed, / [i]n memory only" (22). Association with witchcraft comes in Eliot's poem with the reference to "shifting [...] candles" as in a séance and to the "backward devils" (22) of Dante's *Inferno*, those diviners condemned to forever walk backward for the sin of pretending to divine the future. The rival witch-doctors claim to tell not so much the future as the displaced present; Rabba Kega sees the boy "dead at the bottom of the river" in counter to Bukawai's claim that the boy is "alone and in great danger" (102). Of course their fraudulent nature is proven when Tarzan restores Tibo in the middle of their conning conjurations.

"*Man is inextricably wild and society is the cultivation of that wildness.*"
— "Vile Things Precious" (Cloward 6)

Just as good and evil form a set of necessary contrasts, so do civilization and the wilderness. Each has its necessary drawbacks as well as strengths, though for the most part, in Burroughs' writings nature triumphs over civilization. Cloward asserts: "In wildness are the seeds of the self" (7), a necessary belief for Tarzan to have any hope of survival and an understanding of his identity. Cloward also suggests that nature becomes "culture's mirror and counterpart" (7), a role implicit in the repeated comparisons that Burroughs provides.

What precisely civilization is, must be defined subjectively. Civilization, like beauty, is in the eye of the beholder. For the reader, the "many stages of social evolution and many seemingly bizarre customs and 'superstitions' in the world" (Brantlinger 166) are always something other than the comfortable, what the reader calls civilization.

Civilization, in its positive role, is the result of proper breeding, in Burroughs' worlds. Tarzan is heir to a nobleman's estate, both in land and in character. The narrator informs the reader that Tarzan's father "was the type of Englishman that one likes best to associate with the noblest monuments of historic achievement upon a thousand victorious battlefields — a strong, virile man — mentally, morally, and physically" (*Apes* 8). The son, though he lived with his biological father for only one year, possesses "noble poise" (*Apes* 90) from a "time-honored lineage" (*Jungle Tales* 7), and Jane sees in him a "noble face," the features of which communicate "chivalry" to her (*Apes* 147). His actions are instinctive, not of animal instinct but of the supposed class instinct he has inherited from a long line of noble progenitors. For example, in "The Battle for Teeka," the narrator explains, "In strange ways did heredity manifest itself in the ape-man. Come of an orderly race, he himself was orderly without knowing why" (146). And in "A Jungle Joke," the narrator credits Tarzan's "feeling of repugnance at the sight of unnecessary suffering to heredity — to the germ of British love of fair play which had been bequeathed to him by his father and his mother" (169). It is this aspect of civilization that ennobles him. Grun affirms that "Burroughs emphasizes strongly the fact that his breeding is by no means a product of nature, but of the long line of peers behind him, whose gentility not even complete identity with nature could eradicate!" (134). Innate character, then, exists despite the claims of nature to remake him in animal form. This is shown quite clearly when Tarzan meets Jane. Conrath, in his 1990 dissertation, explains that the hero "is instinctually drawn towards females and though it is almost a commonplace to speak of social acts as kissing as learned, Tarzan has somehow inherited the sexual graces of 'western man'" (38). When he rescues Jane from Terkoz, after fighting for the prize that is embodied literally in Jane, the narrator tells the reader that Tarzan "did what no red-blooded man needs lessons in doing. He took his woman in his arms and smothered her upturned, panting lips with kisses" (*Apes* 141–42). Some readers might suggest that in today's society, kissing would not be the natural impulse Tarzan was dealing with. However, considering the cultural climate that Burroughs wrote in, kissing is perhaps the limit of propriety that could be expressed. It, too, suggests a slightly different moral code than that of today's readers, a code at once more reserved and chivalric.

But civilization is, in many other ways, ignoble. Even before Tarzan is born, the narrator of *Tarzan of the Apes* makes it clear that civilization is peopled by many beastly men that civilization itself cannot control. Before Lord John and Lady Alice ever reach their little harbor, the sailors on board the *Fuwalda* show "just how thin that veneer of civilization is" (Rothstein E1), making the jungle world and the crew under Black Michael distorted mirror images of each other. The events in the shipboard narrative of the first chapter, Holtsmark points out, "are a kind of microcosm of the utter ineffectiveness of the appeals of civilization"— that which is represented by John Clayton and his wife—"to the naked drives of uncontrolled human passion" (65), as represented by the mutineers as well as Captain Billings. First, the unreasonable and inhumane Billings is murdered, then Black Michael, who led the revolt against his inhumanity, finds it difficult to retain any authority over the mutineers. When the reader is introduced to the apes of Kerchak, the tribe clearly represents a variation on the mob that mutinied and set the Greystokes ashore alone. Kerchak's entry into the Greystoke cabin is akin to the former lack of concern the couple was shown aboard the *Fuwalda* when their cabin was ransacked. There appears no difference between the temperaments of Billings and Black Michael, just as there is no difference between the sailors and the apes. In the end, one questions if the rulers and subjects of the unnamed European country whose actions John Clayton is sent to spy out are any different in temperament than these. Rothstein identifies "one of [Burroughs'] main themes" in *Tarzan of the Apes* is just this: "It is difficult to tell the civilized world — with its vicious mutineers, ruthless imperialists and plotting capitalists—from the jungle world" (E1). The theme of a depraved civilization is explored, then, from the beginning of Tarzan's literary life.

Such an idea is explored by Fenton in his biography of Burroughs. When he says, though, "never once did author Edgar Rice Burroughs aver from his conviction that the English were the height of aristocracy, the noblest of souls" (15), he was not thinking of the several comparisons of Tarzan the jungle lord with his reigning cousin in England. In such comparisons, the Englishman always suffers humiliation. In the opening paragraphs of "The Witch-Doctor Seeks Vengeance," the narrator contrasts Tarzan's simple and powerful life with the privileged but impotent life of his reigning cousin. The "imposter" (88) spends his morning "shooting pheasants" while "immaculately and appropriately garbed," with the aid of twenty-three men beating the bushes to flush the birds (87). Tarzan, on the other hand, hunts without elaborate clothing, armed by his own hunger. Later in the story, "in far-off England," one Lord Greystoke tries to sleep, "swearing irritably as a cat meowed beneath his window," while in Africa, the proper Lord Greystoke "composed himself for a night of dreamless slumber, while a prowling lion moaned and coughed beneath him" (91). At the end of the story, by way of completing the frame, the British lord suffers from overeating, while Tarzan once again sleeps well.

The stain of civilization appears to be well-seated in Burroughs. A poem attributed to him, published when he was living in Pocatello, Idaho, parodies Rudyard Kipling. Instead of the white man's burden that Kipling examines, "The Black Man's Burden" asks blacks to give up their own culture for an imported one, where they must adopt European dress and religion, as well as accept unfair laws and taxes. These "Poor simple folk and free" must "Abandon nature's freedom" in order to "Embrace" the white man's liberty, which is placed in quotation marks to indicate that the word is used but the concept is questioned ("Black" 38).

This attitude is apparent in Tarzan's life as well. Once he has experienced civilized life, he makes a conscious choice to stay in Africa, away from civilization's corruption. Tarzan identifies the cities of Europe, as embodied in Paris, as "more dangerous than my savage jungles" (*Return* 31). In *Tarzan and the Golden Lion*, he says, "I [...] have left my jungle and gone to the cities built by men, but always I have been disgusted and been glad to return to my jungle— to the noble beasts that are honest in their loves and in their hates— to the freedom and genuineness of nature" (141). After his experience in Paris, in *Return*, and his betrayal in London, in *Beasts*, Tarzan avoids civilized circles and attempts to create a haven in Africa for Jane and himself, his "vast estate in Uziri" (*Beasts* 7). Stanley Crouch makes an apt comparison, when he says that "Tarzan, like James M. Barrie's Peter Pan, lived in a Neverland where one did not have to grow up and feel his soul eaten away by the responsibilities and rituals of the middle and upper classes" (147). The jungle does sometimes appear a more favorable place to live.

Where civilization fails, nature has a measure of success. Drawing from some of the assumptions of the noble savage motif, Conrath suggests: "The feral child, brought up in the wilds either through the care of a wild beast or on his or her own wits became a ground upon which to debate the merits of civilization, the 'new' Darwinian tenets of environmental conditioning, and role of heredity" (22). Burroughs, though, thought of survival of the fittest not in terms of physical mutations but, as Holtsmark points out, in terms of the creature that is "the most adaptable and the most clever" (115).

Yet nature is not always pure, either. Nature, the narrator affirms, "designed" the horn of the rhinoceros for "frightful work" (*Jungle Tales* 29). The beasts of nature among whom Tarzan lives and moves are "cruel and savage" (108). "All the beasts of the jungle were cruel" (169). Nature, Tarzan understands, "manifest[s] cruel, immeasurable powers" seen for example in the "demoniacal wind" that "threshe[s] the jungle piteously" (110). Nature has made death and suffering commonplace.

So what can be made of this on-off, yes-no swinging of the pendulum between civilization and the world of nature? Frankenstein's creature asks, "Was man, indeed, at once so powerful, so virtuous, and magnificent, yet so vicious and base? He appeared at one time a mere scion of the evil principle and at another as all that can be conceived of noble and godlike" (Shelley 114). Taliaferro invokes Theodore Dreiser's *Sister Carrie*, published in 1900, as a starting place for his biography of Burroughs. Dreiser's narrator claims that civilization is in a transitional and still-unformed state: "Our civilization is still in a middle stage, scarcely beast, in that it is no longer wholly guided by instinct; scarcely human, in that it is not yet wholly guided by reason." The beasts, says Dreiser's narrator, are "aligned by nature with the forces of life," and therefore bear no responsibility. Humans, on the other hand, perceive a sense of responsibility beyond themselves but are unable to break out from themselves to put reason completely above instinct. Dreiser's narrator continues:

> We see man far removed from the lairs of the jungles, his innate instincts dulled by too near an approach to free will, his free will not sufficiently developed to replace his instincts and afford him perfect guidance. He is becoming too wise to hearken always to instincts and desires; he is still too weak to always prevail against them [Dreiser 74].

Civilization, in this view, is an overlay on the natural human. This is clear in several places. Even Jane, one of the most civilized and genteel characters in the series, watches Tarzan battle Terkoz and undergoes a perceptual change, which the narrator describes as "the veil of centuries of civilization and culture [being] swept from the blurred vision of the Baltimore girl" (*Apes* 141). The lack of civilization can be positive or negative, depending on what kind of integrity the character has at his or her heart. "Chivalry is as innate a human quality as brutishness," Taliaferro says (106), and the removal of civilized influence with Tarzan and Jane leaves the character ennobled, whereas the removal of civilized restraints in a character like Snipes leaves a self-centered id. This tension between the jungle and civilization Holtsmark identifies as "Burroughs' most abiding polarity" (49).

Holtsmark concludes: "In the moral judgment which Burroughs passes on the world of Tarzan and the larger world of civilized, especially European society, it is clear that civilization, for all its wonders and achievements, comes off second best to the jungle" (50). Burroughs is "critical of the depths to which the contemporary world has sunk" (Holtsmark 147). Tarzan's choice of the jungle over civilization in Burroughs' fictitious world, is clearly the better one.

One example of this is in the matter of law. Holtsmark contends that Burroughs "draws a distinction between what works in the jungle and what works in civilization in relation to Tarzan's propensity, born of his jungle breeding, to take matters into his own hands" (116). In *The Return of Tarzan*, the narrator makes it clear that context clearly shapes what is right and what is not. The law of Parisian society, in this case representing the civilized world's law, differs from that of the jungle. Tarzan is not outside the law, especially when he is living in civilization. In this case, his friend D'Arnot has taken it upon himself to help Tarzan assimilate to civilization and become his liaison with the police when Rokoff tries to trap him. At the end of that book, when Tarzan is motivated to kill Rokoff, Jane appeals to civilized law again, even though they are in the jungle. She acknowledges that his own strength and code may be sufficient where there is no other form of authority, "but with the strong arm of a civilized government," she says, "it would be murder to kill him now" (*Return* 219). If he did what he viewed was morally justified in this case, because his friends, including Jane, are under the authority of Western governments, they would feel compelled to turn him over to the punishment accorded by civilized law. That Tarzan acquiesces to Jane's appeal "reveals a Tarzan who is learning, even if not approving of, the customs of civilization" (Holtsmark 117). Though Tarzan does plenty of killing, especially in *Tarzan the Untamed*, he does acknowledge the lesson when he is coming to the aid of Meriem, his soon-to-be daughter-in-law. Rather than kill her adversary, he responds, "Once I should have killed him; but not now. I will see, though, that he does not bother you any more" (*Son* 112–13). He acknowledges, "I am not the law" (Son 113), as a way of reconciling to himself his decision to let the man live.

Cheyfitz argues that Jane "holds the most powerful sway over Tarzan, representing for him, like Miranda for that archetypal imperialist Prospero, everything in 'civilization' that must be protected from the apes and black Africans, latter-day Calibans who, in addition to two gangs of mutinous sailors [...] are the villains of the [first] novel" (11). Achebe, too, has connected the image of Caliban to the blacks, claiming that while he has not been identified as African or racially tagged, he does represent "the quintessential colonial subject" ("African" 4).

Cheyfitz, though, is not a careful reader, in that he insists that Tarzan was born "on an island off the African coast" and that the Porters are also "abandoned on the island by mutineers" (12; that this section of his book was also published earlier only compounds the misreading, which should have been caught by readers of *American Literary History*).

And one might argue, as Cheyfitz does, based on the ending of *Tarzan of the Apes*, that the one thing that might "separate the savage from the civilized" is fingerprints (13). He argues further that as a "racist ideolog[y]" the novel blurs the lines "between race and species," and between "the human and the animal" (13). However, the difference between *savage* and *civilized* is not so easily defined. Collingwood takes Freud to task for his dichotomy between the two. He explains that by *savage*, in *Totem and Taboo*, Freud meant "only 'belonging to any civilization markedly different from that of modern Europe'" which makes it clear that the "differences between mental disease and mental health" are defined by "the differences between non-European and European civilizations" (77n).

Conrad frames Marlow's tale of the Congo with a discussion of modern England. In fact, Marlow's first spoken sentence of the story is an enigmatic comparison of the Congo with England: "And this also [...] has been one of the dark places of the earth" (19). The story told about one river, the Congo, is just as true concerning another river, the Thames, where the narration of Conrad's story takes place. The comparison is implicit and explored only as a means of entering the much larger story that Marlow tells. But the comparison is essential in understanding the underlying premise of the book. To ignore the connection is to enfeeble the work that Conrad has done. Achebe points out that superimposition of the two experiences—the colonized Congo upon Roman-controlled Britain—can produce for England "grotesque echoes of its own forgotten darkness" ("Image" 4).

> "Those whom Nature had depicted as merely quaint became grotesque, the grotesque became preternatural; for all was in extremity."
> —*The Return of the Native* (Hardy 19)

In "The God of Tarzan," Tarzan watches over the wall into Mbonga's village and sees "a weird and grotesque figure, a tall figure that went upon the two legs of a man and yet had the head of a buffalo" (52). This "grotesque witch-doctor" (53), unnamed, but in the present stories identified as Rabba Kega, has the attention of the entire village. In Tarzan's mind the grotesque becomes associated with "strange and uncanny powers" (137). And in *The Monster Men*, Burroughs calls those which are grotesque, "caricatures of humanity" (44).

Of all the characters in *Jungle Tales*, Bukawai most clearly fits the criteria. On the first mention of his name, he is called "unclean" (76). Like the lepers of biblical times (and nearly all others), he is shut out from the rest of society. Bukawai is all the more despised because of the "loathsome disease" that is "slowly eating away his face" (76), which made him "almost inarticulate" (82).

In "The Witch-Doctor Seeks Vengeance," the narrator adds that he is "an old, old man, black as the pit, with [...] his sharp-filed teeth [...] showing yellow and repulsive through the great gaping hole where his mouth and nose had been" (94). This external putrefaction is emblematic of the internal decay explored above. Just as the buffalo-headed witch-doctor displays both human and non-human characteristics, Bukawai's "mumbling tones" as he comes into the light to haggle with Momaya "were scarce more human than those of the beast" (82). He has the broad parameters of human form, but, as a caricature does, he shows distortion and misrepresentation. The face is missing its nose and lips, just as surely as his character is missing compassion and solicitude. "Nature had given him few of the kindlier characteristics of man," the narrator reveals, "and these few Fate had eradicated entirely. Shrewd, cunning, cruel, vindictive, was Bukawai, the witch-doctor" (95). He has become "the hideous semblance of a man" (113). His desire for power is extreme, in an effort to compensate for the ostracism he has felt. He has become grotesque, inside and out.

In "A Reminiscence of Mr. Sherlock Holmes: The Singular Experience of Mr. John Scott Eccles" (re-titled "The Adventure of Wisteria Lodge," when it was reprinted in *His Last Bow*), Sherlock Holmes and Watson have a brief exchange. "How do you define the word 'grotesque'?" Holmes asks after examining a telegram for some time. Watson, predictably, provides a pedestrian suggestion: "Strange — remarkable." Holmes is unsatisfied.

> "There is surely something more than that," said he; "some underlying suggestion of the tragic and the terrible. If you cast your mind back to some of those narratives with which you have afflicted a long-suffering public, you will recognize how often the grotesque has deepened into the criminal. Think of that little affair of the red-headed men. That was grotesque enough in the outset, and yet it ended in a desperate attempt at robbery. Or, again, there was that most grotesque affair of the five orange pips, which led straight to a murderous conspiracy. The word puts me on the alert" [745].

The reader is likely, also, on the alert whenever Bukawai is present in the narrative. As Holmes suggests, Bukawai moves from the grotesque to the criminal; in his quest for power he becomes a kidnapper, extortionist, and would-be murderer. In "The Adventure of the Red-Headed League," alluded to above, John Clay uses the innocent Jabez Wilson to cover his own crime, taking advantage of his gullibility and relative powerlessness. Likewise, Bukawai attempts to take advantage of Momaya, and by extension the whole village, through his deception, which he hopes will be gullibly believed, and through the uncertain immunity he bears in his disease. The tragedy included in "The Five Orange Pips" is wrapped up in the murder of three men, the last of which was Holmes's client. Bukawai, likewise, intends to kill Tibo, in a sense Tarzan's client, if he is unsuccessful in his ransom attempt. Where Holmes fails, however, Tarzan succeeds and rescues Tibo from the cave where the hyenas are ready to make him their next meal.

Bukawai is Tarzan's self-appointed nemesis, but symbolically he is already dead, residing in what is just as readily perceived as a tomb, marked by "the mouth of a cave between two rocky hills" (95). It is "very dark" (95) and filled with death; the crater deep within is called the "cold, dead mouth of hell" (112). Momaya calls him a "rotting fragment of a man" (99), indicating that his difference from a corpse is only in his animation; his flesh is decaying and his human qualities have begun to fall way. He has lost foremost the capacity for joy and delight. After the rainstorm in "The End of Bukawai," he cannot smell "the clean-washed air" nor see any "beauty in the fresh sweetness of the revivified jungle" (111). And when he finds his enemy, Tarzan, apparently dead, he rages instead of rejoicing, because even in his enemy's death he feels "cheated of the revenge he had so long dreamed upon" (111).

"An element of the grotesque" is typically present in Burroughs' writing, Holtsmark claims (135). A reader might see this in other places, in Jane's abduction by Terkoz, for example, or its parallel in Tarzan's attraction to Teeka in "Tarzan's First Love." In both cases Burroughs relies on a certain element of shock in the reader at the potential, a certain inhumanness. This inhuman incongruity is present from the moment John and Alice Clayton are marooned on the African shore. Lady Alice sees the mangani and asks in her confusion and uncertainty, "What is it, a man?" (*Apes* 22). Again, when Kala nurses Tarzan upon his adoption, the grotesquery of the situation charges the scene.

Holtsmark cites Burne Hogarth for giving visual form to the grotesqueness inherent in Burroughs' writing. Hogarth created "his own strongly expressionistic accentuation of gnarled landscape forms and contorted figure anatomy that is at times in bizarre defiance of realistically possible poses" (Holtsmark 133). In the illustration on page 26, for example, the tree branch separating Tarzan from Taug is knobby and twisted; the leaves are characteristically pointed. Muscle and movement everywhere in the frame are pushed to their extremes.

Though Holtsmark meant the word *grotesque* in its general sense, the word will push some readers to consider more specialized usage. Sherwood Anderson, in "The Book of the Grotesque," a kind of introduction to his landmark, and (to Burroughs) contemporary, classic *Winesburg, Ohio*, uses the word as a noun, as Holtsmark does, but with a very precise meaning incorporating the indefinite article, *a*, rather than the definite *the*. So, Anderson speaks of *a* grotesque rather than *the* grotesque. Anderson is not the first though. H.G. Wells used it in just such a fashion in *The Invisible Man*. Thomas Browne, in *Religio Medici* (1643), is one of the first to employ a related form of this usage.

The fictitious writer in the opening story of Anderson's book describes people by the distortions of character that occur within them. "It was his notion," Anderson writes, "that the moment one of the people took one of the truths to himself, called it his truth, and tried to live his life by it, he became a grotesque and the truth he embraced became a falsehood" (*Winesburg* 24). He is careful to use a lowercase *t* in *truth* to distinguish it from any absolute truth, by contrast *Truth* with a capital *T*, for in this hypothetical world it is people's absorption of the lowercase truths which brings distortion.

6. The Problem of Good and Evil 155

Bukawai is the most distorted character in *Jungle Tales*. Aristotle claims that "he who is unable to live in society, or has no need because he is sufficient for himself, must either be a beast or a god" (*Politics* 1.2 1253a [55]). In the case of Bukawai, the first is his reality, while the second is his delusion. While the villagers believe he "was in friendly intercourse with gods and demons" (76), just as Rabba Kega warns Tarzan, "the demons of the jungle are my slaves" (55), no one calls either witch-doctor a god. Aristotle goes on, as the case of Bukawai shows, claiming that if one is "separated from law and justice," as is in this case represented by Mbonga's village, "he is the worst [animal] of all" (1.2 1253a [55]). That he keeps company with hyenas tells the reader the beastliness of his character. Jackson declares that "an animal may epitomize the essence of personhood" (265); in this case the characteristics of the animal and the person are interchangeable. The "truth" of his self-reliance is but a cover for his ostracism. When Browne writes, "There are no grotesques in nature" (30), one of the earliest uses of the word in this sense, he means that perversion of nature makes one a grotesque. This self-reliance that Bukawai insists on, by default, distorts his sense of community; his quest for power is domination, first over nature, represented by the hyenas, and second over the village, shown in his attempt to manipulate its people to his own profit.

Sherlock Holmes ends "The Adventure of the Wisteria Lodge" with the claim that "there is but one step from the grotesque to the horrible" (764). It seems that last step is Bukawai's reversal of fortune, where that which he has grasped too tightly returns to bring his death, in this case the domination over the companion hyenas. In "The End of Bukawai," Tarzan is tied to a tree in the crater where Bukawai keeps his hyenas at times. He does this in a curious way; the narrator says he tied him in such a way that his hands remained free but could not reach the knots. Thomas Yeates shows one such way that this might be accomplished by securing his upper arms to the bole of the tree in a preliminary sketch for *Tarzan: The Lost Adventure*. The purpose is clearly so that Tarzan can find some limited defense against the animals to prolong the struggle. The narrator points out that the hyenas "had been fed in this manner before" (113). The narration implies that Bukawai's perverted sense of delight can be found in watching the destruction of others. When Tarzan wears the rope thin and breaks free, Bukawai's reversal of fortune begins. Tarzan ties Bukawai in his place and leaves him to the fate that the witch-doctor had intended for Tarzan, knowing that the kicked and cuffed hyenas will, of habit, return, but that Bukawai will not be able to fend them off. Farmer calls Bukawai's death "horrible, but poetically just" (*Tarzan Alive* 286).

The next most appropriate candidates for the label *grotesque* are the male Oparians, not present in *Jungle Tales*, but related by their grotesquery to the witch-doctor. In the previous novel, twice Burroughs referred to the priests of Opar as grotesque: first, when Tarzan is stealing the gold and remembering his previous experience in Opar (*Jewels* 24), and next when La is fuming at Tarzan's rejection of her and comparing his form to the priests (65). In *The Return of*

Tarzan, the narrator describes these men as "grotesque parodies upon humanity who inhabit the ruins of Opar" (206); even their city is a parody of what a city should be. These are the truly hyphenated ape-men, for it was rumored that there had been interbreeding with apes in generations past which caused them to be deformed and bestial. Opar epitomizes the truth grasped too tightly in its eon-long isolation and its perpetuation of ritual even after meaning had crumbled away.

Both Bukawai and the priests of Opar show their distortion physically. Not all grotesques, as Anderson suggests, are identifiable by physical deformity. One of the best examples of a grotesque, in Andersonian terms, is Mbonga. He sees one way to lead his people, through manipulation and deception, and, just like Bukawai, he does not let concern for others keep him from his "truth."

Before Anderson defined this type of grotesque, Henrik Ibsen created one in the character of Gregors Werle. Gregors is much the opposite of Mbonga in terms of plot, but suffers from the same inflexibility that distorts their sense of place. Gregors finds that

An early draft by Thomas Yeates of Tarzan tied to a tree for *Tarzan: The Lost Adventure* published in *Twixt Two Worlds* No. 2. Copyright Thomas Yeates. All rights reserved.

his friend Hjalmar has been deceived into marrying a woman pregnant by Gregors's father. Hjalmar and Gina are happily married, but Gregors insists, when he discovers the truth, that their marriage is based on a lie and that the lie must be exposed, which brings tragedy to the couple through the death of their daughter. It is Gregors's insistence on his own way, to the harm of others, that connects him with Mbonga. When Tarzan defeats Rabba Kega in "The God of Tarzan," Mbonga is concerned not for the health of the witch-doctor but the economic ramifications that will come to him through a loss of respect for the establishment. Though Mbonga was the village chief, and should have had the

6. The Problem of Good and Evil   157

welfare of the community foremost, the narrator reveals that he "used the superstitious fears of his people to his own ends through the medium of the medicine-man." Scams were frequent by Mbonga and the witch-doctor, who "worked together and divided the spoils" (57). His creed is the inverse of Gregors, who insists that the truth be revealed; for Mbonga, the truth of the witch-doctor's inefficacy must never be revealed. It is from grasping this "truth" so tightly that his village suffers. And this is but one mark of the grotesqueness marking Mbonga, who is more recognizable in civilization, perhaps, than the more extreme Bukawai.

"The hyenas are hungry— they howl for food"
—*King Solomon's Mines* (Haggard 96)

Holtsmark says, "With the possible exception of [...] Dango the hyena, no animal is wholly 'bad' in Tarzan's universe" (85). In the natural world, of course, the hyena has an important place. While it is known for its scavenging, the hyena is also a capable hunter. It has been known to send lions and leopards away from their kills prematurely, and makes its own kills at least as often as it takes the already-dead. Its teeth are particularly well-suited to crushing bone, which allows it to eat where other animals have been unable.

Hyenas are generally seen as a symbol of subservience and dangerous cowardice. They are traditionally known as "filthy, sly nocturnal scavenger[s]" (Tembo 53). When they approach Tibo, a little boy, they do so with "caution and cowardice" (103), as the lone hyena in "The Battle for Teeka" does the body of Gazan. Yet, these same animals attempt to take down Tarzan in their familiar crater, in "The End of Bukawai." Teddy Roosevelt, along with Edmund Hiller, wrote in *Life-Histories of African Game Animals*, "[T]he hyena is a singular mixture of abject cowardice and the utmost ferocity." These animals "often hesitat[e] to attack even the weakest animal if it is unhurt and on its guard," but it will sometimes "assail very formidable creatures" (215).

A scene in *Tarzan and the Jewels of Opar* depicts them in their stereotypical reserve:

> [A] pair of hyenas slunk presently into view. They trotted to a point a few yards from the gorging ape-man, and halted. Tarzan looked up, bared his fighting fangs and growled. The hyenas returned the compliment, and withdrew a couple of paces. They made no move to attack; but continued to sit at a respectful distance until Tarzan had concluded his meal. [... H]e walked slowly off in the direction of the river to quench his thirst. His way lay directly toward the hyenas, nor did he alter his course because of them.
>
> With all the lordly majesty of Numa, the lion, he strode straight toward the growling beasts. For a moment they held their ground, bristling and defiant; but only for a moment, and then slunk away to one side while the indifferent ape-man passed

them on his lordly way. A moment later they were tearing at the remains of the zebra [*Jewels* 61].

The patience demonstrated here, while attributed to fear, may also indicate the intelligence of the animal, in weighing its options. Patience can come more easily to those who will have food when others can no longer eat. The hyena watching over Harry in Hemingway's "The Snows of Kilimanjaro" marks not so much the cowardice of the animal but the intelligent patience that tells it dead men make no resistance.

In the folklore of the Beng people of Côte d'Ivoire, the hyena "always displays greed coupled with stupidity," says Alma Gottleib. This "stupidity prevents him from indulging his greed to his full satisfaction" (488). The association between Bukawai and the hyenas is mutually significant. Bukawai's greed gets him into trouble, and his lack of forethought (a kind of stupidity, perhaps) in dealing with Mbonga and Tarzan leads to his downfall. The hyena of African mythology is also identified as "morally bankrupt" (Gottleib 488), a characteristic that most readers would readily ascribe to Bukawai as well. Jackson verifies: "The hyena's stupidity lies in his inability to empathize with others; therefore he cannot form moral judgments by putting himself in another person's place" (112). The irony, in this application, though, is that Bukawai does literally get put in another's place. Even though Burroughs insisted that "Tarzan does not preach" ("Tarzan Theme" 29), the ready lesson of these stories is as apparent as that of traditional folktales. The temptation to add a moral is strong in many places, as David Anthony Kraft does at the end of "The Fangs of Death," Marvel's adaptation of "The Lion": "Today, young Tarzan learned the folly of carrying a joke too far" (31). The problem, according to Jackson, is that the hyena, and the reader can readily add Bukawai here, "lives in a world of emotion and impulse, a world pervaded by his own subjectivity" (112). Bukawai is unable to see himself as part of something larger. His subjective world does not extend beyond his own dying senses. Regarding the hyena, Gottleib summarizes, "The implication is that in the end, greed, which is incompatible with wisdom, will always be thwarted. The temptation to satisfy unreasonable desires at the expense of others is doomed to defeat" (489). Gottleib may just as well have been commenting on the stories of Bukawai. His attempt to profit from the misfortune of others, sometimes of his own doing and sometimes not, marks a greed devoid of wisdom. His greed, that avarice found in the Seven Deadly Sins, is the predominant force compelling him to his grisly end.

To be related to a hyena is a traditional insult. When Taug and Tarzan are fighting over Teeka, she "call[s] them vile names, [including] Dango, the hyena" (11). Tarzan, likewise torments the lion, "calling him eater of carrion and brother of Dango, the hyena" (25). Tarzan finds disgust in the hyena (along with his own kind), because "[o]nly man and Dango ate until they swelled up like a dead rat" (131). Bukawai's choice of companion, then, reflects his low status outside the community. The man and the animal lend derision to each other's reputations. In "The Witch-Doctor Seeks Vengeance," the animals are introduced in the following manner: "[B]eside [Bukawai], equally hideous, stood two powerful hyenas—carrion-eaters consorting with carrion" (94). Likewise in "Tarzan and the Black Boy," the narrator calls them "the most repulsive of beasts with the most repulsive of humans" (82). In the previous book, Burroughs had melded the image into one, when Tarzan comes across a witch-doctor who wears "the skin of a hyena about his shoulders and the dried head mounted upon his grey pate" (*Jewels* 19). This unnamed man had been a witch-doctor in Mbonga's village when Kulonga was slain, if his testimony is to be trusted. Since both Bukawai and Rabba Kega die in *Jungle Tales*, it cannot be either of them. That there were multiple witch-doctors in the village is never verified, though when Rabba Kega dies, "[a]lready Tubuto, young, agile and evil-minded, [...] was practicing the black art" (167). The timeframe is sketchy. Both Hanson and Farmer indicate that Mbonga's village existed in Tarzan's part of the jungle for a little more than two years (26 and 28 months, respectively), and both agree that Rabba Kega's death occurred in the second half of this time. Whoever followed Rabba Kega could have practiced in Mbonga's village from one year (Hanson) to less than eight months (Farmer), before French soldiers decimated the place. This young man may have survived and misremembered or exaggerated his precise coming to power. The important connection is his wearing of the hyena skin, complete with head, marking his position.

The two hyenas living with Bukawai have other associations. In Mbonga's village, they "were commonly known to be devils masquerading" (76). The hyena has long been associated with witchcraft in African folklore. Because of this, they have been seen as shape shifters, and many consider killing a hyena to bring bad luck. Bukawai's choice, then, seems even more appropriate than it first may have appeared.

The witch-doctor is forced to live alone far to the north of Mbonga's village, because of his disease. The hyena of African folklore is also regarded as anti-social, certainly the condition of Bukawai. Where he came from originally is never identified. But his hyenas, not the people, are his companions. David J. Sapir has suggested that the "hyena and leper are similar" (527). In Kujamaat Diola tradition (Senegal), the dead body of a hyena is treated as if it were a person; one of Sapir's sources confirmed "it might be a person" (527). It is treated with respect out of fear of the "spirit acting on behalf of the dead hyena" (532). This is the only animal treated so. The leper's corpse, on the other hand, is buried much as a dog would bury something, by backward dragging of the feet to cover it with dirt. No fear of the leper's spirit is shown. This transference of character connects the leper and the hyena symbolically, just as Burroughs does literally in these stories. In Kujamaat belief, "a leper might well be a hyena" and a "hyena at any time might in fact be a transformed human" (Sapir 533). The trio formed by Bukawai and his hyena companions, then, is in belief potentially three people. The purposes, though, of a human taking on the hyena form are largely twofold, in Kujamaat belief, for the killing of cattle and for the exhuming of dead people, neither a quality appreciated by the community. Conceptually the crossing of the leper and hyena identities comes this way, for Sapir: "A leper is conceptually dissimulated from his humanness just as a hyena [...] is conceptually dissimulated from its animalness" (537). The eeriness of this combination makes Bukawai all the more unapproachable. The hyenas, more than just a visual symbol of carrion, represent the moral and social decay that all mark the villain of this story. And who is to say that Bukawai was not a hyena all along.

Chapter 7

Painful Laughter in "The Lion" and "A Jungle Joke"

Both "The Lion" and "A Jungle Joke" deal with Tarzan's attempt at disguise, with both humorous and serious ramifications. These stories are paired more for their thematic relationship than for matters of continuous plot, though the lion and its skin do join these stories at several points.

"The Lion," the eighth published in the cycle, "describes Tarzan's exciting attempt to teach the lesson of preparedness to the ape-tribe — and the painful consequences to himself," as the *Blue Book* (April 1917) contents page said in luring readers. Burroughs wrote the story over Christmas (22–29 December 1916), his last writing of the year. The *Des Moines Sunday Register* confusingly re-titled the story as "Jungle Joke"; the story that Burroughs titled "A Jungle Joke" was renamed "Tarzan's Prank." The story has been adapted to comic form in Charlton's *Jungle Tales of Tarzan* #4 (July 1965) and Marvel's *Tarzan* #12 (May 1978), re-titled "Fangs of Death."

In the first of these stories, Tarzan unites the ape tribe against an invading lion. They pursue the lion and retrieve the body of the slain comrade, Mamka. Tarzan urges his fellow apes to post sentries, so that others do not suffer similarly. While watching Rabba Kega perform in the village with a buffalo head, Tarzan spots a lion skin. He procures it and returns, with Manu, the monkey, to the ape tribe. Tarzan dons the lion skin and strolls into the area. (This same lion skin takes on an important role in "A Jungle Joke.") Gunto, a fellow ape, sounds the alarm and begins stoning him. A large stone thrown by Taug renders the disguised ape-man unconscious. Before the apes can pulverize the corpse, Manu flies into their midst and reveals the ruse. Tarzan rouses, embarrassed that he did not receive his expected laugh but pleased the apes had heeded his instruction, and almost swears off practical joking.

The impulse to teach others through disguise here is similar to Odysseus's return to Ithaca, as Holtsmark points out. Homer's Odysseus wants to determine who has been loyal to him while he was away. He adopts a disguise, must fight to make his way, and in the end determines the faithfulness of his wife, son, and dog. The second half of *The Odyssey* details Odysseus's efforts, disguised as a beggar, to infiltrate his own home. This same impulse is Tarzan's as he attempts to enter his own tribe disguised as a lion to determine if they have been attentive to his instruction to post sentries. Odysseus must fight an entire hall of betrayers, detailed in Book 22. Just as in Pope's translation "Up rose the throngs tumultuous" (22.28) at the dangerous stranger in their midst, so too does Tarzan endure the apes "pelting him unmercifully" (127). Odysseus is aided by his son, Telemachus, against the others, just as Tarzan is aided by Manu, the monkey, and in the end by Taug and Teeka.

Blue Book editors warned their readers that the second story here, "A Jungle Joke," "show[ed] the jungle-bred white boy revealing a grim and disturbing sense of humor to a hostile native tribe" (contents page, July 1917). The *Philadelphia Evening Public Ledger* added the subhead: "Tarzan Changes Himself From a Man to a Lion and Saves Numa" (9 August 1919). The story has been adapted to comic form in Charlton's *Jungle Tales of Tarzan* #4 (July 1965), Gold Key's *Tarzan of the Apes* #170 (Aug. 1967), and Marvel's *Tarzan* #13 (June 1978) re-titled "The Changeling."

In this story, Tarzan watches Mbonga's tribesmen building a lion trap. Tarzan remembers seeing lions tortured in the village previously and decides he will set free the lion that the trap apprehends. After taking the bait from the trap, Tarzan follows the warriors who are returning to the village. Among them is Rabba Kega. Tarzan resists twitching while a poisonous insect investigates him; the insect leaves Tarzan and alights on Rabba Kega who squashes it at the moment of its sting. While the poison might bring slow death, Tarzan has other plans. Tarzan abducts the witch-doctor and binds him in the lion trap. The next morning, the tribesmen find a black-maned lion in the trap with Rabba Kega's mauled corpse. The villagers haul the filled trap back to the village. Tarzan takes his lion skin to the village and amid the dancing, steps out into the crowd, roaring. Panic strikes, and, as they flee, Tarzan sloughs off the skin and reveals himself. Though frightened, the villagers realize that Tarzan can transform himself into a lion, or vice versa. Tarzan frees the caged lion and takes to the trees to watch the warriors try to provoke the lion to take his human form, at the cost of many tribesmen.

The character of Mbonga's villagers has already been found morally questionable. The capture of the lion is perhaps understandable, but the intent to torture rings despicable in most cultures. "To torment, for no good reason, a creature which is captive and helpless," writes Midgley, "does seem to most people objectionable in itself" regardless of circumstances (17). This circumstance sets readers against Mbonga's people, even if they know nothing of the previous grievances Tarzan has against them.

Burroughs wrote "A Jungle Joke" between 12 February and the end of the month, 1917. He mailed it 16 March. Ray Long objected to the ending by overnight lettergram, noting that he needed a "new ending making this [a] complete story" and asking for a new revision by special delivery. Burroughs telegraphed his response that the next story was on its way, which Long might substitute, or Long could change the story himself. Long did print "The Battle

7. Painful Laughter in "The Lion" and "A Jungle Joke"

for Teeka" next, presumably to allow time for someone to edit "A Jungle Joke." Early in the story the reference to "his recent battle with Bolgani, the gorilla, the wounds of which were but just healed" and to the "strange sleep adventures," both of which occurred in "The Nightmare" (161), supports the original order of composition, which Hanson accounts for in his chrono-log by restoring its place before "The Battle for Teeka." (Farmer, on the other hand, puts this story as the last of the tales, within weeks of Tarzan's ascendency to the kingship of the tribe.)

Burroughs was tying up loose ends in Los Angeles and preparing to return to Chicago as U.S. involvement in World War I grew more imminent, and he had no wish to be further burdened by the short stories. Though he did not say so in his telegram to Long, his journal indicates that he had already finished the twelfth story as well, and he was likely not in the frame of mind to pull the project back out. Too, he had determined earlier, when working out unsatisfying revisions on *The Outlaw of Torn*, that rewriting was more difficult for him than the original effort, more stressful and more time-consuming. At that point, he had told Metcalf, his editor, "I hate patching [...] and this may have accounted for the poor results" (letter 20 December 1912).

From the present ending, which Burroughs retained for book publication, Long's objection is unclear. What changes Long made are not documented. Apparently, Burroughs did not keep or receive in return a copy of his version of the story, since his usual pattern was to restore changes made by his magazine editors when the book version went to press, as he did with the opening paragraphs of "The Witch-Doctor Seeks Vengeance." Likely, with a cross-country trip looming, he kept no copy to carry back to Chicago.

Typically Burroughs resisted changes in his manuscripts, with the exception of spelling and grammar. It would not be until much later in his career that he would agree to changes in his stories; ironically, again, with a Tarzan short story, this one entitled "Tarzan and the Jungle Murders." Leo Margulies, editor at *Thrilling Adventures*, wrote that Burroughs had "a good story in the yarn," but that "its present shape" was unacceptable; Margulies had an editor revise the story, indicating that "most of the changes have been in re-arranging the story" to make Tarzan's presence more prominent, which he asked Burroughs to approve (letter 25 October 1939). In 1939, near the end of his career, Burroughs accepted the tampering without a fight, indicating by return mail that he had "changed the names of some of the animals [...] to conform with [the] other Tarzan stories" as his only adjustment (letter 30 October 1939).

These two stories provide a number of areas of interest leading from the exploration of the nature of the lion to the mythological figure of the trickster.

"He might have passed for a lion, but for his ears."
—*Narrative of the Life of Frederick Douglass* (Douglass 83)

The lion, for Burroughs, is always black-maned. Darwin suggested that the lion developed a mane as a way to pad the effects of frontal attack. Scientists now consider that conclusion suspect. According to Peyton M. West and Craig Packer, the color, or more precisely the darkness, of the mane is an indicator of health. "Dark-maned males," they conclude, "enjoy longer reproductive life-spans and higher offspring survival" (1339). The darker the mane is, the more virile the animal. The length of the mane, they say, is related to the temperature of the habitat. One lion, believed to have descended from the Cape lion subspecies, based on the size and darkness of the mane, was identified at the beginning of this century, after more than a century of "extinction"; the Cape lion, which should have been geographically south of Tarzan's range, is noted for the huge dark mane that wraps behind the shoulders and covers parts of the stomach. The Barbary lion, now extinct but not in Burroughs' day, also is known for its size and long dark mane; its range was farther north than Tarzan's assumed location. It may have been the largest of the lion subspecies, and Burroughs could have had either of these specimens in mind. Tarzan doesn't battle anything but the most powerful lions, it seems. Also, since Tarzan meets lions in the jungle, rather than the open plain, the dark mane may be a useful adaptation for camouflage in the shadows of the trees.

Literature is characterized by comparisons, both explicit and implicit. Of the wild animals often compared to humans, the lion is perhaps the most frequently invoked. The comparison of a person with a lion is instructive. As Holtsmark points out, in Homer's *The Iliad*, lions are characterized as strong and aggressive attackers. Tydides, for example, fights like "a hungry lion [that] has o'erleape'd / The sheepfold" (5.163–64; see also 10.539–42), and every hemmed-in Greek, like a cornered lion, "firm he stands / With suicidal courage" (12.49–50). When Achilles comes against Aeneas in battle, he charges [f]ierce as a rav'ning lion" (20.190) ; then, wounded Achilles advances

> [...] with gaping jaws,
> And frothing fangs, collecting for the spring,
> His breast too narrow for his mighty heart;
> And with his tail he lashes both his flanks
> And sides, as though to rouse his utmost rage;
> Then on in pride of strength, with glaring eyes
> He dashes, if some hunter he may slay,
> Or on the foremost rank himself be slain [20.194–201].

Achilles here takes on the characteristics of the lion in his mannerisms and recklessness. Likewise, when Tarzan rushes upon Mbonga, in "The God of Tarzan," the narrator gives to Tarzan the characteristics of the lion. In the confrontation, the explicit comparison with the lion is reserved for the end of the pursuit. Tarzan "sprang" at Mbonga and "covered the distance between them in great leaps" (58), before the narrator adds "at the speed of a charging lion." To ground the comparison, the narrator adds: "He was growling, too, not at all unlike Numa himself" (58).

As referent, the lioness's bravery is also linked to Lady Alice, Tarzan's mother, as she comes to the aid of her husband, who is under attack. She not only overcame her fear of guns, but also "rushed toward the ape [that was attacking John] with the fearlessness of a lioness protecting its young" (*Apes* 23). It is after this attack that Lady Alice collapses and gives birth to her son, never to regain her complete awareness again. Holtsmark points out that many writers before Burroughs employed "a paradigm of the exemplary courage of a parent protecting its offspring" (56) through the image of the lion. The fact that her offspring is in utero at the time actually enhances the comparison, because she believes the child cannot grow without the protection and provision of the father, who is the direct object of Lady Alice's protection. As a further extension of the idea, Tarzan is indeed protected later by Kala in the very image invoked here, when she snatches him from the cabin during Kerchak's rampage.

In Proverbs 30.30, Agur identifies the lion as "strongest among beasts, [who] turneth not away for any." It is one of four things that "go well" and are "comely in going" (30.29). The lion's natural majesty is inherent in the narrator's statement in "The End of Bukawai." The "ragged streamers" of clouds "whipped" by the wind "reminded Tarzan of frightened antelope fleeing the charge of a hungry lion" (109). The sound of the wind is compared to the "moaning" of lions, and Tarzan says to himself, "The lions seek their prey" (110). Tarzan speaks metaphorically here. He does not believe the sound comes from a literal lion. Instead he sees it as a likeness, a spiritual manifestation. When these lions of nature arrive in the form of the storm, flattening the treetops, Tarzan murmurs, "The lions pass" (110). The lightning and thunder represent the spring and the kill of the unseen lions and the rain is the blood of their many victims. Similarly, in "Tarzan Rescues the Moon," the stars are the eyes of animals, particularly Numa and Sabor, the lion and the lioness.

Many authors have invoked animal parallels in characters in their works. Dickens, in *A Tale of Two Cities*, profits from the comparison to animals when he refers to Mr. Stryver and Sydney Carton by their predatory characteristics. In regard to Carton's character flaw, the narrator writes, "[A]lthough Sydney Carton would never be a lion, he was an amazingly good jackal" (65). Here, of course, it is the jackal that eventually displays the noblest character, despite his low-light introduction.

More than ten years after naming the lion Numa, Burroughs said in a letter to his brother, "Sometimes I must unconsciously use a word or name that I have read and forgotten, as for instance Numa the lion. There was a Roman emperor, Numa, of whom I had forgotten until I was recently rereading Plutarch's *Lives*" (letter to Harry Burroughs; qtd. in Porges 194). This is a case of an unconscious association where the magnificence that Burroughs attached to the lion, its kingly quality especially, is linked to the Roman conqueror and ruler. And in English history, no one forgets Richard, the king with the heart of a lion.

At the Chicago World's Fair, young Burroughs quite likely visited Carl Hagenbeck's Arena of Wild Animals which included "a giant lion riding [...] on horseback" (McDowell 409). In *The Son of Tarzan*, Burroughs incorporates a scene where the tutor to the young Greystoke reports the boy intelligent though uninterested in his studies, preferring to read about "savage beasts" and "uncivilized peoples"; the tutor continues: "[U]pon two occasions I have found him sitting up in bed at night reading Carl Hagenbeck's book on men and beasts" (14). Taliaferro's speculates that the interest Burroughs gave to lions in his fiction may have grown directly from his experience at the Chicago Exposition.

In "Tarzan and the Black Boy," Tarzan imagines the lion "straining futilely" against the ropes (64). David Adams claims this is because of his subconscious understanding that "Numa's capture or death would signal the coming of his manhood" ("Twelve"). Mark de Brito has pointed out that among West African peoples, a lion-headed mask is used as a part of the circumcision ceremony, that is the formal introduction for a young man to be seen as an adult warrior. Similarly, Adams urges the reader to consider the cub that has died (*Jungle Tales* 80) "as the ending of Tarzan's youth" ("Twelve"). This parallels the struggle with Numa, where Tarzan saves Tibo, the first lion kill recorded for Tarzan in his literary chronology. When Tarzan lets loose the lion near the end of "A Jungle Joke," and its roar apprises the villagers of its all-too-real nature, Burroughs recapitulates a portion of the manhood ceremony, during which the spiritual leader wearing the lion head "roars through the village, terrifying the candidates and everyone within earshot" (de Brito 174). Tarzan's superiority is marked by his victory over the lion. While he did not kill the lion in "A Jungle Joke," as early as "Tarzan and the Black Boy," he has defeated Numa. When Blanch, in Shakespeare's *King John*, says, "O, well did he become that lion's robe / That did disrobe the lion of that robe!" (2.1.143–44), the point is clear that anyone who defeats the lion in combat is worthy of the accolades accorded the lion itself, in this case represented by the very taking on of the skin. Mbonga's warriors, faced with the opportunity to become "men," as the manhood ceremony suggests, fail to overcome, taking refuge instead in the trees outside the village.

The idea of someone disguised as a lion has been used interestingly by later writers. In particular, C.S. Lewis employs the lion-skin disguise as a major motif in the concluding book of his Narnia tales, *The Last Battle*. The ape, Shift, and his sidekick, Puzzle the donkey, discover a lion skin that had been prepared by a hunter then lost. Shift sees the possibilities of it, over Puzzle's hesitation. Puzzle objects fragmentarily "the other beasts might think—" (6), without completing his precise thought, if he had a precise thought. It is Shift's idea to pass Puzzle off as a lion. In this case, the holy fear of the lion comes from the deified form of Aslan, who appears frequently as a lion. The impersonation of a lion, then, is also the impersonation of God. Similarly, Tarzan's appearance in Mbonga's village as a lion, incorporates a supernatural element. The cover

7. Painful Laughter in "The Lion" and "A Jungle Joke" 167

The cover of the June 1978 Marvel comics featuring Tarzan disguised as a lion. Art by John Buscema and Rudy Mesina. Copyright Edgar Rice Burroughs, Inc. All rights reserved.

of Marvel's adaptation, re-titled "The Changeling," shows Tarzan threatening with arms outstretched, his back, arms, and head covered by the lion skin. The speech bubble boasts: "Men of Mbonga! Your spears will avail you nothing—when the lion-god strikes!" (Thomas). Interestingly, this scene does not exist inside the comic book, which holds closer to Burroughs' text. The sham that Shift perpetrates, in Lewis's book, is precisely the kind of hypocrisy that Burroughs denigrates in his writing, where one pretends to spiritual power to gain personal authority and material. In Lewis's book, the ape takes advantage of the beliefs of the other inhabitants to provide for his own comfort and wealth—until the real Aslan arrives. In a sense, this is what Rabba Kega does with his buffalo head, not until a real buffalo arrives, but until one arrives who sees the difference between the buffalo head and the buffalo, between the lion skin and the lion. Tarzan's removal of Rabba Kega from the village sets the scene for Shift's removal from Narnia. The ape dies when he is devoured by the monster-god Tash, whom he has said Puzzle also represents, destroyed by the powers he tried to manipulate.

The lion leads the list of animal comparisons, both positive and negative, whereby a reader comes to understand a little deeper the nature of humans. Tarzan's lion traits get him both into and out of trouble.

> "Ah! Of course, you must have a leader. And I did not think of that before!"
> — the Comtesse de Tourney, *The Scarlet Pimpernel* (Orczy 34)

The absence of Kerchak in these tales makes it possible to highlight the training ground that the tribe provides for Tarzan. Tarzan's growth in leadership is an important part of the collection as a whole. In "Tarzan's First Love," the ape-boy—a term used 16 times in that story, but only twice thereafter (in "The God of Tarzan" and "The End of Bukawai")—is portrayed as a distinct but far-from-important member of Kerchak's tribe of apes. The use of the term "ape-boy" affirms his undeveloped identity. From *Tarzan of the Apes*, the reader knows that Tarzan's role as king of the apes comes after his defeat of Kerchak, an event which must occur after the events of *Jungle Tales*, though Kerchak himself does not appear here. Rather, the apes are referred to by Kerchak's name throughout; a reader who begins with this collection must wonder what this referenced name is, while a reader who has read *Tarzan of the Apes* must wonder at his personal absence. Tarzan's role as leader is initiated, though, in the first story when he tries to direct the actions of his fellow apes in rescuing Teeka from the panther attack. Here, no one listens, and Tarzan is left to defend Teeka on his own, setting an unheeded example.

Much more prominent is Tarzan's role by the final story of the collection,

"Tarzan Rescues the Moon." In this story, along with Taug, Tarzan stands up to the rest of the tribe in protecting the — from the apes' point of view — enemy of the tribe, Bulabantu. After this confrontation, Tarzan retreats to the cabin from which he is later summoned by Taug to save the moon, which has apparently entered into an eclipse (though Hanson suggests less believably the perception may have been caused by a cloud). After the visible success of Tarzan's actions in restoring the moon, the narrator notes: "[H]e took a long stride toward the kingship, which he ultimately won, for now the apes looked up to him as a superior being" (190–91). The reference to Tarzan's ultimate defeat of Kerchak cues the reader back into the original narrative from *Tarzan of the Apes* (80–82), just as reference to the death of Kala in the first story (*Jungle Tales* 16–17) served as a marker for the readers' exit point from that same narrative.

This collection of twelve stories, at least on some level, serves as Tarzan's more detailed rise in leadership, glossed over in the first novel. Departing as it does with the death of his foster mother, the reader can see Tarzan working out his grief simultaneously with his development of leadership. Sharon Olson has pointed out that "[g]rief has the potential to be a *transformative process* [...]," changing someone "into a wiser and quite different individual" (viii). It is no accident that Kala's death predates the first story. It is an important catalyst for Tarzan's maturation, as he must learn to rely on himself and the tribe instead of parental protection. John Schneider, in his foreword to Olson's book, points out that when a person "experience[s] a significant loss, the protective veneer of [...] self-image can be stripped away," leaving her or him "lonely, helpless, empty" (ix). The grieving process, though, "with time and support," leads one to discover "what it takes to empower" (ix). Tarzan's growing leadership abilities, culminating after the collection with the ascendancy to the leadership of the tribe, come through his personal processing of the grief and resulting alienation that begins the collection.

Holtsmark claims that his leadership of the apes is beneficial because Tarzan's "greater intelligence can both conceive and execute plans that are conducive to the betterment of their life" (96). That Holtsmark uses the plural pronoun for "life" indicates that the tribe works as a single unit, that what is good for the community is good for the individual. The most important event to demonstrate this comes in "The Lion," when Tarzan sees the death of Mamka as both corporate and personal. Though the ape cannot be revived, the tribe can profit from teaching at least one lion that there is a price to pay for preying on the mangani. He also knows that removing the reward, the feast Mamka's body will make, will go far in dissuading Numa from seeing apes as fair game. Getting the apes to cooperate with him, though, represents an abnormal collaboration. Rather than reason with them, he must provide an example that they will understand and readily follow. The narrator explains the situation in this manner: "He knew that when once they had seen him carry out his idea they would be much quicker to follow his lead than to obey his instructions" (119), because Tarzan was an abnormality, not an authority in the tribe. He knew the apes' propensity for mimicry. So Tarzan sets the example of how he wants the apes to respond, while telling them the reasons for his strange behavior. "So now Tarzan led where he could not yet command" (120). The most difficult part of Tarzan's plan is finding a reliable decoy, a dangerous role for any of the tribe, someone agile and "equally as brave" as Tarzan (121). In the collection, no bull ape approaches Tarzan in intelligence and reliability more closely than Taug. His cooperation is crucial in the rescue. The effective recovery of the body is gratifying to the tribe. The success of this daring rescue raises Tarzan's corporate authority, because the benefit is to the tribe rather than to an individual. When in later weeks, a child is taken by a panther, Tarzan, because of the leadership he showed in recovering Mamka's body, is able to argue with authority for the implementation of a sentry system.

The by-product of this system is that the apes "scattered less than had been their wont" (124). The refusal to follow whim above parameters set by the sentries is the beginning of maturity. It requires self-control. Self-control is an essential quality of any leader, and the rudiment shown by the apes at this point serves to highlight the greater proportion of that quality in Tarzan. Tarzan is, after all, the example for the rest in this matter. It requires, on his part, the conscious choice to let reason rule over emotions. "Dealing with the emotions is not an easy task for any man," David Adams points out ("Folklorist" 6). But it is just such self-mastery that Tarzan is able to accomplish that allows him to rise above his world. Holtsmark believes that Tarzan "has mastery over the environment to a large extent, but more important, over himself" ("Classical Line" 4). In "A Jungle Joke," Tarzan shows such self-mastery when he follows Mbonga's warriors rather than eat the meat he has taken from their lion trap. The narrator explains: "He was hungry. Had he been all beast he would have eaten; but his man-mind could entertain urges even more potent than those of the belly, and now he was concerned with an idea [...] which permitted him to forget that he was hungry" (164). Tarzan makes a conscious choice in the matter that overrules instinct. Jackson points out that "[t]he problem of choice therefore resolves itself into a problem of moderation, and the problem of controlling the world becomes the same as the problem of self-control" (232). Tarzan's ability to master his jungle surroundings is directly related to his self-control. His moderation keeps him from making mistakes that would subjugate him to raw nature. The triumph of reason over instinct is crucial.

That the apes retained their sentry system longer than Tarzan expected their short-sighted brains to allow credits Tarzan's influence on this particular tribe of apes. And, at the end of "The Lion," it is nearly his undoing. "[A]s the leader is, so will his followers be" (Scott 279), Ivanhoe says as a principle of human nature or, in the mangani's case, quasi-human nature; Tarzan's beating was of his own making because he suffers from the very principle he had taught. Just as he had taught them to defy the lion at the taking of Mamka, so now his own assailing reflects the exact training he had given.

With a little imagination, a reader might well see a genteel mirroring of the rule by example at work in Jane Austen's *Mansfield Park*. As if in Greystoke castle, Edmund tells Maria, when he learns of an upcoming private performance of a play, of which he disapproves, "[I]t is *you* who are to lead" in dissuading the others from continuing; "*You* must set the example" (114, italics original). Maria, as one of the cast, has no power to cancel the production, nor, she tells Edmund, could she "undertake to harangue all the rest" (114). Edmund counters her with the principle that Tarzan understands, at the literal level, when he says to her "let your conduct be the only harangue" (115). Just as a mirror reverses the direction of the image within, and just as the effete Lord Greystoke seems to run the opposite in disposition from his jungle cousin, so Maria chooses to follow peer pressure rather than take up Edmund's challenge to amend the present course. Edmund understood the way to lead, though he failed to transfer that successfully to Maria.

Tarzan has better success in his venture of the sentries. It is this event that serves as the pivotal point in his ability to lead. When he rises to the position of king, he already has the respect of the tribe and their cooperation. The title of kingship is as notable as much as Kerchak's presence in this collection, that is, a name only.

"Fine fellows — cannibals — in their place."
— *Heart of Darkness* (Conrad 50)

Cannibalism was generally attributed to the unknown world in the nineteenth century. Baroness Orczy wrote in her historical novel *The Scarlet Pimpernel*, that at the time of the French Revolution the "typical rural John Bull" believed "the rest of the world an unexploited land of savages and cannibals" (14). Darwin reports, in *The Voyage of the* Beagle, that the inhabitants of Tierra del Fuego resort to cannibalism to supplement dwindling food supplies. There, when necessary, it is the least able to aid the group that is selected to become the next meal, typically the old women. Darwin also reported cannibalism in New Zealand. Livingstone, Stanley, and du Chaillu all refer to the African inhabitants as savages and cannibals. Angene Wilson points out that "[a] 1911 geography" textbook, the same year that Burroughs wrote his first novel, attached "'a general prevalence of cannibalism'" (43) to Africans. Burroughs' readers, then, would have given little thought to the presence of cannibals in Tarzan's jungle.

Other literary sources had adopted the cannibal as an exotic character in fiction. The first popular novel, *Robinson Crusoe*, included Friday and the band of cannibals from whom he was rescued. Queequeg, half a century before Burroughs wrote, represented the cannibal in *Moby Dick*. And Tonga, in Conan Doyle's *The Sign of Four*, appeared 25 years before Burroughs' first book.

The image of the cannibal was one of many riding the surf of the popular imagination at the end of the nineteenth century. Kilgour writes: "The definition of the other as cannibal justifies its oppression, extermination, and cultural cannibalism (otherwise known as imperialism) by the rule of 'eat or be eaten'" (148).

As a part of the imperialistic mindset, the shorthand of the stereotypical cannibal became well grounded. The mention of sharpened teeth, for instance, in a work signaled the suspicion of cannibalism. Heathcliff, in *Wuthering Heights*, is described as having "sharp cannibal teeth" (Bronte 161), where the code is explained. Bronte may have remembered such a description from Olaudah Equiano's *Interesting Narrative*, where he passed into a people who "ornamented themselves with scars and likewise filed their teeth very sharp" (52). Burroughs does the same thing in "Tarzan and the Black Boy," when he introduces Momaya: "Her teeth were filed to sharp points, for her people ate the flesh of man" (69). Bukawai, likewise, is noted for "his sharp-filed teeth, the teeth of a cannibal" (94). Once the code is revealed, the mention of the teeth for the cannibal streamlines the description. In "The Nightmare," an old man is identified by "his filed teeth" (131), just as Conrad identifies his native worker's "filed teeth" (*Heart* 52) as a marker of his ultimate indomesticability.

As noted in chapter five, the prisoner of war is the victim most often identified for the cannibalistic celebration. In a bellicose society, this is a reasonable indicator of a warrior's prowess. Montaigne, in his early essay "Of the Caniballes," points out that such a person "brings home the head of the enemie he hath slain as a Trophey of his victorie, and fasteneth the same at the entrance of his dwelling place" (248). The reader of Conrad will recognize this situation played out at Kurtz's fortress, where decapitated heads top the poles surrounding the office, "smiling continuously at some endless and jocose dream of that eternal slumber" (Conrad 74). Whether Kurtz learned to do so from the people he was living with is not revealed. Similarly, Tarzan finds a human skull in Kulonga's hut. Apparently the heads of deceased people become invested with importance in both these cultures.

Much has been made in recent years of the role of eating in literature and in society that can be applied to the issue of cannibalism. Kilgour points out that "eating is a means of asserting and controlling individual and also cultural identity" (6). This cannibalistic identity is not one that Tarzan wants to own. But it is one area of exploration, eventually, by which he can separate himself from the villagers. No one in Mbonga's village refuses human flesh; Tarzan always does.

Mikhail Bakhtin, Kilgour says, "notes [that] one of the most important characteristics of eating is its ambivalence" (7). It provides a tension between sustenance and dominance. It is an admission of human frailty as well as an assertion of human dominance. As "an act that involves both desire and aggression, [...] it creates a total identity between eater and eaten while insisting on the total control" (Kilgour 7). When one considers eating in such terms, cannibalism becomes both a social and personal indicator. "Cannibals?"

Melville's narrator asks. "[W]ho is not a cannibal?" (321). That is, who does not attempt to dominate another?

The feast that Tarzan witnesses and then joins across Mbonga's palisade, in "The Nightmare," when read in a Bakhtinian manner, "is an indication of openness" (Kilgour 89) on the part of Mbonga, whether Tarzan is an invited guest or not. This openness reveals the inherent ambivalence, because while it shows potential friendliness (not realized in these stories) it also reveals a vulnerability. Tarzan's inclusion brings death to one villager.

The feasting reaches great excess, showing the lack of self-control among the villagers. They are the offensive type that Paul warns the Roman believers about, the type who "serve [...] their own belly" (Romans 16.18), the idolatrous type, that he warns the Philippians, "Whose end is destruction, whose God is their belly, and whose glory is in their shame" (Phil. 3.19). This god is figuratively Milton's Comus, where, as Kilgour says, "the belly is associated with fraud" (111). The act of eating, ostensibly an act of nurture, becomes its opposite, an act of destruction.

The cannibal figure in Western literature is typically an evil force to be overcome. Defoe establishes this idea when Robinson Crusoe, after twenty-some years of solitary life on the island, sees a human footprint. Rather than hope of rescue, his reaction was "the dread and terror of falling into the hands of savages and cannibals" (140). As he feared, he later comes upon the scene of the interlopers' feast, strewn "with skulls, hands, feet, and other bones of human bodies" (141). His response, as mirrored in "The Nightmare," was, as he writes, that "nature discharged the disorder from my stomach; and having vomited with uncommon violence, I was a little relieved [...]" (141). Tarzan, likewise, after visiting the scene of Mbonga's feasters (and partaking belatedly of the elephant meat), finds relief only after "nature and an outraged stomach relieved themselves in their own therapeutic manner" (*Jungle Tales* 136). Thus the cannibal is represented as incompatible with Western civilization.

Both Robinson Crusoe and Tarzan (vicariously, through his parents) have been lost — separated from the place of belonging. Robinson's shipwreck and the Greystokes' marooning set up the loss of place, which is the cousin to loss of identity. Both attempt to assert their civilized identity on the new place with limited success. Their success is limited by their lack of resources, making their new dwellings primitive compared to the country from which they came. Kilgour points out that "where shipwreck occurs, cannibalism often follows, as an even more horrifying image for the loss of human identity" (149). In both of these cases, the cannibalism is located in some other, and the hero is able to overcome its detrimental effects. Burroughs comes closest to Kilgour's claim in *The Return of Tarzan*, when Jane, Rokoff, William Clayton, and three of the sailors from the *Lady Alice*, escape the yacht's sinking. After days adrift, the suggestion of cannibalism, at first unacceptable, becomes the only rational hope, and Clayton (after he is picked/tricked by lottery) agrees to allow Rokoff to kill him so that Jane might live. But the sacrifice does not occur as planned.

Metcalf, Burroughs' editor at *All-Story*, wrote a long paragraph in response to the scene in the proposal, where it appears the cannibalism was accomplished: "I'm afraid that I must definitely taboo your suggestion concerning the cannibalism of the people in the boat where Jane and Clayton are." He continues that "it seems to be both inhuman and bad art to work the cannibal stunt to any definite fashion." Metcalf called the story idea as whole a "corker," in this letter of 9 November 1912, then ironically rejected the story when it was completed, saying it was "not well balanced" (letter 27 January 1913). Burroughs sold it to rival *New Story Magazine* presumably without a change.

While the cannibalistic quality of Mbonga's villagers is present among several unfavorable traits, it is notable for being symbolically the one major force that keeps them from being assimilable into larger society. It is their attempt to eat D'Arnot, in *Apes*, that brings about the ultimate ruin of the village. Tarzan's refusal to join Mbonga's village at this level allows him to remain separate, and therefore free to join civilization, through the assistance of D'Arnot.

"*The ape and the savage, while they may be laughable, do not laugh.*"
— *The Joys of Being a Woman* (Kirkland 70)

In "The End of Bukawai," the narrator tells the reader: "It was not that he was more cruel or more savage than they that they hated him [...]" (108). It is clear that the cruelty of apes like Tublat or the village's practice of torture far exceed Tarzan's cruelty. The trait that brought Tarzan the most animosity from the apes "was the possession and practice of a characteristic which they had not and could not understand — the human sense of humor" (108–09). Like his literary predecessor Sherlock Holmes, whose "ideas of humour" Watson tells the reader "are strange and occasionally offensive" (Conan Doyle 818), Tarzan finds delight often at the unexpected expense of his companions. Holmes, for example, frames his client Lord Cantlemere, in "The Adventure of the Mazarin Stone," as the fence of his own stolen property. When the ruse is revealed Lord Cantlemere, says that Holmes's idea of a joke is "somewhat perverted" (Conan Doyle 978). In a similar manner, Tarzan returns Kulonga's headdress to Kulonga's hut fastened to a skull as a joke, since its owner was now dead. Holtsmark calls Tarzan's sense of humor "sparkling"; "a serious and stern streak in his makeup answers to an almost frivolous engagement in practical jokes and pranksterism" (120). Lest the reader in current culture think practical jokes occur only at the level of embarrassment, Mathias Guenther, an anthropologist of African cultures, reports that such tricks "are usually quite nasty practical jokes that seriously harm their victim" (115). The laughter evoked from such events is uneasy, sometimes callous, and sometimes more akin to jeering.

Writers have tried to define humor in a number of ways. The narrator of *Anne of Green Gables* explains that "a sense of humor [...] is simply another name for a sense of fitness of things" (Montgomery 71). Screwtape, the senior devil instructing Wormwood in C.S. Lewis's *The Screwtape Letters*, explains, "The Joke Proper," a category that causes laughter in humans, "turns on sudden perception of incongruity" (50). Reinhold Niebuhr explains further: "Humour is concerned with the immediate incongruities of life" rather than "the ultimate ones" (112). He goes on, "Laughter is our reaction to immediate incongruities and those which do not affect us essentially" (112). The key to understanding humor is in what one does with the incongruity. Niebuhr claims the end of humor is found when "humour manages to resolve incongruities by the discovery of another level of congruity" (113). Dark humor occurs when that other congruity is at an injurious level.

One of the difficulties that modern readers find with these stories and the "jokes" that Tarzan plays is the role of murder. The presence of these killings prompts Newsinger to suggest by comparison that the collection "reads like the case-study of a dangerously deranged mind" ("Lord" 63). In *Jungle Tales*, Mbonga's villagers are the only people in the narrative; they are the murdered. In *Tarzan the Untamed*, it is not the blacks but the German soldiers who suffer the homicidal "jokes" that Tarzan perpetrates. Skin color is clearly not the determiner. But the humor is weakened because murder *does* affect people essentially, which for Niebuhr calls not for laughter but for faith. In order to laugh, the reader must make a judgment. When the judgment is fitting, as when homonyms are substituted, the laughter is acceptable. It is that "sense of fitness of things" that Montgomery identifies. But, Niebuhr says: "We can not laugh at death" (127). Niebuhr concludes that "the sense of humour remains healthy only when it deals with immediate issues and faces the obvious and surface irrationalities" (130–31). The tacit opposite is that it is an unhealthy humor that brings laughter to bear on issues that affect people essentially, a condition for which death more than qualifies.

Collingwood makes several important distinctions. The first is "amusement"— his term for humor, though it is not precisely the same as Niebuhr's— "implies a bifurcation of experience into a 'real' part and a 'make-believe' part, and that the make-believe part is called amusement in so far as the emotions aroused in it are also discharged in it and are not allowed to overflow into the affairs of 'real' life" (94). The distinction "is no doubt as ancient as man himself" (Collingwood 94); which is why a reader might identify it in Mbonga's village as readily as modern Paris or the Neocene cliffs of Nu's people in *The Eternal Lover*. He claims the distinction between life and fantasy must be maintained not only conceptually but emotionally. People find humor in the twist from an expectation to a different level of completion, what Niebuhr identified as the alternate congruity. Viewers laugh at Moe, of the Three Stooges, getting punched in the face because it is a fantasy, Collingwood's make-believe world. When the same thing occurs in reality, immediately everyone present is alert to the danger that violence represents. The laughter is appropriate only in its make-believe context.

In the next paragraph, Collingwood takes this idea a step further: Danger is established, he continues, "when by discharging their emotions upon make-believe situations people come to think of emotion as something that can be excited and enjoyed for its own sake, without any necessity to pay for it in practical consequences" (94). The thrill of an exciting book, a gripping film, a wild roller-coaster ride — these are the kinds of false emotions that Collingwood marks as dangerous. He seems to negate any positive aspect of catharsis, which the Greeks identified millennia ago. For Collingwood, the humor a reader may find in any unreal situation is dangerous when it laps over into real experience. Yet, these works are created for just such a purpose. These things cannot be enjoyed, in Collingwood's terms because "[a]musement is not the same thing as enjoyment; it is enjoyment which is had without paying for it" (94).

This sets up a question when reading any work of fiction. Is this to be perceived as part of the real world or is it from a make-believe world? Clearly by definition, fiction is not real. Yet the demands of life-likeness, of verisimilitude, cause readers to evaluate fiction by real-life standards. Herein lies the dilemma of the murder that Tarzan employs in his pranks. Can a reader distance the reality of it by keeping it strictly within the fictive world of the story? The discomfort that many readers feel with Tarzan's transgression of the ethical law of justice in these pranks suggests that the two worlds must be joined. Congruity at the alternate level must have at least a tenuous connection to the congruity of the expected level. While a reader can rationalize that Tarzan knew no better, the effect is still as alarming.

Yet a significant element of literature takes its definition from just these kinds of deathly jokes. Black humor, as this kind of situation has come to be called with no intended reference to ethnicity, deals with "grotesque and morbid situations, which often deal with suffering, anxiety, and death" (Harmon and Holman 67). This kind of humor requires more than shock value, typically relying on some underpinning of irony. As a literary movement, black humor coalesced after Burroughs' lifetime, beginning to be identified in the 1950s; one of the earliest works, in retrospect, to base its entire plot on such humor is Joseph Kesselring's 1939 play, *Arsenic and Old Lace*. But the seeds may be imperfectly identified in Tarzan's pranks. Often, as the genre developed, the setting became a dysfunctional society. In many ways, Mbonga's village represents this because it fails to function successfully. In literary reality, it will die. In *The Return of Tarzan*, the narrator reveals that the village has been abandoned and overgrown since Tarzan left the jungle near the end of the first novel. The depravity of the village leadership, likewise, sets up the village for failure. A second feature often identified with black humor is the quest for something which is harmful. Tarzan does this in "The Nightmare," when he takes the meat from the pot which brings on his own sickness.

The role of humor is secondary to the plot in these stories. What Tarzan sees as humorous, is neither amusing nor enjoyable to his ape companions. Neither will many readers be amused because of the real-world implications.

But this is not the first instance where readers have been offended by what they read because of how such actions would be perceived in reality. In the fictive world, the narrator brings excuse. In *Tarzan the Terrible*, the narrator addresses the reader: "Horrible? But you are judging a wild beast by the standards of civilization" (52). The narrator explains that Tarzan's disposition is not the same as the reader's. As an adult, Tarzan "still retained what the other beasts lost as they grew older—a sense of humor, which he gave play to when the mood suited him. It was a grim humor and sometimes ghastly; but it satisfied Tarzan" (*Untamed* 38–39).

> "It was the voice of a trickster now."
> —*Far from the Madding Crowd* (Hardy 216)

Trick in Greek is *dolos*, writes Hyde, in his book-length study *Trickster Makes This World*. This word in its earliest usage is a precise image, that of "baiting a hook to catch a fish" (Hyde 18). It commonly represents that which appears to be true but is not. This ties directly to Niebuhr's discussion of incongruities, where "the sense of humour is a recognition of incongruity" (Niebuhr 608). In one of Aesop's fables, as the apprentice of Prometheus, Dolus (the embodiment of the Greek word), creates a statue in the exact semblance of his master's Truth, except the copy has no feet. When given life, Truth can walk but the fraudulent copy cannot. It is only a trick.

There seems to be the trickster's dark humor at play in the death of Rabba Kega. Burroughs softens the harshness of his demise by allowing him first to be stung by an insect—the narrator points out: "The virus of its sting spelled death for lesser things than [Tarzan]" (164). The implication is that Rabba Kega will die (whether Tarzan does anything) from this bite, though his death may be preceded by "days of anguish" (164). Tarzan's caging of the witch-doctor may, in fact, spare him anguish, but only by transferring it to another, more immediate, anguish. When Tarzan refurnishes the baited lion trap with the witch-doctor, he does so for the trickster's delight in disruption, the incongruity named above. When the villagers find the body of one of their own in the cage, they respond with "rage" and "terror," both responses validating the "self-pride in [Tarzan's] ability as a practical joker" (*Jungle Tales* 168). A similar story is reported by Hyde from Zulu folklore. This trickster figure, called Thlókunyana, will take the edible bait from a trap without springing the mechanism, leaving the snare baitless. Even more to the point is Hyde's exploration of the behavior of the coyote, which will similarly take the bait from a trap, eat it, then leave its feces in the bait's place as a sign of its superiority over the trapper. Both the coyote and Thlókunyana are what Hyde calls "bait-thief tricksters" (22). Tarzan's replacement of the bait with Rabba Kega is the insult similar to the coyote's disdainful replacement. Such a trickster, Hyde goes on, "feeds his belly while standing just outside the conflict between hunter and hunted" (22) — in this case the lion and the villagers. After re-baiting the trap with Rabba Kega, Tarzan eats the goat that had originally been tethered to the trap himself and then watches the warriors from a tree overlooking the trap. This is no passive watching, where Tarzan fills his belly and goes to sleep in a tree, but an active watching. The interest is too keen even for him to sit down, as Yeates shows. Tarzan must see how the reactions of the duped warriors manifest themselves.

Thomas Yeates illustration of Tarzan. Copyright Thomas Yeates. All rights reserved.

"From that position," Hyde continues, "the bait thief becomes a kind of critic of the usual rules [...] and as such subverts them, so that traps he has visited lose their influence" (22).

Holtsmark says that "both his inventiveness and curiosity speak to some degree to that part of his literary origin that is the Trickster" (107). The trickster, say Harmon and Holman, "plays an important role in the zone between individual and society" (561). The trickster is known for "engagingly employing laughter and deception to break rules and violate norms in mischievous ways that facilitate communication and provide escape from danger" (Harmon and Holman 561). "We find ourselves somewhere near the diminishing point of civilization, not far from the trickster's bag of tricks," Joy Harjo writes ("Postcolonial" 104). It is just such a world that Tarzan lives in. And perhaps that was Burroughs' world as well. Atamian suggests that Burroughs himself "has as strong a trickster archetype as his own Tarzan" (13). Harmon and Holman identify Hamlet as one of the notable exemplars of the trickster type. Hamlet feigns madness to deceive the court regarding his inquiry into his father's death. Likewise, Tarzan pretends to be a lion in order to test the apes' sentry system.

Tarzan "sought amusement and adventure and such humor as the grim and terrible jungle offers to those who know it and do not fear it — a weird humor shot with blazing eyes and dappled with the crimson of lifeblood" (*Jungle Tales* 124). One joke that Tarzan practices is injecting decapitated heads into gatherings. In *Apes*, he lobs a skull that he had pilfered earlier into Mbonga's village. This initiates "the seed of fear" (78), which ever after lingers in the people. In *Tarzan the Untamed*, he remembers the havoc he had caused with his tricks in Mbonga's village and uses the decapitated head of one of the antagonists to frighten Bertha Kircher's captors. In *Tarzan the Terrible*, he cuts the head from his dead guard and ties it to the branch of a tree. Later, in *Tarzan, Lord of the Jungle*, he takes the head of a slain enemy and follows his cohorts. "Suddenly something fell heavily upon the ground [...] and rolled [...] among them" (172). How amusing this tactic is to Tarzan is not clear. It becomes expedient, though, in producing a debilitating apprehension among those he seeks supremacy over. After all, the narrator explains, "[I]t was fear of him that had made Tarzan master of many jungles — one does not win the respect of the killers with bonbons" (*Terrible* 53).

One aspect of the trickster is that his cunning often gets ahead of his reason, which leads to an unforeseen negative consequence. In his attempt to become the instrument of experiential learning for the apes, he forgets, or fails to anticipate, that the learner may be himself. Tarzan wants to appear to the apes as a lion. The blending of identities is skillfully accomplished in the illustration by John Buscema and Rudy Mesina for the Marvel comic adaptation entitled "Fangs of Death." The lion's head fits snugly over Tarzan's own hair, like a wig, his own face appearing where the lower jaw of the lion should have been. Colorization (done by George Roussos) gives the lion pelt a bit less red, allowing a fine distinction between it and Tarzan's skin, but imperceptible with-

A panel from the May 1978 Marvel comics adaptations of *Jungle Tales of Tarzan*. Art by John Buscema and Rudy Mesina. Copyright Edgar Rice Burroughs, Inc. All rights reserved.

out conscious attention. A large stone, thrown by one of the mangani, is directed precisely at the intersection of the two identities, as if to destroy the unnatural, and ultimately artificial, joining of the lion with the man.

The embedding of one thing within another was smartly indicated by the layout of the "The Lion" when it first appeared in *Blue Book*. The illustration by Herbert Morton Stoops shows the title and author lines to the left of a line drawing of Tarzan in a tree, turned looking over his right shoulder down the

The New Stories of Tarzan

The Lion

by Edgar Rice Burroughs

NUMA the lion crouched behind a thorn-bush close beside the drinking-pool where the river eddied just below the bend. There was a ford there, and on either bank a well-worn trail, broadened far out at the river's brim, where for countless centuries the wild things of the jungle and of the plains beyond had come down to drink, the *carnivora* with bold and fearless majesty, the *herbivora* timorous, hesitating, fearful.

Numa the lion was hungry; he was very hungry, and so he was quite silent now. On his way to the drinking-place he had moaned often and roared not a little; but as he neared the spot where he would lie in wait for Bara the deer or Horta the boar or some other of the many luscious-fleshed creatures who came hither to drink, he was silent. It was a grim, terrible silence, shot through with yellow-green light of ferocious eyes, punctuated with undulating tremors of sinuous tail.

It was Pacco the zebra who came first, and Numa the lion could scarce restrain a roar of anger, for of all the plains-people, none are more wary than Pacco the zebra. Behind the black striped stallion came a herd of thirty or forty of the plump and vicious little horselike beasts. As he neared the river, the leader paused often, cocking his ears and raising his muzzle to sniff the gentle breeze for the telltale scent-spoor of the dread flesh-eaters.

Numa shifted uneasily, drawing his hind quarters far beneath his tawny body, gathering himself for the sudden charge and the savage assault. His eyes shot hungry fire. His great muscles quivered to the excitement of the moment.

Pacco came a little nearer—halted, snorted and wheeled. There was a pattering of scurrying hoofs, and the herd was gone; but Numa the lion moved not. He was familiar with the ways of Pacco the zebra. He knew that he would return, though many times he might again wheel and fly before he

Copyrighted, 1917, by The Story-Press Corporation. All rights reserved.
1211

The first page of the original *Blue Book* publication of "The Lion."

page. Directly below the branch on which he stands is the text of the right column, beginning the third paragraph of the story. Between the left and right columns of type, however, the illustration continues with the black-maned lion, creating a well around which the text wraps. The lion's tail connects this part of the illustration to the text by aligning with the beginning line of text of the story, and joins to the remainder of the illustration, lying juxtaposed with the base of the tree in which Tarzan is standing. The lion is literally embedded in the text as the interior margins undulate around his form. This blending of text and illustration represents the theme of the story where the lion and the human take on the appearance of one thing.

The stoning that Tarzan receives in this disguise eventually renders him unconscious, and his life is in the balance, a high price for a lesson in vigilance. Yet, that is precisely the point of the lesson that Tarzan intends to teach, that lack of vigilance is a life-and-death matter. Such high stakes are often tied to trickster tales. Burroughs' incorporation of these trickster elements corresponds to such elements in African and Native American predecessors. But Burroughs does not incorporate the attributes of the trickster into Tarzan's personality wholesale. Like all sources, the trickster elements are used where helpful and ignored where their emphasis runs counter to Burroughs' conception of his character. Tarzan lacks two important elements of the major trickster typologies, a lack of self-control with food and with sex. Regarding the first, in "The Nightmare," Tarzan finds nothing but disgust with the villagers who eat far beyond their need, so much so that he kills the last one rather than watch him continue to gorge himself. And the sexual element, only hinted at in the first story, is effectively put aside.

One element of the trickster figure is his ability to take on other shapes. Hyde says that "sometimes tricksters alter the appearance of their skin; sometimes they actually replace one skin with another" (51). This is not a simple substitution, though. The transformation is possible, according to traditional African belief, because identity is not located in a single entity. Rather, as Jackson says, "[t]hese transformations involve relocations of consciousness and reapportionments of moral and intellectual properties" (266). The possibility of Bukawai and the hyenas being essentially the same makes it possible for one to become the other in shape. Tarzan's metamorphosis is less magical than Ovid's characters depict or than do the myriad tricksters in world folklore. He simply pulls a pelt over his body as did Puzzle in C.S. Lewis's *The Last Battle* or as may have Snug the Joiner in *A Midsummer Night's Dream*. That when Tarzan stole the pelt from Mbonga's village he is called an apparition by the narrator indicates the supernatural attachment to such transformations. Mark de Brito points out in his book-length study *The Trickster's Tongue* that the lion head as a ceremonial mask is important in certain West African countries, where it is believed to represent and embody the ancestors. The fusing of human and animal is common among many African heritages. "Hybrid forms representing ancestral spirits," de Brito says, in this case the lion-man merger, may derive from "the interplay between two oppositions: life against death and society against the bush" (169). That Mbonga's village represents society and both the lion and Tarzan represent the bush is an imposed but satisfactory connotation. The life-death dichotomy is embedded within the very object, that is, the living lion now dead having left only the outer shell, to be inhabited by another. The dead lion covering the living Tarzan nearly brings a greater unity in a dead Tarzan.

In the end of "The Lion," Tarzan lies half-dead from the beating the apes have given him, and he realizes there is more potential harm in his actions than he had previously granted. His response is dual: "[H]e almost swore a solemn oath forever to forego practical joking—almost; but not quite" (128). Holtsmark comments, "The concluding tag typifies the attitude of the trickster, who can no more give up his prankish ways than he can stop breathing" (123). He continues, saying that such an expectation—that Tarzan would learn his lesson by the severity of the prank's consequences—is "to misapprehend the essence of the trickster" (124).

"Trickster isn't a run-of-the-mill liar and thief," writes Hyde. "When he lies and steals, it isn't so much to get away with something or get rich as to disturb [...]" (13). When Tarzan dons the lion skin in "A Jungle Joke," his purpose is not to gain food or weapons, his usual booty from the village; instead, he takes on the task purely for the disruption that his false appearance will bring to the villagers. The trickster that Tarzan becomes in this episode "belongs," as Hyde notes, "to the periphery, not to the center" (13n). He is an outsider. The palisade wall marks the point at which Tarzan is clearly out of his own territory and in the jurisdiction of another.

"The trickster myth," as alluded to earlier, Hyde writes, "derives creative intelligence from appetite. It begins with a being whose main concern is getting fed and it ends with the same being grown mentally swift, adept at creating and unmasking deceit, proficient at hiding his tracks and at seeing through the devices used by others to hide theirs" ([17]). Many trickster tales, Hyde writes, "are filled with examples of trickster's hunger and its consequences" (28). In these stories, the uncurbed appetite "lead[s] willy-nilly to some sort of disaster" (32), which the reader witnesses in "The Nightmare." While in one place, Tarzan is able to defer his hunger, ultimately it is because Tarzan is hungry that the story occurs at all. The story is precipitated by Tarzan's hunger and his improper appeasement of it. Hyde goes on to suggest that the "trickster's inventive cunning" is a natural outgrowth of "the body's needs" (63).

Beyond the straightforward desire to slake his hunger, the desire to win at the tit-for-tat relationship he enjoys with Mbonga's villagers drives him to take from them. Hyde says, "Behind trickster's tricks lies the desire to eat and not be eaten, to satisfy appetite without being its object" (37). That Tarzan was destined for just such an end was clear earlier, in "The Capture of Tarzan." There the cannibalistic tribe all but roasted the hero before Tantor's boisterous rescue sent the villagers scattering for their lives.

The role of the trickster in Native American folklore also benefits from what Edward W. Huffstetler called a "layering quality" (11) derived from the number of stories associated with the character type. The collection of *Jungle Tales*, more than any other in the Tarzan canon, is similar to the folktales of any given culture. That the stories are synergistic is evident when Huffstetler writes that recurring elements in a body of work can confer on "the entire work a deeper, more profound level of meaning" and the aggregation of the stories into a cycle creates "a single complex, layered saga" (11). The collection of the stories in *Jungle Tales* simulates this synergy, at least in a small way, through the incorporation of mythological echoes, such as those represented by the trickster.

The character of the trickster is ambivalent. "Ambiguity," Guenther writes, "is the fundamental characteristic" by which a trickster can be identified. As a nature figure, the trickster is as changeable as the weather. "Trickster," continues Guenther, can be "at one time human or animal, at another animal or tree or plant" (115) While sometimes kindly and good, the trickster can also be "mischievous, even vicious, acting without regard to the impact his behavior has on either himself or others" (Huffstetler 72). Jackson points out that there is an "ethical ambiguity inherent in cleverness" (116). One aspect of cleverness, that certainly applies to Tarzan, is rooted in "attentiveness which consists in discernment and intelligent observation" (Jackson 232). Just as Tarzan's humor is sometimes found suspect, so his role as trickster leaves him morally imprecise. He uses his intelligence in ways that his civilized counterpart finds untenable. But the trickster, like Tarzan, is really outside civilization.

CHAPTER 8

What You See
Lessons in Appearance and Reality in "The Nightmare"

Burroughs wrote "The Nightmare," the ninth in the series, in just two days (7 and 8 February 1917). Ray Long called it "a peach of a Tarzan story" (letter 15 February 1917). Holtsmark calls this dream exploration "one of the more intellectually appealing passages" (109) in all of the Tarzan stories, arguing that Tarzan's grappling with this experience "takes on strongly Platonic overtones" (110). The *Des Moines Sunday Register* retitled the story "A Night of Terror." A comic version of the story appeared in Charlton's *Jungle Tales of Tarzan* #3 (May 1965), in *Golden Comics Digest* #4 (August 1969), and in DC's *Tarzan* #214 (Nov. 1972), reprinted in DC's *Tarzan the Untamed* #257 (Jan. 1977) and *Edgar Rice Burroughs' Tarzan: The Joe Kubert Years* #1 (Dark Horse, 2005).

In brief, Tarzan is hungry and Mbonga's village is feasting. Tarzan watches the villagers eat themselves into a stupor. He drops into the unconscious mass of bodies and strangles a man determined to gorge himself. Tarzan takes some of the elephant meat, not knowing it is carrion from a days-old-dead animal. He finds the taste appalling but forces himself to eat some to stave off his hunger. He goes to sleep in a tree, ill from the experience, and begins to dream, first of a tree-climbing lion, then of a strange bird that carries him away. Later he is accosted by a snake with the head of the man he had killed earlier in the night. As morning comes, he crawls into a thicket where he expects to die. After waking, sickness passed, he goes to the cabin and looks at books. He dozes off and awakes to find Bolgani the gorilla standing in the doorway. Thinking the harm no more imminent than his dreams had been, he allows the gorilla to carry him off. When he feels the pain of the gorilla's teeth he galvanizes into action and kills the abductor with his knife, much as he had done years before when he first found the knife. Tarzan is confused about appearance and reality, and can only conclude naively that he will never again eat elephant meat.

This story, as *Blue Book* readers discovered, developed a plot "wherein Tarzan tries—with surprising results—to discover what 'stuff dreams are made on!'" (contents page). The invocation of Shakespeare in the quotation takes the reader to Prospero in *The Tempest*. Ferdinand has just witnessed the supernatural wedding pageant performed by Ceres, Iris, and Juno and stares in disbelief as they fade away. Prospero explains:

> These our actors
> As I foretold you, were all spirits and
> Are melted into air, into thin air:
> [..........................]
> Yea, all [...] shall dissolve
> And, like this insubstantial pageant faded,
> Leave not a rack behind [4.1.148–50, 154–56].

The dream is apparently initiated from Tarzan's indigestion. The biblical injunction against eating "any thing that dieth of itself" (Deut. 14.20) was not a part of Mbonga's heritage nor apparently picked up in the reading material in the Clayton cabin. The resulting sickness can be instructive at both a moral and a psychological level. John E. Mack observes that "nightmares can be of unique value in conveying the conflict over murderous impulses [...]" (86). This is important when considering that the literary use of dreams often will contain "[e]lements from the preceding passages of the story" (Mack 86).

The importance of understanding the difference between appearance and reality is the first concern in understanding this story. Tarzan "considers [it] an abnormality [that h]e does not stay to fight those monsters and great beasts who populate his dreams" (Holtsmark 56). His apparent fear contradicts the reality he knows. Also of concern in this chapter is the codification of behavior; Tarzan begins to consider not just what is and what isn't but also what should and should not be.

The narrator employs a simile to show how uncharacteristic Tarzan perceives his action to be: "Tarzan of the Apes seemed to be a different Tarzan, sluggish, helpless, timid — wishing to flee his enemies as fled Bara, the deer, most fearful of creatures" (137). Bara is shy, noted in "Tarzan's First Love." The chapter considers comparisons both as similes and symbols as preparation for understanding Tarzan's dreams.

> "*What now appeared certain and tangible [...] might soon dissipate into an airy dream*"
> —*Frankenstein* (Shelley 182)

The age-old theme of appearance versus reality is worked out in literal detail in this story, the demands of what, in "Animula," T.S. Eliot called "the imperatives of 'is and seems'" (71). The theme is central to many of the great writers. Shakespeare, for example, works this theme in multiple forms in *A Midsummer Night's Dream*. It is seen in its extremity in the play rehearsal by the rustics. Their play-within-a-play calls for a lion. When Tom Snout asks, "Will not the ladies be afeard of the lion?" (3.1.25), he believes the viewers will be unable to discern the difference between an actor in a lion's skin and a real beast, the very kind of "audience" in both Kerchak's and Mbonga's tribes. In Shakespeare, though, this is laughable. Snout suggests that the audience be told beforehand that the lion is not real. Bottom amends the suggestion to include exposing a portion of the actor's face and concludes, "[L]et him name his name, and tell them / plainly he is Snug the joiner" (3.1.42–43). Presumably, this verbal identification coupled with the visual confirmation is enough to dispel the "illusion." But if the distinction were so easy, its place in literature would be gone. The fact is, illusion and reality are not always readily divisible.

When Tarzan dreams, he sees no differently, it seems, than he does when he is awake. Only the content of the dreams differs. Mack points out that it is a natural tendency for "nightmares to be accompanied by at least a temporary loss after waking of the capacity to distinguish inner and outer reality" (86), and that some schizophrenics "have lost the capacity to distinguish where dreams leave off and waking reality begins" (218). While most adults are able to distinguish the difference after momentary confusion, in children, or first-time dreamers, this ability may be slower to develop.

The crux of the appearance-reality distinction, for Tarzan, comes the following day, when he is sleepily reading in the cabin. Inattentiveness brought on through the throes of sickness the previous night cause him to leave the cabin door unlatched. Bolgani enters, and Tarzan's first fright of the sight gives way to a calmness borne of experience, that is the dream experience he has just come through. Tarzan identifies Bolgani as one of the "empty things which came while he slept," and so is "sure that no flesh and blood gorilla stood before him" (*Jungle Tales* 139). When the pain of Bolgani's attack causes Tarzan's rapid re-evaluation of the situation, reality spurs the young protagonist to resist and defend himself. When he has vanquished his enemy, he remains alive but so does his confusion. The narrator relates that "he did not know what was real and what was not" (141). The distinction dividing real from unreal, Holtsmark points out, is the basis from which many Greek thinkers begin, and Burroughs' narrative in this story invokes "strongly Platonic overtones" (110).

Dostoevsky's narrator in *The Idiot* comments on the illogical nature of dreams.

> We sometimes have strange, impossible dreams, contrary to all the laws of nature. When we awake we remember them and wonder at their strangeness. You remember, perhaps, that you were in full possession of your reason during this succession of fantastic images; even that you acted with extraordinary logic and cunning while surrounded by murderers [...]. You remember how you escaped them by some ingenious stratagem [...]. You remember all this quite clearly, but how is it that your reason calmly accepted all the manifest absurdities and impossibilities that crowded into your dream? One of the murderers suddenly changed into a woman before your very eyes; then the woman was transformed into a hideous, cunning little dwarf; and you believed it, and accepted it all almost as a matter of course [...] [436–37].

The narrator goes on to point out the profound impact of the dream and the confusion that it brings because it "carried with it some enigma which you have failed to solve" (437). But in the end, "what it means, or what has been predicted [...] in it, you can neither understand nor remember" (437).

Tarzan's dream matches the description Dostoevsky gives. It also parallels Raskolnikov's situation in *Crime and Punishment*. After committing murder, Raskolnikov finds that "[d]isjointed scraps and fragments of ideas floated through his mind, but he could not seize one of them, or dwell upon any, in spite of all his efforts ..." (83). This disjointedness is the inability to distinguish appearance from reality. The next day Raskolnikov confuses night and day and blames the "feverishness" that plagued his sleep (84). He also wonders "how he could have omitted to fasten his door when he came in" (84). It is the unlatched door through which Bolgani approaches Tarzan in his confused state. Mack observes: "Dostoevsky has used the nightmare as a deliberate invention to dramatize his hero's profound struggle to deal with terrifying murderous wishes" (88). In Tarzan's case, the struggle is not conscious but unconscious.

The crux of the issue is that Tarzan has always lived by his senses. That he could do otherwise is unthinkable. The senses are stimulated by both real and imaginary sources. The senses themselves cannot be, as Collingwood points out, "divided into real sensations and imaginations" (194). The bizarre sensations that Tarzan sees, hears, and feels during his nightmare are real sensations. It is not the senses that are false in dreaming, but, as Collingwood says, the way in which the senses are "related to the interpretive work of thought" (194). The real importance is in what Tarzan does with the sensations experienced in the dream.

Kilgour claims that a person, whether viewer or reader, cannot know a person or an object simply by seeing it; rather, to truly know anything, the person "must violate its outward form" (28), that is, get beyond the surface to the heart. An excellent example of such a character in the Tarzan books is Anderssen, the ship's cook in *The Beasts of Tarzan*. "[H]is close-set, shifty eyes and repulsive features" (*Beasts* 74) cover an interior of self-sacrifice, demonstrated in giving his life trying to save Jane from Rokoff. In tribute, Tarzan holds the man in his arms while he dies rather than abandon him or kill him.

The nightmare event, coupled with its real-life sequel with Bolgani, puts Tarzan's reasoning ability to the test. Tarzan is, in Hyde's words, "living on the cusp of reflective consciousness" (56). As a trickster figure, Tarzan "embodies reflection coming into being; in him we see both the need for reflective consciousness (without it he suffers) and the rewards of that consciousness" (56), where he triumphs over dangerous adversity.

One method Burroughs uses to set jungle and civilization apart is through food. In the jungle, Tarzan and the beasts eat their food raw. In civilization, even the rudimentary civilization of Mbonga's village, people cook their food. To the readers' senses, civilization seems superior in this regard. Burroughs, however, inverts the usual expectations and identifies the raw meat as the more wholesome. In "The Nightmare," "the great cooking pot in the center of the village" (130) attracts a hungry Tarzan. This may well be the first instance of cooked meat that Tarzan has eaten — and with disastrous consequences. Tarzan always prefers his meat uncooked. Even later in life, when out of politeness he eats his meat cooked with the Waziri, he does so with what the narrator identifies as "the virus of hypocrisy" (*Jewels* 15). Burroughs uses the dichotomy between raw and cooked food as "a springboard for talking about the reality and the appearance of civilized behavior" (Holtsmark 50).

Holtsmark says, "Appearances are truly deceiving" (150), as was demonstrated by the character of Anderssen. The cooked food of Mbonga's village disguises the treachery within, while the abhorrent raw meat belies the mercy demonstrated in Tarzan's final gesture to Anderssen. Anderssen's appearance is raw meat, but his actions are "truly chivalrous" (*Beasts* 91).

"*For ethics boast a syntax of their own*"— Querkopf Von Klubstick
(Coleridge 78n)

Another set of contraries that Eliot identifies in "Animula" are "may and may not" (71). When, in "The Nightmare," Tarzan finds Mbonga's villagers preparing for a feast of elephant meat, Tarzan, the narrator states, "was assailed by no doubts as to the ethics of his doing likewise [...]" (129). Tarzan, in Eliot's terms, *may* eat elephant meat, at the beginning of the story. In this one area, though, his ethics are changed during the course of the narrative, so that when the reader reaches the end, Tarzan *may not*.

"Now the moment a man's voluntary actions are determined by conscious or unconscious reference to a standard outside of himself and his selfish motives," writes Fiske (104), "he has entered the world of ethics[;] he has begun to live in a moral atmosphere" (104–05). Just where this first occurs is difficult to determine. That Tarzan had begun to assimilate some rudimentary ethics is evident at least from the time of Kala's death. In fact, Holtsmark claims that "[o]nly when Tarzan has reached maturity"— and here the reader can define the term in many ways including emotionally and morally—"and can stand alone does Kala die" (155). The anthropomorphic qualities that Burroughs gives to the apes make Tarzan's development of an unconscious code of ethics quite reasonable. For example, in *Apes*, the narrator points out that "Terkoz knew that it was against the laws of his kind to strike this woman of another" (86); it is this violation which causes Tarzan to challenge Terkoz's behavior. And Holtsmark points out that in Burroughs' work, the animals "are morally quite superior to" people (86). Burroughs gives this impression in *The Return of Tarzan*, when Tarzan thinks: "But the brutes are more chivalrous than man — they do not stoop to cowardly intrigue" (96). It is just such development that allows Vernon to conclude: "Tarzan has evolved into his full humanity by becoming the supreme moral animal" (18).

Anthropomorphism aside, some scientists claim that the beginning of morality can be seen in some ape communities. Nicholas Wade cites chimpanzees that "[drown] in zoo moats trying to save others" and rhesus monkeys which choose to deny themselves in order to aid others. The beginnings of ethical decision-making, Wade argues (drawing from the primatological work of Frans de Waal), is found "in [a] concern for others and the understanding of social rules as to how [others] should be treated." Marc Hauser argues that "the brain has a genetically shaped mechanism for acquiring moral rules, a universal moral grammar similar to the neural machinery for learning language" (qtd. in Wade). When a reader accepts Tarzan's linguistic abilities, as explored earlier, that reader implicitly, according to Hauser, accepts Tarzan's abilities for ethical progress as well.

After Tarzan killed Kulonga to avenge the death of his foster mother, Kala, he examined the body and was intrigued by the various items of ornament and weaponry. After his curiosity had been addressed, though, the reader is shocked to read that Tarzan "prepared to get down to business, for Tarzan of the Apes was hungry, and here was meat; meat of the kill, which jungle ethics permitted him to eat" (*Apes* 68). Just what does Burroughs mean by "jungle ethics" and where do they come from?

The First Book of Ethics, while not likely resembling any of the books that Tarzan finds in his father's cabin, provides for juvenile readers a definition of the law of the jungle:

> Every animal must learn to run, or hide, or fight for its life. The strong feed on the weak, the fast on the slow, and the tricky ones on those who are witless, or careless or asleep.
> At first, the early men probably lived much like the animals [Black 3].

When Crouch writes, "Tarzan has no codes and understands none," he cannot be correct. No one, not even a created character, can work outside of a moral framework of some kind; even the trolls in Ibsen's *Peer Gynt* have a moral guideline: "[T]o thine own self be — all-sufficient" (42), or as Christopher Baker phrases it, "Be true to thine own self — ish" (qtd. in Murphy). Donn B. Murphy further explains, "Overtly or by implication, intentionally or by force of circumstance, the hero [...] is involved in the development of moral codes, manners and philosophy by which he or she will live thereafter." To probe into Tarzan's moral framework, then, should be neither surprising nor fruitless. Rather, it will provide a schematic that, despite Tarzan's unusual circumstances, fits the human condition.

In building a consistent approach to decision-making, Tarzan relies on three primary sources. Burroughs gives Tarzan an unconscious heritage, which acts like moral DNA to cause him to respond in situations as if he had the accumulated morals of his parents. At other times, Tarzan is able to create a balance of right and wrong based on things that he has learned from the books in the cabin where he was born. The third source is his human reason, which allows him to create comparative ethics using earlier responses as a framework for a new situation.

Several writers have identified an unwritten code of behavior behind Tarzan's actions. Burger pejoratively identifies "the antique moral code" ("Forty" 255) in Burroughs' work as characteristic of the author, despite the ability of the books to retain and regain readership. Holtsmark has claimed "Burroughs created a whole world in which there are certain codes of behavior and moral laws [...] very definite codes of behavior according to which they measure themselves as being men" (qtd. in Jacobs 5B). Tarzan, as representative of such a world, presents a working out of such ethical reasoning. Soumille, a French critic, insists that all of Tarzan's behavior is presented in moral terms (*"Tout le comportement de Tarzan est présenté en termes de morale"*) (302). He goes on to say: "One cannot make morals only with muscles" (*"On ne fait pas de la morale avec des muscles"* [302]). Beyond strength of body, strength of character makes a man.

Bozarth identifies four stages through which the character of Tarzan matured. The first stage, the feral child with few human instincts ("Tarzan's Growth"), corresponds to the first area of consideration, the decision-making process that comes naturally to Tarzan through heredity, that which we often call instinct. Bozarth's second and third stages—"the ape youth, discovering humanity" and "the human adult, discovering human character"—may be attained in the second method of moral attainment, roughly labeled education. Hauser claims, "At the most basic level, there must be some innate capacity that allows each child to build a specific moral grammar" (Hauser 49). The process of maturity is largely unconscious moral-building. Bozarth's fourth level, where Tarzan becomes a "modern, educated, and rough philosopher" is attained through reason. The example of Tarzan's response to the corpse of Kulonga provides evidence of all three stages, though they are demonstrated individually elsewhere in Tarzan's story.

Decisions during this first period were, as Bozarth says, "based upon exterior forces rather than any premeditation or cognitive thought" ("Tarzan's Growth"). Hauser affirms that "there are hidden parameters underlying people's intuitions [...]" (158). These parameters are often inexplicable because "the guiding principles are inaccessible, tucked away in the mind's library of unconscious knowledge" (Hauser 2). The narrator notes, for example, in "The Fight for the Balu," when Tarzan faces the threats of Taug, that it is "the blood of his English ancestors" (39) that resists the thought to flee, not any reasoned stand on Tarzan's part. Such a belief in mysterious hereditary predispositions was common. For example, in Oscar Wilde's *The Picture of Dorian Gray*, the titular character "was a gentleman, and he [James Vane] hated him for that, hated him through some curious race-instinct for which he could not account" (Wilde 55). In this case, Wilde surely means class rather than race, but the term was readily understood by his reading public.

In the example of Kulonga's death, the narrator asks: "How may we judge him, by what standards, this ape-man with the heart and head and body of an English gentleman, and the training of a wild beast?" (*Apes* 69). This dual identity creates both the problem and the solution. Tarzan is able to use the animal instinct for survival, but in matters unessential for life, he is able to call on the human characteristics that Burroughs posits as innate. Thomas A. Pendleton reconciles these two competing forces by subjugating raw nature to civil nature: "Yet environment — knowing no fellows but animals for his first eighteen years — does not prevail over a human heredity that makes him unselfish, chivalrous, abstemious, chaste [...] — hardly animal traits" (691).

When it comes to killing, Tarzan must make distinctions. Bozarth divides Tarzan's reasoning in this manner: "When Tarzan kills a jungle beast, it is a matter of live or die, but when he kills a human being, it is justified, beyond a shadow of a doubt, that person deserves to die under the ordinary social laws which have driven human culture since time began" ("Code"). Tarzan's murder of Kulonga is the transliteration of the ancient idea from the law of Moses (Exodus 21.22–25, Leviticus 24.17–21, Deuteronomy 19.16.21) or the Code of Hammurabi, that a murderer will pay with his own life. The twist here is that Kulonga would in no way consider the death of Kala as murder, any more than his slaying of Horta the boar would have been. Both were considered legitimate food sources. Tarzan, with his dual identity, however, sees a vast difference. He gives no moral thought to Kulonga's killing of the boar, while his killing of Kala is the equivalent of killing his own mother. In a later novel, when Tarzan comes upon the corpse of an ape with whom he had been raised, "[t]here was no doubt in his mind but that plain murder had been committed [...]" (*Tarzan and the Golden Lion* 33).

A further irony is incorporated into this scene. Mbonga's tribe, which has only recently moved into Tarzan's territory, is cannibalistic, as explored earlier. (Mbonga, Kulonga's father, is identified in "The Lion" as "the jet cannibal of the jungle primeval" [124], and Tibo and Momaya, for all the sympathy they evoke, are also identified as cannibals.) Kulonga, it seems, would have no such qualms if the situation were reversed between Tarzan and himself. Kulonga's ethical framework had been educated along different principles.

But Tarzan is not a part of Mbonga's tribe, and at this point in the story has never even seen it. His decision must come from the three areas identified earlier. And Burroughs clearly placed the bulk of the decision into the first category, when the narrator says, "hereditary instinct, ages old, usurped the functions of his untaught mind and saved him from transgressing a worldwide law of whose very existence he was ignorant" (*Apes* 69). Beyond that when Tarzan attempts to violate this instinct, another instinct intervenes without the aid of reason: "a qualm of nausea overwhelmed him" (69). Bederman carefully qualifies this decision on Tarzan's part: "[T]he impulse to avoid cannibalism," she says, "was a racially superior man's inherent masculine instinct" (225). Something within him — something that his parents knew but could not communicate to him — will not let him transgress the law of cannibalism.

The second moral database from which Tarzan draws is his education. Wade cites philosopher Jesse Prinz in advocating the claim that "moral sentiments are shaped by culture, not genetics." Tarzan's cultural education comes through two sources: his integration into the tribe of Kerchak provides a cultural underpinning, while Tarzan's more traditional education comes by way of the books he discovers in the cabin of his parents. The narrator relates that "Tarzan had learned from his books but scattered fragments of the ways of human beings" (*Apes* 76). Discarding the "but" for a moment, we recognize that these books, however they are interpreted by Tarzan, become another influence on the choices that he makes. The scene is a literary descendant of the education of the abandoned creature in *Frankenstein*. Mary Shelley gives readers a character who is, as Tarzan is later, left to find values and behavioral cues from the world around him. The creature, again as Tarzan will be, is "more agile" than his fellow creatures and admits to "subsist[ing] upon a coarser diet" (Shelley 115), giving a number of other precedents to the character that Burroughs creates. Nature by itself, though, is insufficient to provide a moral code for the creature. When he has adapted to life in the wild, he realizes there is more to life through the books. The creature learns to read them and his moral framework is established through such works as *Paradise Lost* and Plutarch's *Lives*.

"The God of Tarzan" begins: "Among the books of his dead father in the little cabin by the land-locked harbor, Tarzan of the Apes found many things to puzzle his young head" (48). The most important discovery is that he is an M-A-N, while his companions are A-P-E-S (*Apes* 50). While he cannot divorce his kinship with the apes, he recognizes himself as something other than them which goes by the label M-A-N. While at first this distinction troubles him, by his late adolescence "he [is] very proud of the distinction" (*Jungle Tales* 187). It is this realization that deepens the dilemma that Tarzan faces in eating the body of Kulonga. Johnston notes: "Tarzan's discovery that he is a member of the human species [...] lands him in a beautiful ethical dilemma." Johnston describes the situation this way: "Having killed an African tribesman, Tarzan is about to help himself" (59), but he hesitates because he does not know if this new creature is literally fair game. Johnston's reasoning errs in claiming that the apes do not eat their own kind. The first Dum-Dum that the narrator describes is to celebrate the "killing of a giant ape, a member of another tribe" (*Apes* 52). The question, though, is not whether apes eat other apes, because Tarzan has disassociated himself in terms of species from the apes. Johnston continues: "Tarzan now knows himself to be a man, and he recognizes the dead African as a man. [Contrarily] Tarzan is hungry, and his political sympathies are all with the apes. It is a pretty case of conscience, and Burroughs does justice to it" (Johnston 59). His education has led to a moral behavioral stance.

The final assistance in creating a moral framework that Tarzan uses is a kind of synthesis of the two previous sources. When instinct and education fail to provide a direct answer, Tarzan must use his reasoning ability to arrive analogously at an answer. Wade argues that of the many common primate traits, the areas of judgment and reason have no parallel between humans and apes.

Such a claim leads a reader to conclude, as Holtsmark does, that "[i]t is his man's mind, his human intellect, which always triumphs over the [...] beasts" (72). This is applicable not only to ability but also to motivation. One area this is evident, again, relates to Tarzan's killing.

The narrator notes: "Sheeta, the leopard, alone of all the jungle folk, tortured his prey. The ethics of all the others meted a quick and merciful death to their victims" (*Apes* 76). When Tarzan kills Kulonga, it is quick: he "plunged his hunting knife into Kulonga's heart" (*Apes* 68). (Some argue that the pseudo-lynching of Kulonga — Tarzan ropes him and pulls him into the tree before dispatching him with the knife — is a form of torture. The intent from the protagonist's point of view, though, is clearly a matter of expediency; no pleasure is derived from the process, unlike the pleasure that is identified with the villagers, who taunt, prick, and beat various captives, including D'Arnot in chapter 21 of *Apes*, "The Village of Torture," the lion in "A Jungle Joke," and Tarzan himself in "The Capture of Tarzan." And there is no elation analogous to that felt by Mike in John Steinbeck's "The Vigilante," where the torture and killing of a man is given pleasurable overtones.) Likewise, in *Tarzan the Untamed*, the narrator points out, "Like all brave men and courageous beasts[,] Tarzan had little natural inclination to torture — none, in fact; but this case was unique in his experience" (*Untamed* 27). The exceptional case is when he is avenging the death of Jane. Note here that it is placing the event of the death of his wife outside the parameters of previous experience that leads to a different response than normal. The impulse to avenge Jane's death is not outside his realm of experience. When Kala, that other significant female in his life was killed, he likewise tracks down the killer and exchanges a life for a life. And when Teeka had been abducted and presumed dead, Tarzan finds, "though to a lesser degree, he was moved by the same passion" (*Jungle Tales* 151). The narrator continues, in the passage concerning Jane's death, "[a]n inherent sense of justice called for an eye for an eye [...]" (*Untamed* 27). While the inherited sense of right and wrong prods Tarzan to seek the life of Major Schneider, the enormity of the situation, that the murdered one was his own wife, places his response into an undefined moral void, where neither his instinct nor his education gave him a clear answer. So, he must reason from analogy.

This principle is at work in "The Lion." When Numa has killed one of the apes of the tribe, Tarzan must formulate a proper response. He understood, as did the apes, that the lion would leave all the other members of the tribe alone while he fed upon the body of the fallen comrade. For the apes, that was a sufficient consolation; the matter was individual. Their ethic is like that of Peer Gynt's trolls: serve yourself first, and do not worry about future repercussions. For Tarzan, though, the affront was corporate. He had seen the event in times past and realized that if the lion found no negative consequence to attacking the ape tribe, then such response would be tacit encouragement for a return later. So Tarzan "determined to prevent Numa from profiting in any way through his attack upon the tribe" (121). His defense of the ape corpse was proper as a means of safeguarding the tribe against future attacks.

In the case of Major Schneider, while the reasoning is similar, the result cannot be, because with Numa, the lion will have an opportunity to hunt again and presumably choose not to kill apes. Major Schneider will have no such opportunity. The memory of the charred corpse bearing Jane's rings drives him further. Beginning with "the inherent sense of justice," Tarzan recognizes that "the creature must suffer even as he had caused Jane Clayton to suffer" (27). While Tarzan is confident that death is the appropriate end of his pursuit, he believes such atrocities demand "even more" (27). His desire to add emotional pain to physical pain is clear in his choice to leave Schneider treed by a lion in an inaccessible valley.

The dichotomy of ape and man within Tarzan creates an additional tension. "If you are an ape you will do as the apes would do—leave one of your kind to die in the jungle if it suited your whim to go elsewhere," explains the narrator in *Apes*. The corollary follows: "If you are a man, you will return to protect your kind. You will not run away from one of your own people, because one of them has run away from you" (*Apes* 176).

To return a final time to the conundrum of whether to eat Kulonga, Tarzan must first identify Kulonga as a human like himself. Because of his upbringing, he recognizes him as something other than himself. At this point in the story, Tarzan has seen no human since his adoption into the ape tribe some decade or more before. From the picture book, he tentatively identifies the *negro* for comparison, "but how different had been the dull, dead print to this sleek thing of ebony, pulsing with life" (*Apes* 66). This is insufficient to convince him though of the creature's humanity. Rather he uses reason, in connecting this information with another picture, that of the Archer. He is certain the Archer is human. Therefore, Kulonga who resembles the Archer only in his weaponry, is sufficiently associated with humanity for Tarzan to ask the troubling question: "Did men eat men?" (69), the place where the ethical dilemma began.

Reason led Tarzan to identify Kulonga as a man based on the information he had learned from the books in his father's cabin and instinct completed the decision to eschew instead of chew the flesh of his victim. Philosopher Immanuel Kant argued that morality rose from reason. Burroughs tacitly acknowledges this but adds in the nature-versus-nurture debate as well through the invocation of education and heredity. One might paraphrase the Apostle Paul and say: These three things remain—reason, education, and heredity—but the greatest of these is heredity.

Summatively, Pendleton claims that Tarzan "achieves the highest of human moral natures" (691). Tarzan becomes a moral exemplar of sorts. Bozarth claims that Tarzan's "sense of morality and fairness, as well as [his] compassion, decency, and [...] very real capacity for loyalty and love," ranks "above the majority of men anywhere or in any time" ("Code"). Tarzan is able to synergize the rudimentary beast and the human seed to become something greater than either. This may be observed at a physical level as well as a moral level. Pendleton continues, "He combines the beast's absolute freedom, self-assertion and power with the man's absolute commitment to virtue; from roots in the sub-human and the human, he becomes a superhuman" (691). Such superhumanity is all the stronger for its longevity to the present day. "[T]he heroes created by ERB with their highly developed codes of honor and senses of right and wrong come across as a breath of fresh air in a sea of darkness. A character who will only do the right thing and refuses to compromise his integrity is often considered quaint and archaic" to today's readers (Van Hise 6).

"Let me discern, compare, pronounce at last"
—"Rabbi Ben Ezra" (Browning, 249 [l. 99])

The distinction between the two Tarzans, identified earlier in the chapter is the distance Eliot identifies, in "Animula," between "desire and control" (71). When he "seemed to be a different Tarzan" (*Jungle Tales* 137), it is the lack of control that bothers him. He finds himself "sluggish, helpless, timid," desiring the opposites—speed, power, and courage; the comparison can be accomplished only through the simile—"wishing to flee his enemies as fled Bara, the deer" (137).

Comparisons come in a number of forms in literature. Each form functions in a slightly different manner, and each can be profitable in its own way.

A simile makes an explicit connection within the sentence by using a connection word, typically *like* or *as*. In "The Capture," the narrator employs a standard simile: "Yet they were alone, for the teeming jungle with all its myriad life, like the swarming streets of a great metropolis, is one of the loneliest spots in God's great universe" (24). Similes are, perhaps, the easiest of the comparisons to recognize because of the signal word. In Burroughs' writing, the simile is frequent, usually dealing with animals, either as subject or referent.

In this story, for example, Burroughs provides the complex simile of the gluttonous hyena and its human counterpart whose sin causes him to bloat "like a dead rat" (131). In his sickness, Tarzan shudders "like a frightened deer" (135). Often the comparison is made in terms of action. When Bolgani takes Tarzan from the cabin, he does it "as easily as you or I might lift a babe in arms" (139). The visual image is important in all these similes. In another example, the contentment of Tarzan sleeping is evoked through simile when the narrator adds the comparative image: "as quickly as a dog after it curls itself upon a hearthrug before a roaring blaze" (132). To list all the similes in even one Tarzan book would require page upon page. And the simile is but one type of comparison.

The choice of the eagle bearing Tarzan away may be a relation of the simile, the allusion. Here, the classically educated reader will likely see the analog in Zeus's abduction of Ganymede. Ganymede is the representation of human physical perfection, and Zeus takes him to live with the gods, though as an honored servant, the cupbearer. Ganymede is given immortality as well, something later bestowed on Tarzan on at least two occasions: through the pills created by the Kavuru in *Tarzan's Quest*, and through the "vile brews," some "solemn rituals," and a blood transfusion, given to Tarzan sometime in his youth (*Tarzan and the "Foreign Legion"* 159).

A metaphor makes similar comparison but in an inferential way and is meant figuratively. It is sometimes used as a general term for a figure of speech. Aristotle says: "Metaphor is the application of an alien name by transference [...]" (*Poetics* 99). This speaking of one thing in terms of another is one of the standard marks of literature. It comes from the nature of words to be, as Aristotle says, "simple or double" (*Poetics* 98). A word can mean one thing, as all but nonsense words do, or it may mean more than one thing. A metaphor takes advantage of these multiple meanings to shift the connotations of one thing to another unlike it in nature. For example, Tarzan is described as "a very hungry wild beast whom caution was holding in leash" (130). Literally, Tarzan is not a wild beast, though the fiction of the story makes that connection quite plausible. Caution cannot hold a leash, however. The leash is a metaphor for the restraint that Tarzan observes. The word *leash* is taken from its physical meaning and applied figuratively.

In the opening sentence of "The Nightmare," Tarzan is described as "empty" (129). The word is meant literally, as the next sentence begins, "Hunting had proved poor that day [...]" (129). But the word must be examined for its doubleness because it occurs in a list of adjectives that deal not with a physical condition, but with attitudes: "grim, terrible, empty, and envious" (129). Tarzan's emptiness is an indicator of the alienation that he has been fighting throughout the series of stories. The word occurs thrice in the first three paragraphs of the story. Burroughs picks up on the word, then, later in the story, when Tarzan is trying to process the dream sequence he has had. Tarzan reckons Bolgani to be imaginary and determines that he will not allow himself to "be fooled by empty things" (139). The emptiness that Tarzan feels physically and emotionally is now turned rationally. The actual emptiness of the belly becomes an image of the emptiness of intangible things, represented first by the dreams and the emotions, then finally by a rational negation.

Berglund identifies "the cabin itself as a metaphor for the English book — locked, silent, closed, containing mysteries, possible pleasures" (63). At first all Tarzan can do is "peek into the curtained windows" (*Apes* 41). He learns to open the book when he "stumble[s] upon the right combination" (42). Likewise, he learns how to open the books and stumbles upon the right combination in working out linguistic patterns. As education comes through reading books, so Tarzan's education comes also in "reading" the things found in the cabin. The skeletons, the knife, the locket all provide latent semiotic meaning.

He reads about his identity as a man and uses that knowledge to ameliorate his situation among the apes and the blacks. It takes D'Arnot, ultimately to finish this task, both in reading the French diary and in "reading" the importance of the fingerprints.

Cannibalism, likewise, becomes a metaphor. Kilgour claims that "the image of cannibalism is frequently connected with the failure of words as a medium, suggesting that people who cannot *talk* to each other *bite* each other" (16, italics original). The word *bite*, of course, can be literal or figurative. She cites Nicholas Abraham and Maria Torok in claiming that "cannibalism is the ultimate 'antimetaphor'" (16) because it takes the figurative and makes it literal.

Another type of comparison occurs in personification of non-human elements. The jungle, which was examined in chapter 1, is given a personality of sorts, or at least a metaphoric belly. "The hunger of the jungle is most clearly brought out in those phrases in which it 'swallows' someone"; Holtsmark claims such a usage causes a reader "to think of the jungle as itself alive" (57). In "Tarzan Rescues the Moon," the narrator explicitly says, "[T]o Tarzan of the Apes the flowers and the vines and the trees were living creatures" (181), and though he could not understand their replies, "[H]e knew that the whispering of the leaves was the language of the leaves—they talked with one another" (181). In order for a metaphor of this sort to have resonance, the otherness of the two objects must remain viable. For example, if one were to suggest that London's Buck was a wolf, in *Call of the Wild*, the sense of otherness is so weak as to render the comparison relatively powerless. But when London calls another of his short stories "The Sea-Wolf" and names the protagonist Wolf Larsen, the sense of otherness is maintained and Larsen's actions are read both as human and animal. (This character is not to be confused with the Tarzan actor Wolf Larson [nee Wolfgang von Wyszecki]).

Carey-Webb points out that the chapter titles in *Tarzan of the Apes* provide "various metaphorical and allegorical possibilities for reading the novel, [as] has been done for so long with *Heart of Darkness*" (131). There is much a thoughtful reader can glean from thoughtful reflection on the chapter titles, when they provide information beyond the obvious. He argues, though, that Conrad has more "complexity of symbolism" compared to Burroughs' "complexity of plot" (132). Comparatively Burroughs may incorporate his symbols at a simpler level than Conrad, while using plot as the motivation to read. Conrad's plot is relatively simple compared to the outrageous twists that Burroughs takes a reader through. None of this negates Burroughs' use of metaphor and other comparative literary devices. It merely moves him toward the easier end of the continuum. For example, Creed suggests that "the jungle becomes a metaphor for the mother's body. The jungle, like the figure of the mother[,] signifies danger and security, life and death" (169). And Newsinger claims that the jungle of "[d]arkest Africa is a powerful metaphor for the whiteman's own repressed fears which he embodies in the form of the peoples and creatures that inhabit its vast unfathomed forests" ("Lord" 59–60).

A less popular kind of comparison is what Holtsmark labels priamel: "the listing of a series of prefatory statements or attributes against the backdrop of which one is meant to view the final element in the catalogue" (60). The word is related to the word *preamble* and functions in a similar way. For example, in *Tarzan of the Apes*, the narrator writes: "Quick was Sabor, the lioness, and quick were Numa and Sheeta, but Tarzan of the Apes was lightning" (61). Rather than a direct comparison to lightning, which is achieved by the ending metaphor, the extended comparison to the animals with which Tarzan competes intensifies the reader's understanding of value and degree of his quickness. This technique is shown in detail at the end of "Tarzan's First Love," where Tarzan identifies and codifies his singleness. There Tarzan catalogues the other denizens of the jungle, each with its mate, naming five specific "others" followed by the summative "all the beasts and the birds" (23). He follows with the statement: "Only for Tarzan of the Apes is there none." Holtsmark points out, "[T]he cumulative effect of [this] is to throw into high relief Tarzan's aloneness [...]" (62).

One of the most complex forms of comparison is the analogy, where the relationship of two items in one plane of thinking corresponds to the relationship of two items on another plane. Tarzan does this in "Tarzan and the Black Boy." The narrator calls it "[t]hat strange functioning of the mind which sometimes is called association of ideas" (80). The understanding Tarzan has of the relationship between Teeka and Gazan he transfers first to the relationship of Sabor to her cubs and then to the relationship of Tibo to Momaya. He realizes reluctantly, by analogy, that he has intruded into the precious mother-bond. As David Adams points out, "Momaya has become the hero of this tale, while Tarzan is the villain" ("Jungle Tales"). It is through analogy that Tarzan comes to understand his unwitting role.

Another type of comparison is made by direct inference, usually through the juxtaposition of two contrasting characters. At the beginning of "The Witch-Doctor Seeks Vengeance," the narrator depicts a Lord Greystoke "shooting pheasants" (87). The third paragraph shifts to "another Lord Greystoke" who hunts with his hands "in a matted equatorial jungle" (87). The reader is never asked to compare the two, but by using the same name in contrasting situations, the comparison is implicit. Holtsmark uses the classical term synkrisis for this type of comparison. It is used, he says, "for the explicit purposes of contrastive judgment, of individual animals, humans, or events"; "the comparison is inferential and, in effect, unavoidable" (51). He further points out that this syntactic tool is useful for displaying and focusing "underlying attitudes" (53) of each character. Here, the civilized Lord Greystoke is portrayed as wanton and wasteful — he kills "many more birds than he could eat in a year" (87) — while the jungle lord is shown simply, and by implication frugally, "quench[ing] his thirst" (88). A similar scene is set up in *Apes*, where the English title-holder sends back his food because it is "underdone" while the other "gobbled [...] raw flesh" (67) Holtsmark contends that such a comparison celebrates the manners and methods of Tarzan's primitive existence while "those of London and the larger world of civilization are implicitly decried" (53).

But metaphors can betray as well as inform. That is, a reader may read a metaphor that the author did not intend. Singh, Carey-Webb reports, claims that Conrad fails "to distinguish between the metaphors of evil blackness and black skin" (124). This failure, however, is read into the text, both for Conrad and for Burroughs. When Burroughs refers to the black skin of the villagers, it is not in the same manner as the similes and metaphors that have been explored in this chapter. When Burroughs uses *black* in *Jungle Tales*, he is careful to use it as a signifier of color, specifically avoiding the metaphoric connotations that Singh accuses Conrad of. The one possible exception is in the use of the synonyms "black magic" (76, 77) and "black art" (77, 104, 167), which likely were terms devoid of color but unavoidable in their cliché pattern. Critics who claim that readers that have not protested the racial stereotyping have "colluded in the alleged racism of the text" (Carey-Webb 124), fail to see that such condemnation narrows the reading of the text rather than allowing it flexibility. The issue though, as Carey-Webb presents it, is not the relative racism perceived in the use of words like *black* or *darkness*, but what does a modern reader read in the text. These, though, are two fundamentally different questions. The second question says little about the author and a great deal about the reader. A fuller treatment of racism was made in chapter 5.

The use of comparisons leads naturally to the incorporation of symbols. In fact, what one reader might call a metaphor, another may call a symbol. The two are related, and separated only by relative depth of resonance. The *Jungle Tales* collection is read profitably in a straightforward manner. But this is not the only way to read. "The Nightmare" brings to the forefront the possibilities of symbolic readings as well. "The most telling readings of these tales," David Adams writes, "look into their symbolic inner structure" ("Folklorist" 3). Symbols provide a way to read events or images on multiple levels.

It is important to note that a symbol must first represent its literal self. A lion is first a lion and only after the literal meaning is established may it also stand for something else. When this doubling occurs, it "combines a literal and sensuous quality," as Harmon and Holman point out, "with an abstract or suggestive aspect" (539).

The animal figures which feature prominently in Tarzan's dream afford an important and accessible case study of symbols. The lion, Crisp says in his *Dream Dictionary*, represents "[t]he power of our physical strength, of our temper, of our emotions" (35). The eagle, in addition to signifying "dominance," also signifies "the ability to develop an integrated vision or perception out of a wide range of experience" (Crisp 63).

The uses of the lion and the eagle are not arbitrary. Burroughs follows the curse laid out against Gog in the book of Ezekiel. The prophet speaks in the divine voice: "I will give thee unto the ravenous birds of every sort, and to the beasts of the field, to be devoured" (Ezekiel 39.4). This is the curse that falls on those who attack peaceful people (Ezekiel 38.14), thinking to gain from the unsuspecting. It is the same curse that Goliath pronounces on David in the famous battle between the Israelites and the Philistines in 1 Samuel 17. Goliath shouts: "Come to me, and I will give thy flesh unto the fowls of the air and to the beasts of the field" (17.44). The same two kinds of oppressors are given.

If these two animals represent a curse, the reader must delve to discern the reason for the curse. That Tarzan has stolen from the village is easily proven. That he has murdered some of the villagers is also shown, first in Kulonga, but most readily in the old man at the pot, preceding this nightmare. One might justifiably read this latter, unprovoked murder as the cause of the curse that falls upon Tarzan in the form of the sickness and nightmare. This could be read as an authorial punishment for actions that the character has yet to learn are improper.

Burroughs, though, is not characterized by such authorial interjections of moral recompense. The offense seems to lie elsewhere. The other offended party is Tantor, the elephant. As seen earlier, the elephant is a symbol of peace. By taking this symbol and making it into the object of consumptive celebration, the symbol is defied. Logically, the meat could have been from any source; but, that the meat was from the elephant becomes symbolically important. Tarzan, in a sense, attacks the peaceful by partaking of the elephant meat in the village pot. That this is the more notable area of transgression might be supported by the final line of the story where Tarzan determines to "never again [...] eat the flesh of Tantor, the elephant" (141), an otherwise shallow observation.

Modern science has divided and subdivided the animal kingdom into a number of classifications. In a simpler division, all mobile creatures fall roughly into three categories: runners, flyers, and swimmers. In the first dream, the lion is a runner; the eagle is a flyer; and, thus, two-thirds of the animal kingdom assault Tarzan in his first nightmare. The lion, as king of the beasts, represents all land animals. The eagle, as king of the skies, known only through the books in the cabin, represents all flying animals. The only adversary missing is Gimla the crocodile. That Burroughs did not include an aquatic threat to Tarzan could be read to show that the curse is not total but only partial, more a reprimand than a punishment.

Helmut Kuhn calls these two, the lion and the eagle specifically, "[t]he two royal animals," and he goes on to interpret them as designators of "the middle part of the soul instead of the ruling part as the seat of their virtue" (73). This distinction (that the anima in the classical sense — the seat of virtue, as Kuhn says, but also of action and even anger — is separate from the more contemplative reason) is central to the corrective representation of Tarzan assaulted by lion and eagle. His oversight of proper hospitality, that of eating the meat of his friend the elephant, requires correction. Neither does it distort the symbolism, though, to suggest the spirits are reprimanding him for his treatment of the villager at the pot, whom he throttled in his impatience, his lack of virtue. Tarzan's actions, representing his anima, need purgation, symbolized in the nausea and vomiting of the sickness that follows.

The subsequent dream provides the reptile class of the animal kingdom. The snake, apparently metamorphosed from a caterpillar (of the insect class), has been identified earlier as "the most hated and loathed of all the jungle creatures" (*Jungle Tales* 61). His struggle against it in "The God of Tarzan" leaves him concluding that "Histah was not an animal" (63), so different its legless slithering and cold-blooded physiology. In psychological terms, the snake is an ambiguous symbol. Initially it must be seen as a death-bringer. Tarzan, even in his sleep, identifies it as a mortal threat as the jaws gape open to swallow him up. In Tarzan's world it is never seen in a positive role. However, as with most symbols, it can be read positively as well. Crisp points out that the snake can "depict many different things [including] the life process" as seen in the traditional physician's symbol (322).

To suggest that the snake might be life-giving rather than destructive in this dream at first seems counterintuitive. But recognizing the elements of the dream as aspects of Tarzan's anima becomes crucial. The lion as representative of physical strength, the eagle as representative of superiority, the snake as representative of the life force: all these indicate a struggle within Tarzan where these aspects have been perverted. Tarzan's prowess, like the lion's strength, has failed at the beginning of the story. He has not been able to secure food for himself. Tarzan's superiority is negated when he finds himself a scavenger, taking leftover scraps of food from the village. And finally, the image of the snake/villager represents the wrongful termination of the life force. Each of these areas must be restored. In fact, in the remaining stories of the collection, Tarzan finds success in each of these arenas. He begins to reestablish his strength in this story with the victory over Bolgani. And tellingly, when he voices the ape cry over the gorilla's corpse, "[f]ar in the distance a lion answered" (141) as a kind of confirmation. In "A Jungle Joke," the next story written though not the next one printed, Tarzan no longer relies on the village for food, but hovers above them — the eagle totem — while they struggle against the inhospitable jungle. He not only eats the bait they had used in their lion trap, but also terrorizes them with calm aplomb, a much different picture from the sneaking filcher in "The Nightmare." Finally, in the last of the twelve stories, Tarzan redeems his perversion of the life force. This has been the hardest lesson to learn, and this story only hints at the beginning of his understanding. Here, the reader witnesses Tarzan's first act of reasoned compassion toward one of Mbonga's warriors. Bulabantu's stand against the night fears and against the threat of the apes so impresses the ape-man that he intercedes on Bulabantu's behalf, giving him life rather than hastening his death.

To take the interpretation to a political reading, Tarzan is fighting off not the savagery of the jungle, but the representatives of civilization. The three antagonists with which he grapples in the nightmare represent the three people groups that most impact him.

The first is the lion. Baker affirms that "the image of the lion stands for Britain [and] the image of the bald eagle stands for the United States [in] almost a textbook case of [...] metonymic relation" (108). The royal lion of Britain has been present at least since William the Conqueror took the British throne from King Harold in 1066. He goes on to claim: "The symbol of the eagle simply stands for the [United States]; it is uniquely associated with it; and because of its familiarity [...] the symbol is effectively invisible — effectively drained of its animality" (109). Burroughs takes the inherent invisibility of the symbol and restores the animality of it through its aggression toward Tarzan.

The snake with the head of the murdered tribesman represents the "country" of Mbonga's jurisdiction. The snake, identified earlier as that seed of evil in the Garden of Eden, marks the treachery that Tarzan feels for and from Mbonga's village. It is the spoiler of original perfection. The Hebrew word in the Genesis account is *Nahash*, which Crisp identifies as not only a word for the literal snake but also "can be translated as blind impulsive urges" (322). As a political entity, then, the snake represents a government of self-service, or a disregard of others. Regardless of the objective reality, Tarzan has internalized the sense that Mbonga's warriors, and by extension all of the villagers, represent callous disregard to others epitomized by the killing of Kala. The double-edged nature of the dream, however, points to the fact that Tarzan himself suffers from this same kind of disregard, epitomized in this case by the callous strangling of the old man beside the pot whose head now crowns the dream snake. Of all the Tarzan stories, this murder may be the most egregious breach of humane consideration. Kubert, in illustrating the event, chooses to allow the old man to live after seeing Tarzan and identifying him as a hallucination. The narrative box reads: "The old man will never know how close he came to sleeping ... permanently" (5). It is easy to amend the story in this way, though to do so weakens the effect of the snake bearing the murdered man's head.

The actions of the snake are psychologically important. Crisp suggests that to dream of a snake coiling up the tree, as Tarzan sees it, represents "the blind instinctive forces of life emerging into the conscious experience" (323). The importance of interpreting this dream is that very movement from the unconscious to the conscious level. Tarzan spends the remainder of the story attempting to integrate the two in his questions of appearance and reality, in his questioning of the primacy of sight. This is an important moment of maturity. The illness that Tarzan experiences is a part of "the process of personal growth" that takes him "beyond old attitudes or situations" (Crisp 324).

The snake attempting to bite Tarzan is also significant. Crisp argues that to dream such indicates "unconscious worries about our health, frustrated sexual impulse, our emotions turned against ourselves as internalised aggression"; these things, he argues, "can poison us and cause very real illness" (323). All these are implicitly present in Tarzan's situation. First, his health is affected by his betrayal of eating elephant meat. The frustration of his loss of Teeka has caused him, secondly, to repress his embryonic sexual urges. The third characteristic Crisp identifies is at the heart of the story; Tarzan's improper use of force is dealt with by turning the aggression that Tarzan has shown to the old man beside the pot back upon himself in the form of the three attackers. That the poison of betrayal has caused a physical illness, as well, as Burroughs shows by Tarzan's vomiting, fits the pattern that Crisp has identified independently.

In interpreting the symbols, the reader comes far in interpreting the dream itself. "Every Tarzan novel is a dive into the unconscious" (Adams, "Folklorist" 4), and the dream, according to Mortimer, is "a synthesis of unconscious forces" (115). Dreams are, in the words of Bakhtin, "something standing on the boundary between reality and fantastic invention" (160). "We suffer through dreams and are cured by dreams," Bachelard says (4). How much popular psychology Burroughs might have known is unclear. But it is clear that Burroughs expected at least minimal interpretation of the dreams that Tarzan has in "The Nightmare." The series of events in Tarzan's nightmare become a kind of psychological manifestation to show, in an exterior (narrative) way, what is normally only interior and accessible through an omniscient narrator. Tarzan lacks the sophistication to say, as Leonato does in Shakespeare's *Much Ado About Nothing*, that he will "hold it as a dream till it / appear itself" (1.2.18–19). He does not know the difference, as is evidenced by the question, "Where did sleep adventures end and reality commence?" (*Jungle Tales* 140).

"Dreaming is a process of making connections," says Ernest Hartmann (3). The connections are made, though, not at the conscious level. The connections are manifestations of concerns that may continue to be disconnected in the dreamer's conscious life. Hartmann claims that "dreams indeed deal with our emotions and our emotional concerns" (2). He details this process, saying, "[D]reams deal with them by making a pictured metaphor of our concerns" (2). This is important because in literary terms an interesting dream is insufficient cause for the dream's existence. The dream is a tool of the author. Mortimer explains, "The dream permits emphasis through the recall, repetition, or rearrangement of events or through the dramatization of abstract ideas"; and then adds, "The psychological value of the dream is evident, since the dream allows portrayal of the unconscious of a character" (107). An application of the dream is required of any dream in a literary source. The question must be asked: what does the dream emphasize? In the case of Tarzan, as a character and as a representative human, the dream must be functional. The function, in Hartmann's words, is that "[d]reaming cross-connects or weaves in new material, which helps us adapt to future trauma, stress, and the problems of life" (2). In connecting the emotional state of the character with the physical circumstances the character is experiencing, dreaming "pictures or provides a *context* for the emotion" (Hartmann 4, italics original). In order to be effective as a literary device, then, "there must be a line of thought," says Mortimer, "which is released, revealed or explained in the dream" (107). In such a contextualizing function, then, Hartmann suggests that a "dream explains metaphorically the overall state — especially the emotional state — of the dreamer [...]" (12). "This metaphor making" Hartmann says later, shows up particularly "in certain cases of illness when the mind is trying to describe something that is very disturbing physically" (100). Mack summarizes this concept in his claim that "[n]ightmares occur in response to the characteristic danger situations that human beings confront in the course of development [...]" (224).

Burroughs himself suffered from nightmares throughout his life. Porges reports that he "would twist about, moan and cry out loudly and awaken the family" (196). In particular the sense of helplessness was prominent in his dreaming. Porges, based on interviews with Burroughs' sons, says his nightmares "involved the kind of situation [...] where some fearful creature or unidentified peril was approaching the room, and the individual, aware of his danger, tried desperately to move but found himself paralyzed" (196; a sadly ironic precursor to the Parkinson's disease that affected him, his son, and grandson later in life). Tarzan, too, finds himself unable to respond in the way he desires, a condition to be examined shortly.

The strange sensations, primarily visual, that Tarzan experiences in this episodic nightmare are the result of some toxin ingested from the elephant stew. "[T]hat the elephant had died of sickness several days before" (129) clues the reader to the source of the toxin. Just as Caliban, in Browning's poem, says "maggots scamper through my brain" (254 l. 72) after drinking gourd-fruit mash mixed with honey and pods until "froth rises bladdery" (254 l. 71), so Tarzan finds his senses abnormally assaulted after eating from the nasty mess he steals from Mbonga's village. In one case study, Mack speculates concerning a patient who exhibited both fever and delirium that while the disease "had induced the delirium, the hallucinatory state did not occur at the height of the fever, suggesting that a toxic agent associated with the septic illness and not simply the fever itself may have brought about the delirium" (62). Likewise in Tarzan, it seems reasonable to conclude that the toxin in the food brought on both the sickness and the nightmare. The effects are apparent when he wakes to find that "[c]old sweat stood out from every pore, [and] there was a great sickness at the pit of Tarzan's stomach" (*Jungle Tales* 134). The narrator in Dostoevsky's *Crime and Punishment* explains,

> A sick man's dreams are often extraordinarily distinct and vivid and extremely lifelike. A scene may be composed of the most unnatural and incongruous elements, but the setting and presentation are so plausible, the details so subtle, so unexpected [...] that the dreamer could not invent them for himself in his waking state [...]. Such morbid dreams always make a strong impression on the dreamer's already disturbed and excited nerves, and are remembered for a long time [51].

The activeness of Tarzan's waking brain is identified repeatedly. It is his "fertile brain" (8) and "fertile man-mind" (37) that allows him to invent games in "Tarzan's First Love" and "The Fight for the Balu"; he relieves the "sameness" of his quotidian existence with "activities of his own invention" in "A Jungle Joke" (159). In "The End of Bukawai," the narrator identifies Tarzan "as active in brain as he was in body" (106). Such an active conscious brain has a parallel activity in its subconscious level, shown by the intensity of his nightmare. That this is the *first* dream he has ever had may be questioned, despite the narrator's claim. Hartmann points out that adults who "are tough [... and] have learned to handle or ward off or keep away danger [...] recall few of their dreams" (66). It does no injustice to the text or to verisimilitude to read that this is the first dream that Tarzan recalled.

When the narrator states: "Tarzan of the Apes had dreamed his first dream" (134), he refers to the uncontrolled dreams of the subconscious. Earlier, in *Apes*, the narrator indicates that Tarzan's reading brought him "many strange and wonderful dreams" (91). And, in "Tarzan's First Love," Tarzan has "the delectable dream" (8) of becoming as hairy as his foster family. Such dreams must be read as daydreams, those flights of fancy that characterize wonder and conscious manipulation of known or suggested facts. The thinker is in control of such dreams.

In "The Nightmare," the thinker is not in control, and in fact the loss of control is a large part of the terror that the dreamer experiences. Mack indicates that the nightmare in general is characterized by an "intense anxiety of overwhelming proportions, the sense of danger and helplessness, and the occurrence or threat of violent attack, directed especially at the dreamer" (12). Hartmann reports that "nightmares of being chased or attacked by monsters or strange animals are extremely common" in children; in fact, "the most common themes are being chased or hurt" (65). In particular, Hartmann says later, the particular emotion at the fore here is "not being quite in control of their world" (72). Though Tarzan is beyond the child category that Hartmann identifies, his development aside from the physical may be plausibly understood as delayed. Burroughs himself may have remembered the type of nightmares he had as a child and transposed them into Tarzan's realm of experience. The centrality of "life-and-death matters" (Mack 16) in nightmares makes Tarzan's experience a textbook example. That Tarzan is affected sensorially and cognitively accords with psychological observation. Mack claims, "The ego in the nightmare reacts with the kind of anxiety consistent with the perception of intense actual danger threatening survival, that is, as if the threat to the dreamer were absolutely real" (17).

Bachelard writes that "since dreams are most often studied only for the development of their forms, no one realizes that above all they *mime* the *life of matter*, that their life is strongly rooted in the material elements" (129, italics original). He continues, "The dynamics of dreams cannot be understood if we separate it from the dynamic quality of the material elements that dreams work over. [...] In the final analysis, forms are shifting because the unconscious becomes disinterested in them" (130).

Freud believed that multiple symbols and multiple sources mixed together in dreams. Because of this a single symbol might represent several antecedents, or multiple symbols might represent a single source. A Freudian analysis of Tarzan's dream and its variations of interpretation might conceivably fill a book of its own. Jung, on the other hand, believed in what he called the collective unconscious, a kind of species memory that is passed on through generations. This, too, meshes with the role that heredity credits to Tarzan's responses.

Parkers' Complete Book of Dreams says, "If in your dream you were hunting an animal with a view to killing it, it may represent a personal characteristic that you may feel you should eliminate. If an animal is chasing you in a dream, this may suggest that in waking life you are in flight from some area of your personality that is stubbornly demanding expression" (42). That a dream might be instructive is evident from the utterings of the ancient book of Job, wherein Elihu says, "For God speaketh once, yea twice, yet man perceiveth it not. In a dream, in a vision of the night, when deep sleep falleth upon men, in slumberings upon the bed; Then he openeth the ears of men, and sealeth their instruction, That he may withdraw man from his purpose, and hide pride from man" (33.14–17).

This instructive dream is employed in several of Shakespeare's works. The most prominent is the pre-death visitation in *Richard III*. He develops, according to Mack, its use "to recapitulate the past, enabling him thereby to construct the dream from actions of his characters and thus to make it consistent with their natures and motives" (90). Richard is confronted in his sleep by the ghosts of those whom he has killed. First Prince Edward enters with the intention of "sit[ting] heavy on [Richard's] soul" (5.3.118) as do the ghosts of Clarence and Rivers a few lines later. The two young nephews whom he ordered smothered while held in the Tower (akin to Tarzan's strangulation of the old man at the pot) proclaim themselves to be "lead within [his] bosom" (5.3.152). And the ghost of Lady Anne intends to "[fill his] sleep with perturbations" (5.3.161). After the visitations, Richard wakes suddenly and calms his agitation with the ambivalent claim, "I did but dream" (5.3.178). All the images from the dream are part of Richard's past and are used by the author to establish blame within the perpetrator. Richard identifies his conscience as the source of the dream, and its "thousand several tongues" (5.3.193) the reason for the number of people in its torment. Mack credits Shakespeare for the incorporation of three distinct elements into literary dreams: to show "[1] the internal structure of conflict, [2] of the warring elements within the personality, and [3] of the dissection of the inner 'conscience' into various hate-filled voices, attitudes, and qualities of objects from the past" (91). Each of these can be applied in understanding Tarzan's dream.

The question must be asked, "Why *this* dream?" What in Tarzan's experience brings these images to the surface? Hartmann reasserts that dreams are subconscious attempts at problem-solving: "*unresolved* emotional concerns" Hartmann says, are the seeds from which dreams come (71, italics original). The dream then is an attempt by the subconscious to deal with "a nagging problem that has been pushed out of waking consciousness and not thought about a great deal" (Hartmann 71). Burroughs gives clues to this unidentified problem at the beginning of the story. The initial list of adjectives attributed to

Tarzan begins with *grim*. This dour, dismal demeanor indicates an internal dissatisfaction with life. His hunger is ostensibly the reason, but reflection on his failure to secure food must surely feed the hunger as well. The last item of the list is the most pointed, *envious*. His hunger may be uncomfortable, but watching others feast while he is left hungry fuels a determination to get even. Envy leads to covetousness, which ends in theft and murder. Tarzan wants to be accepted; when he is not, he finds ways to irritate those who have caused his isolation.

Even after making some reasonable connections or interpretations of the nightmare that Tarzan experiences, it is important to note that no interpretation of this dream (or of this text, or of any text) is absolutely definitive. Hartmann hedges—"[T]here is not necessarily one absolute meaning to a dream" (145). Nor does this concession, however, negate the connections that have been made. While it might be tempting to provide a full-scale psychological explication of Tarzan's nightmare sequence, Mack points out the difference between real dreams and those created for literary purposes. He concludes: "It is often not profitable to interpret the latent meaning of a dream in a fictional work beyond specific evidence provided in the work itself" (89). Determining what is implicit in the text and what is added to it, though, is not an easy separation to make.

The illness that precedes the dream should not be overlooked. Crisp suggests that illness might represent Tarzan's "intuitions about the physical condition of someone else" (219). Before Tarzan murders the villager, he watches the feast and concludes "of all the beasts of the jungle, then, man was the most disgusting" (131). "[H]is contempt for man increased" when he tasted the native beer; not even a hyena would ingest "such filthy tasting drink as that" (131). What Tarzan considers improper eating becomes true of himself as well. His physical condition reacts to his own transgression, hidden to himself but so evident in others.

Obododimma Oha suggests another way to view this situation, that the nightmare represents "the horror [...] of the Black person's existence, as perceived from a Western-Tarzanist standpoint." Their tastes, exemplified by the diseased meat and the "filthy tasting drink," put them beneath the animals, lower than even Dango, who would have enough sense to forego the native beer.

A final consideration of the dream includes the spatial arrangements of the elements. Tarzan begins his dream in a tree, above a roaring lion. Tarzan is spatially above the lion but also authoritatively above the lion; in the previous chapter his masquerade within the lion's skin showed his superiority. The near-fatal ending of that story showed how tenuous that superiority might be. The dream opens with the challenge of that superiority. Tarzan scrambles to stay above the lion. The next important spatial movement is when the eagle lifts him from the treetop and carries him skyward. Tarzan "knew that there existed in the jungle no such bird" (135). The eagle represents the books, or education, which ought to elevate him but from which he falls, a much greater fall than he would have had from his physical promontory. This is an intellectual fall or a betrayal of the mind, rather than the body. The third spatial arrangement comes in the second dream. Just as had the lion, the snake threatens Tarzan from below. Again the issue of superiority is at stake. In this instance, the head of the murdered man makes clear the ethical question. What is large and threatening in the subconscious though is merely "flicked" (135) away by the conscious mind, in the form of a caterpillar. Bakhtin affirms that the spatial identifier "assumes additional significance" (169) in such symbolic situations.

It seems, then, that a profitable reading of this story requires a number of symbolic assignments. The claim that the dream "serves as a warning to him, a warning which he partially realizes" (Mortimer 111), as did Raskolnikov's dreaming in *Crime and Punishment*, appears trustworthy. The story's conclusion, though, must go far beyond the physical lesson that Tarzan "never again would eat the flesh of Tantor, the elephant" (141). The story says a great deal about the unconscious (collective or otherwise), or to espouse Burroughs' nomenclature, the hereditary. The ethical warning concerning murder seems to elude the dreamer's consciousness, no matter how forceful the dream images are. It is not until the final story that a conscious change is evident.

CHAPTER 9

Allegiance and Apathy
Community in "The Battle for Teeka"

The story returns to Tarzan's affection for Teeka, though not in the rivalrous fashion of "Tarzan's First Love." The contents blurb from *Blue Book*—"a primitive love-affair wherein the white boy Tarzan interferes at great hazard"—misleads somewhat. It deals with the fraternal concern that Tarzan takes toward Teeka when she is abducted.

Burroughs wrote the story 5–11 March 1917 as his stay in Los Angeles was coming to a close, the penultimate story in construction, though not in publication sequence. The *Philadelphia Public Evening Ledger* added the subhead: "Teeka Saves Her Own Life, Aided by Tarzan and Taug" (2 August 1919). The *Des Moines Sunday Register* re-titled the story "Rescue!" with a subhead reading "Tarzan and Taug Save Teeka." The story has been adapted to comic form in Charlton's *Jungle Tales of Tarzan* #2 (Feb. 1965), and in Marvel's *Tarzan* #14 (July 1978), re-titled "The Battle for the She-Ape." The story was also reprinted in *Ellery Queen's Mystery Magazine* (May 1964) and *Ellery Queen's 1970 Anthology* (1969).

Teeka is alone with Gazan in the jungle, when Toog, a bull from another ape tribe, tries to kill Gazan. In defending him, Teeka interposes herself. Toog manages to shake Gazan from the tree where he had taken refuge and carries Teeka off. A hyena begins to investigate Gazan's body; Taug sees the two and kills the hyena. Tarzan finds rifle cartridges in the cabin by the sea and, curious as to what they might be, carries some with him. When he discovers what has happened to Teeka, he orders Mumga to care for Gazan and takes Taug with him to pursue Teeka's kidnapper. Toog shows off his new prize "wife," and his tribe is warned by a monkey of Tarzan and Taug's approach. The foreign apes hide in ambush. Teeka manages to get out a warning to her rescuers. Melee ensues. In the fighting Tarzan loses his knife and the pouch in which he had put the cartridges. Teeka picks them up. She throws a number of the cartridges, which explode upon impact with a boulder. The sound frightens the enemy tribe and they all flee, leaving Tarzan and Taug with Teeka.

The abduction provides what Holtsmark calls Burroughs' "ancillary erotic theme" (132), begun with Terkoz abducting Jane in the first novel and duplicated in numerous places thereafter, including Taglat's attentions to Jane in *Tarzan and the Jewels of Opar*, printed three to four months earlier in *All-Story Weekly*, and an unnamed ape's desire for Meriem in *The Son of Tarzan*, which came out in hardback the week that Burroughs was writing the story. The theme is an undercurrent from the beginning of the *Jungle Tales* collection, beginning with the allusion to Helen, the abducted woman who sparks the Trojan War.

That the story was later picked up by *Ellery Queen's Mystery Magazine* is remarkable. There the story was billed on the front cover as "Something Different." Burroughs did not consciously frame the story as a mystery, so much as a chase story. Much later he tried to mine the idea of Tarzan as detective. In a letter to Jack Byrne, at *Argosy*, he wrote that he was thinking of "making Tarzan something of a jungle Sherlock Holmes" (qtd. in Taliaferro 308). The resultant story was "Tarzan and the Jungle Murders," sold not to *Argosy* but to *Thrilling Adventures*. Vernon suggests, though, that Tarzan flirted with the conventions of detective fiction from the very beginning. In the search for Tarzan's heritage, Tarzan provides clues through the locket and the cabin itself and D'Arnot uses the then-new practice of fingerprinting to prove that the Greystoke title belongs to the ape-man (Vernon 29).

"The Battle for Teeka" provides the reader's last glimpse of Gazan, the mischievous balu of Teeka and Taug. He takes part in four of the stories, unnamed in "The Fight for the Balu." Gazan is retained in the Decca production of *Tarzan and the Little Black Boy* as a representative of the object of maternal care for Tarzan. Because children are unable to provide for themselves, they must be tended by mothers. But when the mother is absent (as occurs in this story) the duty falls to another within the tribe, because every ape is considered an asset to the community, unless extreme conditions warrant its exclusion. When Gazan is left unprotected because of Teeka's abduction, Taug takes over the protective role and saves him from the prowling hyena. When Taug prepares to leave with Tarzan, Gazan's body is given over to Mumga, an old and broken-fanged ape, for her to tend while the parents are away. The apes are not shy at tending one another's calls for help. When Teeka and Gazan are wrapped in Histah's coils, her cries bring the entire tribe on the run. It is just such a scene that Thomas Yeates illustrates. When Taug bellows out his chagrin at finding Gazan's body, again, the whole tribe comes. Such response is admirable; but the reader may easily overlook that in both cases only Tarzan does anything to help. The lesson in "The Lion" begins to show the community how to come together in mutual benefit. When Tarzan leaves little Gazan in Mumga's charge, the reader believes he is alive, though unconscious, and the embryonic sense of community will see him through to recovery. Though Gazan does not reappear, Mumga does as tacit proof that Gazan lives as well.

Thomas Yeates's illustration of Tarzan with the apes, published in *Erbania* in 1988. Copyright Thomas Yeates. All rights reserved.

"But ah! united, what reverse we have!"
Emma (Austen 51)

As the ring theory that Holstmark puts forth (discussed in chapter 2) would anticipate, when the reader arrives at the concluding stories of the collection, a general reversal of motifs occurs. The familiar reader sees this, for example, in the relationship of Lucie Manette and her father in Dickens's *A Tale of Two Cities*. After Lucie nurses her father back to health and sanity, the narrator notes: "The preceding relative positions of himself and Lucie were reversed, yet only as the liveliest gratitude and affection could reverse them, for he could have had no pride but in rendering some service to her who had rendered so much to him" (211), and he devotes himself to her protection. The same occurs in her relationship with Sydney Carton. He is first seen as "reckless in his demeanor" and bearing "a disreputable look" (57). He identifies himself as "a disappointed drudge" and states plainly: "I care for no man on earth" (63). Lucie, though, has a revolutionizing effect upon him, as he comes, through his association with her, to care for many people. Lucie's influence is instrumental in Carton's reversal of attitude. Mary Riso describes the change: "A fire soon burns where a cold black hearth had been; by the end the fire has become a beacon" (174). The *hearth* invoked by Riso might just as profitably and accurately have been *heart*. The compassion that Lucie models in the book is subtly planted and nurtured to fruition in Carton. His final thoughts, conjectured by the narrator, reveal the reversal of his attitude as he gives his life for Charles Darnay, that Lucie might be happy: "It is a far, far better thing that I do, than I have ever done; it is a far, far better rest that I go to than I have ever known" (293). Lucie is able to bring out the humaneness that was buried in the animal nature, a movement, if you will, from Toog to Tarzan. And Sydney Carton's sacrifice is echoed in the end of the first Tarzan novel.

Most notable is the ending of "The Battle for Teeka," where it is Teeka who is the savior more so that her rescuers. In "Tarzan's First Love" and again in "The God of Tarzan," Teeka needs to be rescued from first the panther then the snake. In "The Battle for Teeka," the motif ripples upward again, as Teeka is in need of rescue from the rebel ape. Tarzan, true to form, pursues and attempts to bring justice. But just as a mirror sends a message in reverse, so does Burroughs choose to let Teeka save Tarzan (though Tarzan would never admit it). The one who needed rescue becomes the rescuer in a satisfying reversal of expectations.

Even at the level of syntax, Burroughs uses the reversal of form on numerous occasions. For example, Burroughs writes, "Toog was a fine, big male, resembling in many ways Teeka's mate, Taug" (143). Why Burroughs chose two names so similar for these apes is conjectural. The alliteration and consonance makes them pararhymes. The sentence is thirteen words long, beginning and ending with the pararhyming names Toog and Taug. The center word of the sentence is *resembling*. That word in effect is the fulcrum for the two extremities, the names. The fulcrum word is also the foundational idea connecting the two. The reversal, of course, is based on the rivalry between the mate and the would-be mate. The sentence itself reveals the reversal that takes place at the end of the story, when Toog loses Teeka and she is returned to Taug.

Holtsmark has examined such techniques, found frequently in Greek and Latin writings, in Burroughs' narrative. One important stylistic effect, called chiasmus, is where the words are arranged so as to illustrate the principle "A is to B as B is to A" (Holtsmark 15), in effect setting one pattern then reversing it for emphasis. This chiasmus is seen in the description of Gazan, near the beginning of "Tarzan and the Black Boy." The narrator shows a syntactic double reverse. After establishing Gazan's difficulty remaining focused, becoming side-tracked by edible tidbits, the narrator says, "the caterpillars he always caught, and sometimes the beetles, but the field mice never" (65). Each of the three nouns — *caterpillars*, *beetles*, and *field mice* — is paired with an adverb of frequency — *always*, *sometimes*, and *never*. In a straightforward, parallel structure, the order of the words' appearance — where A represents the noun and B represents its modifier — would be AB AB AB. While Burroughs often uses such parallel forms, the idea of distractibility is enhanced by the chiasmus. Here Burroughs sets up the first AB set, then reverses the pattern to BA in the second instance by placing *sometimes* ahead of *beetles* rather than after. The new pattern is then reversed a second time by placing the modifier *never* at the end of the sentence. This rapid switching of word order matches the idea of Gazan's rapidly shifting attention. Holtsmark summarizes his claims by crediting Burroughs' "remarkably accurate sense of how language can underscore or undercut the psychology of characters or add to the internal drive of the narrative" (21).

The chiasmus is one technique of several and is often combined with others into a complex arrangement of conscious or unconscious emphasis. For example, Holtsmark identifies Teeka's escape from Sheeta in "Tarzan's First Love":

> And just as Teeka sprang for the lower limb of a great tree, and Sheeta rose behind her in a long, sinuous leap, the coils of the ape-boy's grass rope shot swiftly through the air, straightening into a long thin line as the open noose hovered for an instant above the savage head and the snarling jaws [13].

Holtsmark explicates the sentence by pointing out that the independent clause, "the coils of the ape-boy's grass rope shot swiftly through the air," is buttressed by two dependent clauses. The dependent clauses, though, differ in structure. The opening clause is made of two clauses of time, indicating the simultaneity of action, beginning with *as* (the second *as* is implied before the word *Sheeta*). Holtsmark schematizes the clause this way:

> And just as
> > Teeka sprang for the lower limb of a great tree
> and
> > Sheeta rose behind her in a long, sinuous leap [24].

He points out what is visible in the schematic, that the length in syllables of each part (true, in terms of letters and words also) is nearly the same. He identifies the "parallel vowel sequences" (24) in the beginning name of each clause as showing a conscious manipulation while preparing the reader for similar patterns. The clauses continue their parallelism with verbs describing each character's rising movement immediately modified by prepositional phrases. The coordinate conjunction *and* precedes both clauses and emphasizes the parallel nature of the pursued and the pursuer, as Sheeta moves from the latter position to the former by the sentence's end. After the main clause, the sentence again employs two joined dependent clauses. Again, one of the clauses is introduced literally with an *as*, while the other is not, but in inverted order — ABBA. Of course, the sense of time is maintained because all four of the clauses are to be understood as concurrent. The final clause ends alliteratively, Holtsmark points out, where the *s* and *g* of *savage* is echoed in the *s* and *j* of *snarling jaws*. This type of double alliteration, following in this case an ABAB pattern, is like the cynghanedd in Welsh poetics, and is held together with the assonance of the repeated short-*a* sound. In the center of the sentence is the independent clause. This is where Tarzan's action occurs. As Holtsmark says, this is to be anticipated because Tarzan is "[c]entral to this little drama" and so "the centrality of his role in this sentence" (24) reflects his centrality in the action as well.

Once these effects are identified, readers begin to see a multitude of uses and variations. Victor Frankenstein potentially speaks for the reader when he admits, "I prepared myself for a multitude of reverses" (Shelley 52). A linguistic analysis of Burroughs' writing becomes a fecund field for consideration.

"[A]lthough I am a woman [...] Come! treat me fairly."
— Bathsheba, *Far from the Madding Crowd* (Hardy 257)

That Burroughs should make some tacit comment regarding the role of women should not surprise readers. His attention to racial concerns earlier lays the groundwork. In fact, Midgley says that "the position of women, of slaves, or other races, and of non-human animals" bear a connected history in their particular subjugations (74). Newsinger, in "Reader, He Rescued Her: Women in the Tarzan Stories," claims that "a key element" in Burroughs' writing is "[t]he helplessness of [...] women characters" (42), especially when they are threatened. This may be especially true in the first Tarzan books. Esmeralda faints when Terkoz steals Jane, and when she hears or sees a lioness. When Jane fires her revolver in weak defense, she also faints. Both women are rescued by Tarzan. William Cecil Clayton, Olga de Coude, Akut, Bulabantu — all, whether male or female, ape or human, white or black, benefit from Tarzan's rescue. But, admittedly, throughout the series, most of the people in need of rescue are female, and nearly always white. The reader finds the role of female characters in *Jungle Tales*, though, to be more substantial, perhaps because no white females appear.

When Toog abducts Teeka, he expects that she will be submissive, as in general the female apes are. But she is no Mumga, an ape so old that Tarzan calls her "no good" (151) for anything but nursing the injured. Instead Toog finds a she-ape with a strong will, so strong that Holtsmark compares her to Hera (68), the meddlesome, head-strong wife of Zeus. She refuses "the proper humility of a loving and tractable spouse" to such a degree that when Toog joins his companions he is "disfigured and mutilated" (*Jungle Tales* 155) from her resistance. Teeka's reversal from rescued to rescuer puts her in the dominant position. Just as Tarzan sometimes stumbles upon success (as he did in discovering the full Nelson in fighting Terkoz), so Teeka does in flinging the twenty-year-old, unstable, rifle cartridges.

The other female figure in *Jungle Tales* is Momaya, discussed at several points previously, especially chapter 3. She is, like Teeka, a fighter, something of Kurtz's African mistress, but with more personality. When Tarzan abducts Tibo, she is ready to give her life in retrieving him, whether at the hands of the jungle god or through the demonic influences of Bukawai. She even disobeys the patriarchal authority in the tribe to get her son back. Her bravery is impressive. And of all the villagers, she is the first to earn Tarzan's ambivalent respect. This respect comes despite Tarzan's initial revulsion to her appearance. She is described as having filed teeth, slit nose and lip, metal ornaments hanging from various places on her head, and tattoos "mellowed now by age" (69). These observations are made objectively. Most illustrations modify Momaya's appearance to include one or two of these details. The most thorough is Hanlon's drawing for the *Evening Public Ledger* (28 June 1919). In the story, it is Tarzan's viewpoint of her that provides a judgment that her appearance was "very hideous and frightful" (70). The narrator reveals, contrarily, that "she was very beautiful in her own estimation and even in the estimation of the men of Mbonga's tribe" (69). The judgment comes from one who, in the first story, saw Teeka, the ape, as "a most alluring picture of young, feminine loveliness" (7). Tarzan's pool of visual images is distorted because of his upbringing. While readers and artists might consider Teeka as having a dignity or even charm, beauty is not typically the word chosen for such a form. Duane Adams has presented viewers with the paradox of such a claim in his limited edition print of Teeka posing as if for a glamour photographer.

Though Burroughs used two female examples in this collection, he strikes against the charge of sexism in these few instances. Women can have an integral role in what takes place. When Tarzan first discovers Mbonga's village, he sees that the women prepare the poison for the arrows the warriors use. Needham says that from an anthropological viewpoint, such a privilege would be "unusual anywhere" (23). But Burroughs documented the creative value of women from his first novel, *A Princess of Mars*, where "[t]hey make the powder, the cartridges, the firearms; in fact everything of value is produced by the females" (47). The women play an important role in whatever society Burroughs imagines them in.

Graham Murphy argues that sexism is implicit in every Tarzan story, regardless of the presence of female characters. For him, "[t]he archetypal feminine body is the African terrain" and "Tarzan repeatedly takes possession of this feminine environment by asserting his dominance [...]" and ownership. When he leaves the area of his birth with D'Arnot in *Apes*, he refers to the area as "my jungle" (191), and again in *Return* tells him "I think that I shall go back

Hanlon's illustration for the 28 June 1919 *Evening Public Ledger*, showing Momaya in some detail.

Portrait of Teeka by Duane Adams. Limited edition print.

to my own jungle" (49). Such possession, though, seems less a byproduct of masculine dominance or female inferiority and more a claim of ill-defined nationality. Tarzan, in his attempt to understand his identity, uses this important geographical icon as a beginning point, not as a form of gendered dominance.

So, Newsinger's claim that women in Burroughs' fiction "have an urgent need to be dominated" ("Lord" 69) is not supported by the evidence in *Jungle Tales*. Quite the opposite, the few female facets that Burroughs shined are strong

9. Allegiance and Apathy

and respected. Even Jane, who wrings her hands in terrified stupor while Tarzan fights Terkoz for her, becomes, in later books, more than "a useless cypher" (Newsinger, "Reader" 45). Burroughs understood, eventually that Jane needed to take on a higher level of resourcefulness to remain "a credible partner" (Newsinger 45) in this jungle duo. While her resources are different from those of Tarzan, she is able to employ them to her advantage, especially in such books as *Tarzan the Terrible* and *Tarzan's Quest*. Burroughs could write about women in strong roles and many rise out of the pool of stereotypical women in his books. When Newsinger admits that La, the High Priestess of Opar, in the course of several of the Tarzan novels, "achieves a kind of dignity," he dismisses her strength as "presumably accidental" ("Reader" 48). But La is not alone in rising above the typecast. Newsinger identifies Jana, in *Tarzan at the Earth's Core*, as the only female character in the Tarzan series who "had the possibility of [becoming] a convincing heroine" ("Reader" 49). When Jason Gridley, Tarzan's expeditionary companion, offers to protect her, she scoffs: "'You protect me!' she exclaimed, her tone caustic with sarcasm. 'You do not even know the dangers which beset the way'" (109). Jana leads Jason through a series of ordeals which eventually show her that he is her equal. Jana is indeed an admirable character. But La and Jane, as well as Teeka and Momaya, suggest that a number of female characters possess considerable strength. In *Jungle Tales*, where Teeka and Momaya represent the gender, the weak female stereotype is simply not at work.

"There is no branch of detective science which is so important and so much neglected as the art of tracing footsteps."
—*A Study in Scarlet* (Conan Doyle 61)

Collingwood says, "[N]owadays the identification is with the detective" for "the intellectual excitement of solving a puzzle" (86). The ratiocination that Tarzan performs, in the abduction of Teeka and of Jane, is perhaps of a simpler level than what C. Auguste Dupin does in Poe's "The Murders in the Rue Morgue," or what Sherlock Holmes does in Conan Doyle's *The Sign of Four*. But editors at *Ellery Queen's* claim that Tarzan "outdoes" ("Old" 67) every other modern detective, including Poe's. And the process of observing details that lead to a valid conclusion is the same. Just as the detective's goal is to follow the footsteps of the criminal, either literally or figuratively, so Tarzan sets out in this story to follow Toog.

In *The Sign of Four*, Sherlock Holmes identifies the three detective keys needed, by way of a French follower, Francois le Villard: "He possesses two out of the three qualities necessary for the ideal detective. He has the power of observation and that of deduction. He is only wanting in knowledge, and that may come in time" (Conan Doyle 65). In "The Greek Interpreter," he describes his brother, Mycroft Holmes, as his "superior in observation and deduction" (Conan Doyle 399); but Mycroft fails as a detective, not because he lacks knowledge but because he has "no ambition and no energy" (Conan Doyle 400). The aggregate of the two passages leaves the reader with five key ingredients for the detective's role: observation, deduction, knowledge, ambition, and energy. Each of these areas can be identified in Tarzan in "The Battle for Teeka."

Observation is the beginning point of every detective case. Without observation, the clues will be overlooked. Watson, the fictional chronicler of Sherlock Holmes, has the power of observation. When Holmes asks him to examine a hat in "The Adventure of the Blue Carbuncle," he is able to observe the wear on the hat, including the discolored band, the owner's initials, and the missing elastic. He sees the hat is dusty and some attempt has been made to ink over some discoloration. These are the observations necessary to determine what kind of man the owner is. Likewise, Tarzan, when he discovers Teeka's kidnapping, searches the ground with eyes and the air with his nose. It is his nose which finds the first clue, and he announces to the apes that a stranger has been there.

Sherlock Holmes relies on Toby, the bloodhound, for specific sensory information, but Tarzan is able to gather olfactory evidence for himself. In "Tarzan and the Jungle Murders," Tarzan sees the evidence necessary to understand the crime — the footprints of the people who left the downed plane and the angle of the bullet that killed the pilot. But it is what he smelled at the crash site that clinches his investigation. When he apprehends the parties involved, he is able to determine the murderers by scent, but because such evidence will not convince the other parties, he supplies substantiation through throat "imprints" ("Jungle Murders" 190), the angle of attack, and finally the presence of a limp in the footprints leaving the plane. Holmes, like Ramsgate in "Jungle Murders," is accustomed to the visual dominance of civilization and would consider absurd Tarzan's claim: "I carried in my memory the smell of Zubanev" (191). In "The Battle for Teeka," the narrator claims that the sense of smell is more accurate than "photographs and Bertillon measurements" (154), a system of cataloging of physical features for forensic purposes.

After noting the smell of the stranger ape, Tarzan says he will follow the outsider and bring Teeka back. The narrator claims that "[h]ad the stranger bull been within sight they would have torn him to pieces; but it did not occur to them to follow him" (150). Livingstone reports, concerning the soko, that "an intruder from another camp is beaten off with their fists and loud yells. If one tries to seize the female of another, he is caught on the ground, and all unite in boxing and biting the offender" (*Last* 325). This is a variation of theme in "The Lion," where Mamka is avenged and Numa is taught a lesson. The apes all volunteer to pursue Toog as well, but Tarzan points out that if the bulls all leave, the females and children will be unprotected and more abductions might occur. Tarzan takes only Taug as his accomplice.

Observation alone is insufficient, though, to make a detective. The second criterion Holmes identifies is that of deduction. The observer must understand what the clues mean. In the case of the hat, Watson fails. He tells Holmes, "I can see nothing." Holmes responds: "On the contrary, Watson, you can see everything. You fail, however, to reason from what you see" (203). The deductions Holmes makes regarding the owner of the hat seem as remarkable as Tarzan's claim to have known a man by his smell. Yet, in both cases, the reader believes. Tarzan deduces from the unconscious form of Gazan and the absence of Teeka that Teeka has been kidnapped rather than having gone of her own whim. In the first novel, when Jane is abducted by Terkoz, Tarzan follows by deducing the meaning of clues. The narrator combines the observation with the meaning in an extended passage:

> Here, on this branch, a caterpillar has been crushed by the fugitive's great foot, and Tarzan knows instinctively where that same foot would touch in the next stride. Here he looks to find a tiny particle of the demolished larva, ofttimes not more than a speck of moisture.
> Again, a minute bit of bark has been upturned by the scraping hand, and the direction of the break indicates the direction of the passage. Or some great limb, or the stem of the tree itself has been brushed by the hairy body, and a tiny shred of hair tells him by the direction from which it is wedged beneath the bark that he is on the right trail [*Apes* 140].

Knowledge comes into play in two ways, the knowledge of nature and the knowledge of individuals. In the case of the hat, Holmes deduces that the hat owner is intellectual and that his wife has ceased to love him. The first is a claim of science and the second a claim of psychology. The natural science that Conan Doyle had in mind is called anthropometry, a part of Alphonse Bertillon's measurement scheme. While its general intent was to identify repeat criminals, one belief contained in it was that head size was an indicator of intelligence. Holmes tells Watson that the hat-owner's intelligence is proven by the hat's "cubic capacity" (203). Burroughs, likely, would have understood; he had been at the Chicago Exposition where Frank Boas had provided head measurements to fair-goers to help establish their level of intelligence. The aspect of the wife's affections comes from Holmes's "knowledge" that a woman who loves her husband will regularly brush his hat. While the reasoning in both cases may be suspect, the pattern is established. When Tarzan follows Jane, he uses the knowledge that a squashed caterpillar will cling to the object with which it comes in contact; thus, "a speck of moisture" is a viable clue. The apes being creatures of habit, Tarzan is able to guess where the apes are likely to move next and look for clues there, because of his knowledge of their psychology. Even after the rain, Tarzan follows Toog by knowing the "well-marked trails" were "the most logical path for the thief to follow" (*Jungle Tales* 153).

Mycroft Holmes fails as a detective because he is sedentary. Tarzan leads no sedentary life. He is constantly active, both in body and in spirit. He has the ambition needed, in this case, because Teeka is more than a cow of Kerchak's tribe. His affection for Teeka, though muted, is established in the first story. His affection for her balu is shown in "The Fight for the Balu" and "The God of Tarzan," as well as his admonition to Mumga that her life would pay for any mistreatment or inattention that Gazan received while he and Taug were away. His motivation to retrieve Teeka is stronger than it would have been had it been any other member of the tribe.

The final quality that Holmes identifies is energy. This is likely the easiest of the five qualities to document in Tarzan. He not only begins the pursuit immediately, without rest, but, when he senses the rain approaching, he "accelerate[s] his pace" (152). He follows for two days, then fights along with Taug to free her from now three captors, who are joined by unnumbered reinforcements. His energy is notable.

While Tarzan may possess the requisite characteristics to succeed as a detective, following Holmes's rationale, the story itself holds little mystery. That it was republished in *Ellery Queen's* (given a new title: "Tarzan, Jungle Detective") might be considered a mystery. It contains detection without mystery, and the detection is accomplished largely in a manner that cannot include the reader because of Tarzan's reliance on smell. This negates what E.T. Guymon, Jr., says is crucial in a mystery or detective story, the reader's "matching of wits" (362). To accomplish this, the reader must be given the same evidence that the detective has. Because the smell of a criminal is not transferred to the reader when Tarzan encounters it, that clue fails to engage the reader. The narrator gives visual clues—"the imprint of a huge handlike foot and the knuckles of one great hand were sometimes plain enough for an ordinary mortal to read" (153)—but the smells of Toog or any of the apes are left undescribed. Ordinary mortal readers are left to take it by faith that Tarzan's nose is infallible. Near the beginning of "Jungle Murders," the narrator explains that "the sense of smell never failed" and "it always told a man what was what" (149), that is, if the man is Tarzan. But any avid mystery reader will leave "Jungle Murders" saying the author didn't play fair. Sherlock Holmes identifies this type of situation in Watson's narratives of his own adventures. When Watson admits that Holmes deductions are nothing short of remarkable, Holmes says that they only seem so "because the [onlooker] has missed the one little point which is the basis of the deduction"; and he continues, "The same may be said [...] for the effect of some of these little sketches of yours, which is entirely meretricious, depending as it does upon your retaining in your own hands some factors in the problem which are never imparted to the reader" (378). Such withholding is precisely the breaking of Guymon's rule, and this violation has been leveled against Sherlock Holmes as well as Tarzan. For these reasons, "The Battle for Teeka" just doesn't sit square as a mystery.

"All for one, one for all."
—*The Three Musketeers* (Dumas 89)

In the first story, "Tarzan's First Love," Tarzan looked to Teeka to provide meaning in his life. He began what has been called his "masculine journey."* While it seemed natural to Tarzan, and to most males, that the female is a vital source for male identity, John Eldredge claims "the masculine journey always takes a man *away* from the woman" (*Wild* 115, italics in original). First, Eldredge explains elsewhere, "[a] man's need for validation is one of his most desperate longings" (*Way* 128). This longing is foundational in Tarzan's turning to Teeka after the loss of his mother. "Until we have that validation," Eldredge goes on, "we live with an uncertainty down deep inside. As men we need to know who we truly are, and what we are destined to become" (*Way* 128). This knowledge seems wrapped up in the male-female relationship as a means of validation and empowerment. These first inclinations, though, led in the earlier case to frustration and self-denial. The reason, Eldredge goes on, that the male identity must come from a source other than the female is that "[a] man does not go to a woman to get his strength; he goes to her to *offer* it" (*Wild* 115, italics in original). While Tarzan has returned to Teeka in just such a role in earlier stories, it is here that the paramount example occurs. And this time, he has done so with the complicity of Taug, who has become something of a bond-brother, or at least a willing ally in a common cause.

The relationship that has developed over this course of stories between Tarzan and Taug is demonstrated by Taug when he discovers the body of Gazan. The narrator writes: "Of all the bulls of the tribe, Taug held affection for Tarzan only. Tarzan he trusted and looked up to as one wiser and more cunning" (149). Tarzan may be smaller in bulk, but Taug recognizes that his smooth-skinned companion, "playmate of his balu days" and "companion of innumerable battles" since childhood (150), offers a resource that none other of the tribe can offer. The wisdom that Taug identifies in Tarzan is pragmatic and faithful. It sees consequences far beyond his own ability to project cause-and-effect situations. This awareness has created in Taug — as well as in Tarzan — an allegiance that makes their pursuit of Teeka fitting.

The man cannot come back to the female with strength of character, though, until he has answered the question of his identity. At this point Tarzan has only partially answered that question, as the resolution of the story shows. It will not be until the proper female arrives in the form of Jane, that the answer is completed and Tarzan is able to fully give of his identity and character to the woman. After *Jungle Tales*, Teeka plays no role in Tarzan's life; after Jane arrives his life is forever changed, and she is, arguably, never completely absent from his consciousness.

Because Tarzan is relatively confident in who he is and of his perceived role in the tribe, he is able to enlist Taug in the unheard-of scheme to rescue

---

*I discovered the term in John Eldredge's book *Wild at Heart* (2001) but later found it used in a number of earlier writings dealing with masculine studies, perhaps most prominently Robert Hicks's *The Masculine Journey* (1993). The idea of masculine studies took its impetus from Robert Bly's *Iron John* (1991).

Teeka from her abductors, a partnership that began in the rescue of Mamka in "The Lion." The allegiance that Tarzan builds depends on his appeal to the more human qualities of the apes. The "super-intelligence" (75) that the narrator refers to in "Tarzan and the Black Boy" is used here to draw Taug beyond the lessons of team work that Tarzan had begun earlier.

The narrator's comments upon the "community instinct" (150) in this story are, at first, puzzling. This innate characteristic, says the narrator, "sent them huddling into a compact herd where the great bulls, by the weight of their combined strength and ferocity, could best protect them from an enemy" (151). This musk ox behavior is demonstrated nowhere in the *Jungle Tales* collection. Perhaps Kerchak can be credited with some influence here. In the first novel, Kerchak calls the tribe together when the sounds of Tarzan's titanic struggle against Bolgani are heard. Some mile distant, the narrator notes, Kerchak assembles the tribe "for mutual protection" and "to see that all the members of the tribe were accounted for" (*Apes* 45). The specific formation is not described, nor do they come to Tarzan's rescue when they discover he is missing. In *The Beasts of Tarzan*, when Tarzan joins himself to Akut's tribe he must teach them to call and respond whenever one of the group voices "the hideous cry with which the tribe of Kerchak had been wont to summon its absent members in times of peril" (32); so, the practice is not general to the apes. In "The Battle for Teeka," Toog expects that the bulls of this alien tribe "will fight a stranger to the death in protection of the mate or offspring of a fellow, precisely as they would fight for their own" (142). In the *Jungle Tales* collection, though, the evidence of their actions suggests the opposite. In "Tarzan's First Love," the rule was every ape for him- or herself, as they run from Sheeta's entrance. In "The Lion," when Numa enters the glade where the tribe is eating, "the apes turn and flee, huge bulls trampling upon little balus" (118), in their effort to reach the trees. It is after this event that Tarzan teaches them through the retrieval of Mamka's body. This story, "The Lion," is the first where a community effort is shown by the apes to fight against an enemy, which is referenced in the narrator's claims regarding community instinct. The pummeling of Sheeta's body in "The Fight for the Balu" seems inadmissible in this regard because Tarzan's attack had weakened the animal and made the encircling apes actions somewhat risk-free, though the narrator does allow some interpretive room here. This is the approach Joe Kubert gives in his DC rendition, where the inset double panel shows Tarzan, left, struggling with the panther (while a second panther added by Kubert prepares to join the fray), as the apes, right, stand watching. But the narrator notes that the novelty is "following up an enemy offender to wrest his prize from him and punish him" (150) rather than the apes working together for a common offense or defense. The claim that "they had as yet not reached a mental plane which would permit them to work as individuals" (150–51) seems backwards. The individual instinct is the more primitive of the two. As suggested in chapter 3, the first counter to individualism is the maternal instinct. From that, eventually, Fiske theorizes, cooperation

Joe Kubert's full-page panel with insets depicting the apes as bystanders while Tarzan fights Sheeta. DC Comics 213 (October 1972), "Balu of the Great Apes," *Tarzan of the Apes.* Copyright Edgar Rice Burroughs, Inc. All rights reserved.

rises and altruism can be born. The progression is more logically, then, from individual, to parent, to community member.

In "The Lion," Tarzan considers the apes' behavior:

> He recalled how ludicrous the great bulls had appeared in their mad scramble for safety that day when Numa had charged among them and seized Mamka, and yet he knew them to be fierce and courageous. It was the sudden shock of surprise that always sent them into a panic; but of this Tarzan was not as yet fully aware [125].

To make some sense, then, of the narrator's claim regarding the community instinct, a reader may suppose that an unwritten phrase, "when the apes are not surprised," precedes the claim. If the apes had had time to prepare for battle, they would have taken up just such a position, instead of running for the trees. It is more believable, as the narrator claims, that "[t]he idea of separating to do battle" (151) was new to them. That was the lesson Tarzan taught them in "The Lion," where Taug acted as decoy while Tarzan' stole the body. When, in "The Battle for Teeka," the bulls all desire to join with Tarzan in tracking down the interloper, this is change for the better. Tarzan must remind them, though, that teamwork and allegiance have multiple faces. The allegiance to the tribe requires that no one be left vulnerable. It is with that in mind that Tarzan and Taug take the rescue of Teeka upon themselves—two or three against one it would seem—and leave the others to care for the remainder of the tribe. In this way, their allegiance to each other as members of the same tribe shows the rightful dispersal of duties that benefits them all.

CHAPTER 10

Shooting in the Dark
The Role of Imagination in "Tarzan Rescues the Moon"

This last story of the series, written 14–18 March 1917, showed the ambivalence of Tarzan's superiority. Tarzan's reason sets him apart from the others, but it provides only partial answers to his questions. As the series of stories concluded, the editors of *Blue Book* seem to have lost their enthusiasm when they simply labeled the story as containing "some of the most surprising but typical adventures" of the ape-man. The story has been adapted to comic form in Charlton's *Jungle Tales of Tarzan* #2 (Feb. 1965), *Golden Comics Digest* #4 (August 1969) and Marvel's *Tarzan* #7 (Dec. 1977).

One night, Tarzan watches a party of men around a fire. They have erected a thorn barrier around them to keep lions at bay. One of them is taken by a lion, however, despite their throwing lit branches at the prowling carnivores. Later, Tarzan muses about the nature of life, the universe, and death. He tells Taug that the stars are the eyes of beasts, analogous to the eyes of the lions he had witnessed outside the fire of the tribesmen. A meteor is the firebrand thrown by the moon to keep the beasts away. Taug wonders skeptically about what Tarzan has said. When he tells the other apes, they feel threatened by Tarzan's otherness and plot to kill him. One of the black tribesmen enters the territory of Kerchak's apes. Tarzan recognizes him as one who had stood up to the lion attack with a burning branch. Because he admires the bravery the man has shown, he interposes himself to keep the apes from attacking. Taug joins him. The other apes circle. Before a battle can take place, Tantor interrupts and disperses the apes. The tribesman flees. Tarzan goes to the cabin, abandoning the company of the untrustworthy apes. After a month of separation, Taug witnesses the beginning of a lunar eclipse. Thinking the sky-beasts are eating the moon, he rushes to the cabin and calls Tarzan out to help. Tarzan shoots arrows into the sky and soon the moon begins to wax again. For his heroic deed the apes welcome him back to the tribe. Only Tarzan lacks faith in his ability to rescue the moon.

Related to the trickster's propensity to let his cunning run ahead of plan-ning is his unhesitating gambling. In "Tarzan Rescues the Moon," after the apes have called Tarzan back from the cabin to address the calamity of the disappearing moon, Tarzan gambles that, according to his analogy-based understanding of the universe, he can frighten away the destroyer, just as he would frighten away a nocturnal predator in the jungle. Tarzan, of course, has never dealt with such an occurrence and is gambling that his actions will mesh with some other workings of the universe. Holtsmark points out that this story is related to an event among the Apaches, where the white men threatened to shoot the moon with a cannon (a telescope); during the eclipse the leader grew quite concerned and peace came only after the eclipse began to reverse (125–27).

Holtsmark calls this ending to the collection "a witty and amusing note" (87). In it, Burroughs provides an "adaptation of theories current in his day about the mythmaking capacities of 'primitive' peoples on the basis of the observation of natural phenomena" (124–25). Anthropologically, Burroughs wrote in line with current understanding of non–Western people groups.

> "I never cared much about moonlight before."
> –Phoebe, *The House of the Seven Gables* (Hawthorne 189)

The moon is central to this story, though this is not the first time Tarzan has speculated concerning it. The moon runs as a silent background in many of the stories and images of Tarzan, as Charles Vess shows in his illustration for *Tarzan: The Lost Adventure*. In "The God of Tarzan," Numgo advances the theory that Goro, the moon, is responsible for "the lightning and the rain and the thunder" (49), and offers as evidence the unrelated fact that Goro's light presides over the Dum-Dum. It, arguably, holds for the apes the aura that Conrad describes in *Lord Jim*, "the dispassionateness of a disembodied soul" (159), an entity both within and outside their world. "[T]he belief of the apes in Goro and the moon as high god," Barnard says (actually the narrator calls it "the brilliant god of their savage and mysterious rites" [*Jungle Tales* 190], not a "high god"), is a connection between Burroughs' apes and authentic African culture, in particular "that his ape world has part of its inspiration in early Khoisan ethnography" (108). Stephen Watson, in his poetic representations of Khoisan* (or more accurately /Xam) beliefs entitled *Return of the Moon*, for example, affirms the belief that the moon walks across the sky, though he says in his notes that not all the beliefs ascribed to these people by Westerners can be corroborated. He cites Guenther, who writes in *Bushman Folktales* that no indicators

---

*Wylie writes succinctly, "Just what to call this panoply of related but scattered peoples, speaking a multitude of mutually unintelligible languages, remains controversial" (*Elephant* 63). The variations *Bushman, Khoi, Khoikhoi, Khoesan, Khoesaan, Khoisan, Saan, San, /Xam* all relate to some segment of this people group. When the source does not show a preference, I have used the term *Khoisan*.

Tarzan silhouetted against a huge equatorial moon by Charles Vess, published in *Tarzan: The Lost Adventure* (Dark Horse 1.2, February 1995). Copyright Edgar Rice Burroughs, Inc. All rights reserved.

point to a belief "that the moon was regarded as the bringer of rain, game[, or] food, let alone the object of worship" (82). But Guenther confirms that the moon is often given human characteristics by some African groups, often male, though sometimes female, and that rituals are more often performed under a full moon (for visual reasons), as the apes perform their Dum-Dum. In one Bushman story, the moon sends the hare with the message of rebirth or life after death, which the hare, a trickster figure, reverses. In consequence the moon tells the hare that she will be cursed with a split lip and timidity — "Having said this, the moon remained silent" (Guenther 75). The silence of the moon is frustrating to Tarzan in "The God of Tarzan," and consistently maintained in "Tarzan Rescues the Moon." For all the invention that Burroughs is famous for, his incorporation of bits of contemporary knowledge is notable (even when later that knowledge appears discredited). When Tarzan confronts the moon, he believes that he has frightened Goro into hiding "when a cloud came and obscured her face" (51). At this point no one seems concerned at the disappearance of the "full, [...] great, glorious, equatorial moon" (50). Tarzan, at least, has observed that sometimes the moon "sleeps late into the night, or [...] wanders through the sky by day" (181). At the time of "The God of Tarzan," the ape-boy has not planted the seed of fear in the idea that the moon can be eaten and thus removed from their world forever.

After Tarzan's attempt to locate God in the moon, he finds his intelligent reasoning brings a more well-supported answer to the moon's existence, this time by analogy, in "Tarzan Rescues the Moon." (Aside from these two stories, Goro is mentioned only once in the collection.) After watching the fire of the camped warriors with its satellites of beasts' eyes, he identifies the moon with the fire and the warriors. The stars remind him of the lions prowling about the native's fire, which corresponds to the moon. The danger, of course, is that the lions are present because of their desire to devour the men. So the eyes represent a threat. When he relates this idea to the apes (via Taug), they scoff and determine that Tarzan is the greater danger, causing Tarzan to choose the cabin over the tribe as a place to live. Because of Tarzan's warning, Taug later identifies the slowly perceptible disappearance of the moon, consistent with a lunar eclipse, as the prophesied devouring by Numa of the sky.

One of the most ancient uses of the moon is for measuring time. Even in this story, when Tarzan leaves Kerchak's tribe, his absence is "a moon" (189). Many ancient peoples have used the moon similarly. The moon, as Diana Brueton says, "was a far easier to see and [a] more effective measure of time than was the Sun's slow journey over a year" (136). It has been called "the earliest timepiece" (Brueton 224). American folklore named each full moon of the year as a way to reckon the passing of time and the place of the cycle. To today's general reader only the Harvest Moon (September's) may sound familiar among such others as the Strawberry Moon (June's) or the Beaver Moon (November's).

The most insistent and frightening application of the passage of time occurs, of course, in an eclipse. In Thomas Hardy's *Return of the Native*, when Clym and Eustacia sneak out to meet by moonlight, it is the night of an eclipse. As Eustacia pleads for Clym to give her a better life, the moon is slowly disappearing. In mournful recognition, she says, "[S]ee how our time is slipping, slipping, slipping!"; then to emphasize the relationship between themselves and the cosmos, she points with resignation "towards the half-eclipsed moon" (Hardy 170). And as the premonition suggests, the relationship fails. Eclipses are seen in many cultures as "an omen of some catastrophic event" (Brueton 222). The terror of the eclipse to Taug is grounded well in anthropology and folklore. Though his understanding of what the moon is may be ill-informed, his dread of the unnatural disappearance is quite real.

The moon is many things. It is a light. It is a clock. It is at times an adversary. It is an ambiguous symbol, one of several, in this story. Bachelard describes the moon as "matter before being form" (121), that is, as the stuff that something is made of. The moon in this story is emblematic, then, of the human that Tarzan is becoming out of the simply animal matter that he has grown in among the apes. Bachelard says also, the moon clearly is a cosmic influence that at times "impregnates the universe and gives it a material unity" (121). The moon represents an egg-like function. The "huge, swollen moon" (175) that opens the story sets up this pregnancy image. It is, as Watson says in "The Sun, the Moon and the Knife," "full of moon-children" (30). The egg likeness informs the image of rebirth, first when Tarzan emerges from the cabin at Taug's call and then when the moon emerges out of its own absence. The Tarzan at the end of the collection is ready to be a human, ready for the imminent arrival of European civilization and to take his place at a higher level.

Similarly, Marie Bonaparte identifies the moon as "a mother symbol" in Poe's writing, especially in "Annabel Lee" (130) and in "The Unparalleled Adventures of One Hans Pfaall" (643). In "Annabel Lee," the moon is the dream-bringer, and the stars represent the eyes of the beloved. In Tarzan's situation, he mis-identifies the eyes as enemies of the moon. When the moon has returned to full, and the stars remain, the narrator provides a unified picture, a prophecy of what is to come, when the eyes of the beloved and the bringer of dreams work together. The prophetic change in Tarzan occurs with the arrival of Jane to the jungle nine months later (Hanson reckons the time as 30 April 1908 to 2 February 1909).

Just as the moon becomes a kind of womb image, so the cabin, as mentioned, becomes the protective womb, nest, cocoon, or eggshell that Tarzan needs to develop his identity. When Tarzan leaves Kerchak's tribe, after preserving Bulabantu's life, it is for a time of spiritual and emotional reflection. The leaders of the tribe had charged him with differentness, with not belonging. Tarzan had made the same observations in the first story, "Tarzan's First Love." There, however, the alienation was predominantly self-inflicted. At this late point in the collection, Tarzan has put together a rudimentary identity. When the apes call it into question, it prompts Tarzan to examine his and their assumptions. The cabin is his place of safety, his personal cocoon. None of the apes can understand the latch mechanism, so the door can be opened only by Tarzan.

In some respect, the cabin is a symbol of, as Bonaparte says, "that primal dwelling in which we all originally abode; the mother's body" (516), and as she says elsewhere, "one of man's universal symbols; that which represents a woman as a building" (643). The return to the cabin is a return to his human parentage. This retreat, superficially a break with his ape identification, is a time of introspection. The statement in "Tarzan's First Love," "Tarzan is a man. He will go alone" (23), essentially an admission of alienation, lacks the positive connotation of this later departure. Here the isolation is constructive, strengthening his confidence and sense of self, not in giving him an answer — it takes D'Arnot's intervention to provide that — but in the security of asking questions. Tarzan finally comes to accept that questions can go unanswered without undermining the answers he has already accepted. This return to the cabin, as symbol of human heritage, connects Tarzan to his human identity and answers him, even in his ignorance.

That the cabin is surrounded by jungle with an opening through the harbor to the ocean (another womb image) is instructive here as well. "Emotionally, nature is a projection of the mother" ([115]), Bachelard says. He identifies

Bonaparte's study of Edgar Allan Poe as helpful. Bonaparte, for example, claims: "[T]he sea [...] is the universal, phylogenetic 'mother' symbol" (130). Bonaparte identifies bodies of water with the mother figure in many ways. In Poe's early poem "The Lake," she says, the water "would seem to have been the symbol of his dead mother which lured him on and beckoned him to return and once more merge in her" (37). Bonaparte claims that "the sea is an ancient, universal symbol of the mother [...]" (91); and, "Of all the mother symbols common to mankind, the sea is one of the most constant and fundamental" (290). Tarzan's return to the cabin by the sea can be read as his mythic return to the mother and to all the life-giving properties associated thereto.

But the sea is much more than a mother symbol. It often represents the unknown or the subconscious, or as Crisp says, "the boundary between the unconscious and the conscious" (340). That the cabin is at the sea is important also because it is here that Tarzan attempts to plumb his own identity. Crisp avers that "[t]he sea, with its surface and hidden depths, lends itself to depicting this human experience of known and unknown regarding self" (339). Crisp identifies the importance of the sea as a boundary, a fluid one, if you will, between the real and the imagined. "The enormity of the sea," Crisp continues, "is also a visible image of the enormity of our own inner world, most of it unknown, and also the relationship we have with the universe, which we exist in yet know so little about" (339). It is this plumbing of the depths that a reader might infer occurs in Tarzan's month alone. "Water is, in a sense, embodied coolness," Bachelard says (31–32); it is the image of the stasis that precedes change. But its "coolness [has] a power of awakening" (Bachelard 31) Tarzan to possibilities that he has never before considered.

Tarzan cannot drink of the sea as he can of the rivers and streams that flow into it. Bachelard points out that "sea water is an inhuman water, [because] it fails the first *duty* of every revered element, which is to serve man *directly*" (152, italics original). Sea water is much the same in appearance as fresh water, but it fails to nourish. While it addresses thirst, it cannot satisfy it. "Water, the substance of life," Bachelard says, "is also the substance of death for ambivalent reverie" (72). In "Annabel Lee," the sea becomes the place of bereavement and the womb of marriage becomes a tomb of death. The speaker of the poem spends endless nights pining the loss of his beloved, "[i]n this kingdom by the sea" (Poe 957). The proximity to the sea water in this story symbolizes the difference between Tarzan and the apes that he has grown up beside. The apes have become sea water to him, not able to nourish and strengthen him. And though he has survived many years, with some metaphoric sea water, he cannot thrive in this context alone. This idea looms essential in this last story before the arrival of Professor Porter's party, which represents the fresh water that Tarzan has been craving.

The moon, supported by a number of other symbols, represents the change that is taking place within Tarzan. The story is only superficially about the moon. Its depth is the personal rebirth that Tarzan undergoes as represented by the eclipsed moon coming to life again out of itself.

10. Shooting in the Dark

> "I want to see life, to travel the world, and write things like Kipling [...]."
> — Richard Hannay, *The Thirty-Nine Steps* (Buchan 40)

Many readers have assumed that Burroughs used Kipling's *Jungle Books*, written less than two decades earlier, as a starter for *Tarzan of the Apes*, as do Fenton, Taliaferro, and Conrath, who says Burroughs has "often been (unfairly) accused of poorly parodying" Kipling (30). Early comparisons lauded Kipling. For example, A.B. Noble asserted that Kipling's superiority is shown in the treatment of the animals, that is in his "fidelity to actual traits" (58). Just what those traits are remains to be made explicit. This claim leads Noble to conclude that Tarzan's narrative "has imagination without truth, and hence leads to nothing" (60). "The main difference between Kipling and Burroughs," Altrocchi claims, similarly, "is a question of art" (94). Altrocchi lauds Kipling's "correct and vigorous English" while disparaging Tarzan readers as "hav[ing] the mental caliber of children" (94). Nesteby, on the other hand, comes down on the other side of the issue. "The *Jungle Books* lack Burroughs' force of the primitive [...]" ("Tenuous" 483), he says. "Posterity has, thus far, chosen Tarzan over Mowgli [...]" ("Tenuous" 484). William G. Hale, a British librarian, defended Burroughs' writing, in 1922, as "no worse than the speech with which Kipling endows his animals" (letter to the *Wisconsin Library Bulletin*, 24 May 1922; qtd. in Porges 364). Ray Bradbury puts a rhetorical question to use when he asks what our world would be like if Burroughs had never written about Tarzan; would our world be similarly altered by someone else? He answers: "Kipling had his chance, and didn't change the world, at least not in the same way" (xvii). He notes that Kipling's Mowgli stories "are known and read and loved around the world, but they didn't make most boys run amok pull their bones like taffy [...]" (xvii–xviii). Answers vary from reader to reader as who was the better writer, because "better" is a subjective term. Bradbury suggests that Kipling is a "liked" author but Burroughs is a "loved" one (xviii). To the objective question, who has sold more books, the answer is clearly Burroughs.

The story of Tarzan in general, what Kenneth Kidd calls "the folkloric-turned-literary story of a child raised by animals" (124), is the bed from which Kipling's *Jungle Books* sprang as well. Both stories lead to the challenge of confused identity. Just as Tarzan concludes that he must become human in these stories, Mowgli determines to himself, "If I am a man, a man I must become" (*Jungle* 57); and, just like Tarzan, Mowgli concludes at the end of "Tiger-Tiger!": "Man pack and wolf pack have cast me out [...]. Now I will hunt alone in the jungle" (*Jungle* 71).

As the source for his Tarzan idea, Burroughs himself typically referred to the myth of Romulus and Remus, the founders of Rome, as he does, for example in a 1931 radio interview for KTM, Los Angeles. This is the same year that questions of plagiarism were voiced in England. Porges says that Burroughs wrote to the editor of *The Bristol Times*, 13 February 1931, in response to a claim that he had stolen his ideas from several British writers, including Kipling. He wrote: "To Mr. Kipling [...] I owe a debt of gratitude for having stimulated my youthful imagination and this I gladly acknowledge," though he insisted that nothing was stolen, that Mowgli himself was based on earlier characters (qtd. in Porges 130). But the charge rankled Burroughs. He wrote in his letter: "It is all very silly, and perhaps noticing such charges is sillier yet, but no man enjoys being branded a thief" (qtd. in Porges 132). This is an issue that Burroughs took personally. As Atamian points out, this was not perceived as a claim regarding "one's talents as a writer" but "one's integrity as a man" (12). And the claim that the *Jungle Books* were the source Burroughs used for any of the Tarzan stories, Atamian says, "is farfetched" (85).*

Later, Kipling actually referred to Tarzan in his autobiography, *Something of Myself*, saying that "the genius of all the genii was the one who wrote a series called *Tarzan of the Apes*" (235). Porges suggests that Kipling's attitude "achieves an air of condescension and lofty tolerance" (132), in calling Burroughs an imitator, but it nonetheless affirms Burroughs' achievement (and Conrath, like Bradbury, points out that Tarzan has had far more imitators than Mowgli ever did). Burroughs, on his side, told the Bristol editor, the controversy "has reawakened my interest in my set of Kipling, which I have not opened for many years," despite the rumored "disparaging remarks" attributed to Kipling concerning Burroughs (qtd. in Porges 132). And earlier, in a letter to his editor at Volland dated 26 January 1929, he called himself "an ardent Kipling admirer" (qtd. in Porges 429).

The acknowledgement of Kipling's influence seems to come easier to Burroughs, with the passing of time. In correspondence with Altrocchi, Burroughs adds to his list of remembered sources of the Tarzan character: "Then, of course, I read Kipling" (letter 31 March 1937; qtd. in Porges 130). Oliver Poole, also, quotes Burroughs as adding in 1938, "and I loved too, the boy Mowgli in Kipling's 'Jungle Books.' I suppose Tarzan was the result of those early loves" (13). Porges later reports that Burroughs found Kipling's fiction "boring" (194), preferring his poetry.

The question of probability often comes up when either Tarzan or Kipling's Mowgli is discussed. Because the topic spans both literature and sociology, proofs are sometimes tendered regarding the plausibility of either Tarzan or Mowgli ever reaching adulthood. Midgley, an important scholar on animal nature, writes regarding species differentiation that "it is often possible for an infant placed in an alien group to grow up imprinted on it, and to imitate many of its habits" (105). The principle, then, if not the specific, is sound in both these stories. This is the idea that propelled the plot of *Greystoke* to its unusual interpretation of the Tarzan story.

Midgley herself demurs when the adopted species is human. "It seems

---

*Atamian has his own belief that the origin of the Tarzan idea comes from a passage in Du Chaillu where a white-faced apeling mourns the death of its mother; the natives tease Du Chaillu noting the resemblance between the baby ape and the European explorer. See Atamian's full explanation, 95–106.

impossible that a child should be brought up from the start by wolves or any other terrestrial species, because the sheer physical work is beyond them" (107). Being adopted at one year (Tarzan) or at two (Mowgli) is "remarkably early," Midgley says (107). "If [...] the thing could be done," Midgley goes on, the adopted human would "have mixed imprinting" and be comfortable in neither birth nor adoptive environments (107). Both Burroughs and Kipling sieze on that "If." Both authors set aside the realities of biology and sociology to explore the metaphoric existence of their respective hero.

In the case of Tarzan, Midgley's earlier commentary seems especially appropriate: "If brought face to face later with members of its own species, it may transfer its allegiance to them, or more often reach an uneasy compromise between the two" (105). Midgley is writing long after Burroughs, but the observation seems aptly predicated on Burroughs' Tarzan stories. After the events in *Jungle Tales*, Tarzan is ready to transfer allegiance to Professor Porter's party and European civilization in general. But his pendulum swings back at the end of *Apes* and beginning of *Return* to show an uneasy compromise in his behavior.

> *"See the value of imagination."*
> — Sherlock Holmes, "The Adventure of the Silver Blaze"
> (Conan Doyle 300)

When Burroughs wrote, "[I]magination is but another name for superintelligence" (*Jungle Tales* 75), he affirmed the French philosopher Bachelard, who claimed (later than Burroughs) that imagination was a "superhuman faculty" (16). Bachelard said, paradoxically: "A man is a man to the extent that he is a superman. A man should be defined by the sum of those tendencies which impel him to surpass the *human condition*" (16, italics original). He goes on to say, "The imagination invents more than objects and dramas— it invents a new life, a new spirit; it opens eyes which hold new types of visions" (16). Additionally, he says imagination "is the faculty for forming images which go beyond reality" (16). Dennis Brutus, similarly, claims that creativity must be considered "a quintessential part of being human," that the ability to create is rooted in human nature (9). Don Maclennan, likewise, identifies the vivifying nature of the imagination, in *Notes from a Rhenish Mission*: "Imagination gave me / eyes and ears / with which to live" (21).

Sherwood Anderson claims: "It is imagination that drives us on, that can destroy us, that sometimes makes a man do heroic deeds, that produces all of our art and our poetry, that has produced all of the inventions that make modern life so strangely different from life a few generations ago" ("Man" 39). He provides by way of example: "our railroads, our automobiles, the telephone and telegraph, the radio" ("Man" 39). This is the same impulse that causes the narrator in "Tarzan and the Black Boy" to claim: "Imagination it is which builds bridges, and cities, and empires" (75). Anderson says further, "The imagination of man is the attribute perhaps least of all understood" ("Man" 39.) In a passage that sounds much like Burroughs himself, Anderson writes:

> But I am not going to try here to set myself up as a thinker. I have never put a very high valuation on myself as a thinker. I am, however, a man in love with the art of writing, and if I am anything of any importance at all to my fellows it is as a story teller and a story teller must always be concerned, first of all, with human life ["Man" 39–40].

Elevating the role of the storyteller to a place above the thinker is a way to value as real that which is more than cerebral, that which addresses the emotional and visceral in the human response. Later, Anderson makes the insightful claim that human life is experienced "on two planes," made up of what is real and what is imagined (44). He theorizes: "These roads do not cross each other but the road of the imagination constantly touches the road of reality" (44). These roads are the land and the sea illustrated by Bachelard earlier. It is the interplay of these two worlds/roads that inform human perception and quantify that which is called life.

What Tarzan does in the cabin for the month of his absence is not recorded. The narration remains with the apes and Tarzan's departure and return are seen from the same viewpoint. The reader knows, though, that Tarzan is "filled with [...] curiosity" (*Jungle Tales* 19). Bachelard contends, "Curiosity sets the mind of man in motion" (27). The reader also knows that on earlier occasions, Tarzan has explored the books more often than anything else when he has spent his time there. Such study "arous[es] his curiosity, stimulat[es] his imagination and fill[s] his soul with a mighty longing for further knowledge" (*Jungle Tales* 48). It would be reasonable to assume that this month away is a time of intensive study, uninterrupted by the squabbles of the tribe. This is a time for the education of Tarzan's imagination, a nearing of Anderson's two roads. Hyde writes: "Imagination assembles the disparate elements of our experience into coherent, lively wholes" (138n). It is just such an assembling stage that Tarzan encounters in his month at the cabin. When the narrator cites the imagination as the area stimulated when Tarzan is puzzling through the letters in the children's primer, the reader infers that it is just such stimulation that Tibo lacks in the earlier story, either from culture or from aptitude, which gives rise to the contrasting situation that Tarzan represents. When Tarzan emerges from the cabin's cocooning influence, his understanding of himself is changed. No longer does he believe that he "is greater than God" (56); instead, he is "skeptical" that he has the power others ascribe to him (191). He has honed his reasoning, creative, imaginative power and arrived, paradoxically, closer to humility.

Tarzan is different from every other creature that he knows, especially the mangani tribe where he has grown up. As Hank Morgan said of his medieval compatriots, so might Tarzan observe of Kerchak's apes: "Their very imagination was dead" (Twain, *Connecticut* 124). The civilized analog of this is embodied in Miss Pross, the no-nonsense caretaker in the Manette household, in *A*

Tale of Two Cities. When Mr. Lorry asks her about what she might imagine, she retorts: "Never imagine anything. Have no imagination at all" (Dickens 73). The lack of subject in each sentence requires the reader to interpret whether these two sentences are declarative or imperative. Does she mean "*I* have no imagination at all"? Or, is she giving direction, as in "*You should* have no imagination at all," as a kind of life philosophy? Both might be true of the mangani, as shown by their distrust of Tarzan's use of his imagination.

Imagination is crucial, but impotent without some kind of application. Tarzan excels in application as well. Like Victor Frankenstein, he might well reflect, "My imagination was vivid, yet my powers of analysis and application were intense" (Shelley 200–01). It is interaction with the world, the treading of both Andersonian roads, that gives imagination meaning.

> "I once had a friend, the most noble of human creatures, and am entitled, therefore, to judge respecting friendship."
> — Victor Frankenstein, *Frankenstein* (Shelley 27)

In "Tarzan Rescues the Moon," this last story of the collection, Taug's friendship with Tarzan is solidified. Taug, who had been Tarzan's rival in "Tarzan's First Love," becomes his greatest ally. This "symmetrical reversal," as Holtsmark calls it (42), enhances the reader's appreciation for Taug's commitment. Most notably, Taug alone accompanies Tarzan to rescue Teeka from Toog and his associates. When Taug senses danger in the moon's disappearance, he turns to Tarzan rather than the tribe.

Tarzan's acceptance by Kerchak's apes has been always tentative. In "Tarzan's First Love," the narrator identifies for the reader, after Tarzan's abrupt entrance into the midst of the tribe, "the bristling neck hair which remained standing long after the apes had discovered the identity of the newcomer" (20). His difference makes the apes "nervous and unstrung for a considerable time," (20) each time he enters unexpectedly. And, the narrator goes on, even after visual identification, "all found it necessary to satisfy themselves that he was indeed Tarzan by smelling about him a half dozen or more times before they calmed down" (20). The species identifiers missing in Tarzan make for a continual tension among the apes. As Midgley points out in cases of cross-species adoption, the outside member "will never be fully integrated into its foster-species because many of the appropriate signals are impossible to it, and it has innate tastes of its own that will set it apart" (105). Tarzan's sense of humor, for example, as shown in "The Lion," is alien to the mangani, and becomes a cause for tension among them. Likewise, his desire for play, which is spurned by the adult apes, continues long beyond childhood in Tarzan.

While the question of Tantor's ability to understand gratitude is debated in "The Capture of Tarzan," the apes' ability is shown developing in Taug and

Teeka throughout. The exploration begins in "The Fight for the Balu," when the narrator asks, "Is gratitude a possession of man only, or do the lower orders know it also?" (46). In "Tarzan's First Love," Tarzan rescues both Teeka and Taug from death. In "The Fight for the Balu," he rescues their child, Gazan. In "The God of Tarzan," again, he rescues Teeka and Gazan. In "The Lion," it is Taug who joins in Tarzan's plot to rescue Mamka's corpse, and Taug who joins him in the pursuit of Toog, in "The Battle for Teeka." A reader might infer that these latter actions on Taug's part result from some gratitude that he feels toward Tarzan from the events of the earlier stories. When Tarzan leaves Kerchak's tribe to live in the seaside cabin, he singles out Taug and Teeka alone as less "foolish than Manu" (188), and gives them permission to visit him.

Taug represents the possibility of the entire tribe joining under Tarzan's leadership. Augustine has written, "The bond of human friendship has a sweetness of its own, binding many souls together as one." (*Confessions* [book 2, chapter 5] 25). The narrator writes that during Tarzan's absence from the tribe "there were those who missed him more than Tarzan imagined" (189). While the plural pronoun *those* might represent Teeka and Taug, named in the next sentence, the ambiguity remains that others in the tribe may have borne amity toward the ape-man. Friendship becomes to the tribe what maternal love is to the family. It is a beginning point for cooperation. It is the cornerstone from which civilization grew. As did men under Childe Harold, they can become a fraternal band: "their friendship sure, / When Gratitude or Valour bids them bleed, / Unshaken rushing on where'er their chief may lead" (Byron ["Childe Harold's Pilgrimage" 2.65.7–9] 29). But they are not there yet. The final two paragraphs of the story point out the imputed value of his actions in saving the moon. The "remarkable rescue" caused the apes to believe that Tarzan was "a superior being" (191). Tarzan's ascendance to the leadership of the tribe after Kerchak is the high water mark of the apes' civil behavior. Tarzan does not remain long as their king, and their advancement stalls as Tarzan's attentions turn toward the arrival of the tarmangani to answer his questions.

"And besides, the last word is not said — probably shall never be said."
— Lord Jim, *Heart of Darkness* (Conrad 145)

Centeno, in his introductory essay of *The Intent of the Artist*, points out that any work of art, in this case the specific form of the short story, "is not meant to be a corroboration of our actual sense of experience, but an expansion of it, and also a liberation, a sudden disclosure of new perspectives in human existence" (32). Thoughtful readers can affirm that each story carries a meaning of its own. Burroughs set out to polish each little jewel in its own setting. His bent toward novel-length prose tripped him up on occasion, but in the main he succeeded. Tarzan grows in each story, and he grows in the accumulation of the stories. David Adams verifies that "[e]ach story is in a sense a search for the integration of his personality[;] after all, this is the essence of the ape-man legend" ("Folklorist" 4). And speaking of some later writing (*Tarzan and the Forbidden City*), Adams adds: "These stories are actually a search for a missing or undeveloped part of Tarzan's personality, and make the most sense when they are read in this way ("Folklorist" 5). Such a claim is central to *Jungle Tales* as well. Holtsmark wrote privately that Burroughs "had a genuine feel for literature and what it can say about the human condition [...] and man's sense of himself in the larger scheme of things" (letter to Hyde).

In Burroughs' many books, he follows a well-developed pattern, comprised of three essential elements, according to Thomas D. Clareson: "[S]urvival in a hostile world epitomized by a jungle; physical victory in combat over a variety of loathsome creatures, animal or man; and the unquestioning adoration of primitive and sensual women" (190). In *Jungle Tales*, Burroughs, perhaps unwittingly, removed the third element because of his premise. Each story has survival and victory, but each victory is a little hollow without the attention of the woman. Once Teeka is given over to Taug, Tarzan spends the rest of the book looking for some replacement, and finds there is no substitute. In this respect, the collection is a twelve-story priming of the romantic pump, so that Jane's arrival, in *Tarzan of the Apes*, provides unparalleled satisfaction.

Noble trashed *Tarzan of the Apes* as "mere bosh" in 1921. The trash which he warned readers to avoid was, as previously stated, anything that contained "imagination without truth." (60). In typical self-deprecating fashion, Burroughs responded that Noble was "attempting to treat seriously something that was never intended to be serious" (qtd. in Taliaferro 184). The study made here shows Noble's assessment falls short for a reader willing to look beyond the fast pace and formulaic structures. Rather, many forms of truth lie embedded in Burroughs' work, and rather than becoming sense-deadening drugs, as Noble claims, his words leave much for the reader to bring alive. Holtsmark indicates that Burroughs' "peculiar literary skill is [...] his ability to combine fantastic and unbelievably exciting adventure stories with commentary on man and his condition" (6).

Conrath suggests that the multi-media manifestation of tarzan will never have a "last word" (14). Conrath uses the lowercase version to distinguish from the more well-defined text written by Burroughs in much the same way that Vernon coins the word Tarzania to refer to all things related to the Tarzan phenomenon. This multi-media character, Vernon acknowledges, "is and isn't Burroughs' Tarzan; he only started there" (5). It may be true for even the Tarzan that Buroughs created that a last word will never occur as each generation probes and applies the thoughts that Burroughs set down not only in *Jungle Tales of Tarzan* but in the two dozen books that chronicle his literary life.

Bibliography

Achebe, Chinua. "African Literature as Restoration of Celebration." *Chinua Achebe: A Celebration.* Ed. Kirsten Holst Petersen and Anna Rutherford. Studies in African Literature. Portsmouth, NH: Heinemann, 1991. 1–10.

_____. *Home and Exile.* New York: Oxford University Press, 2000.

_____. "An Image of Africa: Racism in Conrad's *Heart of Darkness.*" *Massachusetts Review* 18.4 (Winter 1977). Rpt. *Hopes and Impediments.* New York: Doubleday, 1989. 1–20.

Adams, David A. "Burroughsian Language Banks." 11 July 1996. *ERBzine* 0327. ERB-APA Archive. 2000. n. pag. 24 November 2007.

_____. "A Folklorist Reading of *Tarzan and the Forbidden City.*" *Burroughs Bulletin* New Series 62 (Spring 2005): 3–12.

_____. "The Jungle Tales of Tarzan: A Morphological Study Based Upon Vladimir Propp's Structural Theory of Folktales." *Fantastic Worlds of Edgar Rice Burroughs* 47 (Spring–Summer 2000). Rpt. *ERBzine* 1369. 2005. n. pag. 24 November 2007.

_____. "The Twelve Lunar Labors." Part III: Jungle Tales of Tarzan — A Novelistic Reading. *ERBzine* 0671. 2002. n. pag. 14 September 2007.

Adams, Duane. *Tarzan Shoots Goro.* *ERBzine* 0297. 2000. n. pag. 20 February 2000.

Adkins, Patrick H. Introduction. *Forgotten Tales of Love and Murder.* By Edgar Rice Burroughs. [New Orleans]: Guidry & Atkins, 2001. 9–16.

_____. "*Tarzan Forever*: A Study in Moral Imbecility." The Dream Vaults of Opar Website. 1999. n. pag. 2 March 2006.

"A.J.J." Letter to the Editor. *All-Story Magazine* Dec. 1912: 958.

Altrocchi, Rudolph. *Sleuthing in the Stacks.* Cambridge: Harvard University Press, 1944.

Anderson, Poul. "Apes and Martians." *Boy's Life* September 1972: 20, 46–47.

Anderson, Sherwood. "Man and His Imagination." Centeno 39–79.

_____. *Winesburg, Ohio.* 1919. Rpt. New York: Penguin, 1976.

Andrews, Clarence A. "An Introduction to Upton Sinclair's *The Jungle.*" *The Jungle.* By Upton Sinclair. New York: Airmont, 1965. 3–9.

Aristotle. *Aristotle's Poetics.* Trans. S.H. Butcher. New York: Hill and Wang, 1961.

_____. *Politics.* Trans. Benjamin Jowett. New York: Modern Library, 1943.

Ashe, Frank. *Happy Birthday, Moon.* New York: Scholastic, 1982.

Atamian, Sarkis. *The Origin of Tarzan: The Mystery of Tarzan's Creation Solved.* Anchorage: Publication Consultants, 1997.

Augustine. *The Confessions of St. Augustine.* Trans. Albert Cook Outler. New York: Dover, 2002.

Austen, Jane. *Emma.* 1816. Rpt. New York: Airmont, 1966.

_____. *Mansfield Park.* 1814. Rpt. New York: Bantam, 1983.

Bachelard, Gaston. *Water and Dreams: An Essay on the Imagination of Matter.* 1942. Trans. Edith R. Farrell. Dallas: Dallas Institute of Humanities and Culture, 1999.

Bailey, Seth T. "Dignity Complex, Author's Foe." *Oakland Tribune Magazine* 3 June 1923: 4.

Baker, Steve. *Picturing the Beast: Animals, Identity, and Representation.* Urbana: University of Illinois Press, 2001.

Bakhtin, Mikhail. *Problems of Dostoevsky's Poetics.* Ed. and trans. Caryl Emerson. Theory

and History of Literature 8. Minneapolis: University of Minnesota Press, 1984.
Balasopoulos, Antonis. "Progress, Regression, Repetition: Edgar Rice Burroughs' *Tarzan of the Apes* and the Ambivalences of Imperial Modernity." *Imaginaires* 9 (October 2003): 199–213.
Ballantyne, R.M. *The Gorilla Hunters*. New York: American News, 1886.
Barnard, Alan. "The Lost World of Laurens van der Post?" *Current Anthropology* 30.1 (Feb. 1989): 104–114.
Beale, Howard K. *Theodore Roosevelt and the Rise of America to World Power*. Baltimore: Johns Hopkins University Press, 1956.
Bederman, Gail. *Manliness & Civilization: A Cultural History of Gender and Race in the United States, 1880–1917*. Chicago: University of Chicago Press, 1996.
Bell, John. "A Charles R. Saunders Interview." *Black American Literature Forum* 18.2 (Summer 1984): 90–92.
Berglund, Jeff. "Write, Right, White, Rite: Literacy, Imperialism, Race, and Cannibalism in Edgar Rice Burroughs' Tarzan of the Apes." *Studies in American Fiction* 27.1 (Spring 1999): 53–76.
Bevington, David, ed. *The Necessary Shakespeare*. 2d ed. New York: Pearson-Longman, 2005.
Birell, Francis. "The Glories of Excess." *The New Statesman and Nation* 21 May 1932: 661–62.
Black, Algernon D. *The First Book of Ethics*. New York: Franklin Watts, 1965.
Blake, William. *Blake's Poetical Works*. Ed. John Sampson. London: Oxford University Press, 1928.
Bleiler, E. "Edgar Rice Burroughs." *Science Fiction: The Early Years*. Kent, OH: Kent State University Press, 1990. 95–111.
Bonaparte, Marie. *The Life and Works of Edgar Allan Poe: A Psycho-Analytic Interpretation*. London: Imago, 1949.
Bozarth, David Bruce. "The Code of Tarzan." Tangor Responds Column. March 1999. *ERBmania*. 5 October 2005.
_____. "Interracial Marriages: The Lie of ERB's Racism Exposed." Tangor Responds. 2000. *ERBmania*. 18 June 2007.
_____. "Jungle Tales: Seriously Understated." Tangor Responds. 2002. *ERBmania*. 3 Feb. 2004.
_____. "Tarzan: Man or Beast?" Tangor Responds. 1999. *ERBmania*. 5 October 2005.
_____. "Tarzan's Growth: How Tarzan's Character Changed 1912–1944." Tangor Responds. 2000. *ERBmania*. 3 Feb. 2004.
Brackett, Leigh. "Barsoom and Myself." *ERBANIA* 19 (1966). Rpt. *Edgar Rice Burroughs' Fantastic Worlds*. Ed. James Van Hise. Yucca Valley, CA: Van Hise, [1996]. 9.
Bradbury, Ray. "Tarzan, John Carter, Mr. Burroughs, and the Long Mad Summer of 1930." Introduction. *Edgar Rice Burroughs: the Man Who Created Tarzan*. Porges xvii–xix.
Brantlinger, Patrick. "Victorians and Africans: The Genealogy of the Myth of the Dark Continent." *Critical Inquiry* 12 (Autumn 1985): 166–203.
"Bringing the Legend to Life — Behind-the-Scenes Featurette." *Tarzan II* (DVD). Disney, 2005.
Brontë, Emily. *Wuthering Heights*. 1847. Rpt. Case Studies in Contemporary Criticism. Boston: Bedford-St. Martin's, 1992.
Browne, Thomas. *Religio Medici*. 1643. Rpt. *The Writings of Sir Thomas Browne*. Boston: Ticknor and Fields, 1862. 1–155.
Browning, Robert. "Caliban upon Setebos." Loucks 252–59.
_____. "Rabbi Ben Ezra." Loucks 246–51.
Brueckel, Frank J. "The Lost Years of Tarzan." *The Barsoomian* 11 (1966). Rpt. *Edgar Rice Burroughs' Fantastic Worlds*. Ed. James Van Hise. Yucca Valley, CA: Van Hise, [1996]. 43–46.
Brueton, Diana. *Many Moons*. New York: Prentice Hall, 1991.
Brutus, Dennis. *Still the Sirens*. Santa Fe: Pennywhistle, 1993.
Buchan, John. *The Thirty-Nine Steps*. 1915. Del Mar, CA: The Mystery Library [Publisher's Inc. and University of California], 1978.
Buel, J. W. *Heroes of the Dark Continent*. New York: Hunt & Eaton, 1890.
"Bukawi's Revenge." *Tarzan of the Apes* 18 (29 Oct. 1971): 10–17.
Bulfinch, Thomas. *Bulfinch's Mythology*. Ed. Edmund Fuller. New York: Laurel-Dell, 1959.
Burger, Phillip R. "Forty More Years of Adventure." Afterword. *Master of Adventure: Edgar Rice Burroughs*. Lupoff 224–61.
_____. "Glimpses of a World Past: Edgar Rice Burroughs, the West, and the Birth of an American Writer." Thesis. Utah State University, 1987. Microform.
Burroughs, Edgar Rice. 1922. *At the Earth's Core*. Rpt. New York: Ace, 1962.

_____. *The Beasts of Tarzan.* 1916. Rpt. New York: Ballantine, 1963.
_____. "The Black Man's Burden." *Pocatello Tribune* 8 April 1899.
_____. "Creator of Tarzan Speaks." *Los Angeles Times* 7 Jan. 1923. Rpt. *ERBzine* 1366. 2005. 20 April 2009.
_____. "Edgar Rice Burroughs Tells of Success of His Famous Fiction Character That This Newspaper Helped to Popularize." *The Tacoma News Tribune* 12 January 1934. Rpt. *ERBzine* 1788. 2007. 20 April 2009.
_____. "Evolution Held Undeniable — Nature's Law, Says Author." *New York American* 6 July 1925. Rpt. *Edgar Rice Burroughs Tells All.* Ed. Jerry Schneider. 3d ed. Rialto, CA: Pulpville Press, 2008. 76–77.
_____. *Forgotten Tales of Love and Murder.* [New Orleans]: Guidry & Atkins, 2001.
_____. "How I Wrote the Tarzan Books." *Washington Post* 27 Oct. 1929: 19.
_____. "The Illustrator and the Author." *The Authors' League Bulletin* October 1927. Rpt. *ERBzine* 0035. 20 April 2009.
_____. *Jungle Tales of Tarzan.* 1919. Rpt. New York: Ballantine, 1963.
_____. Letter to Fred Anger. 21 July 1934. [Correspondence files, ERB, Inc.]
_____. Letter to George A. Barrett. 5 November 1928. [Correspondence files, ERB, Inc.]
_____. Letter to George Vaughan. 7 June 1934. [Porges papers, Ekstrom Library, University of Louisville.]
_____. Letter to H.E. Jacobs of the *Brooklyn Daily Eagle.* 9 June 1919. [Correspondence files, ERB, Inc.]
_____. Letter to J. John Munson. 19 October 1935. "Lost Words and Letters of Edgar Rice Burroughs, Pre–World War II." *ERBzine* 1039. 2003. 14 December 2007.
_____. Letter to Joan Burroughs. 24 January 1941. *ERBzine* 1022. 2003. 12 July 2008.
_____. Letter to Leo Margulies. 30 October 1939. [Correspondence files, ERB, Inc.]
_____. Letter to Leo Margulies. 30 January 1940. [Correspondence files, ERB, Inc.]
_____. Letter to Ray Long. 13 October 1916. [Correspondence files, ERB, Inc.]
_____. Letter to Ray Long. 16 October 1916. [Correspondence files, ERB, Inc.]
_____. Letter to Ray Long. 30 October 1916. [Correspondence files, ERB, Inc.]
_____. Letter to Robert Davis. 24 January 1916. [Correspondence files, ERB, Inc.]
_____. Letter to Robert Davis. 20 December 1916. [Correspondence files, ERB, Inc.]
_____. Letter to Robert Davis. 15 December 1917. [Correspondence files, ERB, Inc.]
_____. Letter to Thomas Newell Metcalf. 6 March 1912. [Correspondence files, ERB, Inc.]
_____. Letter to Thomas Newell Metcalf. 20 September 1912. [Correspondence files, ERB, Inc.]
_____. Letter to Thomas Newell Metcalf. 20 December 1912. [Correspondence files, ERB, Inc.]
_____. Letter to Thomas Newell Metcalf. 9 January 1913. [Correspondence files, ERB, Inc.]
_____. Letter to Thomas Newell Metcalf. 24 January 1913. [Correspondence files, ERB, Inc.]
_____. *Llana of Gathol.* 1948. Rpt. New York: Ballantine, 1963.
_____. *The Monster Men.* 1929. Rpt. New York: Ace, [1963].
_____. Night Letter to Robert Davis. 17 March 1916. [Correspondence files, ERB, Inc.]
_____. *A Princess of Mars.* 1917. Rpt. New York: Ballantine, 1963.
_____. *The Return of Tarzan.* 1915. Rpt. New York: Ballantine, 1963.
_____. *The Son of Tarzan.* Chicago: McClurg, 1917.
_____. *The Son of Tarzan.* 1917. Rpt. New York: Burt, 1918.
_____. *The Son of Tarzan.* 1917. Rpt. New York: Grosset & Dunlap, 1927.
_____. *The Son of Tarzan.* 1917. Rpt. New York: Ballantine, 1963.
_____. *Tarzan and the City of Gold.* 1933. Rpt. New York: Ballantine, 1964.
_____. *Tarzan and the "Foreign Legion."* 1947. Rpt. New York: Ballantine, 1964.
_____. *Tarzan and the Golden Lion.* 1923. Rpt. New York: Ballantine, 1963.
_____. *Tarzan and the Jewels of Opar.* 1918. Rpt. New York: Ballantine, 1963.
_____. "Tarzan and the Jungle Murders." 1940. *Tarzan and the Castaways.* New York: Ballantine, 1964. 148–91.
_____. *Tarzan and the Leopard Men.* 1935. Rpt. New York: Ballantine, 1964.
_____. *Tarzan at the Earth's Core.* 1930. Rpt. New York: Ballantine, 1964.
_____. *Tarzan, Lord of the Jungle.* 1928. Rpt. New York: Ballantine, 1963.
_____. *Tarzan of the Apes.* 1914. Rpt. New York: Ballantine, 1963.
_____. *Tarzan the Invincible.* 1931. Rpt. New York: Ballantine, 1964.

———. *Tarzan the Terrible.* 1921. Rpt. New York: Ballantine, 1963.

———. *Tarzan the Untamed.* 1920. Rpt. New York: Ballantine, 1963.

———. "The Tarzan Theme." *Writer's Digest* 12 (June 1932): 29–32.

———. *Tarzan's Quest.* 1936. Rpt. New York: Ballantine, 1964.

———. *The War Chief.* 1927. Rpt. New York: Grosset & Dunlap, n.d.

———. "The Witch-Doctor Seeks Vengeance." Ed. Ray Long. *Blue Book* Feb. 1917: 744–53.

Buscema, John, and Rudy Mesina, illustrators. "Fangs of Death." David Anthony Kraft and Roy Thomas, writers. *Tarzan, Lord of the Jungle.* Marvel Comics 12 (May 1978).

———. "The Changeling." Roy Thomas, writer. *Tarzan, Lord of the Jungle.* Marvel Comics 13 (June 1978).

Byrne, Eleanor, and Martin McQuillan. "Walt Disney's Ape-Man: Race, Writing, Humanism." *New Formations: A Journal of Culture/Theory/Politics* 43 (Spring 2001): 103–16.

Byron, Lord George Gordon. *The Complete Poetical Works of Lord Byron.* Boston: Houghton Mifflin, 1905.

Carey-Webb, Allen. "Heart of Darkness, Tarzan, and the 'Third World': Canons and Encounters in World Literature, English 109." *College Literature* 19.3 (Oct. 1992): 121–41.

Carpenter, Stanford W. "The Tarzan vs. Predator Comic Book Mini-Series: An Ethnographic Analysis." *International Journal of Comic Art* 1.2 (Fall 1999): 195–215.

Caruso, Charles. "Lord of the Pulps: Edgar Rice Burroughs." *MD* April 1982: 100–07.

Centeno, Augusto. *The Intent of the Artist.* Princeton: Princeton University Press, 1941.

Cheyfitz, Eric. *The Poetics of Imperialism: Translation and Colonization from The Tempest to Tarzan.* New York: Oxford University Press, 1991.

Clareson, Thomas D. *Some Kind of Paradise.* Westport, CT: Greenwood, 1985.

"Classical Line: From Homer to Tarzan." [University of Iowa] *Spectator* 11.3 (1977): 4.

Cloward, Tim. "Vile Things Precious: Variations on the Wild Man Myth." Diss. University of Texas at Dallas, 2002.

Coleridge, Samuel Taylor. *Biographia Literaria.* 1817. Rpt. Everyman's Library. New York: Dutton, 1906.

Collingwood, R. G. *The Principles of Art.* Oxford: Clarenden, 1947.

Conan Doyle, Arthur. *The Original Illustrated "Strand" Sherlock Holmes: The Complete Facsimile Edition.* Ware, Hertfordshire: Wordsworth, 1996.

Conrad, Joseph. *Heart of Darkness.* 1902. Ed. Ross C. Murfin. 2d ed. Boston: Bedford-St. Martin's, 1996.

———. *Lord Jim.* 1900. New York: Bantam, 1958.

Conrath, Robert E. "Rethinking the Ape-Man: Approaching Tarzan as Object of Critical Discourse." Diss. McGill University. Ottawa: National Library of Canada, 1990. Microform.

Cooper, Brenda. "A Boat, a Mask, Two Photographers and a Manticore: African Fiction in a Global Context." *Pretexts: Literary and Cultural Studies* 9.1 (2000): 63–76.

———. *Weary Sons of Conrad: White Fiction against the Grain of Africa's Dark Heart.* New York: Peter Lang, 2002.

Cooper, James Fenimore. *The Prairie.* 1827. Rpt. New York: Signet-NAL, 1964.

Coriell, Vernell W. Letter to the editor. *Other Worlds* Nov. 1956: 94–96.

Corliss, Richard. "Him Tarzan, Him Great: Disney's Animators Triumph by Turning the Ape-Man into a Questing Kid with a Surfer's Agility and an Identity Crisis." *Time* 14 June 1999: 220–21.

Cowart, David. "The Tarzan Myth and Jung's Genesis of the Self." *Journal of American Culture* 2.2 (Summer 1979): 220–30.

Creed, Barbara. "Me Jane: You Tarzan!—A Case of Mistaken Identity in Paradise." *Continuum: The Australian Journal of the Media* 1.1 (1987): 159–74.

Crisp, Tony. *Dream Dictionary: An A to Z Guide to Understanding Your Unconscious Mind.* New York: Wings, 1990.

Crist, Kenneth. "Tarzan's Father." *Los Angeles Times Sunday Magazine* 27 June 1937: 7, 26.

Crouch, Stanley. "Swing That Vine, White Boy!" Rev. of *The Tarzan Collection* DVD. *Slate* 23 June 2006. 26 June 2006.

Crowder, E.H. *Second Report of the Provost Marshal General to the Secretary of War on the Operations of the Selective Service System to December 20, 1918.* Washington, D.C.: GPO, 1919.

Cullinan, Patrick. "The Text." *The Paperbook of South African English Poetry.* Ed. Michael Chapman. Parklands [South Africa]: Ad. Donker, 1986. 215–16.

Daiches, David. "Some Aspects of T.S. Eliot." *College English* 9.3 (1947): 115–22.

Dale, Alzina Stone. *T.S. Eliot: The Philosopher Poet*. Wheaton, IL: Harold Shaw, 1988.

Dante. *Inferno*, 1314. Trans. Allen Mandelbaum. New York: Bantam, 1982.

Davison, Richard Allan. "Edgar Rice Burroughs, Tarzan, and Hemingway." *North Dakota Quarterly* 63.3 (Summer 1996): 34–39.

Day, David. *A Burroughs Bestiary*. London: New English Library, 1978.

de Brito, Mark. *The Trickster's Tongue: An Anthology of Poetry in Translation from Africa and the African Diaspora*. Leeds: Peepal Tree, 2006.

Defoe, Daniel. *Life and Adventures of Robinson Crusoe*. 1719. Rpt. New York: Butler, 1888.

Dickens, Charles. *A Tale of Two Cities*. 1859. Rpt. Mineola, NY: Dover, 1999.

Dodds, Georges T. "Burroughs' Sailor Among Apes." *ERBzine* 1474. 2005. 14 November 2005.

Doniger, Wendy. "The Mythology of Masquerading Animals, or, Bestiality." *Social Research* 62.3 (Fall 1995). Rpt. *Social Research* 71.3 (Fall 2004): 711–32.

Dostoevsky, Feodor. *Crime and Punishment*. 1866. Ed. George Gibian. Trans. Jessie Coulson. Norton Critical Edition. New York: Norton, 1964.

———. *The Idiot*. 1868. Trans. Eva M. Martin. Geneva: Edito-Service S.A., [1956?].

Douglass, Frederick. *Narrative of the Life of Frederick Douglass[,] an American Slave*. 1881. Cambridge, MA: Belknap-Harvard University Press, 1960.

Dreiser, Theodore. *Sister Carrie*. 1900. Rpt. New York: NAL-Signet, 1980.

Du Chaillu, Paul. *Explorations and Adventures in Equatorial Africa*. London: John Murray, 1861.

Dumas, Alexandre. *The Three Musketeers*. Trans. anon. 1888. Rpt. New York: Tor, 1994.

Earle, Ralph. *The Gospel According to Matthew*. Special ed.; excerpt from Volume 6 of *Beacon Bible Commentary*. Kansas City: Beacon Hill Press of Kansas City, 1964.

Eastman, John C. "Village Life at the World's Fair." *The Chautauquan* 17 (1893): 602–04.

Eastman, P. D. *Are You My Mother?* 1960. Rpt. New York: Beginner-Random, 1998.

"Edgar Rice Burroughs, Tarzan Creator, Was Never In Africa." Associated Press 9 July 1939. Rpt. *ERBzine* 1788. 2007. 20 April 2009.

Eldredge, John. *The Way of the Wild Heart*. Nashville: Nelson, 2006.

———. *Wild at Heart*. Nashville: Nelson, 2001.

Eliot, T.S. *The Complete Poems and Plays*. New York: Harcourt Brace, 1952.

———. "Hamlet and His Problems." *Atheneum* 4665 (26 Sept. 1919): 940–41. Rpt. *The Sacred Wood: Essays on Poetry and Criticism*. London: Methuen, 1920. 95–103.

Equiano, Olaudah. *The Interesting Narrative of the Life of Olaudah Equiano*. 1791. Boston: Bedford-St. Martin's, 1995.

Euripides. *Helen*. *Three Great Plays of Euripides*. Trans. Rex Warner. New York: Mentor, 1958. 127–92.

Evans, Arthur B., and R.D. Mullen, comp. "North American College Courses in Science Fiction, Utopian Literature, and Fantasy—Addenda: The Books, Authors, and Films Most Widely Assigned." *Science-Fiction Studies* 70 (November 1996): 525–26.

Farmer, Philip José. Introduction. *Mother Was a Lovely Beast*. New York: Pyramid, 1976. ix–xiii.

———. "A Language for Opar." *ERB-dom* 75 (1974): [14–16].

———. *Tarzan Alive*. 1972. Rpt. Lincoln: Bison-University of Nebraska Press, 2006.

Fenton, Robert W. *Edgar Rice Burroughs and Tarzan: A Biography of the Author and His Creation*. Jefferson, NC: McFarland, 2003.

Fiedler, Leslie. *What Was Literature?: Class Culture and Mass Society*. New York: Simon & Schuster, 1982.

Fiske, John. *Through Nature to God*. Boston: Houghton Mifflin, 1899.

Foster, Harold, illus. *The Illustrated Tarzan Book No. 1 Picturized from the Novel Tarzan of the Apes by Edgar Rice Burroughs*. New York: Grosset & Dunlap, 1929.

Fowler, Alistair. "Sherlock Holmes and the Adventure of the Dancing Men and Women." *Addressing Frank Kermode: Essays in Criticism and Interpretation*. Ed. Margaret Tudeau-Clayton and Martin Warner. Urbana: University of Illinois Press, 1991. 154–68.

Freud, Sigmund. *The Ego and the Id*. 1923. Trans. Joan Riviere. New York: Norton, 1962.

———. *Totem and Taboo*. 1913. Trans. James Strachey. New York: Norton, 1950.

Galloway, Stan. "Teeka." *Burroughs Bulletin* New Series 65 (Winter 2006): 33.

Gingerich, Owen. "The Real Issue: Is There a Role for Natural Theology Today?" 14 July

2002. Leadership University. 12 January 2004.

Gottlieb, Alma. "Hyenas and Heteroglossia: Myth and Ritual Among the Beng of Cote d'Ivoire." *American Ethnologist* 16.3 (August 1989): 487–501.

Griswold, Jerry. "Ur of the Ur-Stories: *Tarzan of the Apes*." *Audacious Kids*. New York: Oxford, 1992. 104–20.

Grun [Shafer], Nina. "From Hesiod to Tarzan: A Study of the Noble Savage in Relation to Romanticism with Special Reference to the Eighteenth Century." Thesis. Smith College, 1939.

Guenther, Mathias. *Bushman Folktales: Oral Traditions of the Nharo of Botswana and the /Xam of the Cape*. Stuttgart [Germany]: Franz Steiner Verlag Wiesbaden, 1989.

Gunn, James. "The Education of a Science Fiction Teacher." *Kansas Quarterly* 10.4 (Fall 1978). Rpt. *Inside Science Fiction*. San Bernardino, CA: Borgo, 1992. 9–15.

Guymon, E.T., Jr. "Why Do We Read This Stuff?" *The Mystery Story*. Ed. John Ball. Del Mar, CA: The Mystery Library [Publisher's Inc. and University of California], 1976. 361–63.

Habblitz, Harry. Young Tarzan illustration. *Fantasy Illustrated #3* (Winter 1964): 4.

Haggard, H. Rider. *King Solomon's Mines*. 1885. *King Solomon's Mines — She — Allan Quartermain*. London: Octopus, 1979.

Hamilton, Edith. *Mythology*. New York: Mentor, 1969.

Hammond, Dorothy, and Alta Jablow. *The Africa That Never Was: Four Centuries of British Writing about Africa*. New York: Twayne, 1970.

Hanson, Alan. *A Tarzan Chrono-log*. 2d ed. Spokane: Waziri, 2003.

Hardy, Thomas. *Far from the Madding Crowd*. 1874. New York: Signet, 1960.

_____. *The Return of the Native*. 1912. 2d ed. Ed. Phillip Mallett. Norton Critical Edition. New York: Norton, 2006.

Harjo, Joy. "The Book of Myths." *How* 82–83.

_____. *How We Became Human: New and Selected Poems: 1975–2001*. New York: Norton, 2002.

_____. "A Postcolonial Tale." *How* 104–05.

Harmon, William, and Hugh Holman. *A Handbook to Literature*. 11th ed. Upper Saddle River, NJ: Pearson-Prentice Hall, 2009.

Hart, James D. *The Popular Book: A History of America's Literary Taste*. Berkeley: University of California Press, 1961.

Hartmann, Ernest. *Dreams and Nightmares: The New Theory on the Origin and Meaning of Dreams*. New York: Plenum, 1998.

Hauser, Marc D. *Moral Minds: How Nature Designed Our Universal Sense of Right and Wrong*. New York: ECC-HarperCollins, 2006.

Hawthorne, Nathaniel. *The House of the Seven Gables*. 1851. Rpt. New York: NAL-Signet, 1961.

Herrick, Robert. "His Age." *Selected Poems*. Manchester: Carcanet, 2003. 29–34.

Higgins, Jonna. "Tarzan of the Apes: An Ecofeminist Perspective." Utz, *Investigating* 15–29.

Hillman, Bill. "Edgar Rice Burroughs' Remarkable Summer of '93." Edgar Rice Burroughs Personal Library Project. *ERBzine* 1275. 2004. 19 December 2007.

_____. "ERB Houses: The Family Tree from 1875–1950." *ERBzine* 250. 1999. 17 February 2004.

_____. "The ERB / Jack London Connection I." *ERBzine* 1271. 2005. 5 May 2007.

_____. "Joan Burroughs Pierce, Part 1." *ERBzine* 1102. 2004. 16 September 2005.

_____. "Major George Tyler Burroughs, Sr." *ERBzine* 0942. 2002. 19 July 2008.

Hogarth, Burne. *Jungle Tales of Tarzan*. New York: Watson-Guptill, 1975.

Holtsmark, Erling B. *Edgar Rice Burroughs*. Twayne's United States Author Series. Boston: Twayne, 1986.

_____. Letter to Clyde [Bob] B. Hyde. 17 March 1978. [Burroughs Collection, Ekstrom Library, University of Louisville]

_____. Letter to Martin Williams of *Smithsonian*. 8 Oct. 1984. [Burroughs Collection, Ekstrom Library, University of Louisville]

_____. *Tarzan and Tradition: Classical Myth in Popular Literature*. Westport, CT.: Greenwood, 1981.

Holy Bible. King James Version. 1611. New York: American Bible Society, n.d.

Homer. *The Iliad*. Trans. Edward, Earl of Derby. 1864. Ed. Ernest Rhys. New York: Dutton, 1910.

_____. *The Odyssey of Homer*. Trans. Alexander Pope. 1726. New York: Heritage, 1942.

Howard, Allan. "ERB — Victorian!" *Burroughs Bulletin* Old Series 32 (Winter 1973): n.p.

Huffstetler, Edward W. *Tales of Native America*. Myths of the World. New York: Metrobooks-Friedman/Fairfax, 1996.

Hugo, Victor. *Les Miserables*. 1862. Fantine, vol. 1. 5 vols. Boston: Estes and Lauriat, n.d.

Hyde, Lewis. *Trickster Makes This World*. New York: North Point, 1998.

Ibsen, Henrik. *Hedda Gabler. The Wild Duck / Hedda Gabler*. Trans. Michael Meyer. New York: Norton, 1997.

_____. *Peer Gynt*. Trans. Christopher Fry and Johan Fillinger. New York: Oxford University Press, 1989.

Jackson, Michael. *Allegories of the Wilderness: Ethics and Ambiguity in Kuranko Narratives*. Bloomington: Indiana University Press, 1982.

Jacobs, Gary. "Tarzan of the Apes — Trashy or Classy?" *Cedar Rapids Gazette* 26 Feb. 1978: 5B.

Johnston, Alva. "How to Become a Great Writer." *Saturday Evening Post* 29 July 1939: 5–7, 58–60.

Jurca, Catherine. "Tarzan, Lord of the Suburbs." *Modern Language Quarterly* 57.3 (September 1996): 479–504.

Jusko, Joe. *Joe Jusko's Art of Edgar Rice Burroughs*. Pittsburgh: FPG, 1996.

Kanyandekwe, Daniel. "Dreaming of Africa: American Writers and Africa in the Twentieth Century." Diss. State University of New York at Buffalo, 1996. Microform.

Kennicott, Donald. Letter to Edgar Rice Burroughs. 12 December 1927. [Correspondence files, ERB, Inc.]

Kidd, Kenneth. "Psychoanalysis and Children's Literature: The Case for Complementarity." *The Lion and the Unicorn* 28 (2004): 109–130.

Kilgour, Maggie. *From Communion to Cannibalism: An Anatomy of Metaphors of Incorporation*. Princeton: Princeton University Press, 1990.

Kipling, Rudyard. *American Notes*. 1891. Rpt. New York: Arcadia, 1950.

_____. "The Hyænas." *Rudyard Kipling's Verse: Inclusive Edition 1885–1918*. Garden City, NY: Doubleday, 1919. 365.

_____. *The Jungle Books*. 1895. Rpt. New York: Signet-NAL, 1961.

_____. *Something of Myself: For My Friends Known and Unknown*. Garden City, NY: Doubleday, Doran, 1937.

Kirkland, Winifred Margaretta. *The Joys of Being a Woman and Other Papers*. 1918. Rpt. Freeport, NY: Books for Libraries Press, 1968.

Kraft, David Anthony, writer. "The Fangs of Death." *Tarzan, Lord of the Jungle*. Marvel Comics 12 (May 1978).

Kreuzer, James R., and Lee Cogan. *Literature for Composition*. New York: Holt, Rinehart and Winston, 1965.

Kubert, Joe. "Balu of the Great Apes." *Tarzan of the Apes*. DC Comics 213 (October 1972).

_____. "The Captive." *Tarzan of the Apes*. DC Comics 212 (September 1972).

_____. "The Nightmare." *Tarzan of the Apes*. DC Comics 214 (November 1972).

Kuhn, Helmut. "The True Tragedy: On the Relationship between Greek Tragedy and Plato, II." *Harvard Studies in Classical Philology* 53 (1942): 37–88.

Lacon-Watson, E.H. "'Tarzan' and Literature." *The Fortnightly* 119 (23 June 1923): 1035–45.

LeGuin, Ursula K. "Myth and Archetype in Science Fiction." *Parabola: Myth and the Quest for Meaning* Fall 1976. Rpt. Schechter and Semeiks, *Patterns* 442–48.

Levin, Martin, ed. *Love Stories*. New York: Quadrangle, 1975.

Lewis, C.S. *The Last Battle*. 1956. Rpt. New York: Macmillan, 1988.

_____. *The Screwtape Letters*. 1942. Rpt. New York: Macmillan, 1977.

Livingstone, David. *The Last Journals of David Livingstone, in Central Africa, from Eighteen Sixty-Five to His Death*. Ed. Horace Waller. New York: Harper, 1875.

_____. *Missionary Travels in South Africa*. 1857. 2 vols. Rpt. Santa Barbara, CA: Narrative Press, 2001.

_____. *The Zambesi Expedition*. 1865. Rpt. Santa Barbara, CA: Narrative Press, 2001.

Logan, Rayford W. "Negro Youth and the Influence of the Press, Radio, and Cinema." *The Journal of Negro Education* 9.3 (July 1940): 425–34.

London, Jack. *Before Adam*. 1906. Rpt. New York: Ace, n.d.

_____. *The Call of the Wild*. 1903. Rpt. New York: Dover, 1990.

Long, Ray. Letter to Edgar Rice Burroughs. 17 July 1916. [Correspondence files, ERB, Inc.]

_____. Letter to Edgar Rice Burroughs. 16 November 1916. [Correspondence files, ERB, Inc.]

_____. Letter to Edgar Rice Burroughs. 15 February 1917. [Correspondence files, ERB, Inc.]

_____. Letter to Edgar Rice Burroughs. 2 October 1918. [Correspondence files, ERB, Inc.]

_____. Letter to Edgar Rice Burroughs. 7 October 1918. [Correspondence files, ERB, Inc.]

_____. Lettergram to Edgar Rice Burroughs. 20 March 1917. [Correspondence files, ERB, Inc.]
Loucks, James F., ed. *Robert Browning's Poetry.* Norton Critical Edition. New York: Norton, 1979.
L[ovecraft], H.P. Letter. Letters to the Editor. *All-Story Weekly.* 7 March 1914. Rpt. "Lovecraft: A Burroughs Fan." *ERBzine* 1137. 2004. 9 April 2004.
Lupoff, Richard. "Barsoom!" *Heavy Metal* September 1982: [55–63].
_____. "The Case of the Doctor Who Had No Business, or The Adventure of the Second Anonymous Narrator." *Startling Mystery Stories* Winter 1969: 66–75.
_____. *Master of Adventure: Edgar Rice Burroughs.* Lincoln: University of Nebraska Press, 2005.
Mack, John E. *Nightmares and Human Conflict.* Boston: Little, Brown, 1970.
Maclennan, Don. "In a Pot on the Window Sill." *Solstice.* Plumstead [South Africa]: Snailpress, 1997. 8.
_____. *Notes from a Rhenish Mission.* Plumstead [South Africa]: Carapace, 2001.
Manning, Russ. Letter to the editor. *The Register* 25 June 1972 (Orange, CA). Rpt. *ERBzine* 0277. 2000. 21 July 2008.
_____. Untitled drawing. *Burroughs Bulletin* Old Series 15 (1964): n.p.
Manson, Cynthia, and Charles Ardai, eds. *High Adventure.* New York: Barnes & Noble, 1992.
Margulies, Leo. Letter to Edgar Rice Burroughs. 25 October 1939. [Correspondence files, ERB, Inc.]
Marlowe, Christopher. *The Tragical History of the Life and Death of Dr. Faustus. Christopher Marlowe's Dr. Faustus: Text and Major Criticism.* Ed. Irving Ribner. New York: Odyssey, 1966.
Marquis, Don. "The God-Maker, Man." 1915. *Dreams and Dust.* Pinkmonkey. 30 March 2004. 47–49.
McDowell, Edward B. "The World's Fair Cosmopolis." *Frank Leslie's Popular Monthly.* 36.4 (October 1893): 407–16.
McGreal, Dorothy. "The Burroughs No One Knows." *World of Comic Art* May 1966: 12–15.
McWhorter, George T. *Burroughs Dictionary.* Lanham, MD: University Press of America, 1987.
_____. "No Racism Intended, Bwana." *Fantasy Review* 84 (October 1985): 34.

Melville, Herman. *Moby Dick; or, The Whale.* 1851. Rpt. Norwalk, CT: Easton, 1977.
Merwin, W.S. "The Judgment of Paris." *The Carrier of Ladders.* New York: Atheneum, 1984. 22–24.
Metcalf, Thomas Newell. Letter to Edgar Rice Burroughs. 18 September 1912. [Correspondence files, ERB, Inc.]
_____. Letter to Edgar Rice Burroughs. 11 October 1912. [Correspondence files, ERB, Inc.]
_____. Letter to Edgar Rice Burroughs. 9 Nov. 1912. [Correspondence files, ERB, Inc.]
_____. Letter to Edgar Rice Burroughs. 10 Dec. 1912. [Correspondence files, ERB, Inc.]
_____. Letter to Edgar Rice Burroughs. 27 Jan. 1913. [Correspondence files, ERB, Inc.]
Meyer, Michael. Afterword. *Tarzan of the Apes.* By Edgar Rice Burroughs. New York: Signet Classics, 2008. 295–306.
_____, ed. *The Bedford Introduction to Literature.* 8th ed. Boston: Bedford-St. Martin's, 2008.
Midgley, Mary. *Animals and Why They Matter.* Athens: University of Georgia Press, 1983.
Miller, Walter James. "Burne Hogarth and the Art of Pictorial Fiction." Hogarth 7–35.
Milne, A. A. *Three Stories from Winnie-the-Pooh.* 1926. Rpt. New York: Scholastic, 1966.
Montaigne, Michael. *The Essayes of Michael Lord of Montaigne.* 1580. Vol. 1. 3 vols. Trans. John Florio. 1603. Rpt. London: Oxford University Press, 1904.
Montgomery, L.M. *Anne of Green Gables.* 1908. Everyman's Library. Rpt. New York: Knopf, 1995.
Morris, John D. "What's a Missing Link?" *Acts & Facts* 35.4 (2006). Institute for Creation Research. 23 September 2008.
Mortimer, Ruth. "Dostoevski and the Dream." *Modern Philology* 54 (Nov. 1956): 106–16.
Moskowitz, Sam. *Under the Moons of Mars: A History and Anthology of 'The Scientific Romance' in the Munsey Magazines, 1912–1920.* New York: Holt, Rinehart and Winston, 1970.
Murphy, Donn B. "Peer Gynt by Henrik Ibsen." Georgetown University. <http://www.georgetown.edu/faculty/murphyd/Zhistory/ibsen-peergynt.htm>. 4 January 2006.
Murphy, Graham J. "Layered Imagings and Colonial Fantasy: Possession, Penetration, and Tarzan Comic Books." *Images: A Journal of Film and Popular Culture* 7 (1998). 21 March 2006.
Murray, Paul T. "Blacks and the Draft: A His-

tory of Institutional Racism." *Journal of Black Studies* 2.1 (1971): 57–76.
Mwikisa, Peter. "Conrad's Image of Africa: Recovering African Voices in *Heart of Darkness*." *Mots Pluriels* 13 (April 2000). 20 September 2005.
Needham, Rodney. "Tarzan of the Apes: A Reappreciation." *Foundation* 28 (July 1983): 20–28.
Nesteby, James Ronald. "The Tarzan Series of Edgar Rice Burroughs: Lost Races and Racism in American Popular Culture." Diss. Bowling Green State Univ., 1978. Microform.
_____. "The Tenuous Vine of *Tarzan of the Apes*." *Journal of Popular Culture* 13 (1980): 482–87.
Newsinger, John. "Lord Greystoke and Darkest Africa: The Politics of the Tarzan Stories." *Race & Class* 28.2 (1986): 59–71.
_____. "Me Disney, You Tarzan." *Race & Class* 42.1 (2000): 78–81.
_____. "Reader, He Rescued Her: Women in the Tarzan Stories." *Foundation* 39 (Spring 1987): 41–49.
Niebuhr, Reinhold. "From Humour and Faith." 1946. *The Questing Spirit: Religion in the Literature of Our Time*. Ed. Halford E. Luccock and Frances Brentano. New York: Coward-McCann, 1947. 608.
Noble, A.B. "Stepping Stones to Correct Taste." *Iowa Library Quarterly* Dec. 1921: 56–61.
Nye, Russell B. *The Unembarrassed Muse*. New York: Dial, 1970.
Oha, Obododimma. "Eating Raw Nothing, Committing Suicide: The Politics and Semiotics of Food Culture." *Mots Pluriels* 15 (Sept. 2000). 6 Sept. 2005.
"The Old Frontier: Anthropoid Epic." *Ellery Queen's Mystery Magazine* May 1964: 67–68.
Olson, Sharon. *Into the Light*. Minneapolis: Bolger, 1993.
Orczy, Baroness [Sara Orczy-Barstow Brown]. *The Scarlet Pimpernel*. 1913. Rpt. Everyman's Library Children's Classics. New York: Borzoi-Knopf, 1999.
Orwell, George. *Nineteen Eighty-Four*. 1949. Rpt. New York: Penguin-Plume, 2003.
Paley, William. *The Works of William Paley*. Philadelphia: J.J. Woodward, 1836.
Parker, Julia, and Derek. *Parkers' Complete Book of Dreams*. New York: DK, 1995.
Pendleton, Thomas A. "Tarzan of the Papers." *Journal of Popular Culture* 12.4 (Spring 1979): 691–93.

Poe, Edgar Allan. *The Complete Tales and Poems of Edgar Allan Poe*. New York: Modern Library, 1938.
Poole, Oliver. "Romance Isn't Dead." *Writers' Markets & Methods* March 1938: 12–13.
Porges, Irwin. *Edgar Rice Burroughs: The Man Who Created Tarzan*. Provo: Brigham Young University Press, 1975.
Queenan, Joe. "Tarzan's Children: Why Movies About Africa Require White Saviors." 14 January 2007. *Los Angeles Times*. 18 January 2007.
_____. "A Whiter Shade of Guile." 5 January 2007. *The Guardian*. 22 February 2008.
Ransby, Barbara. "*Blood Diamond*: A Film Review." *The Black Commentator* 211 (21 December 2006). 22 February 2008.
Reade, W. Winwood. *Savage Africa: Being the Narrative of a Tour in Equatorial, Southwestern, and Northwestern Africa; with Notes on the Habits of the Gorilla; on the existence of Unicorns and Tailed Men; on the Slave Trade; on the Origin, Character, and Capabilities of the Negro, and on the Future Civilization of Western Africa*. New York: Harper, 1864. Rpt. Landmarks in Anthropology. New York: Johnson, 1967.
Rebarber, Theodor. "Helping Your Child Learn Responsible Behavior with Activities for Children." 1993. KidSource Online. 6 Sept. 2005.
Rice, Andrew. "Me Tarzan, You Bride." June 1997. *Salon*. 21 October 2005.
Riso, Mary. *Heroines*. Grand Rapids, MI: Baker, 2003.
Robinson, Frank M. "The Story Behind the Original Story." *Zoetrope: All-Story*. 4.1 (2005). 28 October 2005.
Romøren, Rolf. "The Light of Knowledge — In the Midst of the Jungle: How Tarzan Became a Man." Presented at the conference "Tradition and Innovation: Fairy and Folk Tales as Social and Cultural Agents." 18 August 2000. Children's Literature Research Unit, University of South Africa. 21 December 2005.
_____. Personal e-mail to the author. 13 January 2006.
Roosevelt, Theodore. Rev. of *National Life and Character* by Charles H. Pearson. *Sewanee Review* 2 (May 1894): 353–76.
_____, and Edmund Hiller. *Life-Histories of African Game Animals*. New York: Scribner's, 1914.
Rothstein, Edward. "From Darwinian to Dis-

neyesque." *New York Times* 15 July 1999: E1, 8.

Rousseau, Jean Jacques. *Emile.* 1762. Trans. Eleanor Worthington. Heath's Pedagogical Library. Boston: D.C. Heath, 1899.

Rubanowice, Robert J. "The Tarzan Series: A Twentieth-Century Case Against Civilization." *Proceedings of the Sixth National Convention of the Popular Culture Association.* Chicago. 22–24 April 1976. 563–80.

St. John, J. Allen. Illustration for "The Fight for the Balu." *Jungle Tales of Tarzan.* By Edgar Rice Burroughs. Chicago: McClurg, 1919.

Sapir, David J. "Leper, Hyena, and Blacksmith in Kujamaat Diola Thought." *American Ethnologist* 8.3 (1981): 526–43.

Schechter, Harold, and Jonna Gormely Semeiks. "The Helpful Animal and the Holy Fool." Schechter and Semeiks, *Patterns* 265–70.

_____, eds. *Patterns in Popular Culture: A Sourcebook for Writers.* New York: Harper & Row, 1980.

Schneider, John M. Foreword. Olson ix–xi.

Scott, Walter. *Ivanhoe.* 1819. Rpt. Everyman's Library. London: Dent, 1959.

Serpell, James. *In the Company of Animals: A Study of Human-Animal Relationships.* 1986. Rpt. New York: Cambridge University Press, 1996.

Shakespeare, William. *Hamlet.* Ca. 1600. Bevington 552–604.

_____. *King John.* Ca. 1596. Rpt. New York: The University Society, 1901.

_____. *Macbeth.* Ca. 1606. Bevington 715–47.

_____. *The Merchant of Venice.* Ca. 1600. Bevington 74–112.

_____. *A Midsummer Night's Dream.* Ca. 1595. Bevington 46–73.

_____. *Much Ado About Nothing.* Ca 1599. Bevington 113–49.

_____. *The Taming of the Shrew.* Ca. 1592. Bevington 5–41.

_____. *The Tempest.* Ca. 1611. Bevington 849–78.

_____. *The Tragedy of King Richard the Third.* Ca. 1592. Bevington 274–325.

_____. *The Winter's Tale.* Ca. 1610. Bevington 805–44.

Shelley, Mary. *Frankenstein.* 1818, 1831. Rpt. New York: NAL-Signet, 1965.

Simonson, Walter. "Part One: World within Worlds." *Tarzan Versus Predator at the Earth's Core.* Illus. Lee Weeks. Milwaukee, OR: Dark Horse, January 1996.

Smith, Herbert F. *The Popular American Novel 1865–1920.* Boston: Twayne, 1980.

Soumille, Gabriel. "Tarzan, l'homme-singe." *Educateurs* [Paris] 46 (July–August 1953): 299–306.

Southam, B.C. *A Guide to the Selected Poems of T.S. Eliot.* 6th ed. San Diego: Harvest-Harcourt Brace, 1996.

Spradley, David William. "The Tarzan Phenomenon." Thesis. Stephen F. Austin State University, 1972. Microform.

Stanley, Henry M. *In Darkest Africa.* New York: Scribners, 1891.

Starr, Frederick. "Anthropology at the World's Fair." *The Popular Science Monthly* 43 (September 1893): 610–21.

Steele, Joel Dorman, and Esther Baker Steele. *A Brief History of Ancient, Mediaeval, and Modern Peoples.* New York: American Book Company, 1883.

Stevenson, Robert Louis. *Dr. Jekyll and Mr. Hyde.* 1886. *Dr. Jekyll and Mr. Hyde and Other Stories.* New York: Masterpiece Library-Magnum, 1968.

Stoker, Bram. *Dracula.* 1897. Rpt. Boston: Bedford-St. Martin's, 2002.

Street, Brian V. *The Savage in Literature: Representations of "Primitive" Society in English Fiction 1858–1920.* London: Routledge & K. Paul, 1975.

Stroud, Joanne H. Foreword. Bachelard [vii]–x.

Taliaferro, John. *Tarzan Forever: The Life of Edgar Rice Burroughs, Creator of Tarzan.* New York: Scribner, 1999.

Tapper, Richard L. "Animality, Humanity, Morality, Society." *What Is an Animal?* Ed. Tim Ingold. Unwin Hyman: London, 1988. 47–62.

"Tarzan, Lord of the Jungle." *Blue Book* 46.1 (November 1927): 5.

Tarzan II. Dir. Brian Smith. Disney, 2005. DVD.

Tembo, Mwizenge. *Legends of Africa. Myths of the World.* New York: Metrobooks-Friedman/Fairfax, 1996.

Tennyson, Alfred. *Idylls of the King.* 1885. Rpt. New York: New American Library-Signet Classics, 1961.

Thomas, Roy, writer. "The Changeling." Illus. John Buscema and Rudy Mesina. *Tarzan, Lord of the Jungle.* Marvel Comics 13 (June 1978).

"Through the Looking Glass." *Chicago Tribune* 1 November 1893: 9–10.

Torgovnick, Marianna. *Gone Primitive: Savage Intellect, Modern Lives.* Chicago: University of Chicago Press, 1990.

Tozer, A.W. *The Pursuit of God*. 1948. Rpt. Camp Hill, PA: Christian Publications, 1982.
Trigilio, Tony. "Staring Back in the Classroom: Genre, Identity, and the Power in Looking." *Modern Language Studies* 26.4 (Fall 1996): 99–107.
Trimble, Irene. *What Makes a Hero*. Random House PICTUREBACK Books. New York: Random, 2003.
Tucker, Betty Jo. *Tarzan II* DVD Review. *The Z Review-UK*. 22 June 2005.
Tucker, John I. "Tarzan Was Born in Chicago." *Chicago History* Spring 1970: 18–31.
Twain, Mark. *A Connecticut Yankee in King Arthur's Court*. 1889. Rpt. New York: Signet-Penguin, n.d.
_____. *The Adventures of Huckleberry Finn*. 1885. Rpt. New York: NAL-Signet, n.d.
Utz, Richard J. "Introduction: Reading/Teaching Against the Grain: Literariness and *Tarzan of the Apes* in the Literature Classroom." Utz, *Investigating* 1–13.
_____, ed. *Investigating the Unliterary: Six Readings of Edgar Rice Burroughs' Tarzan of the Apes*. Regensburg [Germany]: Ulrich Martzinek, 1995.
Van Hise, James, ed. *Edgar Rice Burroughs' Fantastic Worlds*. Yucca Valley, CA: Van Hise, [1996].
_____. "Why Edgar Rice Burroughs?" Van Hise 6.
Vernon, Alex. *On Tarzan*. Athens: University of Georgia Press, 2008.
Vess, Charles. Untitled illustration. *Tarzan: The Lost Adventure*. Dark Horse 1.2 (February 1995): 1.
Volman, Daniel. Rev. of *The Farther Frontier: Six Case Studies of Americans and Africa, 1848–1936*. The International Journal of African Historical Studies 26.3 (1993): 680–81.
Wade, Nicholas. "Scientist Finds the Beginnings of Morality in Primate Behavior." 20 March 2007. *New York Times*. 6 August 2008.
Wahl, Greg. "Me Hero, You Dupe: Gender and the Narrative Division of Labor in *Tarzan of the Apes*." Utz, *Investigating* 31–48.
"War and Literature." [by "J.B."] *Oak Park Events*. 3 Nov. 1917. [Porges papers, Ekstrom Library, University of Louisville]

Ward, James. "Sense-Knowledge (II)." *Mind* NS 28.112 (Oct. 1919): 447–462.
Washington, Booker T. *Up from Slavery*. Garden City, NY: Doubleday, 1901.
Watson, Stephen. *Return of the Moon*. Cape Town: Carrefour, 1991.
West, Peyton M., and Craig Packer. "Sexual Selection, Temperature, and the Lion's Mane." *Science* 297 (23 August 2002): 1339–43.
Whitman, Walt. *Leaves of Grass*. 1892. Rpt. New York: Airmont, 1965.
Wilde, Oscar. *The Picture of Dorian Gray*. 1891. Ed. Donald A. Lawlor. Norton Critical Edition. New York: Norton, 1988.
Wilder, Thornton. "Some Thoughts on Playwrighting." Centeno 83–98.
Williams, J.H. *Elephant Bill*. Garden City, NY: Doubleday, 1950.
Wilson, Angene. "Taking Tarzan Out of the Text Books." *Africa Report* 13.5 (May 1968): 43–44.
Wolfe, Gary K. "Coming to Terms." *Speculations on Speculation: Theories of Science Fiction*. Ed. James Gunn and Matthew Candelaria. Lanham, MD: Scarecrow, 2005. 13–22.
Wyatt, Neal. Rev. of *The Burroughs Cyclopaedia* and *Edgar Rice Burroughs: The Exhaustive Scholar's and Collector's Descriptive Bibliography*. *Library Journal* 122.1 (January 1997): 84.
Wylie, Dan. *Elephant*. London: Reaktion, 2008.
_____. *Original Forest*. Grahamstown: n.p., 2001.
_____. Personal interview. 23 August 2001.
Yeates, Thomas. *Tarzan*. Tarzine 82 (1983): back cover.
_____. *Tarzan with Apes*. Erbania 58 (1988): back cover.
_____. Untitled sketch. *The Edgar Rice Burroughs Art of Thomas Yeates*. ECOF 2002 program booklet [Twixt Two Worlds No. 2]. 35.
Zeuschner, Robert B. "Religious Themes in the Novels of Edgar Rice Burroughs." 2004. *ERBzine* 1120. 2004. 19 July 2008.
Zins, Henryk. *Joseph Conrad and Africa*. Nairobi: Kenya Literature Bureau, 1982.

Index

Numbers in ***bold italics*** indicate pages with photographs.

abduction 137, 162, 185, 197, 210–211, 220; of Jane 38, 109, 154, 211, 219, 221; of Teeka 63, 194, 210–211, 216, 219–221, 224; of Tibo 74, 109–110, 216
Abel (biblical character) 144
abstract 89, 93, 103, 147, 200, 204
Achebe, Chinua 51, 110, 112–114, 116, 121, 132, 151–152
Achilles (Homer character) 31–32, 164
Adam (biblical character) 6, 40–43, 103; *see also* American Adam
Adams, David A. 29, 38, 46, 49, 65, 91, 103, 128, 135, 166, 170, 199–200, 204, 239
Adams, Duane ***48***, 49, 216, ***218***
adaptability 28, 150, 164, 193, 204
adaptations of Tarzan to other media 6, 13, 23, 31, 44, 70, 82–83, 87, 99, 109, 111, 131, 140, 158, 161–162, ***167***, 168, 179–180, ***180***, 185, 210, 227
Adkins, Patrick. H. 14, 116, 130
adolescence (teen years) 8, 11, 18, 23, 29–30, 33, 39, 61, 82, 84, 87, 102, 125, 136, 137, 192–193
Adonis 32
"The Adventure of Charles Augustus Milverton" (Conan Doyle) 93
"The Adventure of the Blue Carbuncle" (Conan Doyle) 88, 220–221
"The Adventure of the Crooked Man" (Conan Doyle) 222
"The Adventure of the Dancing Men" (Conan Doyle) 105
"The Adventure of the Empty House" (Conan Doyle) 27, 59
"The Adventure of the Greek Interpreter" (Conan Doyle) 219–220
"The Adventure of the Mazarin Stone" (Conan Doyle) 174
"The Adventure of the Red-Headed League" (Conan Doyle) 153
"The Adventure of Wisteria Lodge" (Conan Doyle) 153, 155
The Adventures of Huckleberry Finn (Twain) 76, 79, 112–113

Aeneas (Homer character) 32, 164
The Aeneid (Vergil) 16, 32
Africa 8, 21, 24, 28–29, 33, 54, 56, 60, 67, 74, 78, 80–81, 97, 108, 110, 112–122, 125, 129–132, 134, 140, 145, 149, 151, 154, 157–159, 166, 171, 174, 182, 193, 198, 216, 218, 228–229; *see also* black; specific countries and tribal identities
African American 131; *see also* black
Agamemnon 36
Agur (biblical charcter) 136, 165
Ajax 32
Akut (Burroughs character) 32, 54, 82, 97, 215, 224
Aladdin 99
Alice Clayton (Burroughs character) 52, 64, 83, 133, 148, 154, 165
alienation, estrangement 24, 27, 29–30, 77, 137–139, 169, 197, 231
All-Story Magazine, All-Story Weekly, All-Story Cavalier, Argosy 2, 7–8, 14, 24, 45, 136, 174, 211
allegiance 210, 223–224, 226, 235
allegory 33, 103–104, 198
alliteration 213, 215
allusion 31–32, 35, 38–39, 153, 197, 211; *see also* specific works and characters
Altrocchi, Rudolph 33, 39, 103, 107–108, 233–234
altruism 25, 68, 71–72, 122–123, 226
Amazing Stories 2
ambition 65, 147, 220–221
American Adam 79–80
American Notes (Kipling) 28
Amis, Kingsley 17
analogy 59, 146, 193–194, 197, 199, 227–228, 230, 236
Andersen, Hans Christian 99
Anderson, Poul 56, 95, 112
Anderson, Sherwood 14, 76, 142, 154, 156, 235–237
Andrews, Clarence A. 27–28
Andy MacDuff *see* Shoz-Dijiji

253

Index

anger 201
"Animula" (Eliot) 186, 189, 196
Anne of Green Gables (Montgomery) 174–175
antagonist, villain 54, 59, 68, 71, 112, 129, 133, 151, 160, 179, 199, 202; *see also* specific characters
antelope 165
anthropomorphism 57, 59, 62, 68, 102, 189
Anthropop (Burroughs character) 57
Apache 130, 137, 228; *see also* Native American
Apache Devil (Burroughs) 130, 137
ape language 32, 42, 42n, 44, 105, 107–108, 110, 138
apes: anthropological views 38, 52–56, 60–61, 65, 97, 119, 190; mangani 9, 11, 23–29, 32–33, 38–40, 42–43, 56–65, 70–74, 76, 82–83, 87–88, 90–91, 93, 96–98, 101–102, 104, 109, 126, 133, 136, 148, 154, 156, 161–162, 168–170, 174, 176, 179–180, 183, 189, 193–195, 210–211, 213, 216, 220–221, 224, 226, 227–232, 236–238; *see also* specific characters
Aphrodite 32, 36
Apollo 31
appearance and/versus reality 29, 46, 49, 60, 135, 145, 155, 176–177, 179–180, 182–183, 185–189, 203–204, 232
Ardai, Charles 23
Are You My Mother? (Eastman) 101
Argosy see *All*-Story
Aristotle 155, 197
arrows 11, 49, 216, 227
Arthur Gordon Pym (Poe character) 139
Ashe, Frank 100–101
Aslan (C.S. Lewis character) 166, 168
assimilation, integration 11, 20, 24, 27, 29–30, 40, 71, 99–100, 117, 126, 139, 151, 174, 189, 193, 200, 203, 237, 239
assonance 215
Astounding Stories of Super Science 2
At the Earth's Core (Burroughs) 76
Atamian, Sarkis 29, 38, 52, 54, 91n, 130, 142, 179, 234
Augustine 238
Aunt Sally (Twain character) 112
Austen, Jane 171, 213
avarice *see* greed
"The Avenger" (Burroughs) 14

Bachelard, Gaston 74, 132, 204, 206, 230–232, 235–236
Bailey, Seth T. 15
Baker, Steve 59, 102, 202
Bakhtin, Mikhail 172–173, 204, 209
Balasopoulos, Antonis 29, 59, 73–74, 78, 106–107
Ballantyne, R.M. 52
Balzac, Honoré de 13
Barnard, Alan 57, 72, 228
Barrie, James M. 149
Barsoom, Mars, Martian 2, 60, 112, 125, 130, 145, 216–217; *see also* specific titles and characters
"The Battle for Teeka" (Burroughs) 11, 54, 63, 70–72, 74, 82, 96, 133, 143, 147, 157, 162–163, 194, 210–214, 216, 219–224, 226, 238
Beale, Howard K. 123
The Beasts of Tarzan (Burroughs) 54, 61, 82, 85, 115, 149, 188–189, 224
beauty 23–24, 27, 32, 35–36, 43, 82, 88, 91, 94, 94n, 114, 124–126, 129, 138, 143, 147, 154, 216
Bederman, Gail 60, 72, 98, 121, 192
Before Adam (London) 97–98
Belgium 114, 124
Bell, John 131–132
Bellow, Saul 21
Beng people 158
Berglund, Jeff 79, 98, 104, 107, 197
Berlin Conference 8
Bertillon, Alphonse 220–221
Beyond Thirty (Burroughs) 117
Bible 69, 145, 152, 186; Deuteronomy 186, 192; Ecclesiastes 27; Exodus 135, 192; Ezekiel 146, 200–201; 1 Corinthians 105; 1 Samuel 201; Genesis 40–43, 146, 203; Hebrews 96; Isaiah 69; Job 207; Leviticus 192; Matthew 145; Philippians 173; Proverbs 136, 165; Psalms 90, 143–144; Revelation 139; Romans 88, 173; *see also* specific characters
Billings (Burroughs character) 148
Black, Algernon D. 190
black, blacks, blackness 31–32, 43, 52, 56, 60, 63–64, 69, 75, 109, 112–120, 123–132, 138–139, 149, 151, 153, 159, 175, 198, 200, 208, 213, 215, 227
"The Black Man's Burden" (Burroughs) 149
Black Michael (Burroughs character) 83, 148
Blake, William 27, 92–93
Blanch (Shakespeare character) 166
Blood Diamond (film) 115
Blue Book 13–14, 16, 23, 41, 44–45, 66, 70, 87, 126, 129, 136, 140–142, 146, 161–162, 180, 185–186, 210, 227
body language 63
Bolgani *see* gorilla
Bonaparte, Marie 139, 231–232
"The Book of Myths" (Harjo) 30
books in the Greystoke cabin 87, 90, 92, 94, **100**, 102–108, 125, 185–186, 190, 193, 195, 197–198, 201, 208, 236
bow *see* arrows
Boys' Cinema Weekly 9, 9
Bozarth, David Bruce 14–15, 130, 191–192, 195
Brackett, Leigh 18
Bradbury, Ray 233–234
Brantlinger, Patrick 111, 122, 147
Britain *see* England
Brontë, Emily 172
Browne, Thomas 154–155
Browning, Robert 89–90, 196, 205
Brueckel, Frank J. 11

Brueton, Diana 230
Brutus, Dennis 235
Buchan, John 233
Buck (London character) 110, 198
Buel, J.W. 52, *53*, 112
buffalo 152–153, 161, 168
Bukawai (Burroughs character) 31, 49, 64, 68, 75, 83–84, 86, 110, 140–147, 152–160
"Bukawi's Revenge" 109
Bulabantu (Burroughs character) 92, 127, 169, 202, 215, 231
Bulfinch, Thomas 32, 35
Burger, Phillip R. 21, 39, 65, 79, 116, 123–124, 191
burial 46, 120, 134, 138, 159–160
Burroughs, Coleman (brother) 121
Burroughs, Danton (grandson) *v*, 6, 205
Burroughs, Edgar Rice: childhood 7, 31, 73, 113, 117, 119, 121, 124, 145, 166, 206; health 13, 57, 205–206; military academy and service 17, 57, 119, *120*, 121
Burroughs, George Tyler (father) 17, 132, 145
Burroughs, Harry (brother) 165
Burroughs, Hulbert (son) 19, 205
Burroughs, Joan (daughter) 16–17, 89
Burroughs, John Coleman (son) 205
Buscema, John 179, *180*
Bushman, Khoisan, San, /Xam 228–229
Busuli (Burroughs character) 123, 127
Buto *see* rhinoceros
Buzz Lightyear 99
Byrne, Eleanor 58–60, 80–81, 104–105
Byron, Lord George Gordon 238

cabin built by John Clayton 8, 11, 29, 43, 52, 67, 73, 81–83, 87, 90, 92, 94, 99, 102, 105–106, 108, 125, 128, 139, 148, 165, 169, 185–187, 190, 193, 195–197, 201, 210–211, 227–228, 230–232, 236, 238
cage 23, 29–30, 43, 84, 162, 177
Cain (biblical character) 145
"Caliban upon Setebos" (Browning) 89–90, 205
The Call of the Wild (London) 110, 198
Canler (Burroughs character) 59, 64, 92
cannibalism 15, 44, 54, 64, 79, 89, 98, 104, 107, 112, 118, 123–124, 127, 137, 171–174, 183, 192, 198
Captain Billings *see* Billings
"The Capture of Tarzan" (Burroughs) 9, 9, 28, 34, 44–47, 50–51, 66–69, 78, 89, 92, 118, 137, 143, 150, 158, 183, 194, 196, 237
Carey-Webb, Allen 16, 18, 21, 112–114, 198, 200
Carpenter, Stanford W. 131
cartridges 210, 216–217
Caruso, Charles 103
"The Case of the Doctor Who Had No Business, or The Adventure of the Second Anonymous Narrator" (Lupoff) 12
cave 31, 141, 144, 153–154
Centeno, Augusto 75, 238

character-based fiction 49
Charlton comics 13, 70, 87, 161–162, 185, 210, 227
Charon 32
Cheeta (film character) 133–134
Chekhov, Anton 13
Cherokee 130; *see also* Native American
Cheyfitz, Eric 63, 72, 107–108, 132, 137, 151–152
chiasmus 214
Chicago, Illinois 28–29, 60, 70, 78, 119–121, 141, 163, 166, 221
Chicago World's Fair *see* Columbian Exposition
children's literature *see* literature for children
chimpanzee 54, 54n, 56, 67, 97, 133, 190
chivalry 37, 147–148, 150, 189, 192
"Choruses from 'The Rock'" (Eliot) 27, 46, 93, 142
Christmas 1, 161
Circe 137
circle *see* cycle
circumcision 166
Civil War 2, 129
civilization 20, 27–30, 59, 62, 72, 76–82, 104, 106–107, 113, 117, 120, 122–123, 127–132, 135, 142, 147–152, 157, 166, 173–174, 177, 179, 184, 188–189, 199–200, 202, 220, 231, 235–236, 238
Clareson, Thomas D. 36, 239
Clarke, Arthur C. 17
classroom 16–20
Cloward, Tim 41, 147
Clytemnestra 36
Cogan, Lee 19
Coleridge, Samuel Taylor 67, 189
Collingwood, R.G. 107, 122, 152, 175–176, 188, 219
Collins, Phil 24, 135–136
colonialism *see* imperialism
Columbian Exposition, Chicago World's Fair 119–121, *120*, 124, 166
Columbus, Christopher 119
community 155–160, 169, 210; academic 15, 19; ape 54, 60, 98, 190, 211, 224, 226; human 60, 115–116
compassion 25, 66, 95, 153, 195, 202, 213
Conan Doyle, Arthur 27, 59, 88, 93, 105, 171, 174, 219–222, 235
Congo River 152
A Connecticut Yankee in King Arthur's Court (Twain) 236
Conrad, Joseph 12, 18, 51, 105, 110–118, 123, 131–132, 146, 152, 171–172, 198, 200, 228, 238
Conrath, Robert E. 21, 61, 78–79, 148–150, 233–234, 239
consonance 213
Coogan, Peter M. 20–21
Cooper, Brenda 41, 63, 113–114
Cooper, James Fenimore 108, 137

256 Index

Coriell, Vernell W. 39–40
Corliss, Richard 24
Côte d'Ivoire 158
cowardice 71, 78, 121, 157–158, 189
Cowart, David 33
creator 43, 88–90, 104–105, 122, 138; *see also* God
Creed, Barbara 24, 41, 104, 198
Crime and Punishment (Dostoevsky) 188, 205, 209
Crisp, Tony 63, 65, 200, 202–204, 208, 232
Crist, Kenneth 7, 16
crocodile, Gimla 201
Crouch, Stanley 41, 149, 190
Crowder, E.H. 117, 125
cruelty 121, 124, 126–127, 129, 132, 137, 150, 153, 174
Cullinan, Patrick 7
cunning 28, 32, 45, 78, 83, 153, 179, 183, 187, 223, 227
curse, cursing 143, 200–201, 229
cycle 20, 28, 44–47, **48**, 49–50, 69, 92, 184, 227, 230
cynghanedd 215

Dahomey people of Benin 120–121, 124
Daiches, David 145–146
Dale, Alzina Stone 24, 26, 88
Dango *see* hyena
Dante Alighieri 27, 137, 146–147
Dark Horse comics 70, 185
D'Arnot (Burroughs character) 42, 108, 118, 127–128, 137, 151, 174, 194, 198, 211, 217, 231
Darwin, Charles 61, 79, 90, 128, 164, 171; *see also* evolution
David (biblical character) 201
Davis, Robert 14, 141, 145
Davison, Richard Allan 18
Day, David 54–55
DC Comics 13, 23, 44, 70, 91, 185, 224, **225**
death 11, 23, 27, 30, 32, 38, 42, 44, 46–47, 66, 73–75, 81, 84, 91n, 95–96, 104, 114–115, 126–127, 141, 144, 150, 154, 156, 159, 162, 166, 169, 173, 175–177, 179, 182–183, 189–192, 194–195, 198, 202, 206–207, 224, 227, 232, 238
de Brito, Mark 166, 182
deduction 219–222
deer, Bara 186, 196
Defoe, Daniel 73, 79, 173
Delilah (biblical character) 35
demon, devil 29, 38, 75, 96, 122, 142, 147, 150, 155, 175, 216
dénouement 19, 49, 68
Des Moines Sunday Register (newspaper) 13, 23, 70, 140, 161, 185, 210
detective 211, 219–222; *see also* Sherlock Holmes
deus ex machina 66–67
devil *see* demon
devil-god 96, 139

diary, John Clayton's 11–12, 51, 137, 198
DiCaprio, Leonardo 116
dichotomy 28, 78, 89–90, 134, 152, 183, 189, 195
Dick, Philip K. 86
Dickens, Charles 47, 165, 213, 237
"The Disappearance of Lady Frances Carfax" (Conan Doyle) 174
Disney films and characters 24, 57, 59, 66, 82–83, 99, 101, 111, 135–136
dissertations and theses 20–21; *see also* specific authors
Doc Savage 2
Dr. Doolittle (Lofting character) 2
Dr. Faustus (Marlowe) 35
Dr. Jekyll and Mr. Hyde (Stevenson) 60, 132–133
Dodds, Georges T. 39
dog 28, 54, 60, 66, 101, 110, 118, 159, 161, 196
Doniger, Wendy 39
Dostoevsky, Feodor 133, 187–188, 205
The Double (Dostoevsky) 133
Douglass, Frederick 163
Dracula (Stoker) 45, 65
drama, play 76, 105, 171, 176, 186–187
dreams, nightmares 62, 74, 81, 86, 101, 135, 172, 185–189, 197, 200–209, 231
Dreiser, Theodore 150
duality 29, 77, 98, 111, 132–135, 139, 142, 183, 191–192
DuBois, W.E.B. 117
Du Chaillu, Paul 54, 54n, **55**, 91n, 112, 121, 171
Dum-Dum 61, 65, 96–98, 118, 193, 228–229
Dumas, Alexandre 222

eagle 101, 196, 200–203, 208
Earle, Ralph 142
Eastman, John C. 121, 124
Eastman, P.D. 101
eating 24, 41, 44, 54, 81, 92, 97–98, 101, 137, 141–142, 144, 149, 152, 157–158, 169–170, 172–173, 177–178, 182–183, 185–186, 188–190, 193, 195, 199, 201–203, 205, 208–209, 224, 227, 230; *see also* cannibalism
eclipse 169, 227–228, 230, 232
ecofeminist criticism 65
Eden 40–41, 43, 103, 121, 203
Edmund (Austen character) 171
Eldredge, John 223, 223n
elephant, Tantor 9, 34, 44–47, 51, 65–69, 91, 98, 101, 138, 173, 183, 185, 189, 201, 203, 205, 209, 227, 237
Eliot, T.S. 6, 24, 26–27, 30, 34, 45–46, 93, 142, 145–147, 186, 189, 196
Ellery Queen's Mystery Magazine 108, 210–211, 219, 222
Emile (Rousseau) 76
Emma (Austen) 213
emotion, feelings 29–30, 34–36, 40, 46, 63, 68, 70, 71, 74, 89, 95, 98, 158, 170, 175–176,

Index 257

189, 195, 197, 200, 203–204, 206–207, 231, 236
emptiness 1, 27, 122, 146, 169, 197
"The End of Bukawai" (Burroughs) 9, *10*, 21, 68, 83–86, 140–144, 150, 153–155, 157, 165, 168, 174, 205
energy 220, 27, 118, 222
England 12, 25, 28, 34, 51, 60, 77, 79–82, 102, 109, 113–114, 117, 135, 137, 140, 147–149, 152, 165, 191, 197, 199, 202–203, 233–234
English language 56, 69, 74, 102–104, 107–108, 138, 233
envy 197, 208
epiphany 28, 36, 82, 86, 94, 104
Erebus 32
Esmeralda (Burroughs character) 125, 215
Estaban Miranda (Burroughs character) 133
estrangement *see* alienation
The Eternal Lover (Burroughs) 121, 175
ethics, morals 3, 38–40, 51, 64, 88, 107, 120, 133, 146–148, 151, 158, 160, 162, 176, 182, 184, 189–196, 201, 209
Euripides 35, 67
Europe 8, 29, 35, 52, 60, 84, 106, 108, 110, 113–114, 116–119, 122–123, 132, 148–149, 151–152, 231, 234n, 235
Eve (biblical character) 6, 43
Evening Public Ledger (Philadelphia newspaper) 13, 162, 210, 216, **217**
evolution 21, 28, 60–62, 79–80, 84, 89–90, 92, 94, 106, 114, 119–121, 128, 131, 147, 150, 189
eyes 24, 28, 31, 36, 44, 51, 54, 56, 92–93, 111, 115, 117–118, 132, 143, 147, 164–165, 179, 187–188, 194, 220, 227, 230–231, 235
Ezekiel (biblical character) 146, 200–201

Famous Fantastic Mysteries 2
Fantasy Illustrated 9, *10*, 140
Far from the Madding Crowd (Hardy) 177, 215
Farmer, Philip José 8, 11, 38–39, 56, 78, 91n, 155, 159, 163
father 1–2, 17, 30, 63, 72–75, 79, 81–83, 98, 100, 110, 121, 132, 138, 144–145, 147–148, 156, 165, 192, 213; *see also* specific names
Father Constantine (Burroughs character) 41, 127
Faulkner, William 5, 17–18
feast *see* eating
femme fatale 35
Fenton, Robert W. 17, 149, 233
Fiedler, Leslie 129
"The Fight for the Balu" (Burroughs) 38, 47, **58**, 70–75, 84, 89, 191, 205, 211, 222, 224, 238
fingerprint 137, 152, 198, 211
Fiske, John 60, 71–72, 92–94, 94n, 133–134, 189, 224
Fitzgerald, F. Scott 17
"The Five Orange Pips" (Conan Doyle) 153
flashback 83, 85, 140

Fleis, Charles 31
fog 51, 93
"For the Fool's Mother" (Burroughs) 14
foreshadowing 19, 36, 68–69, 106
Forgotten Tales of Love and Murder (Burroughs) 14
formalist criticism 30
Foster, Harold 56, **57**, 99, ***100***
Fou-tan (Burroughs character) 130
Fowler, Alistair 105
frame story 12, 51–52, 149, 152
France 11, 41, 108, 125, 159, 191, 198, 219, 235
Frankenstein (Shelley) 43, 83, 102, 104–105, 138, 150, 193, 215, 237
French Revolution 171
Freud, Sigmund 64, 90, 98, 122, 139, 152, 206
Friday (Defoe character) 73, 79, 171
Frost, Robert 14
future (n.) 36, 43, 62, 69, 147

G8 and His Battle Aces 2
Galsworthy, John 18
Ganymede 197
Gazan (Burroughs character) 30, 63, 70 72, 84, 109, 157, 199, 210–211, 214, 221–223, 238
Gemnon (Burroughs character) 139
Germany 129, 175
ghosts 207
Gina Ekdal (Ibsen character) 156
Gingerich, Owen 88
The Girl from Hollywood (Burroughs) 39
God 27–28, 41, 43, 46–47, 72, 87–92, 94–96, 101, 107–108, 115, 139, 142–146, 166, 173, 196, 207, 230, 236
god, goddess 31, 34–36, 39, 41, 52, 62–63, 67, 74–75, 90, 94–96, 115, 144, 150, 155, ***167***, 168, 173, 197, 216, 228; *see also* devil-god; specific names
"The God-Maker, Man" (Marquis) 90
"The God of Tarzan" (Burroughs) 13, 21, 34, 47, 74–75, 82, 87–97, 99, 101–108, 109, 125, 142–143, 145, 152, 155–157, 164, 168, 193, 201–202, 213, 222, 228–230, 236, 238
Gold Key comics 13, 44, 87, 109, 162
Goliath (biblical character) 201
good and evil 38, 93, 132, 140, 142–147, 162
Gordon King (Burroughs character) 130
gorilla, Bolgani 9, 67, 82, 163, 185, 187–188, 196–197, 202, 224
gorilla, scientific descriptions 51–52, **53**, 54, 54n, **55**, 56, 97, 118
Goro *see* moon
Gottlieb, Alma 158
Greece 5–6, 31–35, 39, 41, 62, 74, 90, 94, 96, 98, 106, 138, 164, 176–177, 187, 214; *see also* specific characters
greed, avarice 27, 114, 143, 158
Greek language 31–32, 74, 177
Gregors Werle (Ibsen character) 156–157
grief 110, 169
Griswold, Jerry 24, 28

grotesque 142, 152–157, 176
Grun, Nina 20, 77, 80, 148
Guenther, Mathias 174, 184, 228–229
Guido da Montefeltro (Dante character) 27, 30
Guinevere 35
Gulliver's Travels (Swift) 57
Gunn, James 1–3, 17
Gunto (Burroughs character) 161
Guymon, E.T., Jr. 222

Habblitz, Harry 9, *10*
Hagenbeck, Carl 166
Haggard, H. Rider 112, 157
hair 28, 43, 52, 60–61, 95, 99, 103, 118, 124, 129, 179, 206, 221, 237
hairlessness 43, 124
Hamilton, Edith 32, 35
Hamlet (Shakespeare) 136, 179
Hammond, Dorothy 122
Hanson, Alan 8, 11, 85, 159, 163, 169, 231
Happy Birthday, Moon (Ashe) 100–101
Hardy, Thomas 152, 177, 215, 230
Harjo, Joy 30, 179
Harmon, William 50, 68–69, 78, 176, 179, 200
Hart, James D. 7, 56, 77–78
Hartmann, Ernest 204–208
Hauser, Marc D. 190–191
Hawthorne, Nathaniel 13, 228
Heart of Darkness (Conrad) 12, 18, 51, 110, 112–115, 131, 146, 171–172, 198
Heathcliff (Brontë character) 172
Hedda Gabler (Ibsen) 38
Heidegger, Martin 59
Heinlein, Robert 17
Helen of Troy 30, 34–36, 39, 211
Hell 27, 32
Hemingway, Ernest 5, 17–18, 21, 158
Heracles *see* Hercules
Hercules 31, 33–34, 34n, 35, 99
Hercules and the Princess of Troy (film) 34
heredity, heritage, inheritance 30, 37, 51, 73, 77–83, 90, 107, 113, 118, 127, 129–130, 134, 139, 147–148, 150, 182, 186, 190–192, 194–195, 207, 209, 211, 231
Herrick, Robert 36
Higgins, Jonna 65
Hiller, Edmund 157
Hillman, Bill 13, 28, 66, 110, 121, 145
"His Age" (Herrick) 36
Histah *see* snake
Hjalmar Ekdal (Ibsen character) 156
Hoffmann, E.T.A. 13
Hogarth, Burne 25–26, **26**, 56–57, 154
Holman, Hugh 50, 68–69, 78, 176, 179, 200
Holtsmark, Erling B. 5, 16–19, 24, 26, 31–34, 36, 38–40, 43, 46–47, 47n, 49, 57, 59–63, 65–66, 74–75, 78–80, 82, 84, 87, 98, 104, 119, 123, 133–134, 136–137, 148, 150–151, 154, 157, 161, 164–165, 169–170, 174, 179, 183, 185–187, 189, 191, 194, 198–199, 210, 214–216, 228, 237, 239; *see also* Tarzan and Tradition
Homer 30, 32–33, 36, 57, 106, 137, 161, 164; *see also* specific characters and titles
The House of the Seven Gables (Hawthorne) 228
Howard, Allan 38, 116
Huckleberry Finn (Twain character) 76, 79, 112–113
Huffstetler, Edward W. 184
Hugo, Victor 80
humor 40, 83, 161–162, 174–177, 179, 184, 237
hunting 15, 23, 27, 32, 46, 52, 59, 67, 81, 85, 87, 102–103, 109–110, 114, 140, 142, 149, 157, 164, 166, 178, 195, 197, 199, 207, 233
"The Hyænas" (Kipling) 64
Hyde (Stevenson character) 60
Hyde, Lewis 45, 177, 179, 182–183, 188, 236
hyena, Dango 64, 68, 86, 101, 140–142, 144, 153, 155, 157–160, 182, 196, 208, 210–211

Ibeto (Burroughs character) 73, 145
Ibsen, Henrik 38, 60, 156, 190
identity, search for 20, 29, 77–78, 82, 107–108, 111, 135–139, 147, 173, 198, 218, 223, 231–233
The Idiot (Dostoevsky) 187
idiot plot 45
Idylls of the King (Tennyson) 33
The Iliad (Homer) 32, 164
illness, sickness 1, 57, 185, 203–205, 208
imagination 2, 7, 21, 27, 35, 38, 78, 83, 96, 110, 112, 116–117, 128, 132, 145, 171–172, 188, 197, 233–237, 239
imperial(ism), colonial(ism) 12, 51, 73–74, 104, 114, 138, 148, 151–152, 172
"In a Pot on the Window Sill" (Maclennan) 51
inference 12, 39, 88, 94–95, 199
Inferno (Dante) 27, 146–147
instinct 63, 69, 71–72, 74–75, 82, 110, 122, 147–148, 150, 170, 191–195, 203, 221, 224, 226
integration *see* assimilation
integrity 143, 150, 196, 234
intuition 40, 89, 93, 105, 107, 110, 191, 208
The Invisible Man (Wells) 154
irony 7, 18, 28–30, 43, 45, 73, 96, 136, 138, 142, 158, 163, 174, 176, 192, 205
Irving, Washington 13
Ishmael (Melville character) 138
Ivanhoe (Scott) 170
ivory 114–115

Jabez Wilson (Conan Doyle character) 153
Jablow, Alta 122
jackal 59, 165
Jackson, Michael 15, 155, 158, 170, 182, 184
Jacobs, Gary 32, 191
Jane Porter (Burroughs character) 8, 19, 24, 30, 34, 36–39, 41, 59, 92, 94–95, 99, 109,

Index

147–151, 154, 173–174, 188, 194–195, 211, 215, 219, 221, 223, 231, 239
Janus 114
Jason 31
Jason Gridley (Burroughs character) **219**
Jekyll (Stevenson character) 60, 132–133
Jerry Lukas (Burroughs character) 32
Jocasta 33
John Carter (Burroughs character) 129–130
John Clay (Conan Doyle character) 153
John Clayton (Burroughs character) 12, 73, 80, 82, 113, 148
Johnston, Alva 18, 30, 57, 105, 136, 193
joke 32, 83, 158, 161, 174–177, 179, 183
"Journey of the Magi" (Eliot) 27
Jove 139
"The Judgment of Paris" (Merwin) 36
Jung, Carl 207
jungle: as location 14–15, 23, 25, 27–33, 41, 43, 46–47, 63–67, 74, 76–77, 80–81, 84, 90–93, 97–98, 102–103, 107–108, 120, 124, 127, 133–136, 138, 140, 142, 149–151, 154–155, 159, 162, 164, 170–171, 179, 188, 190, 192, 194–196, 199, 202, 208, 210–211, 216, 218, 228, 231; as symbol 27–30, 41, 46, 92, 98, 131, 133, 148–151, 179, 198, 239
The Jungle (Sinclair) 27–29
The Jungle Books (Kipling) 97, 233–234
Jungle Girl (Burroughs) 130
"A Jungle Joke" (Burroughs) 31, 47, 84, 86, 124, 126–128, 133, 137, 139, 143, 147–148, 150, 159, 161–163, 166, 170, 177, 183, 194, 202, 205
Jungle Tales of Tarzan (Burroughs): congruence with *Tarzan of the Apes* 8–9, 11–12, 31, 33, 73, 80–81, 84, 96–97, 105, 124–125, 128, 168–169, 223; publication history 13–14, 23, 41, 44–45, 70, 87, 109, 116, 136, 140–142, 161–162, 185, 210, 227
Jungle Tales of Tarzan (Hogarth) **26**, 57
Juno 32, 186
Jurca, Catherine 82, 108, 132
Jurgis Rudkus (Sinclair character) 28–29
Jusko, Joe 9

Kala (Burroughs character) 5, 9, 11, 23, 33, 52, 54, 56, 61, 63–64, 71–73, 84, 95, 100, 115, 124, 127, 133, 138, 140, 154, 165, 169, 189–190, 192, 194, 203
Kant, Immanuel 195
Kanyandekwe, Daniel 21
Keats, John 2, 35, 106
Kennicott, Donald 103, 129
Kerchak (Burroughs character) 9, 11, 24, 27–28, 42n, 44, 54, 61, 71–72, 82, 98, 102, 108, 124, 126–127, 137–138, 148, 165, 168–169, 171, 187, 193, 221, 225, 227, 230–231, 236–238
Kidd, Kenneth 233
kidnapping *see* abduction
Kilgour, Maggie 104, 137–139, 172–173, 188, 198

King John (Shakespeare) 166
King Solomon's Mines (Haggard) 157
Kipling, Rudyard 28, 64, 97–98, 112, 149, 233–235
Kirkland, Winifred Margaretta 119, 174
kissing 37, 148
knife inherited from John Clayton 9, 28, 34, 67, 73, 81–82, 84, 91–92, 115, 185, 194, 197, 210
knowledge 31, 33, 45, 52, 85, 93, 95, 102, 104, 106–107, 118, 121, 134, 137, 145, 191, 198, 219–221, 223, 229, 236
kooloo-kamba 54, 54n, **55**
Korak (Burroughs character) 32, 34, 66, 97
Korean War 117
Kraft, David Anthony 158
Kreuzer, James R. 19
Kubert, Joe 23, 44, 66, 70, 91, 131, 185, 203, 224, **225**
Kuhn, Helmut 201
Kujamaat Diola people 159
Kulonga (Burroughs character) 11, 73, 84–85, 98, 115, 123, 127, 159, 172, 174, 190–195, 201

La (Burroughs character) 42, 155, 219
Lacon-Watson, E.H. 15, 18
Lady Alice *see* Alice Clayton
Lady Anne (Shakespeare character) 35, 207
Laius 33
The Land That Time Forgot (Burroughs) 2
Lang, Andrew 2
language, linguistic(s) 30, 32, 38, 41–42, 44, 46, 51, 54, 56, 60–62, 87–89, 93, 97, 102–108, 104n, 114, 118, 120, 129, 131, 190, 197–198, 214–215, 228n; *see also* specific languages
Larson, Wolf 198
The Last Battle (Lewis) 166, 182
Latin 16, 31, 45, 65, 214
law 27, 78, 80, 90, 94, 96, 115, 151, 155, 176, 190, 192
leadership 60, 62, 70, 83, 91–92, 91n, 108, 110, 124, 130, 156, 166, 168–171, 176, 219, 228, 231, 238
Leaves of Grass (Whitman) 132
Leda 35, 39
LeGuin, Ursula K. 76
leopard, panther: Sheeta as animal 23, 25–26, 36, 38, 42–43, 63–64, 70, 81, 85, 93, 157, 168, 194, 170, 199, 213–215, 224, **225**; Sheeta as symbol 36, 38, 64
Leopold II 124
leper 152, 159–160; *see also* Bukawai
Levin, Martin 23, 37–38
Lewis, C.S. 88, 166, 168, 175, 182
Lewis, Sinclair 17
Lincoln, Abraham 1
linguistics *see* language
Linnaeus, Carl 61
"The Lion" (Burroughs) 11, 61, 71, 98, 102, 158, 161–162, 169–170, 179–180, **181**,

182–183, 192, 194, 211, 220, 224, 226, 237–238
lion, Numa, Sabor: as animal 34, 43–44, 47, 50–51, 63, 66–67, 71, 73, 81, 85, 93, 102, 110, 128, 135, 149, 157–158, 161–166, 168–170, 178–179, **181**, 182, 187, 194–195, 199–200, 202, 208, 215, 220, 224, 226–227, 230; as symbol 34, 67, 101, 143–144, 157, 162, 164–166, 168, 179–180, 182–183, 185, 187, 199–203, 208–209, 227, 230
lion skin 102, 161–162, 166, **167**, 168, 179, 182–183, 187, 208
literacy 87, 102–104, 104n, 106–108; *see also* language
literature: as accepted body of written work for study 2–3, 15–21, 31, 33, 36, 51, 62–63, 79, 87–89, 104, 114, 125, 172–173, 176, 187, 196–197, 234, 239; as elite writing 15–17, 19–20; for children 87, 99–102; as popular writing 1–3, 37, 86–87
"The Little Door" (Burroughs) 14
Livingstone, David 54, 91n, 97, 121–122, 171, 220
Llana of Gathol (Burroughs) 129
Locke, John 122
Lofting, Hugh 2
Logan, Rayford W. 131
London, Jack 66, 77, 97–98, 110, 112, 198
London, England 27, 29, 81, 149, 200
Lone Ranger (Striker character) 130
Long, Ray 13–14, 87, 109, 126, 141–142, 162–163, 185
Lord Jim (Conrad) 228, 238
Los Angeles, California 13, 109, 163, 210, 233
Los Angeles Times 7, 16, 115
Loucks, James F. 89–90
love story 6, 36–40
Lovecraft, H.P. 24, 103
Lucie Manette *see* Manette family
Lupoff, Richard 5, 8, 12, 14, 17–18, 40, 103, 116, 123

Macbeth (Shakespeare) 103
Mack, John E. 186–188, 205–208
Maclennan, Don 51, 235
Major Schneider (Burroughs character) 194–195
Malaprop (Sheridan character) 125
Malibu comics 23
Mamka (Burroughs character) 161, 169–170, 220, 224, 226, 238
Manette family (Dickens characters) 213, 236
Manning, Russ 25, **25**, 129
Mansfield Park (Austen) 171
Manson, Cynthia 23
Manu *see* monkey
Margulies, Leo 77, 163
Maria (Austen character) 171
Marlow (Conrad character) 12, 51, 113, 115, 118, 152

Marlowe, Christopher 35
Marquis, Don 90
marriage, wedding 39, 130, 156, 232
"The Marriage of Heaven and Hell" (Blake) 27
Mars, Martian *see* Barsoom
Marvel Comics 13, 23, 87, 140, 158, 161–162, **167**, 179, **180**, 210, 227
Marxist criticism 64
masculine journey, masculine studies 223, 223n
The Mastermind of Mars (Burroughs) 60
Maxon, Rex 56
Mbonga (Burroughs character) 47, 73, 82, 87, 90–91, 91n, 92, 115, 123–124, 127, 143–145, 156–158, 164, 173, 192, 203; village and people 11, 23, 29, 34, 37, 43–44, 46–47, 60, 63, 64, 66–67, 69–70, 73–74, 76, 79, 84, 87, 98, 102, 106–108, 110, 115, 119, 123–128, 137–140, 143, 152, 155, 159, 162, 166, **167**, 168, 170, 172, 173–176, 179, 182–183, 185, 187–189, 192, 202–203, 205, 216, **217**
McClurg, A.C., publisher 1, 13, 34n
McDowell, Edward B. 120, 166
McGreal, Dorothy 16, 18, 20, 38
McQuillan, Martin 58–60, 80–81, 104–105
McWhorter, George T. 6, 32, 111–112
Melville, Herman 138–139, 173
Menelaus 35
The Merchant of Venice (Shakespeare) 36
Meriem (Burroughs character) 42n, 62, 151, 211
Merritt, A. 2
Mesina, Rudy 179, **180**
Metamorphoses (Ovid) 32, 39
metaphor 28–30, 57, 59, 64, 144, 165, 197–200, 204, 232, 235
Metcalf, Thomas Newell 7–8, 16, 31, 102, 163, 174
meteor 227
Meyer, Michael 19, 51, 111, 114
Michigan 13, 21, 87, 109
Michigan Military Academy 17, 119, **120**
Midgley, Mary 64–65, 111, 118, 162, 215, 234–235, 237
A Midsummer Night's Dream (Shakespeare) 37, 182, 186
military draft 116–117
Miller, Walter James 25
Milne, A.A. 101
Milton, John 43, 173
Minidoka (Burroughs) 57
Miranda (Shakespeare character) 151
Les Misérables (Hugo) 80
missing link 60–61, 80, 90, 128
Moby Dick (Melville) 171, 138–139
Modernism 6, 23–24, 26–27, 29–30
modifier 32, 56, 75, 113, 137, 214–216
monkey (Manu) 34, 43, 57, 62, 79, 134, 137, 161–162, 190, 210, 238
The Monster Men (Burroughs) 152

Montaigne, Michael 122, 145, 172
Montgomery, L.M. 174–175
moon (Goro) 32, 44, 47, **48**, 49, 61, 87, 89–91, 96–97, 101, 169, 227–232, 237–238
morning 47, 149, 162, 185
Morris, John D. 61
Mortimer, Ruth 133, 204, 209
Moses (biblical character) 33, 135, 192
Moskowitz, Sam 7
motherhood 7, 15, 30, 33, 52, 64, 71–75, 78, 101, 107, 109–110, 127, 148, 165, 169, 190, 192, 198–199, 211, 223, 231–232, 234n
mouth 28, 54, 143, 153–154
Mowgli (Kipling character) 61, 97, 233–235
Much Ado About Nothing (Shakespeare) 204
Mugambi (Burroughs character) 35, 124
Mullargan *see* One-Punch Mullargan
Mumga (Burroughs character) 90, 210–211, 216, 222
murder 36, 115, 143–144, 148, 151, 153, 175–176, 186–188, 192, 194, 201, 203, 208–209, 220
Murphy, Donn B. 60, 190
Murphy, Graham J. 131, 217
Murray, Paul T. 116–117
Muviro (Burroughs character) 124, 131
Mwikisa, Peter 112, 114–115, 121, 123
Mycroft Holmes (Conan Doyle character) 219–221
mythology 3, 7, 20, 31–32, 34, 36, 39, 41, 62, 78, 98, 114, 158, 163, 183–184, 228, 232–233

Narcissus 24
narrative technique: authorial intrusion 16, 50, 67, 177, 187, 191, 201; editorial 52, 59, 126, 173–174, 179, 187, 195, 235, 238; editorial omniscience 31, 34, 41–42, 45–46, 50, 61–63, 65, 67–68, 71–72, 74–75, 78, 84, 89, 91–92, 95, 97, 110, 115–117, 124, 126–129, 133, 147–150, 153, 156, 159, 164–165, 186, 189, 194, 196, 213, 221, 228; first-person 12, 27, 51, 59, 113, 115, 138, 222; objective 50, 84–85, 126, 139, 145, 222, 237; omniscient 11, 26–27, 34, 42–45, 50, 52, 54, 56, 60–61, 68, 72–73, 81–84, 94–96, 98, 102, 110, 123–126, 129, 134, 155, 157, 169–170, 174, 177, 187, 192–194, 198–199, 204–205, 216, 220, 222, 223–224, 226, 238; sensory 50–51; unnamed 12, 51; unreliable 12, 52, 143, 206, 224, 226
Native American 129–130, 138, 182, 184; *see also* specific people groups
natural theology 60, 87–89, 95–96; *see also* theology
Needham, Rodney 65, 124–125, 216
Nesteby, James Ronald 20, 233
Newsinger, John 16, 77, 125, 175, 198, 215, 218–219
Niebuhr, Reinhold 175, 177
night 12, 31, 81, 94, 120, 128, 132–133, 145, 149, 166, 185, 187–188, 202, 207, 227, 229–230, 232
nightmare *see* dreams
"The Nightmare" (Burroughs) 9, 82, 96, 101, 135, 137–138, 143, 152, 158, 163, 172, 173, 176, 182–183, 185–189, 196–197, 200–209
Nineteen Eighty-Four (Orwell) 38
Nkima (Burroughs character) 134
noble savage 20, 71, 76–80, 150
nose 28, 100, 127, 153, 216, 220, 222
Notes from a Rhenish Mission (Maclennan) 235
Numa *see* lion
Numgo (Burroughs character) 90, 96, 101, 228
Nye, Russell B. 18

Oak Park, Illinois 13
objective correlative 34–35
observation 15, 20, 23, 40–41, 49–50, 54, 65, 68, 80, 95, 101, 110, 122, 129, 133, 142, 145, 184, 186, 188, 196–197, 201, 206, 216, 219–221, 228–229, 231, 235–236
ocean, sea 2, 27, 41, 67, 92, 196, 210, 231–232, 236
odor *see* smell
Odysseus 31–33, 137, 161–162
The Odyssey (Homer) 161
Oedipus 33, 98, 138
Oha, Obododimma 208
Old Timer (Burroughs character) 32
Olga de Coude (Burroughs character) 41, 128, 215
Oliver Edwards (Cooper character) 137
Olson, Sharon 169
One-Punch Mullargan (Burroughs character) 15
Opar 34, 39, 42, 136, 155–156, 219
Operator #5 2
Orczy, Baroness [Sara Orczy-Barstow Brown] 168, 171
Orestes 31
Original Forest (Wylie) 134–135
Orion **31**
Orth, Michael 20, 123
Orwell, George 38
The Outlaw of Torn (Burroughs) 163
Ovid 32, 39, 182

Packer, Craig 164
Paley, William 88, 95–96
panther *see* leopard
Paradise Lost (Milton) 43, 105, 193
parallel grammar 214–215
pararhyme 213–214
Paris (Greek hero) 35–36
Paris, France 34, 121, 149, 151, 175
Parkers' Complete Book of Dreams 207
past 2, 62, 82, 138, 156, 194, 207
patience 33, 66, 158, 205
patriotism 71, 121–122

262   Index

peace 65, 132, 201, 228
Peer Gynt (Ibsen) 60, 190, 194
Pellucidar 2, 112
Pendleton, Thomas A. 192, 195–196
Perseus 31
Peter Pan (Barrie character) 149
Philander (Burroughs character) 34
philosophy 3, 14, 16, 24, 27, 59, 76, 88–90, 114, 139, 142, 190–192, 237; *see also* specific philosophers
The Picture of Dorian Gray (Wilde) 191
The Pioneers (Cooper) 137
pit 34, 44, 46, 50, 66–67, 69, 93, 153
play *see* drama
playfulness 42, 65, 83–84, 237
plot 8, 12, 19, 21, 26, 30, 42, 45–46, 49, 73, 103–104, 131, 134–136, 156, 161, 176, 185, 198, 234
plot-based fiction 49
Plutarch 165, 193
Pocatello, Idaho 149
Poe, Edgar Allan 13, 105, 139, 219, 231–232
point of view 43, 50–51, 56, 59, 68, 117, 126, 128–129, 142, 169, 194; *see also* narrative technique
polarity 72, 78, 133–134, 151
Poole, Oliver 234
Porges, Irwin 7, 13–14, 17, 65–66, 79, 165, 205, 233–234
"A Postcolonial Tale" (Harjo) 179
practical jokes 83, 174, 177
The Prairie (Cooper) 108
priamel 199
pride 3, 35, 126, 143, 164, 177, 207, 213
A Princess of Mars (Burroughs) 17, 19, 130, 216–217
Professor Porter (Burroughs character) 43, 151, 232, 235
Prometheus 31, 77, 177
Prometheus Radio Theatre 87, 87n
prophecy 79, 136, 146, 200–201, 230–231
Prospero (Shakespeare character) 105–106, 151, 186
Prufrock (Eliot character) 26–27, 29–30, 146
psychological criticism 3, 20, 24, 26, 62, 64, 90, 133, 136, 186, 202–204, 206, 208, 214, 221
The Puppet Masters (Heinlein) 17
Puzzle (C.S. Lewis character) 166, 168, 182

Queenan, Joe 115–116
Queequeg (Melville character) 171

Rabba Kega (Burroughs character) 75, 84, 133, 137, 140, 145–147, 152, 155–156, 159, 161–162, 168, 177–178
"Rabbi Ben Ezra" (Browning) 196
racism 20, 109, 111–132, 151–152, 192, 200, 215
rain 165, 221–222, 228–229
Ramsgate (Burroughs character) 220
Ransby, Barbara 116
Ras Thavas (Burroughs character) 60

Raskolnikov (Dostoevsky character) 188, 209
rat 59, 158, 196
Reade, W. Winwood 64, 97, 110, 118–119, 122
reality *see* appearance
reason, reasoning 8, 24–25, 27, 34, 38, 40, 43, 45, 60–61, 75–76, 80, 82–83, 86, 88–90, 92–93, 95–96, 98, 101, 105, 122, 128, 133, 142, 145, 150, 169–170, 179, 187–188, 190–195, 201–202, 221, 227, 230, 236
Rebarber, Theodor 102
reed buck 50–51
Religio Medici (Browne) 154
religion 88, 95, 98, 129, 145–146, 149
Rendezvous with Rama (Clarke) 17
rescue 23, 29–30, 33, 37–38, 41, 46–47, 63, 66–67, 70, 74, 79, 87, 91, 131, 140, 148, 153, 168, 170–171, 173, 183, 210, 213, 215–216, 223–224, 226–227, 237–238
The Return of Tarzan (Burroughs) 3, 16, 32, 34, 41–42, 61, 79–80, 92, 97–98, 108, 123–124, 127–128, 149, 151, 155–156, 173–174, 176, 189, 217, 218, 235
Return of the Moon (Watson) 228, 231
The Return of the Native (Hardy) 152, 230
revenge, vengeance 23, 63, 84–85, 98, 109–110, 115, 127, 154, 190, 194, 220
reversal 20, 46–47, 57, 59, 96, 125, 155, 171, 192, 213–216, 228–229, 237
rhinoceros, Buto 44–45, 150
Rice, Andrew 37
Richard I, Richard the Lion-Hearted 165
Richard III *see Tragedy of King Richard the Third*
ring composition 46
rising action 19, 46
Riso, Mary 213
Robin Hood 78
Robinson, Frank M. 36
Robinson Crusoe (Defoe) 73, 79, 171, 173
Rokoff (Burroughs character) 32, 34, 59, 64, 92, 151, 173, 188
Romanticism 20, 76
Rome 31–32, 34, 39, 41, 62, 114, 138, 152, 165, 233; *see also* Bible
Romøren, Rolf 104, 104n, 106
Romulus and Remus 31, 33, 233
Roosevelt, Theodore 78–79, 122–123, 157
rope 26, 28, 70, 74, 80–86, 109, 140–141, 155, 166, 194, 214
Rothstein, Edward 71, 111, 148
Rousseau, Jean Jacques 76–78, 105
Rubanowice, Robert J. 38–39

Sabor *see* lion
sacrifice 34; *see also* self-sacrifice
St. John, J. Allen 56, **58**
Sapir, David J. 159–160
Sarina (Burroughs character) 130
satire 57, 81, 125
Saunders, Charles R. 131–132
savage 28, 33, 59, 63, 72, 76–80, 91n, 96, 98,

Index 263

105, 111, 113, 118, 121–122, 130–131, 149–150, 152, 166, 171, 173–174, 202, 214–215, 228; *see also* noble savage
The Scarlet Pimpernel (Orczy) 168, 171
scent *see* smell
Schechter, Harold 66–67, 133–134
Schneider, John M. 168
science fiction 17, 130
Scott, Gordon 34
Scott, Ridley 86
Scott, Walter 170
The Screwtape Letters (Lewis) 175
sea *see* ocean
"The Sea-Wolf" (London) 198
Sebastian Moran (Conan Doyle character) 27, 59
self-control 15, 115, 170, 173, 182
self-reliance 68, 102, 155
self-sacrifice 66, 71, 91, 173, 188, 213
Semeiks, Jonna Gormely 66–67, 133–134
sense of humor *see* humor
sentence analysis 46, 197, 213–215, 237
Serpell, James 64
sex, sexuality 15, 38–40, 148, 182, 203
sexism 216–217
The Shadow 2
Shakespeare, William 15, 33, 35–36, 51, 89, 103, 105, 136, 166, 186–187, 204, 207
Sheeta *see* leopard
Shelley, Mary 43, 83, 102, 104–105, 150, 186, 193, 215, 237
Sheridan, Richard 125
Sherlock Holmes (Conan Doyle character) 12, 27, 59, 88, 93, 105, 153, 155, 174, 211, 219, 222
Shift (C.S. Lewis character) 166, 168
short story form 5, 13–14, 75, 163, 238
Shoz-Dijiji (Burroughs character) 130
sickness *see* illness
The Sign of Four (Conan Doyle) 171, 219
simile 92, 186, 196, 200
Simonson, Walter 131
Sinclair, Upton 27–28
Singh, Frances 113, 200
Sister Carrie (Dreiser) 150
skin, skin color 25, 50, 52, 95, 100, 107, 118–119, 124–129, 131, 139, 175, 179, 182, 200, 223
sleep, slumber 24, 51, 78, 81, 149, 163, 178, 185, 188, 190, 196, 202–204, 207, 229
smell, odor, scent 51, 81, 94, 154, 220–222, 237
Smith, Herbert F. 18
snake, Histah 34, 63, 74–75, 87–89, 92–93, 95–96, 101, 142, 185, 202–203, 209, 211, 213
Snipes (Burroughs character) 59
"The Snows of Kilimanjaro" (Hemingway) 158
soko 54, 54n, 220
Solomon (biblical character) 27

Something of Myself (Kipling) 234
"Son of Man" (Collins) 136
The Son of Tarzan (Burroughs) 12, 32, 34, 42n, 61–62, 66, 68, 97, 151, 166, 211
soul 29, 32, 65, 132, 134, 139, 143, 146, 149, 201, 207, 228, 236, 238
Soumille, Gabriel 31, 191
Southam, B.C. 146
spatial arrangement 50, 208–209
spirit, spirits 59–60, 62, 87, 93–96, 123, 134, 142, 144–146, 159, 165–166, 168, 182, 186, 201, 221, 231, 235
Spradley, David William 20
Stanley, Henry M. 121–122, 171
Starr, Frederick 119, 121
Steele, Esther Baker 117
Steele, Joel Dorman 117
stereotype 111–116, 125–126, 131, 157, 172, 200, 219
Stoker, Bram 45, 65
Street, Brian 119
strength 28, 31–32, 34, 42, 56, 77, 81, 110, 123, 143, 146–147, 151, 164–165, 190–191, 200, 202, 218–219, 223–224, 231 232
Striker, Fran 130
Stroud, Joanne H. 74, 132
Stryver (Dickens character) 165
style 15, 23, 66, 69
Styx, Stygian 31–32
subconscious *see* unconscious
subjunctive 45, 90
survival of the fittest *see* Darwin, Charles; evolution
Swift, Jonathan 19, 57, 125
Sydney Carton (Dickens character) 165, 213
symbol 38–39, 42, 46, 49, 65, 74, 78, 92, 102–103, 105, 136, 138–139, 145, 153, 157, 159–160, 174, 186, 198, 200–204, 206, 209, 230–232

A Tale of Two Cities (Dickens) 47, 165, 213, 236–237
Taliaferro, John 13, 16–18, 31, 38–39, 50, 52, 57, 60, 78–79, 82, 89, 110, 115–116, 123, 125–126, 129–130, 132, 150, 166, 211, 233, 239
The Taming of the Shrew (Shakespeare) 15, 51
Tantor *see* elephant
Tapper, Richard L. 64, 102
Tartarus 32
Tarzan (film, 1999) 24, 59, 111, 136
"Tarzan and the Black Boy" (Burroughs) 42, 56, 63, 74–76, 84–85, 91, 96, 105, 109–111, 116–117, 126–128, 134, 136, 141–142, 152–153, 155, 159, 166, 172, 199–200, 214, 224, 235
"Tarzan and the Castaways" (Burroughs) 15
"Tarzan and the Champion" (Burroughs) 15
Tarzan and the City of Gold (Burroughs) 67, 84, 135, 139
Tarzan and the Forbidden City (Burroughs) 34, 135, 239

Tarzan and the "Foreign Legion" (Burroughs) 32, 130, 197
Tarzan and the Golden Lion (Burroughs) 67, 149, 192
Tarzan and the Jewels of Opar (Burroughs) 12, 32, 34, 44, 84, 124, 136, 157–58, 211
"Tarzan and the Jungle Murders" (Burroughs) 15, 66, 163, 211, 220,
Tarzan and the Leopard Men (Burroughs) 32
Tarzan and the Lion Man (Burroughs) 24
Tarzan and the Little Black Boy (Burroughs) 109, 211
Tarzan and the Lost Empire (Burroughs) 134
Tarzan and the Lost Safari (film, 1957) 34
Tarzan and the Trappers (film, 1958) 34
Tarzan and Tradition (Holtsmark) 5, 16, 18, 31–32, 47n
Tarzan at the Earth's Core (Burroughs) 95, 219
Tarzan, Guard of the Jungle (Burroughs) 16
"Tarzan, Lord of the Jungle" (*Blue Book* article) 66
Tarzan, Lord of the Jungle (Burroughs) 135, 179
Tarzan of the Apes (Burroughs) 3, 5–9, 11–12, 15–19, 24, 28, 30–34, 36–38, 41–42, 51–52, 56, 59, 61, 64, 71, 73, 80–85, 87, 91–92, 95–96, 98–100, 102, 104, 106, 109–110, 113–114, 118, 122–125, 128, 134, 141, 147–148, 150, 152, 154, 165, 168–169, 174, 179, 189–195, 197–199, 206, 218, 221, 224, 233–235, 239; *see also* Gold Key comics
"Tarzan Rescues the Moon" (Burroughs) 9, 11, 13, 31–32, 47, 65–66, 85, 92, 94–96, 116, 165, 169, 193, 198, 227–231, 236–238
Tarzan II (DVD) 24, 82–83, 99, 135–136
Tarzan Shoots Goro (Adams art) **48**, 49
Tarzan, the Ape Man (film, 1932) 41, 130, 133
Tarzan the Invincible (Burroughs) 16
Tarzan: The Lost Adventure (Burroughs and Lansdale) 155, **156**, 228, **229**
Tarzan the Magnificent (film 1960) 34
Tarzan the Terrible (Burroughs) 128, 135, 177, 179, 219
Tarzan the Untamed (Burroughs) 84–85, 89, 129, 141, 151, 175, 179, 194; *see also* DC comics
Tarzan Versus Predator at the Earth's Core (Dark Horse comics) 131
Tarzania 239
Tarzan's Fight for Life (film 1958) 34
"Tarzan's First Love" (Burroughs) 11, 20, 23–30, 34–44, 47, 50, 60–61, 63, 71–73, 80–81, 83–84–85, 89, 99–100, 135–137, 141, 143, 147, 154, 158, 168, 186, 199, 205–206, 210, 213–214, 216, 223–224, 231, 236–238
Tarzan's Greatest Adventure (film, 1959) 34
Tarzan's Hidden Jungle (film, 1955) 34
Tarzan's Quest (Burroughs) 197, 219
Taug (Burroughs character) 11, 23–25, **25, 26,** 28–29, 31, 35–37, 41, 43, 60–61, 63, 70, 72–73, 82, 84, 96, 137, 143, 154, 158, 161–162, 169–170, 191, 210–211, 213–214, 220, 222–224, 226–227, 230–231, 237–239
teamwork 70–71, 110, 224, 226
Teeka (Burroughs character) 23–28, 34–40, 43, 61, 63, 70–72, 74–76, 82, 84–85, 87, 92, 99–100, 136, 143, 147, 154, 158, 162, 168, 194, 199, 203, 210–211, 213–214, 216, **218**, 219–224, 226, 237–239
"Teeka" (Galloway) 40
teeth 28, 43, 52, 54, 56, 100, 127, 137, 153, 157, 172, 185, 216
Telemachus 31, 162
Tembo, Mwizenge 157
The Tempest (Shakespeare) 89, 106, 186
Tennyson, Alfred 33
Terence X. O'Leary's War Birds 2
Terkoz (Burroughs character) 19, 36–38, 41, 56, 59, 91, 148, 150, 154, 189, 211, 215–216, 219, 221
"The Text" (Cullinan) 7
theology 3, 57, 87, 89–90, 92, 94–96, 99; *see also* natural theology
The Thirty-Nine Steps (Buchan) 233
Thomas, Roy 168
The Three Musketeers (Dumas) 222
"Through the Looking Glass" 120–121
Tibo (Burroughs character) 42, 49, 56, 73–75, 84, 105–106, 108–110, 116–117, 126–128, 134, 140, 142, 144, 147, 153, 157, 166, 192, 199, 216, 236
time 11, 18, 33, 35, 39, 50, 56, 68, 85, 109, 119, 123, 163, 169, 192, 195, 214–215, 219, 226, 230–231, 234, 236–237
Tonga (Conan Doyle character) 171
Tonto (Striker character) 130
Tony Rosetti (Burroughs character) 130
Toog (Burroughs character) 74, 210, 213–214, 216, 219–222, 224, 237–238
Torgovnick, Marianna 132
torture, torment 44, 64, 68, 126–127, 138, 140–141, 158, 162, 174, 194, 207
Tower of Babel 42
Tozer, A.W. 94
The Tragedy of King Richard the Third (Shakespeare) 35, 207
trickster 45, 163, 177–179, 182–184, 188, 227, 229
Trigilio, Tony 20
Trimble, Irene 99
Trojan War 32, 34, 39, 62, 211
trolls 60, 190, 194
Troy 34–36
true love 39
Truman, Harry 117
truth 80, 88, 94, 101, 115, 154–157, 177, 233, 239
Tublat (Burroughs character) 73, 83, 85, 100, 138, 140, 174
Tubuto (Burroughs character) 159
Tucker, Betty Jo 135
Tucker, John I. 28

The Turn of the Screw (James) 51
Twain, Mark 76, 79, 112, 125, 236
2001: A Space Odyssey (Clarke) 17
Tydides (Homer character) 164

Ulysses (Dante character) 137
unconscious, subconscious 24–25, 29, 34, 40, 44, 63, 65, 69, 78, 97, 102, 105, 123, 132, 140, 161, 165–166, 182, 185, 188–191, 203–204, 206–207, 209, 211, 214, 221, 232
understatement 28, 45
underworld *see* Hell
United States 6, 7, 28–29, 78–79, 94, 112, 115–116, 119–121, 123, 125–126, 129–130, 132, 202–203, 230
Up from Slavery (Washington) 111
Updike, John 21
Utz, Richard J. 5, 19

Van Hise, James 18, 196
vengeance *see* revenge
Vergil 16, 32
verisimilitude 21, 67, 101–102, 176, 206
Vernon, Alex 15–16, 29, 38, 102–103, 189, 211, 239
Vess, Charles 228, **229**
viewpoint *see* point of view
villain *see* antagonist
Volman, Daniel 54

Wade, Nicholas 190, 192–193
Wahl, Greg 52
"War and Literature" 23, 30
The War Chief (Burroughs) 129–130, 137
Ward, James 69
Washington, Booker T. 111
Washington, George 1
"The Wasteland" (Eliot) 30
water 45, 51, 59, 74, 81, 91, 232, 238; *see also* ocean
Watson (Conan Doyle character) 12, 27, 59, 93, 153, 174, 222
Watson, Stephen 228, 231
Waz-don and Ho-don 60, 135
Waziri 15, 79, 108, 112, 123–124, 128, 131, 189
Weissmuller, Johnny 31, 41, 116
Wells, H.G. 2, 19, 154
West, Peyton M. 164
White, Hayden 78
whiteness 33–34, 43, 54, 60, 64, 74–75, 107,
109, 112, 114–117, 120–121, 123, 125–126, 128–132, 137–139, 149, 162, 198, 210, 215–216, 228, 234n
Whitman, Walt 132
Whitman Big Little Books 99
"Who Am I?" (Collins) 24, 135
Wichita Billings (Burroughs character) 130
Wilde, Oscar 191
Wilder, Thornton 18
William Cecil Clayton (Burroughs character) 30, 34, 173–174, 215
Williams, J.H. 67, 133
Willis, Connie 17
Wilson, Angene 171
Wilson, Woodrow 117
Winesburg, Ohio (Anderson) 14, 154
Winnie-the-Pooh (Milne character) 101
The Winter's Tale (Shakespeare) 33
witch-doctor 68, 75, 96, 101, 110, 140, 143, 145–147, 152–153, 155–157, 159, 162, 177; *see also* Bukawai; Rabba Kega
"The Witch-Doctor Seeks Vengeance" (Burroughs) 31, 41, 73, 75, 81, 86, 140–147, 149, 153–154, 157, 159, 163, 172, 199, 206
"The Witch-Doctor Seeks Vengeance" (Burroughs; ed. Ray Long) 142
Wolfe, Gary K. 45
wolves 33, 60, 118, 198, 233, 235
women 35–39, 56, 59–60, 65, 72, 75, 110, 127–128, 130, 133, 171, 215–219, 239
Wonder Stories 2
World War I 6, 117, 125, 163
World War II 13, 89, 99, 116
World's Fair *see* Columbian Exposition
Wuthering Heights (Brontë) 172
Wyatt, Neal 18
Wyatt Earp 78
Wylie, Dan 67–68, 134–135, 228n

Xenophanes 90

Yeates, Thomas 155, **156**, 178, 178, 211, **212**
The Young Marooner 39

zebra 118, 158
Zeus 23, 32, 35, 39, 197, 216
Zeuschner, Robert B. 24, 91, 96
Zins, Henryk 132
Zubanev (Burroughs character) 220

www.ingramcontent.com/pod-product-compliance
Ingram Content Group UK Ltd.
Pitfield, Milton Keynes, MK11 3LW, UK
UKHW041931140426
5217IPUK00014B/427